At the Threshold of the Modern Age

Karl König

At the Threshold of the Modern Age

Biographies Around the Year 1861

Karl König

Floris Books

Karl König Archive, Vol. 10

Subject: History and biographies

Karl König's collected works are issued by
the Karl König Archive, Aberdeen
in co-operation with the Ita Wegman Institute
for Basic Research into Anthroposophy, Arlesheim

Translated by Simon Blaxland de Lange

First published in German in 1973 under the title
Geister unter dem Zeitgeist by Verlag Freies Geistesleben
First published in English by Floris Books in 2011

© 2011 Trustees of the Karl König Archive

All rights reserved. No part of this publication may
be reproduced without the prior permission of
Floris Books, 15 Harrison Gardens, Edinburgh
www.florisbooks.co.uk

British Library CIP Data available

ISBN 978-086315-845-2

Printed in Great Britain
by CPI Group (UK) Ltd, Croydon

Contents

Individual Spirit and Spirit of the Age —
A Biographical Question
Foreword by Richard Steel   9

1. A Study of the Year 1861   13
2. Samuel Hahnemann   35
3. Ernst, Baron von Feuchtersleben   57
4. Charles Darwin   91
5. Rudolf Wagner   109
6. Rudolf Virchow   127
7. Carl Ludwig Schleich   143
8. Justinus Kerner   159
9. Josef Breuer   189
10. Sigmund Freud   207
11. Adalbert Stifter   239
12. Wilhelm Dilthey   263
13. Karl Eugen Neumann   282
14. Marie Eugenie Delle Grazie   299
15. Grant, Hildebrand, Dohrn, Marées   321
16. Gustav Mahler   369

17. Alma Mahler-Werfel and Lou Andreas-Salomé	385
18. Robert Owen	401
19. Harry, Graf Kessler	421
20. Helen Keller	433

O Life, Life, Wondrous Time	
Afterword by Alfons Limmbfrunner	459
Notes	467
Bibliography	478
Index	485

Individual Spirit and Spirit of the Age — A Biographical Question

Richard Steel

Over a period of ten years, Karl König explored a number of biographies by writing essays for publication in various German magazines. It was a series of entirely unrelated 'life impressions,' generally commemorating various anniversaries of the different individuals portrayed. Most of the essays were published in the Stuttgart journal, *Die Drei*. (There is a detailed list at the end of the book.)

These short biographies are inspirational in their own right, as they offer the reader insights into the lives and changing fortunes of people who have influenced our culture in manifold ways, covering issues such as medicine and science, social reform as well as literature and music. The essays were written between 1955 and 1965, but were only collated posthumously when it became apparent that, as an entity, they offered unique insights into a phenomenon of the nineteenth century. Their relevance became even more apparent when it was discovered, that, right in the middle of this period, in February 1961, König had written an essay, 'A century ago: a study of the year 1861', in connection with Rudolf Steiner's centenary. All of a sudden, the whole issue seemed to be considered in an entirely new light, as the different individuals came to be seen as heralds of the Michaelic Age, the age of a new consciousness that would introduce anthroposophy through Rudolf Steiner.

This is how the book, which was first published in 1973, came to be called *People of the Time — Biographies at the Threshold of the Modern Age*. This title has been out of print for many years now.

When we considered the 150th anniversary of Rudolf Steiner at the Karl König Archive, it became apparent that this book would be of relevance in this connection, seeing that the exploration of biographies of contemporaries and predecessors provided the historical, social and spiritual contexts for the age during which Rudolf Steiner was born. It therefore seems appropriate that this book should be published during 2011, fifty years after König wrote his essay on the year 1861.

For this edition, the German book of 1973 has been slightly altered: Apart from this introduction and the afterword by Alfons Limbrunner, we have put the essay, 'A study of the year 1861,' at the beginning of the book instead of at the end, as was done originally.

This seems more appropriate for our time because the biographies, taken as a whole, seem to reveal a common background of civilizational and historical issues. It was this situation that necessitated the birth of anthroposophy through Rudolf Steiner as an aid to renew culture. Through observations described in the essay, König offers the following conclusion:

> Thus around 1860 the spiritual need for a new conception of man's being began to awaken in the depths of the souls of civilized mankind. What had been gradually submerged since 1860 BC and has completely vanished in the last few centuries now needs to appear once more.

Considered on the basis of this statement, the biographies of individuals who helped shape the cultural impulses of that time, can be seen in an entirely new light.

Although initially written in honour of Rudolf Steiner's centenary, König's June 1961 essay may well shed some light on our time and ask us contemporaries to focus our attention on the biographical responsibilities now in our hands, fifty years on.

The biographical sketches reflect the extent to which great personalities were struggling towards the end of the 'dark age' (the Kali Yuga) and the changeover to the newly emerging Michaelic age.* It was the destiny of people at that time to have to face the dilemmas that were also to affect our time.

Based on the context of the specific age — and considering the appeal made by the spirit of that time — the destinies König describes seem rather tragic; somewhat lacking when considering that they were to herald the emergence of a truly new age.

Karl König always had an interest in biographies. Even without the manifold depictions on the life of Rudolf Steiner, he gave more than sixty talks on biographies; the first of these, about the life and destiny of Ferdinand Raimund, was held at the Goetheanum in Dornach, on October 6, 1933. And in addition to the contributions in this publication, he wrote another fourteen essays about various prominent people.

During the time he still lived in Vienna, and before the move to Scotland that led to the founding of the Camphill movement, biographies had played an important part in König's life. Right until the fateful date of March 11, 1938, when the Nazis annexed Austria, he regularly worked with a youth group. One of the tasks he set those young people was to study the lives of people who had died during the First World War.

In his 'Autobiographical Fragment' he brings to light this deep-rooted endeavour that could also be called 'historical conscience,' and which also reveals one of the roots of the social

---

* Kali Yuga is a Sanskrit term of Hindu cosmology meaning 'Age of the dark demon, Yuga,' who is a counter-image to Vishnu.
  During a lecture on Feb 2, 1910, *The Christ Impulse and the Emergence of Consciousness,* Rudolf Steiner proposed that 1899 marked the end of this age. He said that the Michaelic Age began in 1879 (lecture of Jan 19, 1915, *Destinies of people and nations.*)

endeavours that ultimately led to the founding of Camphill:

> Of course, at that time I did not know that the core of Camphill would form itself out of this group. So this is how the future prepared itself in 'seed' form — within only a few short months of my return to Vienna. We chose as our first theme of study the work and biographies of individuals who had died early on in the World War: Bernhard von der Marwitz, Otto Braun, Franz Marc, August Macke and others. We sensed that these young people had attempted to prepare the ground for something we should continue. Thus we found our way into the stream of historical evolution. We did not want to remain on the fringes of this endeavour, but wished, on the contrary, to be part of making one of Central Europe's tasks become reality.[1]

In those days — as is the case within the biographies presented here — the motivation was to reveal people's struggling and the experiencing of inner endeavours. Perhaps this allows us to rediscover these deep-rooted impulses and hopes, and to apply them in a new way — relevant to our time and the spirit of our age — as they are still accessible in this world, if we are prepared to look for them.

At the same time, re-enlivening and continuing these endeavours may provide some help to those that had to pass into the realms of life after death without fulfilling their destinies on earth. The healing approach towards unfulfilled destiny, the paths of destiny that are in need of support if they are to unfold — that is what was revealed in such a specific way through Karl König's own destiny, — and it also was what connected him to Kaspar Hauser, who would have been fifty years old the year Karl König was born.[2] In his own words, Karl König expressed it by saying: *This is my future task.*[3]

Easter 2011, Karl König Archive, Berlin

1

A Study of the Year 1861

I

The year of Rudolf Steiner's birth is in many respects a significant nodal point in the history of nineteenth century Europe and the wider world. A great diversity of historical events meet there as in a pencil of rays, flowing together and forming a fascinating panorama in which past and future meet.

One can find almost the entire history of the second half of the nineteenth century concentrated as though in a concave mirror in this year 1861, and from there one can follow the threads that link past and future events with one another. An older period comes to an end and a new one begins in this year. Hence it is understandable that, in his book on German history of the nineteenth and twentieth centuries, Golo Mann begins the sixth chapter, entitled 'Prussia conquers Germany,' with the year 1861. In the ensuing decade Bismarck brought about the dominance of Prussia in Germany; Austria's supremacy was outweighed, and Central Europe thereby acquired a completely new form that did not stand the test in the First World War and led to the collapse of Europe. The seeds of these events are to be found in the year 1861. It is then that the social sickness and the inadequacy of the bourgeois world were manifested in clear signs and symptoms.

II

This year began with an end. King Friedrich Wilhelm IV died on January 2, 1861. With this king, who had not been able to rule for years because of mental deficiencies, one of the last rulers who still experienced himself as the bearer of God's grace passed away. 'And if what a person believes and accepts — as opposed to what the opinion of others might seek to require of him — is indeed true for him, Friedrich Wilhelm IV was king by the grace of God in an unusual and ultimate sense of this word; and so no conviction could be more hostile to him that the notion that all people exist by the grace of God.'[1] But this was what was going on at that time: that not one person or some people but that now after many centuries and millennia every person was included in the condition of having the grace and favour of God. This was expressed with different words, but what was yearned for was precisely to become children of God. And the growing proletariat, was beginning to demand this, although it was led astray in this respect by its theoreticians.

Friedrich Wilhelm IV did not have the least understanding of this. He clung to beautifully sounding phrases and meant what he said, but he could never fulfil what he promised. Hence a Berlin joke about the way he spoke turned *'das gelobe und schwöre ich'* (this I vow and swear) into *'dat gloobe ick schwerlich'* (this I hardly believe').

Golo Mann characterized him thus: 'He was richly cultured, also of good will, well-educated, in need of affection, inspired by beauty, but weak. Ruled by the power of the moment, improvising in a self-satisfied way, dependent on advisers whom he loved to clout round the ears, superstitious, arrogant, disloyal.' This monarch dreamed of a hierarchically ordered state. He still wanted to see himself in the lustre of the divine light as the 'father of his subjects' who should look up to him.

This is also why he refused the crown of Germany when it

was offered to him by the Frankfurt Parliament. 'The thing [as he called the crown] does not bear the sign of the holy cross, does not emboss the head with the stamp "by the grace of God;" it is no crown.' He still expected the 'grace of God,' but this is not what happened to him. He tried to assimilate the new circumstances by endeavouring to collect the increasing flood of liberalism in conservative reservoirs, but his inner strength was not sufficient. Constant wishes paralysed the wings of his efforts, and in the end the powers of destiny sent him the night and the darkness of insanity. From 1857 onwards his brother Wilhelm was Prince Regent, ascending the Prussian throne on the day that Friedrich Wilhelm died. Wilhelm I, under Bismarck's guidance, became the first German Kaiser.

With Friedrich Wilhelm IV the heritage of the classical and romantic period passed away. He was one of the last who, in the new age, still remained as a living symbol from the beginning of the nineteenth century. On September 21, 1860 the philosopher Schopenhauer died, and on July 1, 1860 the physician Gotthilf Heinrich von Schubert; and the scientist Alexander von Humboldt had died a year previously, on May 6, 1859. Thus the last bearers of a spirituality for which the second half of the century seemingly had space were all crumbling.

Bismarck established the new Reich upon the grave of the 'romantic on the royal throne.'

III

In the same decade that brought the unification of Germany, the Austro-Hungarian monarchy broke up. Here, too, the decisive events took place around 1860–61. War against France arose in connection with the Italian freedom movement, the Risorgimento, and Austria was defeated at Solferino on St John's Day 1859. At the armistice of Villafranca, Emperor Franz Joseph I transferred Lombardy to Napoleon III, who handed over this great province to the Italian federation — an important link in the forming of the future Italian monarchy.

In Austria, however, this defeat brought about a further strengthening of those forces which were pressing towards national independence; Czechs and Hungarians, Slovenes and Poles, Croats and Slovaks experienced the Italian victory as a fanfare call for rebellion. Both the crown and the government tried — initially with insufficient means — to counteract this growing tide of nationalism and soon had to resort to more far-reaching methods. The question of the constitution was now to be solved through the *Oktoberdiplom,* the October Diploma.

> This *Oktoberdiplom* was — as the Magyars expressed it — 'the imperial state of the high nobility against the Viennese bureaucracy.' It took the leading political individualities into account. The centre of gravity of legislation was now transferred to the *Landtag* [state parliament] and a far-reaching federalism was established in legislation and administration. The Ministries of the Interior, of Justice and of Education were abolished and in the place of these central authorities there emerged in Austria the Ministry of State, in Hungary the Court Chancellory for Hungary and something similar for Croatia and Transylvania.[2]

It was the first, but mighty step towards transforming the monarchy into a confederation. The centre of gravity of political and cultural life would be transferred to the *Länder* [provinces] and would have furthered the justified aspiration of the individual nations for self-development and self-determination. However, the retarding forces of that Viennese bureaucracy which was led by the centralizing demands of liberal Germanness resisted this. Likewise in Hungary the lower classes rebelled out of an incredible foolishness and pettiness against this generous initiative in the direction of self-government, and so a few months later the *Oktoberdiplom* was replaced by the *Februarpatent,* the

1. A STUDY OF THE YEAR 1861

February Patent. Anton von Schmerling was the father of this new legislative framework. It sought to bring about the solution in a Germanic centralist way. An imperial council was created consisting of two parts: the upper chamber and the parliament. All legislative authority was united in this imperial council, and the state parliaments of the individual countries were left with only few rights and many duties. František Palacký rightly said at the time,

> that parliamentary life, without which in future a nation will neither be able to flourish nor even have a proper life, must in a short space of time completely disappear from the Bohemian state parliament, as one will be dealing here only with a few local needs such as hospitals and hospices, quartering of military personnel etc., with all other matters being hustled off to Vienna, where they will be dealt with one-sidedly in a Germanic way.[3]

Franz Joseph I had turned the tiller of the new constitution in that direction which led away from federalism of a constitutional monarchy, in which all his peoples would have been able to develop a free, nationally-determined cultural life. It was precisely through this that the continuing existence of the Austro-Hungarian Empire was prevented. The Emperor's inability to grasp that he had to hand over to these national groups the rights that he had inherited, which had made him his people's lord and master and entrusted him with an all-powerful commanding voice in questions of government and legislation, made any further progress virtually impossible. The *Februarpatent* was enacted on February 26, 1861, and two days later he gave his ministers an address in which he called upon them 'to defend the throne with all the energy and harmonious application of all their powers against the extracting of further concessions, be it through pressure from the imperial council or the state parliaments, or through revolutionary attempts by the masses.'[4]

17

Eighteen and a half years, one moon-node period later, in the autumn of 1879, Austria formed the alliance with Germany which Bismarck carried through against the will of Wilhelm I. A further moon-node period brought the murder of the Empress Elisabeth, an event which was deeply wounding for Franz Joseph I. At the same time the 'freedom from Rome' movement was gathering more and more power, and this — together with the anti-Semitic and nationalistic German impulses of Georg von Schönerer and his circles — undermined the last secure foundations of the monarchy. The collapse was inevitable and, similarly, arrived at the end of the third moon-node period in the autumn of 1918. Austria disintegrated into separate nation-states, and politically Central Europe had ceased to exist. What began in 1860/61 in 1918 came to a tragic conclusion.

IV

Nationalism, which had led in Germany to the unification of the Reich, brought about the downfall of the Austrian monarchy. However, the seeds for this can be found in the years 1860 and 1861.

In Italy at this time the establishing of an Italian monarchy was nearing completion. What had been happening for decades with the help of the *Risorgimento,* the Italian unification, and the *Irredenta* (annexing territories of Italian speakers) and had been supported by the Piedmontese monarchy now found its magnificent conclusion. Once Lombardy had been united with Piedmont in the autumn of 1859, the conquest of Sicily and southern Italy by Garibaldi and his band of irregulars began in 1860. The campaign of his Thousand Volunteers was so successful that Cavour was forced to advance with an army from Piedmont to Central Italy in order that Garibaldi and his army should not be forfeited to Mazzini. He thereby made it pos-

1. A STUDY OF THE YEAR 1861

sible for Victor Emanuel enter Naples at Garibaldi's side on November 7, 1860. On March 17, 1861 he was then elected 'King of Italy' by the Italian chamber. In this day — for the first time since the rule of Theodoric the Great — a united Italian kingdom came into being, a foretaste of what was achieved in Germany ten years later.

Everywhere in Europe the backwards-looking forces of an awakening nationalism were on the march — in Germany, in Austria and in Italy. France, under Napoleon III, still felt itself to be the lord and master of Europe and was trying to maintain this already lost position. Britain thought on a global scale and was intent on strengthening and expanding its mighty empire.

Both in the East and in the West there were two significant events in the early part of 1861. On March 13 Alexander II proclaimed his manifesto liberating 46 million Russian peasants from the yoke of serfdom.

> They received a small house with a small adjoining plot of land, the right to cultivate estates of their masters and the opportunity to gain possession of them through repurchases supported by the state ... At the same time the tsar set up provincial councils as a kind of preliminary stage to a parliament, he introduced courts with a jury and re-established the philosophical, juridical and political colleges which had hitherto been suppressed at the universities.[5]

However, the most significant of all these reforms was, without doubt, the freeing of the Russian peasants from the bondage of serfdom. Further innovations were made necessary through these measures which had hitherto been completely unknown in Russia. 'A creditor organization had to be put on its feet which allowed the new owners to obtain the sum demanded as immediate payment by the lords of the estates in exchange for yearly repayments. Western institutions afforded the most comfortable experiences of the way that such credit-systems could work.'[6]

Thus western capitalism made its entry into Russia simultaneously with the liberation of the peasants.

The Civil War that arose in the United States of America had similar roots, although the circumstances were completely different. At the end of 1860 Abraham Lincoln was chosen as President and, at the beginning of 1861, saw himself placed by his inauguration in the position of being able to overcome the conflict which had already existed for a long time.

However, this conflict did not only have to do with the question of the black slaves; it had far deeper roots. The feudal Democrats of the south, who needed the slaves for cultivating tobacco, cotton and sugar cane on their huge estates, were defending this culture of luxury and grandiose life-style from being penetrated by northern industrialism. The awakening age of modern technology was vying with the feudal world of landed property. This struggle lasted for four years, and was one of the bloodiest civil wars of the century. The South was beaten, the secession of the states that had deserted the motherland was revoked, and the Negroes received — at least on paper — their human rights. At the end of the war, in 1865, the victorious President, Abraham Lincoln, was assassinated.

Thus in both West and East two events took place which are closely connected with one another. In both contexts the ownership of human labour was abolished. In Russia the peasants for the first time had houses which they were able to make their own. In the United States the Negroes' labour became a commodity which henceforth they could sell, whether monthly or yearly. In this way the first steps were made which were subsequently able to lead to a possible liberation of the individual human being. The individual was no longer to be possessed by other people; he was to have the possibility of freeing himself from ancient ties of blood and race in order to find himself as an individual personality. These events, too, were initiated at the beginning of 1861.

1. A STUDY OF THE YEAR 1861

V

In the same year, at first wholly unnoticed, Johann Jakob Bachofen's monumental book on prehistoric matriarchy, *Das Mutterrecht,* appeared. He wrote in the foreword:

> An unknown world opens up before our eyes. The deeper we go into it, the more strangely everything forms itself around us ... That primordial rule of life to which the maternal law belongs, out of which it has sprung and whence alone it can be explained, appears alien and strange in its tendencies alongside that of the Hellenic world.[7]

With this work a hitherto closed world of human evolution was newly opened. The prehistory of mankind led beyond the Greek and Egypto-Babylonian ages. Completely new horizons of ancient existence suddenly became visible and revealed a world which would become more fully accessible only after sixty further years of research.

But not only was matriarchy recognized in 1861. It was also courageously defended by a remarkable person. The Hungarian physician Ignaz Philipp Semmelweis published his book *Etiology, Concept and Prophylaxis of Childbed Fever.* He had already indicated fourteen years previously in 1847 and 1848, in lectures in Vienna, that the enormous mortality rate (in many hospitals as high as 30 per cent) of mothers through childbed fever must be traced to an external infection of the birth passage. If an adequate policy of cleanliness were to prevail among doctors and midwives, childbed fever could be reduced to a minimum. His own measures proved the truth of his theory. But hardly any of the leading obstetricians recognized the significance of this discovery. Semmelweis was slandered and attacked in a very demeaning way and Paul Diepgen calls this whole affair 'a dark chapter in the history of medicine.' Only gradually, in association with the discovery and use of antiseptics, was the mortality-rate of mothers reduced. By the end of the century it was no longer a danger to give life to a child. Here, too, the year 1861 was a historical landmark.

In the same year Adalbert Stifter was working on *Witiko;* Gustave Flaubert was writing *Salambo* and Victor Hugo was finishing *Les Misérables.* These are three novels which were of great importance for nineteenth century literature. The theme of *Witiko* is justice; *Salambo* has to do with a barbarian revolt against culture. And in *Les Misérables* there is a search to make a higher power of justice available to those who are in misery of have been condemned.

On March 13 Wagner's *Tannhäuser* was performed for the first time in Paris. The wife of the Austrian ambassador, Pauline Metternich, was responsible for arranging this première, which became of the great theatrical scandals of the time. For months there were intrigues in the highest circles of Parisian society against the bringing about of this performance. Berlioz made his contribution to this and wrote after the performance: 'Wagner has clearly gone mad. He will die of apoplexy.'

Tannhäuser had already been put on in Dresden in 1845, but had only been a moderate success. Here in Paris, at the centre of the Napoleonic miracle, amidst the atmosphere of decadent bourgeois pomp, the performance of this opera which tells of heavenly love and compares Venus with St Elisabeth, could only be mocked and scorned. But this event likewise belongs to the astonishingly diverse web of the events of the year 1861.

VI

In the springtime of this year three children were born who were destined to acquire a considerable influence on the further development and evolution of humanity at the end of the nineteenth and the beginning of the twentieth centuries.

1. A STUDY OF THE YEAR 1861

On February 15 the Englishman Alfred North Whitehead was born in Ramsgate, Kent.

On February 27 the Austrian Rudolf Steiner saw the light of this world in Kraljevec in what is now Croatia.

On May 6 the Bengali polymath Rabindranath Tagore entered the earthly world.

In the West, Central Europe and the East there appeared the representatives of an epoch which only now, after a hundred years, has begun to manifest itself in its tragic greatness.

Whitehead was a physicist, mathematician and philosopher. Steiner was a philosopher, seer and the modern scientist of the supersensible. Tagore was a poet, singer, educator and reformer.

Whitehead went from England, where he was Professor of Mathematics and Physics in Cambridge and London, to America and became Professor of Philosophy at Harvard University in Cambridge, Massachusetts. He died there in advanced years, on December 30, 1947.

Steiner spent his life in Central Europe. He studied in Vienna, edited Goethe's scientific works in Weimar, moved as a freelance writer to Berlin and lived during and after the First World War in Dornach near Basle, where he passed through the gate of death on March 30, 1925.

Tagore spent his youth in India, then made a number of journeys to America and Europe but always returned to his native land. There he founded a school which has today become a university; and he died on August 7, 1941 in West Bengal.

It is as though the three regions of the earth, which were being confronted by fundamental decisions, wanted in these three representatives to present themselves in a kind of idealized picture. The most refined thoughts that the Anglo-Saxon world could conceive of were formulated by Whitehead. Steiner created a new picture of the world out of the idealistic thinking of the Classical-Romantic period in Central Europe which led to a way of understanding and contemplating the supersensible world such that all magic was banished from it. Tagore, on the other hand, renewed the religious life of his country; he tried to illumine it with the blossoms of western spirituality and endeavoured to let the expanses of the earthly world stream into the dreamy depths of India.

Whitehead sublimated Western thinking to such a rarefied extent that the breath of comprehending and understanding almost came to a standstill. Steiner, in contrast, gave a new impulse to Central European thinking by establishing a new theory of cognition in which both morality and also the phenomena of nature and its laws have a place. Man became the measure of all things. Tagore imbued the world of facts with grace, beauty and wonder and tried to make all deeds and actions into a religious festival.

In Whitehead's philosophy objects are therefore the determining element, because he objectivizes the whole world. He would like to form everything in a subject-less way, so that it becomes pure mathematics and logic. Objects embody ever-newly unfolding events in mutual relationships, and everything personal and individual is none other than the infinite multiplicity of these relationships between objects. He says in one of his basic works:

> Eternal objects inform actual occasions with hierarchic patterns, included and excluded in every variety of discrimination. Another view of the same truth is that every actual occasion is a limitation imposed on possibility, and that by virtue of this limitation the particular value of that shaped togetherness of things emerges ... God is the ultimate limitation, and His existence is the ultimate irrationality. For no reason can be given for just that limitation which it stands in His nature to impose.'[8]

One can see how an objectified thinking here leads *ad absurdum*, although it makes every effort to do justice to all phenomena, forces and events.

In his later book *Adventures of Ideas* he tries to link everything

1. A STUDY OF THE YEAR 1861

that exists in an all-embracing system, which was to become a philosophy of the present. There he writes: 'Nothing can be omitted: experience drunk and experience sober, experience sleeping and experience waking, experience drowsy and experience wide-awake, experience self-conscious and experience self-forgetful, experience intellectual and experience physical, experience religious and experience sceptical.'[9] And so it goes on, and he names all possible and conceivable experiences. But he forgets the one who is having the experiences. This person, the individuality itself, is completely overlooked.

Whitehead endeavours to construct a metaphysics and philosophy of objects and events, but he loses the architect, the initiator of events and the one who experiences these objects and events. It is a philosophy which has lost the ego and has become completely subject-less and, hence, devoid of initiative.

With Tagore, on the other hand, an entirely different world-picture unfolds. Whereas Whitehead represents the great scholar who has been acquiring vast knowledge since his youth and had already been Professor of Physics and Mathematics at Cambridge for 24 years, Tagore is proud of having learnt as little as possible. In his autobiographical fragment, *My Life,* he writes:

> I suppose it was fortunate for me that I never in my life had what is called an education, that is to say, the kind of school and college training which is considered proper for a boy from a respectable family ... In my versification, vocabulary and ideas I yielded myself to the vagaries of an unbuttoned fancy.[10]

Tagore thereby received a living, ever open and rich feeling life, with which he was able to penetrate the created world. He says:

> I had a deep sense, almost from infancy, of nature, a feeling of intimate companionship with the trees and clouds, and the touch of the seasons. At the same time I

had a peculiar susceptibility to human kindness. These craved for expression, and naturally I wanted to give them my own expression, though I was too immature to give them any perfection of form.

He then tells of his own religious experiences, in which he is able to behold his world of experience imbued and irradiated with light as a 'sensory whole.' For him, the Godhead is manifested in the mantle of the beautiful. 'God does not care to expose His power written in geological inscriptions, but He is proud of the beauty in green grass, in flowers, in the play of colour on the clouds, in the music of running water.'

An awareness of this kind derives not from objects but from personal experiences; everything objective has as though been blotted out for Tagore. He also does not want the object as such, because it barely exists for him at all. All events and objects exist only in the experience of the individuality. 'Somewhere in the arrangement of this world there seems to be a great concern with giving delight, showing that in addition to the meaning of matter and force there is a message conveyed through the magic touch of personality. This touch cannot be analysed, it can only be felt.' For Tagore this experience is the only significant one that a human being can have. 'Facts and power belong to the outer, not to the inner soul of things. Gladness is the one criterion of truth.'

The magic that streams from Tagore's poems is that intimate state of a merging between the world and man. Man has entered into the world and has united himself with it, and it expresses itself through him. Tagore speaks out of this conviction in his essay, *Personality*:

> I believe in a spiritual world — not as anything separate from this world — but as its innermost truth. With the breath we draw we must always feel this truth, that we are living in God. Born in this great world, full of the mystery of the infinite, we cannot accept our existence as a

1. A STUDY OF THE YEAR 1861

momentary outburst of chance drifting on the current of matter toward an eternal nowhere. We cannot look upon our lives as dreams of a dreamer who has no awakening in all time. We have a personality to which matter and force are unmeaning unless related to something infinitely personal, whose nature we have discovered, in some measure, in human love, in the greatness of the good, in the martyrdom of heroic souls, in the ineffable beauty of nature which can never be a mere physical fact nor anything but an expression of personality.

In Tagore and Whitehead the mighty contrasts between East and West become clearly manifest. For the one there exist only objects, as they are encountered and discovered through events. What results is not an individuality but a 'limitation,' and God can be seen as the ultimate 'irrational limitation.' For Tagore, on the other hand, personality is everything. In it nature comes into being and passes away; objects are the abstractions of an ill-formed understanding, which endeavours to comprehend what is comprehensible but can nonetheless be experienced. God is the all-encompassing reality, with whom man can be wedded as a person.

The only bridge that can establish a connection between these two worlds is the spirit of Central Europe. The form in which Rudolf Steiner has grasped, recognized and transformed this spirit forms the arch bridging the gulf between West and East. The concern of Rudolf Steiner, the man of the middle, is the forming of a conception of one's own self, or ego. In his *Autobiography,* he reports of a conversation that he had with one of his friends who at the time had materialist views which the young Rudolf Steiner contradicted. This conversation was about the nature of the human I.

> To me the human I is concrete reality that can be surveyed inwardly. To me, that reality was no less real than any

external fact recognized by materialism. However, it is absolutely nonmaterial. During the following years, my insight and knowledge of the reality and spiritual nature of the I helped me against all the temptations of materialism. I knew that nothing could disprove the reality of the I. And it was clear to me that the I is unknown to those who think of it as a manifest form of something else or as the consequence of some processes.[11]

In one of his principal works, *The Riddles of Philosophy*, he writes in the chapter entitled 'A Brief Outline of an Approach to Anthroposophy':

Man feels himself as a self-conscious ego through the fact that he perceives an external world with his senses, that he experiences himself as being outside this external world and that, at a certain stage of scientific investigation, he feels himself in relation to this external world in such a way that it appears to him as 'illusion.' Were it not so, the self-conscious ego would not emerge.[12]

Whitehead completely ignores the self-aware ego, and the world becomes for him an 'objective' illusion, because he takes seriously only that aspect of reality which can be grasped with concepts. From this he derives external objects. Tagore has knowledge of the ego but he has no time for concepts, because he regards the other aspect of reality, that of perception, to be the only real one. Thus the world becomes for him a subjective experience which has no order.

The insights that are formulated in Rudolf Steiner's *Philosophy of Freedom* represent the bridge across this abyss which separates the Western and Eastern conceptions:

The percept is the part of reality that is given objectively, the concept the part that is given subjectively (through intuition). Our mental organization tears the reality apart into these two factors. One factor presents itself to perception, the other to intuition. Only the union of the two, that is, the percept fitting systematically into the universe, constitutes the full reality.[13]

Here we find the synthesis which alone enables the self-conscious ego to recognize itself in the world, and the world in the ego. What in the East seeks to lose itself and in the West leads to ghostly abstractions has here become experienced reality and truth. The philosopher Rudolf Steiner prepares the path that will lead to anthroposophy, to man's understanding of his own being.

VII

The panorama of the events that took place in and around the year 1861, and the three personalities who were born in this year illustrate what was asserted at the beginning of this chapter: that the events of the second half of the nineteenth century are concentrated around 1861 as though in a concave mirror.

In Central Europe the Austro-Hungarian Empire was beginning to break up under the pressure and thrust of the national movements of the peoples that had been united within it. At the same time the Italians and Germans were uniting these same national forces. This awakening nationalism, which can also be called a Napoleonic quality, thereby overshadowed the burgeoning forces of liberalism which were arising in the 1840s. The year 1848 brought a victory, transformed by the shortcomings of the middle-class into a serious set-back. And the reaction, out of which a further drive towards absolutism arose, prepared the way for nationalism. The focal point of these various currents seems to have been in 1861.

The complete change that occurred in Austria in the time between the *Oktoberdiplom* and the *Februarpatent* is the clear symptom of the forces that were at work here.

AT THE THRESHOLD OF THE MODERN AGE

Deeply underlying these events — not yet discernible but nevertheless present — the forces which would lead in a few years to the onward march of the proletariat were gathering. The proletariat was beginning to awaken, stretch and get into its stride, and as a first act of a growing sense of awareness the Allgemeine Deutsche Arbeiterverein (General German Workers' Association) was founded by Ferdinand Lassalle in 1863, which became the nucleus of the Workers' Party. Because liberalism had become wedded to nationalism and had betrayed its essential ideals, Marxism emerged as the awakener of the proletariat. The Communist Manifesto appeared in 1848; but it had as yet little effect. It was only after a further twenty years that a kindling process began and ignited the fie which is still glowing even today.

Rudolf Steiner described the situation at that time with the utmost clarity. In a lecture on October 25, 1918, he referred to the great significance of the years between 1845 and 1878. He stated that in 1845 the first fifth of the consciousness-soul age, which had begun in 1413, had run its course.

> The 1840s were an important period for the powers that were driving world evolution forward envisaged a significant crisis in this time ... In the 1840s it seemed as if the impulse of the consciousness soul might stream into the political domain of the civilized world in the form of political views.[14]

Then he goes on to describe how the middle class completely slept through this time. The bourgeoisie at this time had no interest whatever in questions pertaining to world-conceptions and failed to take hold of the opportunities that were presented to it. Rudolf Steiner indicates that humanity had been given a span of just 33 years — between 1845 and 1878 — to embrace the new liberal ideas.

> It is of the greatest importance in the context of the historical development of present-day humanity that one

1. A STUDY OF THE YEAR 1861

can gain a proper overview of these decades between the 1840s and the 1870s. One needs to be quite clear that it was in these decades — beginning from the 1840s — that what one calls liberal ideas flowed in an abstract form into human evolution, and that mankind was given until the end of the 1870s to grasp these ideas and relate them to the realities of the time. But the bearers of these ideas — the members of the middle class — missed their opportunity. There is something utterly tragic about the evolution of the nineteenth century. The 1840s and early 1850s seemed to herald the dawning of a new popular movement! ... But by the end of the 1870s, the bourgeoisie had failed to understand liberal ideas. From the 1840s to the 1870s the middle class had been asleep.

Only when looked at in this way does the background of the symptomatology of the year 1861 become fully apparent. This year of 1861 lies precisely in the middle of the period between 1845 and 1878, like the fulcrum of a balance. And we can now clearly see how a dramatic change takes place in the few months between the *Oktoberdiplom* and the *Februarpatent*. The so-called liberals of the German officialdom in Vienna became the instrument of the failure to take hold of the opportunities. They opposed this 'new popular movement' that was stirring and made it impossible for the middle classes to wake up to the new ideals.

It was in these weeks that the child Rudolf Steiner was born in what was then Austria. He would once more make possible and get under way what had so tragically failed to come about in his year of birth.

This is what he himself means in the lecture quoted above when he says 'that in the most productive and fertile years for the bourgeoisie, from the 1840s to the end of the 1870s, they had been asleep, and that afterwards it was too late; for nothing could then be achieved in the way that it would have been possible in the period referred to.' Only one thing was still possible now: 'To achieve something through fully waking up to a scientific experience of spiritual realities.' This is what Rudolf Steiner brought about.

At this time Stifter was writing his *Witiko*. Is he not trying to portray the ideal of the liberal human being through the medium of the story? The first book of this novel is prefaced by a motto: 'It sounded almost like the singing of larks.' Was the author sensing the breath of the *Völkerfrühling* (new popular movement)? Did he feel that new ideas wanted to descend upon people like singing larks? But he, too, was too deeply asleep and was just dreaming the dream of *Witiko*, where the 'divine right' of a human being who has begun to recognize himself as a free citizen comes to realization.

Just as Rudolf Steiner stands between Whitehead and Tagore, so Adalbert Stifter stands between Flaubert and Zola. The latter hears the voices that call from the depths and prepare the march of the proletariat. Flaubert, in contrast, looks back and longs for the old world.

The twentieth century was prepared in America and Russia. Efforts were made to lessen the burden of slavery through war and of serfdom through generous reforms. East, West and Middle were beginning to form themselves in such a way that the tasks of the historical future were becoming visible.

VIII

Rudolf Steiner also made an important observation about the time around 1860 in another context. He indicates that the old ideas under whose sway European humanity still lives are no longer adequate to bring about the establishing of a new culture. For, says Rudolf Steiner, these ideas go far back to the times of the early Middle Ages. 'Europe was founded on really old ideas, hence out of an old spirituality.' And he goes on to say:

1. A STUDY OF THE YEAR 1861

> But in the depths of the soul-region there is a strongly rooted hunger for a transformation of Europe and of the whole civilized world. This is the great struggle that can be observed over the past sixty years or so at the foundations of European culture. Something is wanting to take shape, but it is thrust back by conservative ideas.[15]

As these words were being spoken in 1920, they refer to the year 1860. It is therefore there that those roots are to be sought whence a transformation of Europe will grow.

In the course of the same lecture Rudolf Steiner then points towards a further fact. He describes the soul-condition of man around the year 1860 BC and says:

> In pre-Christian times there had been a feeling for the idea of reincarnation, for there was a knowledge of it only before the year 1860 BC. After the year 1860 there was only an instinctive feeling for it in Egyptian culture as a whole, in the Near East and in Roman times ... Now the time is coming when the view of man as a spiritual being who passes through an evolution between death and a new birth is becoming a living feeling, a living experience, when one must live with the idea of the super-earthly significance of human souls. For without this idea the culture of the earth will become devoid of life.

Thus around 1860 the spiritual need for a new conception of man's being began to awaken in the depths of the souls of civilized mankind. What had been gradually submerged since 1860 BC and has completely vanished in the last few centuries now needs to appear once more. There was a quest for the idea of man's eternal being, which passes through life and death and leads a twofold existence — one between birth and death and another between death and a new birth.

This 'new popular movement' which had not been taken up

and understood by the bourgeoisie and, hence, has not been able to manifest itself politically ever since, nonetheless lives on, though on a different level of our existence. It seeks manifest itself to human souls as a new science of man's being and to lead them to an understanding of their spirit-nature.

In this way the time when a dark night of the soul had weighed down upon mankind for over three thousand years was overcome. The period of darkening began with the evening twilight around 1860 BC and extended until the first ray of the new morning, which became visible in 1860 AD. Michael, the Archangel, appeared in the gentle radiance of this awakening morning light, and in the autumn of the year 1879 took over the leadership of mankind's further evolution and the guiding of the earth's destiny.

Thus Bachofen's *Mutterrecht* appeared in 1861. It reached back to those times which lay 1860 years before Christ, when the cult of the dead was celebrated amidst knowledge of reincarnation. With this work, too, something new was beginning which would gradually conquer the space that it deserved in the cultural life of our time.

The year 1861 was a significant point in the evolution of modern humanity. That it became the year of Rudolf Steiner's birth is now all the more understandable. It was a year of crisis in European history, when certain evolutionary trends that were to lead into the twentieth century took their cue for the future.

2

Samuel Hahnemann

Christian Friedrich Samuel Hahnemann (1755–1843), was a German physician who founded homeopathy.

I

It really is quite extraordinary to call to mind the age that Hahnemann attained. What a destiny! How outrageous and yet also magnificent all at once! How incomprehensible and nonetheless offering a hint of the guidance of what came to expression in it.

In the early autumn of 1834, when Hahnemann was nearly eighty, a young Frenchwoman, Mlle Melanie d'Hervilly-Gohier, came to him for consultation in Köthen. Several months previously she had obtained a copy of this book, *The Organon of the Healing Art,* and read it with a growing admiration. She now had the wish to meet the author of this immortal book in person.

Hahnemann had come to the end of his life's work. The fruit of his old age — the book, *Chronic Diseases,* had been completed and published in five volumes. Nobody understood it, not even his most intimate pupils. What he meant by psoniasis, syphilis and sicosis was also difficult to comprehend; Hahnemann was embittered. His memory had deteriorated, his physical forces were declining, he had become bad-tempered, quarrelsome and tetchy. The solitude of his old age had descended upon him. His wife, who had been at his side for nearly fifty years, was no longer alive. His favourite son had disappeared, his closest pupils had rebelled against him. What was there that still made life worth living?

Mlle Melanie came as a patient; after a few weeks she was Hahnemann's betrothed, and in January 1835 their wedding took place. Hahnemann had been a wanderer throughout his life, until he came to rest in Köthen, a small town in Saxony-Anhalt. Now he sold his house, distributed his possessions among his daughters and grandchildren, and the *Allgemeine Homöopathische Zeitung* of July 13, 1835 carried a brief message: 'Councillor Dr S. Hahnemann left for Paris on June 14.'

The young Frau Hahnemann journeyed with her husband to the capital of France, where at this time everything was full of life and zestful energy; they were the 'golden days of the bourgeoisie.' Louis Philippe, the Citizen-King, slid about on his throne in his efforts to be on good terms with all classes. He administered his kingdom as a company chairman oversees his business; he had to see to it that his customers were satisfied with him.

It was the Paris of Balzac and Victor Hugo; Stendhal's novels were appearing, and Alfred de Musset, George Sand and Chopin were enacting the romantically tragic festival of their lives. The operas of Halévy, Meyerbeer and Adam were 'en vogue.' Berlioz was composing, and Delacroix had started to paint the frescoes in the Chamber of Deputies.

Madame Hahnemann introduced her husband to the great world of the city of Paris. The windows of their house looked out onto the Jardin du Luxembourg. The first patients came, and soon she managed to persuade the government to issue a special permit allowing Dr Hahnemann to practise freely as a physician. The house became too small, and they moved into a larger one in the Rue de Milan.

In the evening they went to concerts, the great opera and playhouses. Hahnemann became young again. In 1840,

2. SAMUEL HAHNEMANN

Samuel Hahnemann

when Hahnemann was 85, a visitor described this as follows: 'Hahnemann's solid form, his great mobility, his hearing which was wholly unaffected by age and his normal powers of vision are indicative of the excellent health that he enjoys. According to all who have known him for some time, his intellectual faculties would appear in every respect to be as they have always been.'

This old man seemed to have been granted a new lease of life. He maintained it until the spring of 1843. Then around Easter he became ill, his powers gradually ebbed away; and he died on July 2. His body was embalmed and only buried on July 11. 'I spent eleven days lying on his bed beside his lifeless body, whose grave I would like to have shared.' Thus did Melanie write to her friend.

Hahnemann was dead; he died in the city and in the arms of the woman that had restored his youth to him. At his death the moon was passing through the constellation of Leo, the Lion, and the sun shone down upon the earth from Gemini, the Twins. Hölderlin had given up his spirit one month before him.

What was it that brought Hahnemann, who had never set foot on French soil before, to Paris? Perhaps an intuitive sense can discern what thinking can no longer comprehend; for this Gallic land was formerly the home of the Druids. A Baroque statue of Veleda, that Gallic priestess who was initiated into the mysteries of the art of healing, can still be seen in the Jardin du Luxembourg today. This man who had endeavoured to renew the art of healing wended his way to the western land where oaks still bear the sacred mistletoe.

At the same time, from 1839 until 1842, Richard Wagner was also in Paris. Whether they met one another has not been recorded; but it is possible, for a reception took place in the Hahnemanns' salon to mark the sixtieth anniversary of his qualification as a physician, and many musicians were present. Clara Wieck-Schumann played on this festive day. There is also a further possibility that the Hahnemanns were present when that remarkable performance of Beethoven's Ninth Symphony that so moved Richard Wagner took place in the Conservatoire. Did the countryside of Brittany and Cornwall shine forth at that time in the hearts of Hahnemann and Wagner?

Melanie has been the subject of much cynical scorn. But she was a chivalrous woman; free, beyond temptation, loving and strong in her intentions. She went her way like a priestess and served her sacred friend.

A young Scot who saw Hahnemann during the last year of his life described him thus: 'His face had a luminous expression; there was something divine in his appearance.' He who throughout his life striven for 'rational therapy' died as a priest of the healing art.

II

Hahnemann was never what one might call a sedentary person. He was a wanderer from his youth onwards, moving restlessly from town to town until finally, as an old man, he settled for fourteen long years in Köthen. Destiny took him away even from there, when as an eighty-year-old he moved to Paris.

Never did he wander so incessantly and under such difficult circumstances as between the years 1789 and 1796. He was virtually driven from one place to the next; his family always came with him, comprising four, then five and six children. Even just to count the places gives a picture of this need to wander; he was homeless, in the true sense of the word.

In 1789 he was still in Leipzig; but since he was really poor he moved to a suburb where living was cheaper. He remained there for over a year and gained his livelihood by translating English and French works about medicine and chemistry. From Stötteritz — as this miserable suburb was called — he went in 1791 to Gotha and from there to Schloss Georgenthal, which was close by. There he set up a sort of humane mental home, which he had to abandon because of a lack of patients. In

1793 he was in Molschleben near Gotha, in 1794 in Göttingen and then, in the winter of the same year, in Bad Pyrmont in Lower Saxony. From there he went to Braunschweig, then to nearby Wolfenbüttel, and in 1796 he finally arrived not far away in Königslutter. Here he remained until 1799, in apparent tranquillity and stability.

The basic idea of homeopathy was born during these seven years of wandering. What had begun to germinate in Stötteritz started to blossom in Königslutter. Now he was able to formulate what he had previously only glimpsed intuitively. The idea of *similia similibus* was to be developed.

It would be erroneous to suggest that he would have had no opportunity for rest, for at least twice he was at this time offered a chair at a university. He declined on both occasions. He preferred to wander about in the northern heart of Germany. He travelled round the Harz region from place to place, searched and wandered, began projects and abandoned them again, until finally he reached the gateway that revealed to him the path to a rational art of healing. It was an inner journey with outer stages of suffering.

However, much besides was happening during these seven years, and Hahnemann seemed to take no part in these events of the time. There was revolution in Paris and France; the storm that the Count of St Germain foresaw broke and had devastating consequences. This was the story in the West.

In the other heart of Germany, in Thuringia, where Jena and Weimar have their lines of communication, the encounter between Goethe and Schiller occurred and ran its course during these seven years and became for each of these two men the central point of his life. Schiller called it the 'most beneficial event' of his life; and for Goethe it was similar. In 1788 the latter had returned from Italy and soon afterwards published his anatomical study about intermaxillary bones. He worked on the theory of metamorphosis in plants and animals and assiduously studied the foundations of the theory of colour. Throughout 1790 Goethe was preoccupied with scientific studies, and in 1791 he established his *Freitagsgesellschaft* (Friday Society), where he regularly reported about his scientific results. The following years were likewise devoted to scientific tasks, and he also wrote the revised version of *Wilhelm Meister*.

For his part, Schiller gave his inaugural lecture in Jena on May 26, 1789. In the ensuing years he worked on the foundations of a new conception of man's being; and he began to present these views in 1793 in the letters *On the Aesthetic Education of Man*.

In 1794 he founded the monthly journal, *Die Horen* (The Horae), and, in a letter of June 11, invited Goethe to participate in it. Goethe gave his assent, and in the following month the memorable meeting marking the beginning of their friendship took place. In the following year, 1795, this journal published Goethe's *Conversations of German Emigrants* (which includes his *Fairy Tale of the Green Snake and the Beautiful Lily),* and Schiller's *On the Aesthetic Education of Man.* In these letters and in Goethe's *Fairy Tale* the seed was sown for a new image of the human being.

Something further was also taking place in this seven-year period. Novalis took the decisive inner steps leading to the unveiling of this spirit-world. His existence began to shine forth through his connection with Sophie von Kühn, which happened between 1795 and 1796. In March of the following year Sophie crossed the threshold of death, and her friend began to 'die after her.' She had revealed to him the gateway to the world of all-powerful night.

Destiny-groups were forming; for not only did Goethe and Schiller find one another but Friedrich Schlegel and Novalis became friends in 1792 in Dresden and thereby formed the core of the first romantic circle, which would grow in the coming years; with Friedrich Schlegel's brother August Wilhelm, and their wives Dorothea and Caroline, Ludwig Tieck and Schelling a group of people emerged amongst whom there was a real sense for the future.

At this time, however, Hahnemann was completely alone. He

was a man of solitude who fumbled about in the dark; he was also one who sought the veiled image at Sais, who wanted to tear aside the veil from the riddle of illness in order to build the temple of the new art of healing.

This period began for him in 1789, when he translated Cullen's *Treatise on Materia Medica*. Through this work he found the point of departure that he had been seeking for so long. Cullen was a famous Scottish physician, the founder of the Glasgow Medical School, who now taught in Edinburgh. In his book on *Materia Medica* he speaks about quinine and the properties of this substance. Hahnemann had doubts about Cullen's indications, and in order to find proofs for them he took quinine himself. What he now experienced was of the greatest significance; for the substance that was used to treat intermittent fever gave rise to intermittent fever if taken by a healthy person. Hahnemann observed himself as he experimented on his own body, and wrote: 'As an experiment I took four pinches of good quinine twice daily for a number of days; my feet, fingertips etc. first became cold, I felt faint and sleepy, then my heart started to pound, my pulse became faster and faster and more pronounced; a sense of exhaustion spread through my limbs; then my head started throbbing, my cheeks grew red and I felt thirsty — in short, all the usual symptoms of intermittent fever appeared one after another ... This paroxysm lasted for two to three hours each time, and was renewed when I repeated this dose, otherwise not. I stopped, and became healthy.'

In this way Hahnemann was tentatively finding the path that he would now pursue unremittingly. He began by testing medicines on a healthy person, and by degrees the idea of homeopathy grew. Seven years after this original experiment he was able to formulate it; and in an 'Essay on a New Principle for Ascertaining the Creative Power of Drugs,' he wrote: 'In imitation of Nature, which cures a chronic illness through another which is added to it, for the [chronic] illness which is to be cured one might use the one remedy which is able to provoke another,

2. SAMUEL HAHNEMANN

very similar, artificial illness, and the former one will be cured. *Similia similibus.*'

This was a discovery of immense proportions. For the first time the equation that Paracelsus had dimly discerned had been revealed to the thinking human mind:

$$\text{Remedy} = \text{Illness}$$
$$\text{Illness} = \text{Remedy}$$

Symptoms were now not merely the picture of the illness but the picture of the remedy. It is not the illness that one must seek but the medicine; the melody of the symptoms sings the song of the medicament.

Hahnemann writes in this article where he formulated his discovery: 'In my additions to Cullen's pharmacology I have already observed that with sensitive, albeit healthy people quinine in large doses causes a proper bout of fever that is similar to that of intermittent fever, and hence probably acts as a counterweight to the latter, which it cures. I now see after my more seasoned experience: not only probably *but quite definitely.*'

This article appeared in 1796 and was published in the *Journal der praktischen Arzneykunde,* edited and published by Hufeland. Hufeland was Professor at the University of Jena and the personal physician of Karl August, Grand Duke of Sachsen-Weimar, as well as being the physician of Goethe and Schiller.

When at the height of his fame Hahnemann looked back once more at the beginnings of his great discovery. In volume three of his *Reine Arzneimittellehre,* the following words appear in the discussion of cinchona bark:

> In the year 1790 I made my first experiment on myself with cinchona bark in connection with its capacity to cause intermittent fever, and with this initial experiment I experienced the dawn of the theory of healing and its shining forth into the full light of day. I learnt that medicines are merely states of illness with the power to

make a healthy person ill, and, moreover, are only able

to cure such illnesses as manifest symptoms which the medicine that is chosen for them can similarly engender in a healthy person.

Hahnemann was fully conscious of his great, revolutionary discovery. He was not conscious of the fact that this re-orientating of any healing art was taking place at the same time as Goethe was developing the theory of metamorphosis, Goethe and Schiller were presenting a comparable picture of man and Novalis was expounding the first ideas of a 'scientific Bible' and, hence, laying the foundations for establishing magical idealism.

All these different, dissimilar initiatives being developed by people with diverse natures nevertheless belonged together. The same star was shining upon these great results of human intellectual endeavour. Although Hahnemann, being a solitary wanderer, never came into direct contact with Goethe and Schiller or Novalis, he was their brother in the spirit; and those coming after him have the duty gradually to gain an understanding of this.

Novalis gave a description of Hahnemann and homeopathy, without knowing them intimately. He said:

> This inspired physician is in tune with himself and the object, but in the sense of mutual perfection rather than mutual confinement. He observes remedy and illness more precisely with every step, becomes little by little increasingly the master of illness and remedies and is the benevolent power who skilfully translates outward charms into a happy enemy of illness, both with regard to a harmonious interaction or structure and to dose (quantity), degree (quality) and frequency (rhythm).

Hahnemann tried hard to fulfil these demands.

III

Hahnemann's decisive article on a new principle for discovering the healing forces in remedies appeared in Hufeland's *Journal der praktischen Arzneykunde* (Journal of Practical Medicine) in 1796. In the same year and in the same volume of the journal another article appeared with the title 'Regarding the State of Health in the Cleve Institute.' The author was the physician of the poor-house of Cleve, a young 24-year-old man who had studied medicine in Jena under Hufeland. His name was Johann Gottfried Rademacher. His way of life was the total opposite of Hahnemann's; for he was truly settled in his abode. In April 1797 he went to Goch as the town physician and stayed there until his death in 1850. In the year of Hahnemann's death, 1843, Rademacher's sole, but important, work appeared; it had a long title, which was expressive of the author's strange position in the intellectual life of that time: *Rechtfertigung der von den Gelehrten misskanten, verstandesrechten Erfahrungsheillehre der altenscheidekünstigen Geheimärzte und treue Mittheilung des Ergebnisses einer fünfundzwanzigjährigen Erprobung dieser Lehre am Krankenbette* (Justification of the Theory of Experiential Healing, Misconstrued by Scholars but Intellectually Sound, of the Old Separatist Physicians Working out of Occult Sources, and a Faithful Sharing of the Result of a Twenty-Five-Year Testing of this Theory at the Sickbed). Such a title in 1843 was a unique event; three hundred years previously it would have been comprehensible and generally accepted. In this book the medicine of Paracelsus reappears unchanged and barely transformed, and Rademacher says in the foreword: 'It will surely not be offensive to the medical scrutiny and liberal attitudes of our time that I confess myself to be an honest man, and better taught by the heavenly world than by all physicians living before and with me.'

This book, although backward-looking, has at the same time a premonition of the future. It exhibits a profound knowledge of man, and the experiences of 'the old man of Goch' are of much greater value than much of what has been produced in the field of medicine since he wrote. For example, he divides his 'organs of healing' into those of the stomach, the chest and the head, hence, anticipating Rudolf Steiner's later ideas of the threefold nature of the human organism.

His 'universal remedies' are saltpetre (potassium nitrate), copper and iron, and so he was giving an indication of what Rudolf Steiner was subsequently to say regarding blood being constantly ill and in need of healing.

Rademacher was much in demand as a physician; he was the physician of the little man, of the poor and the ordinary citizen, and anyone who sought his help would receive it. Born in the same year as Novalis (1772), he died in the middle of the nineteenth century, where he stood out as a last visible sign of a spiritual past. He resembled his master Paracelsus even in his physiognomy, and words emerged from his soul such as the following:

> Who has glimpsed the hidden hearth of the subterranean fire? Who has calculated its influence on the human body? When it shakes the earth and bursts forth from mountains in glowing streams, we know that it brings destruction to man; but we do not know its quiet, homely thundering in the depths. Who has fathomed the influence of the stars on the human body, whether they merely shine before us in the dark night or determine our health, our lives? It would be presumptuous to maintain that the seven stars, the ring of Saturn or the Medusa head of Perseus have an influence on my body; but to deny it would be no less presumptuous.

At the end of his book, on page 1309, he begins his 'Last Words to the Reader' with the sentences:

> My old master Hufeland told me — as I was still almost young and he was not yet old — that I should examine

2. SAMUEL HAHNEMANN

everything and choose the best. This is indeed a very understandable thing to say; but it is impossible for anyone on his own to examine everything unless he has previously thought clearly about what the totality that needs to be examined consists of.

This is how he makes reference to the man at whose feet he had sat as a young student in Jena: Christian Wilhelm Hufeland. Hufeland was probably the most famous physician of his age. He was no reformer but a maintainer and preserver. Nevertheless, he was a focus for all the different threads, and he had a certain understanding of each of these threads.

On March 2, 1792, as a thirty-year old, Hufeland read some extracts from his book, *Makrobiotik,* in the *Freitagsgesellschaft* (Friday Society) founded and led by Goethe. He was immediately — probably at Goethe's suggestion — appointed by Grand Duke Karl August to Jena University as a Professor. He remained there until 1801; then he went to Berlin University, where he likewise became a world-famous teacher of medicine and a practising physician; and he died there in 1836.

He summed up his life as a physician by publishing shortly before his death a work entitled *Enchiridion medicum.* Whereas one might call Rademacher's *Erfahrungsheillehre* a Dionysian book, Hufeland's *Enchiridion* is a thoroughly Apollonian work: a masterpiece in its content, language and structure. The evening twilight of the setting spiritual sun gently illumines this eclectic book. The foreword concludes with these words:

> May it be received in this sense with a ready will and good intentions and achieve its purpose of bringing benefits, and especially of being a sure guide to prospective physicians at the sick-bed! For I shall conclude my literary career with the same motto with which I began it: *Nisi utile est, quod agimus, vana est gloria nostra* [If what we do is not useful, our glory is vain].

A few weeks later Hufeland was dead. But his book continues even today to be a source of that noble spirit who knew of the destruction of the old but approached the unfathomable night with a quiet wisdom.

Hufeland drew a clear line under the medicine of a whole epoch. His book is without hope; it is not inspiring like Rademacher's *Erfahrungsheillehre,* but nor is it pioneering like Hahnemann's *Organon of the Healing Art.* The *Enchiridion* brings together what has been the idea and practice of medicine over the past two thousand years. As one reads individual sections of this book one often does not know whether they are not simply quotations from the *Corpus Hippocraticum.*

Thus the section on 'Diagnostics' begins with a description of the constitutions and then soon proceeds to the four temperaments; and he characterizes the choleric, sanguine, phlegmatic and melancholic temperaments as if he were speaking of blood, of phlegm, of yellow and black gall — and this was one of the pillars of Hippocratic medicine.

He introduces the chapter entitled 'Practice' with maxims which are of a wholly Hippocratic nature: 'Art is eternal, systems are transient.' 'Art belongs to man's inner sanctum; systems belong to time, whose products they are.' 'We have other forms of illness, other means of healing, other concepts and ways of explaining things than in olden times; but the art of healing is still the same, nature is the same, and the same qualities are needed to be a great physician as in the time of Hippocrates.'

The first of Hippocrates's propositions (his collection of aphorisms) is as follows: 'Life is short, art is long, opportunities are fleeting, experience is uncertain, judgment is difficult. Not only must the physician be prepared to do what is required but also the patient himself, his carers and outer life's circumstances.'

This is the same language and the same spirit that has declared itself here. But what in Hippocrates is full of radiant power and is like the light of the morning sun has become quite different in Hufeland; it is irradiated with the light of the setting sun.

2. SAMUEL HAHNEMANN

For Hufeland there were only three cardinal remedies; he calls them 'Heroica' as they were known traditionally: bleeding, opium and emetics. Hippocrates also taught this.

At the beginning of the *Enchiridion* Hufeland says of himself:

> By 'natural healing' I mean the only true art of healing based on eternal laws! It is what from Hippocrates onwards was always the ideal of true physicians and has continued to be that of true practitioners throughout all changes of the school system! This is what I profess myself and what I have always known.

Only a thoroughly Greek-oriented mind could speak in this way; this is why he taught first in Jena and then in Berlin, which was the centre of the Greek feeling for existence at that time. Hence Hufeland was Goethe's doctor and felt himself belonging fully to his circle.

As the motto for his *Makrobiotik* he chose Goethe's words: 'Sweet life! Beautiful friendly familiarity of existence and activity — must I really part from you?' Is this not reminiscent of the adage of the Greek soul that speaks of how it is better to be a beggar on earth than a king in the realm of the shades? The frontispiece shows the Three Fates spinning the threads of life.

Whereas Rademacher looks towards Paracelsus, Hufeland gazes back to Hippocrates. Hahnemann, however, is the third member of the group. He, like Rademacher, had a very friendly relationship with Hufeland. In his letters to him there is an underlying cordial warmth, which was otherwise completely absent in what he said. He begins one of his letters to Hufeland with the words: 'My dearest friend! Not for you but for the sake of yourself and my unimpeded access to your excellent heart must I have the pleasure of pouring out my whole way of thinking and convictions, as I would have liked to have done before the public long ago.' The ensuing sixteen-page letter is a fiery document that Hahnemann — as a man possessed by his idea — gives expression to. He writes:

> If this path which I have found in quiet contemplation
> of nature — once having suppressed all feasible
> preconceptions — that leads with a sure certainty to health
> and well-being flatly contradicts all the dogmas of our
> medical school, just as Luther's Theses which he nailed
> to the door of Wittenberg's Castle Church contradicted
> the hierarchy that was crippling the spirit, neither my nor
> Luther's truths can be blamed for that. Just as he did not
> deserve the venom of prejudice, nor do I.

This has a different sound from Rademacher's nocturnal words and the evening propositions of Hufeland. Here there is a Promethean struggle, protesting and destructive of the old, reaching out of the depths to the light. Whereas Rademacher acknowledges himself to be a pupil of the alchemists and Hufeland looks back to Hippocrates, Hahnemann is indebted to no one. He feels himself to be the first and only one. 'Here I stand, I can do no other,' could also be his words.

And whereas Rademacher wrote his *Erfahrungsheillehre* and Hufeland his *Enchiridion* looking back at their work as doctors, Hahnemann produced *The Organon of the Healing Art,* at the beginning of his homeopathic practice. It appeared in 1810, and Hahnemann was only to die 33 years later; his life's work as a physician still lay before him.

But he recognized himself as an 'only one.' In the foreword to the first edition of the *Organon* he states:

> I give myself credit for being the only one to have carried
> out a serious, honest revision of the art of medicine and
> to have presented the consequences of his convictions to
> the public eye partly in anonymous writings and partly
> under his own name. In the course of these investigations
> I have found the path to the truth that I had to follow
> alone, very far removed from the military road of medical
> observance.

Then comes a long introduction of nearly 90 pages, in which examples of the homeopathic way of healing are cited from medical books of the past two thousand years. And then the *Organon* begins like a mighty cannon. Paragraph after paragraph follow one another in succinct words and apodictic sentences which have the effect of building blocks; one block is placed upon the other until finally the structure of the whole basic principles of homeopathy has been erected.

> [Paragraph 1 states briefly and concisely:] The highest and sole calling of the physician is to make sick people well, which is called healing.

> [Paragraph 2:] The highest ideal of healing is a quick, gentle and lasting restoration of health, or the alleviation and overcoming of illness to its full extent in the shortest, most reliable and least harmful ways, in accordance with clearly perceivable reasons.

> [In paragraph 6 there is a clear statement that] the invisible inner changes brought about through illness and the changes in outward appearance discernible to our senses (embodied in the symptoms) together form before the eye the creative omnipotence that one calls illness; but merely the totality of the symptoms is the side of the illness that is turned towards the healer, this alone is perceptible to him and the only aspect of the illness of which he has knowledge, which he needs for his profession as a healer.

There then follows a description of the significance of symptoms, the referring of symptoms to the remedy that has been chosen, the testing of medicines on healthy people and everything that has since then become the foundation of homeopathic practice.

In these more than 300 paragraphs or building-blocks there is hardly any argumentation. The language is very evocative and assertive, and eloquently imparts the truth that it is seeking to convey. The word-structure has something rhapsodic about it, something that is integral to what is being expressed and manifests the will that underlies it.

Thus the motto which was placed at the beginning of the *Organon* from the second edition onwards is a summons: *Aude sapere* — dare to be wise.

Each of these three books — Rademacher's *Erfahrungsheillehre,* Hufeland's *Enchiridion medicum* and Hahnemann's *Organon of the Healing Art* — has its own language and diction. If one tries to enter into the inner life of these three works and to follow the development of its language and the sequence of its thoughts, they can be transformed in such a way that they become architectonic structures which manifest their authors' minds and spirits.

Then the *Erfahrungsheillehre* becomes a Gothic cathedral in whose darkness the reader intuitively immerses himself until, by raising his head aloft, he can perceive the wonderful play of colours of the glass windows. A deep religious faith fills the crowd of praying people there; the mysterious singing of the choir sounds forth from aloft, raising the spirits.

The *Enchiridion,* however, is transformed into a Greek temple. The sky of Greece opens up over it; the gateway is open and light floods into it. People who affirm the earth are climbing up and down the steps of the temple, and noble columns frame the building. The lines are simply and livingly ordered.

The *Organon* is something else again. It leads back into early times; the building blocks of the paragraphs become separate blocks of stone arranged in concentric circles. Stone stands beside stone on a solitary hill. The crowd is outside, beyond the holy circle, which is the sole preserve of priests offering up the sacrifice in the light of the rising sun. A holy grove of celebrating Druids appears, surrounded by towering stones. What does this mean?

IV

When Hippocrates left the temple of Aesculepius on Cos behind him and made his way through the lands of Greece as a wandering doctor, a new age of medicine began. What had hitherto been embedded in the mysterious working of the mysteries now appeared in the light of day. The sun of the bestowing spirit was extinguished, and independent thinking was beginning to ray forth. What had formerly been encompassed within the words and deeds of priests was now transmuted into the coinage of a thinking and acting born from understanding. Hippocrates betrayed the mysteries and so laid the foundations of a medical art which could be understood by those studying this art. He gave the rules of a physician's activity and conduct, just as Aristotle gave the laws of logic.

He described the effects of nature on man and depicted man himself as an intermingling of soul and bodily natures. Even though what had been so alive within Hippocrates became gradually more and more abstract through the imprint of the Roman and Arabic element, it was nevertheless the same being who continued to exist there: Hippocratic medicine. It lived through two thousand years; then it died. The real mortal hour of this medicine fell in the time of the latter part of the eighteenth century. Rudolf Steiner indicated that each cultural epoch lasts 2160 years. That was also the length of the lifetime of Hippocratic medicine.

In 1805 Hahnemann published a small booklet entitled *Aesculepius in the Balance,*[1] where the following observation appears:

> We were never nearer the discovery of the science of medicine than in the time of Hippocrates. This attentive, unsophisticated observer sought Nature in Nature. He saw and described the diseases before him accurately, without addition, without colouring, without speculation.

In the faculty of pure observation he has been surpassed by no later physician. Of only one important part of the medical art was this favourite son of Nature destitute, else had he been completely master of his art: the knowledge of medicines and their application.

With this Hahnemann defines himself as the fulfiller of what Hippocrates was unable to bring about. He sensed the end of a medical epoch and saw himself as the prophet of one that was newly beginning.

In the same year of 1805 Hahnemann wrote a longer treatise entitled *Medicine of Experience*,[2] which appeared simultaneously in Hufeland's journal and as a book. This treatise was a kind of initial exploration of what appeared before the world five years later as the *Organon*.

If we calculate 2160 years back from that year, we arrive at the year 355 BC, the year of Hippocrates's death. Thus Hahnemann, together with Hufeland and Rademacher, stands at the turning point of the Hippocratic age of medicine. From Hippocrates's death until the time of Hahnemann 72 orbits of Saturn have passed; at this cosmic moment the pulse of the cycle of the planets has beaten 72 times. Medicine stands before a new resolve; three physicians feel the pulse-beat of this turning point and know that the breath of life is expiring.

Hufeland looks backwards; his eye is directed towards Greece and is as though immersed in this memory.

Rademacher brings inwardly to life the seed of that new impulse which had proclaimed itself 300 years previously in Paracelsus. Then in Paracelsus it appeared as an initial glimmer which would come to fulfilment only later.

Hahnemann, however, looks forwards. He carries the impulse to find the right remedy on its way, once he has destroyed the erroneous and outmoded concepts of illness.

The path of Hippocratic medicine went from the south-east to the north-west; it began in Cos and ended in Köthen. It was

2. SAMUEL HAHNEMANN

not a straight path, for it went via North Africa and Spain, intermingling with the Arab element; but the main direction was that from Cos to Köthen. But there at the end of its existence it encountered Hahnemann. He carried another spiritual stream, for in Hahnemann there was a first manifestation of what had hitherto been evident only in the foundations of medicine as an invisible spring. This spring originated in the north-west, where Celtic places for initiation of a Druidic nature in Ireland and Scotland, Gaul and Wales had preserved the mystery of medicine. What in the course of the Middle Ages had sometimes come to light in the form of herbal books now became openly apparent with Hahnemann.

Just as the south-eastern stream bore the mystery of illness, so was the mystery of medicine concealed within the north-western stream. Now they converged; the Hippocratic river had become old and empty, whereas that of Hahnemann had remained young and vigorous.

The old river had left a corpse behind it, and this was permeated, conserved and prepared by the agnostic science that became widespread in the nineteenth century and lives among us as the mighty mummy of present-day mainstream medicine.

Hahnemann's stream, however, remained a little brook, because it has hitherto not managed to embrace the spiritual influence of the Hippocratic stream which has been liberated from its sheath. Only if these two unite and acknowledge the third element which has begun to appear in Paracelsus and Rademacher will the true art of healing arise once more. This will then unite the mystery of illness with the mystery of medicine and link this with the Christian healing influence which was truly beheld for the first time by Paracelsus.

However, this will come about only if the gates of the mysteries opened by Rudolf Steiner can be traversed. What Goethe's *Fairy Tale* revealed by way of wisdom and what Schiller's *Letters on Aesthetic Education* expressed in thought-forms could subsequently be made manifest as anthroposophy at the beginning of the twentieth century. At that time, too, the foundations of homeopathy came into being; and they can form a connection with the new spiritual-scientifically orientated medicine if the path to anthroposophy is followed.

Just as Hegel, the Greek, Schelling, the Christian, and Fichte, the Celt, signify the end of philosophy and at the same time anticipate what will later arise as a new science of the spirit, so for the realm of medicine do Hufeland, the Greek, Rademacher, the Christian, and Hahnemann, the Celt, point towards what must be born from the womb of the dying mother as a new medicine of the mysteries. If the crystalline form of the injection of homeopathy can be filled with the substance of a re-born Hippocratic element and takes into itself the radiance of the Paracelsian proclamation, it will be the foundation stone of a restored image of man, an *anthropos* imbued with Sophia.

May Hahnemann's power, Hufeland's devotion and Rademacher's inner depth begin to work amongst physicians of the future.

3

Ernst, Baron von Feuchtersleben

Baron von Feuchtersleben (1806-1849) was born and died in Vienna. He was a physician, poet and philosopher.

I

Feuchtersleben lived in Vienna and its immediate proximity, and his earthly life belonged to the first half of the nineteenth century. This is already enough to characterize a large part of his world, for seldom has a city manifested at any particular time such a unified, all-encompassing and characteristic aspect as did Vienna in the early decades of the nineteenth century. It was as though both were intimately connected: the city and its time. They were so harmoniously matched that the great Vienna Congress could never be held anywhere other than Vienna. This period of history could be experienced at that time as having reached a point of the highest perfection; and it was suitably expressed by the congress in this city on the Danube.

A further reason why the whole period was mirrored with such precision in the Viennese air and in the waves of the river was that Vienna was by then no longer a German city. Ferdinand Kürnberger expressed it thus:

You would be doing this city a real and undeserved injustice if you measured it with a German yardstick and claimed it as a German city. On the other hand, all becomes light and clear, intelligible and understandable, right and reasonable, if you take Vienna for what it is — a city on the frontier between Europe and Asia! ... Europe represents law, Asia capriciousness; Europe has a strict matter-of-fact quality, Asia reflects the purely personal element.[1]

Even though this somewhat crude characterization is not altogether appropriate, it was nevertheless the case that the Near East, Turkey and Syria, Egypt and Persia, Arabia and above all the Balkans communicated to a very intimate degree with Europe through Vienna — particularly at the time when the Orient was beginning to reveal its intellectual treasures, and Persian and Arabic literature was streaming towards Europe instead of Asiatic hordes.

Just as at this time Humboldt and Schopenhauer in Germany were deepening their experience of the literature of ancient India, it was Joseph von Hammer-Purgstall who brought both access and respect to the culture of the Near East. Through him the Ottoman Empire was recognized as a land of high civilization; the songs of Hafiz, the singing of Bakis and the stanzas of the *Rubaiyat* of Omar Khayyam became part of the cultural life of Germany. Through Hammer-Purgstall Goethe found his way to the *West-Eastern Divan,* and Rückert and Platen discovered the sources of many of their writings. Sheherazade began to disseminate her world of magic, and Ferdinand Raimund held his fairies and spirits captive on the stages of the Josefstadt and Leopoldstadt theatres, where thousands cheered him on every week. Here Oriental figures came to life: Tutu and Zoraide, Aladdin and Zephises, Lacrimosa and Borax, Moisasur and Mansur. They mingled without any coquettishness or barrier with Franzl and Mali, with Habukuk and Valentine, for on both

3. ERNST, BARON VON FEUCHTERSLEBEN

Ernst, Baron von Feuchtersleben

sides, in the Arabian land of spirits as well as in the city of Vienna, everything was really somewhat similar, and the boundaries were thoroughly blurred.

This was also the main difference between the romanticism of Heidelberg and Vienna; in the north, in central Germany, the German Middle Ages stood in the background, youth's magic horn *(des Knaben Wunderhorn)* sounded forth, and the children's stories and folk tales of the Brothers Grimm blossomed. But here in Vienna there lived *A Thousand and One Nights,* reflecting the magical world of Arabia. The sultan with his harem, assassins and their mysterious customs, dervishes and the world of Mecca and Medina were interwoven far more closely and directly into life than was the case elsewhere in Europe at that time.

But Vienna was not only this. For the world of music, which is very difficult to express in words, was linked with it. To be sure, Mozart had died in 1791 and Haydn followed in 1809, but their harmonies and melodies pervaded the town houses and the palaces of the nobility, concert halls and many churches. Beethoven was at the height of his powers in this middle period of his life, which began in 1801 with the music for *The Creatures of Prometheus* and ended with the Ninth Symphony. Schubert composed over five hundred songs and also created the endless richness of the melodies that pervade his sonatas, chamber music and symphonic works. Moreover, there was a further circle of other composers — not least Lanner and Johann Strauss I, whose dances and marches wafted as dominant rhythms through the Viennese atmosphere.

In addition, there were the paintings of Schwind and Waldmüller, Danhauser and Führich, who with each one of their strokes and colours tried to capture the scent of that bygone time; and some of them kept the magic breath of this time intact as a legacy until the second half of the nineteenth century.

Alongside Raimund there also lived Nestroy and Bauernfeld, Lenau and Grillparzer, and Stifter spent his younger days in this environment. It is therefore understandable that the editor of the great *Oxford History of Music,* Sir William Henry Hadow, made the following pronouncement: 'If I had to list the three greatest artistic ages in world history, I would give first place to the Athens of Pericles, the second to Elizabethan England and the third without any doubt to Vienna in the second half of the eighteenth and the first quarter of the nineteenth centuries.'[2]

If this Englishman had been a real artist, he would only have spoken of the first quarter of the nineteenth century, for the Vienna of Joseph II and his successors between 1770 and 1800 was by no means the over-ripe, perfected and sweet fruit which matured between 1805 and 1830 on the tree of history and shortly afterwards faded away.

Only in these few years did the magic of music pervade the entire life and existence of this city. But it was no mere charming merriment and amorous courtship; there was also a considerable depth of feeling and a burning urge for freedom. The musical inspiration derived from contact with a spiritual world. Beethoven once declared to Bettina von Arnim that 'music is a higher revelation than all wisdom and philosophy. It is the wine that inspires one to new creations, and I am the Bacchus who prepares this marvellous wine for people and makes it intoxicated with the spirit.'

A similar intoxication is expressed in Grillparzer's lines which he dedicated to Queen Music:

> With the radiant sovereign crown,
> With the sweetly sounding mouth
> And eyes sparkling with madness,
> Brandishing a delicate plectrum ...

It was in this world that the great trilogy *Das goldne Vlies* (The Golden Fleece), with Medea as its central figure, came to Grillparzer's mind. Medea is the queen with 'eyes sparkling with madness'; she comes from Colchis, from those regions of the Near East that border upon Persia and harbour the last memories of the mysteries.

The ardent kiss of this muse had captivated all who were living in Vienna at that time. Life became a strange mixture of dream and reality, so that the title of Grillparzer's play *Der Traum ein Leben* (The Dream, a Life) was entirely appropriate. And in a play by Raimund Fantasy sings:

> In poetic high spirits
> I weave through celestial spheres,
> I stick the sun on my hat
> And play dice with the stars.

'It doesn't get better than this' — these are the restrained high spirits of an epoch which later threatened to suffocate in bourgeois self-satisfaction, exhausted itself in Nestroyan intellectualism and petered out in the dullness of Viennese operetta. But at that time, in the 1820s, something was living in Vienna that made it one of the most beautiful and most enchanting periods of human history.

The decline that rapidly ensued occurred in part because another gift from the Orient invaded Europe. Between 1830 and 1832 cholera spread with frightening speed throughout the European continent. It originated in India, then raged for many years in Persia and came from there to Vienna and Austria and thence to Germany, France and England. The East did not only give its wisdom but also its destiny.

In Raimund's last *Original-Zaubermärchen in drei Aufzügen* (Original Fairy-Tale in Three Acts), the fairy Cheristane says to the 'wastrel' Herr von Flatwell: 'Know this: you have no human being clasped to your breast. Cheristane is my name, I am of fairy lineage and my home is in the distant clouds that drift in eternal magic circles over Persia and Arabia.'

That is the innermost picture of that magical time. People were wastrels, and they held a fairy in their arms which then returned whence it had come: to the distant clouds drifting over Persia and Arabia. The destiny of the Viennese Biedermeier age had come to an end, and a new epoch dawned.

3. ERNST, BARON VON FEUCHTERSLEBEN

II

It was amidst this special and extraordinary time that Feuchtersleben spent his childhood, youth and early manhood. He associated with Schubert, Bauernfeld and Schwind and was a member of this whole circle. He was on intimate terms with Baron von Spaun and Grillparzer. Thus he imbibed with great intensity the mood and life of this period, and — like the majority of his many friends — died young.

He was born in Vienna on April 29, 1806. His father was an imperial counsellor and his uncle, his father's brother, was a Field Marshal. Thus he belonged to a family from the Austrian civil and military nobility.

His father must have been a strange man, probably a somewhat eccentric gentleman who, shortly after his son qualified as a physician, committed suicide and left many debts. In his first marriage he was married to the daughter of the well-known 'Moor' Angelo Soliman. His father-in-law was a rich and well-educated man who moved in the high circles of the imperial city and epitomized the Oriental aspect of Vienna. His first wife soon died, and Feuchtersleben remarried. The first child from his second marriage was a son, Ernst. However, this wife also died early, and the child initially grew up in the country until, at the age of seven, he came to Vienna to be educated at the Theresian Academy.

This educational establishment, the Theresianum, was a Catholic boarding-school for the sons of German and Czech nobility in Austria. It prepared young barons and counts for careers in the higher echelons of the civil service with much Hapsburg tradition and ecclesiastical strictness.

The school lacked any breadth of vision, and its ruling principles were narrowness and suppression. Feuchtersleben remained at this academy for twelve years, and he subsequently said of it: 'Only with reluctance does life go forward. In the school of servitude I learnt to be free, and in the midst of darkness I boldly ignited a spark like Prometheus and nurtured it.'[3] The future dietician of the soul and the philosopher of a practical psychology are already manifesting themselves here.

In contrast to what was generally customary and specifically also against his father's advice he decided not to pursue a career in the civil service but to study medicine. He himself gave the following account of this:

> A citizen's worth is determined by the extent of his activity in relation to his powers. After careful consideration I believe that I am best able to work in accordance with my individuality in the profession of a physician. It seemed to me the most desirable outcome to be able to give my fellow citizens direct access to a state of well-being. With this thought I always carried the image of the physician before my soul, as one who has so evident an influence on people's lives and work.

Thus he thoroughly felt himself to be a citizen; his liberal convictions were already apparent at that time, and he tried to act in accordance with them. When he entered university in 1825 (Karl Julius Schröer, Rudolf Steiner's teacher, was born in the same year) he published two treatises in the journal *Isis:* 'On the Study of Nature,' and 'On Genius.' Both the fundamental trends of his research were already in evidence here. He proceeded from observation of nature and tried to penetrate on this basis into the realm of human soul-activity.

In the course of his studies he not only engaged with medical colleagues but made a deep study of philosophical questions, and took a particular interest in Oriental linguistics. It was said that, together with his friend Romeo Seligman, who was to become Professor of the History of Medicine at Vienna University, he learnt fully to master Arabic and Persian.

He qualified as a physician on June 9, 1834. Shortly afterwards he married a girl with whom he had had an intimate friendship for many years. Helena was to be a faithful wife, who was as devoted as a sister to him until his death. Hebbel had this to say about the early period of their marriage:

> A modest dwelling was rented in a suburb and the medical practice was started. Naturally, every patient who sent for the young physician was poor, so that not only was no payment made for his services but very often the chemist had to be paid on the patient's behalf. This general situation was exacerbated because Feuchtersleben's baronial title, which he had renounced in his youth and then taken up again, inhibited prosperous individuals from offering him ready cash and caused them to send him a superfluous luxury item instead of a few banknotes. When they went to bed in the evening, the young couple were so anxious to economize that they did not allow themselves even a little stump of candle to read themselves to sleep.[4]

As during the time at the Theresianum, a virtue was made of necessity. Feuchtersleben began to write a large number of literary, aesthetic and critical articles and became a much sought-after contributor to various magazines, journals and booklets. In this way he earned his living.

In 1835 a medical treatise on *Das hippokratische erste Buch von der Diät* (the First Hippocratic Book on Diet) appeared. The following year Cotta published the first edition of his poems, and in 1838 his most famous work, *Zur Diätetik der Seele* (Dietetics of the Soul) was published. Immediately after its appearance it made a considerable impression on his contemporaries, and had to be reprinted several times. Many were of the opinion that, since the appearance of Goethe's *The Sorrows of Young Werther,* no book had achieved so direct an influence on its readership as did the *Dietetics*.

The following year a further medical volume appeared: *Über der Gewissheit und Würde der Heilkunst* (On the Certainty and Value of the Art of Healing), which was intended for patients and endeavoured to explain to them the right attitude with regard to the physician and to medicine in general.

In 1840 the meteoric rise of the young doctor began. He was chosen as secretary of the Society of Physicians founded in 1838 and remained in this post for four years. His work in this regard included taking responsibility for correspondence, drawing up minutes and publishing negotiations and lectures. Neuberger said in this regard: 'It is a real pleasure to read the four annual reports which Feuchtersleben presented at the celebratory gatherings; behind the bare figures and unadorned facts one immediately senses the thinker who always discerns the universal in the particular, the author who even knows how to write a chronicle on artistic achievement.'

He resigned from this position as secretary when he was appointed Professor of Psychiatry, and — probably as one of the first in universities at that time — gave the medical students of all years a course of lectures on 'medical psychology.' These lectures appeared in the following year under the title *Lehrbuch der ärztlichen Seelenkunde* (Manual for a Physician's Soul-Science). An immense amount of material was included here, and his lecture courses were so well attended that not only did the largest lecture theatre have to be made available but the other professors demanded that their lectures were not timetabled against his, as otherwise they would have had to lecture to empty chairs.

An invigorating breath of liberal thinking and broad convictions must have pervaded these lectures, for the students were enthusiastically devoted to their professor. The faculty now also chose him as its dean, and he began to reform the entire structure of medical study. He succeeded in this by degrees to such an extent that in 1847 he was appointed 'Vice-Director of Medical and Surgical Studies.' This led him to become chairman of the professorial group of the Faculty of Medicine, and he now began to work in every way he could towards achieving a future freedom for teaching and learning at the university. He presented his views in a remarkably courageous address on

3. ERNST, BARON VON FEUCHTERSLEBEN

April 20, 1847, which he gave in commemoration of the fiftieth jubilee of Vienna University. In the front row of his audience sat Metternich with the other ministers of the reactionary regime. Feuchtersleben then said,

> We are awake, and see with regret how little we have won through edifices of thought and literary works. With bitterness does a man condemn the times in which we are living before the court of humanity, since dreams and abstractions have been imparted to our maturing youth instead of useful knowledge and insights into life.[5]

Then came the year 1848. Feuchtersleben was in direct contact with the rebelling students. He helped them to be properly armed, and after the success of the insurrections in March and July he was chosen by the graduates of the university by acclamation as their representative in the newly formed Frankfurt Assembly. He turned down this nomination and also his appointment as Minister for Teaching and Education in the newly chosen cabinet. His friend, Baron Doblhoff, took on this post, and Feuchtersleben became his first junior permanent secretary. He developed a new structure for education and studies. Many of his memoranda and suggestions became the connecting thread of all educational reform for several decades. For example, it was through him that Latin ceased to be the language of instruction at universities; he tried to free primary and secondary schools from the church concordat and introduced scientific subjects into grammar schools.

He gave up his post in response to the bloody October uprisings in the same year.

> I can only develop, prove myself and be properly active if I am trusted. I am not made for any task that cannot be accomplished with a slow or at any rate calm and collected consistency. A person seeking to lead and create should never be regarded as a mere deputy; he needs

to be given the space to work that he has been allocated through the trust placed in his insight.[6]

He left the Ministry for Teaching so as to resume his place — after a brief holiday — as Vice-Director of Medical Studies. However, the professorial group opposed him, and he had to tender his resignation from the university. At the age of 43 he withdrew into private life.

In response to the October uprisings a reactionary government was brought in which tried to render all reforms that had been achieved null and void; and as the faculty had turned against Feuchtersleben he saw everything that he had striven and hoped for disappear into oblivion. The freedom that he had anticipated had not appeared.

On the morning of March 15, 1848 he wrote a poem that begins with the following words:

> Now stands it there, transfigured before our eyes
> In dawn's red glow, our heart's most ardent yearning.
> The truth is hardly different from the poem,
> The eye blinks, tear-filled as yet with grief,
> Shuts, blinded by the radiance of new life,
> Looks once more — and yes, freedom is truly nigh.

But this freedom did not last. Deeply discouraged and disappointed, Feuchtersleben laid down his intellectual weapons. He submitted to the ingratitude of his contemporaries and succumbed to an ever more all-consuming melancholy. He was soon unable to leave his bed, and in the last weeks before his death he finally refused all nourishment. The forces of the abyss had overwhelmed him. These were the years of darkness and denial of the spirit which now descended upon Europe; Feuchtersleben was their first victim.

His wife cared for him, and a friend from his youth, Romeo Seligmann, treated him medically. He died on September 3, 1849 in total isolation, embittered and withdrawn from the world. The poem that he wrote and which, in Mendelssohn's setting, became a popular song expresses already in its first verse what death was to bring him:

> It is ordained in God's decree
> That one must avoid what one
> Likes best;
> Although nothing in all the world
> Is so difficult for the heart
> As parting, yes, parting!

III

When Feuchtersleben entered Vienna University in 1825, the medical school was no longer what it had been at the end of the previous century: the famous faculty visited by the whole of Europe, where doctors such as van Swieten, de Haen, Stoll and Peter Frank taught. It had some good teachers, but none of them had a capacity for breadth and wisdom.

However, two other medical students studied with Feuchtersleben who, together with him, were to renew the vocation of the Vienna School: Joseph Škoda and Carl Rokitansky. Feuchtersleben was born in 1806, Škoda in 1805 and Rokitansky in 1804; the latter two came from Bohemia, Škoda from Pilsen (Plzen) and Rokitansky from Königgrätz (now Hradec Králové). Neither of these two had the cultural background that filled Feuchtersleben's soul. The Vienna of Schubert's time was alien to them; they were rational people whose destiny it was to bring about the end of Hippocratic medicine.

Škoda was the son of a poor metalworker and spent his childhood and youth in Pilsen. Through the help of a Viennese family it was possible for him to enter the university in 1825, the same year as Feuchtersleben, and he mainly studied physics and mathematics. He had a quite particular gift for these two disciplines, but all the same — guided by his teachers' advice — became a physician. In 1831 he qualified as a doctor of medicine, and after working for a short time in Bohemia treating cholera, he returned to Vienna as an unpaid assistant at the General Hospital. Here he began his fundamental research on auscultation and percussion.

In 1836 he published in the *Medical Annuals of the Imperial and Royal Austrian State* his first work on percussion, which launched a complete re-thinking of the theory developed in France ... In 1837 Škoda made an important contribution 'On the Heartbeat and the Tones evoked by the Heart's Movements' and another one 'On the Use of Percussion for Studying the Organs of the Lower Abdomen.'[7]

In 1839 his comprehensive 'Treatises regarding Percussion and Auscultation' appeared, and in 1841 he became Principal of the Vienna Hospital. Škoda raised physical diagnosis to a teachable method; he developed it in the finest detail, and through him the science of diagnosis became an important part of medicine. In therapy he was tentative, ready to 'wait and see' and careful, and his pupils became therapeutic 'nihilists.' With Škoda mathematical physics entered medicine.

Rokitansky's youth was arduous and impoverished. His father died when the child was only nine years old. He attended school in his father's town and in Leitmeritz (Litomerice), and went to Prague University. Dissatisfied with the teachers there he moved to Vienna in 1824 and qualified four years later at the Faculty of Medicine. Immediately after he qualified he worked in the dissection department of the General Hospital.

> The first of Rokitansky's written records of a dissection is of October 23, 1829. The sequence of his opening up of corpses begins with the number 4781; it ends with his departure from the institute on August 31, 1875 and the number 64,567 is recorded; and there were at least

an additional 25,000 forensic dissections. This signifies an abundance of experience which only a genius can survey, organize and connect. It was not enough for Rokitansky to link his separate findings together; his concern was to discover the physical and physiological connections in the living organism, to trace the changes in the organs ever further back and no longer to leave it to chance whether they would be found. These methods brought something new, clarified what was familiar, answered what was open to question and yielded sharp and clearly discernible pictures of illnesses and types of illness as regards their causes, their development, their course and their consequences.'[8]

Between 1842 and 1846 his *Handbook of Pathological Anatomy* appeared, one of the fundamental works of modern medicine. Rudolf Steiner spoke about it in the following way:

> Interestingly enough, it is possible to point precisely to the two decades in which this transformation came about, when any relics of the legacy of olden times were abandoned and the atomistic and materialistic view inherent in modern medicine was established. If you take the trouble to peruse Rokitansky's *Handbook of Pathological Anatomy,* published in 1842, you will still find traces of the old humoral pathology, remnants of the view that illness arises from an abnormal interaction of fluids. The view that one must pay attention to this blending of fluids — which one can only do if one continues to have some awareness of the supra-earthly qualities of fluids — was very ingeniously incorporated by Rokitansky into his observations of changes in organs ... Thus in 1842, I would say, you have the last manifestation of the legacy of the old humoral pathology.[9]

Humoral pathology is the final legacy of Hippocratic medicine, which had outlived its usefulness by the beginning of the nineteenth century.

When, several years after the appearance of the *Handbook,* a sharp criticism of its theories rained down upon Rokitansky from none other than the young Rudolf Virchow, the older anatomist revised the next edition of his pathological anatomy and restructured it almost entirely upon cellular pathology. This eradicated any last traces of an older view.

All this was taking place when Feuchtersleben become secretary of the Society of Physicians, the dean of the Faculty of Medicine and Professor of Psychiatry. This man, whose youth had been spent in the magical world of the now fading Viennese Biedermeier culture, the friend of musicians, poets and painters, had now been plunged into the inevitable sobriety of the period prior to the revolution in March 1848 and, in his field of medicine, was in the midst of these changes. The teachings of Hippocrates were buried, and modern science with its observation and experiment took its place.

To Feuchtersleben this reorientation was a wholly justified impulse of his time. When, subsequently, he was working at the Ministry of Education, he drew up a far-reaching plan for establishing a giant scientific institute within the Faculty of Medicine. But he could also see the other side (and this was what was so great and unforgettable about him); for he endeavoured to instil a true image of the human being into the scientific views that were being formed. This was one of his central concerns, that the soul-spiritual aspect of man's being should not be forgotten. It was precisely because it was right for a scientific manner of observation to be introduced that a true image of man should be established. If Feuchtersleben had been successful in this aim, the two decades referred to by Rudolf Steiner would have taken a different course. For it would have made a substantial difference if around 1860 there had been a spiritual image of man which did not succumb so easily and without resistance to the hypothesis of the struggle for existence. However, Feuchtersleben's death removed a fighter for the spirit. When his colleagues in the faculty (and Škoda and Rokitansky were the most respected of these) rejected him as Vice-Director of Medical Studies and he was driven by this humiliation and disappointment into the clutches of melancholia, his ruin became inevitable.

Gustav Fechner, similarly, was sick at heart, confused and desolate between 1842 and 1845, only then to recover his alertness to the point of finding a link between physics and psychology. Many similar destinies unfolded between 1842 and 1860, in the eighteen years when the continuing existence of a spiritual view of man hung in the balance. Feuchtersleben was one of many victims. He vanquished Hippocratic teachings by degrees, but he did not want to abandon them without replacing them with a comparable modern view.

In his dissertation 'On Reports of Healing' Feuchtersleben expressed himself in favour of a renewal and enlivening of the Hippocratic world-conception. Neuberger said of this:

> There were always only certain artistically gifted masters of Hippocratism and so few worthy pupils, for qualities associated with outstanding individualities cannot be taught as can the technicalities of modern medicine ... Feuchtersleben likewise recognized the problem, but he still considered traditional Hippocratism to be a structure worth retaining and believed that new goals of great significance could be reached on the old paths, if these were properly developed through further achievements.

Thus when his treatise *Das hippocratische erste Buch von der Diät* appeared in 1835, he was trying to develop his insights regarding the renewal of Hippocratism. It was 'a work which, prompted by dissatisfaction with the vague hypotheses and fanciful systems of contemporary medicine, directed one's attention to the pure source. As a piece of writing it was filled with a strong bias.'[10]

Two further medical texts then appeared. In 1837 he published a treatise in the medical annuals on the 'Attempt at an

Examination of the Most Recent View of Disease as an Anal Organism,' where he most vigorously disputed the theory that disease must be regarded as a pathogen independent of the organism. This view was represented at that time most notably by Schönlein; and Feuchtersleben spoke out against it with the power of his words and of his immense knowledge.

In 1839 his book *Die Gewissheit und Würde der Heilkunst* appeared. Enlightenment and liberalism had here gained the upper hand over the primal sources of Hippocratism. Feuchtersleben now demanded that ordinary people should be given a basic grounding in the theory of disease. It was necessary to have scientific insights, instruction in hygiene and guidance as to what to do in the event of sudden accidents. He protected doctors from all quacks and 'homeopaths' and tried to make it clear to patients that only a physician with an academic training was a true medical practitioner.

With this, the rejection of traditional Hippocratism was complete. In the meantime, however, Feuchtersleben's *Diätetik der Seele* had appeared, where the attempt was made to present a new image of man. This book was, in its succinct brevity, a landmark in the history of medical anthropology. In it, Feuchtersleben's message was expressed clearly and unambiguously.

IV

'Anyone who doubts whether he has a soul should not read anything I say!' These words appear in the first section of Feuchtersleben's most well-known book. This small but weighty volume, which was first published in 1838 and continued in print — in editions of ever-increasing size — until the end of the century, was an attempt to counter the loss of the soul. It could probably be seen as nothing short of providential that this work entered the public arena precisely at the beginning of one of the darkest periods that humanity has ever had to live through.

3. ERNST, BARON VON FEUCHTERSLEBEN

Rudolf Steiner once made the observation that what lay behind the appearance of the *Chymical Wedding* by Johann Valentin Andreae was that through this call 'To the Princes and Heads of States' the Thirty Years' War would have been prevented.

> Johann Valentin Andreae had a great spiritual movement in mind, and had given much thought and preparation to its realization. Two factors were in operation at that time: what Valentin Andreae wanted and what ultimately led to the Thirty Years' War. However, the events that led to the Thirty Years' War rendered the movement that Johann Valentin Andreae wanted to bring about impossible.[11]

Rudolf Steiner's indication in this context could to a certain extent also apply to Feuchtersleben and his *Diätetik der Seele*. It was written in order to counteract the soullessness of newly emerging scientific and psychological views. For modern science originated from the same sources whence the Thirty Years' War was also nurtured. In the seventeenth century humanity was worn down by the destruction and devastation of Central Europe. In the nineteenth century the human soul itself was to be harmed. Both occasions signalled victories for the forces of darkness.

Feuchtersleben's little book derived from the same source as the *Chymical Wedding*. Because it had a spiritual message to impart, it found its way to thousands of people. Many who were awaiting this message received it; but their power was not sufficiently great to withstand the growing storm-tide of materialism. And Feuchtersleben himself was beaten down, dying in a state of mental derangement.

His little book is a call to human beings to practise contemplation through inner schooling. It consists of eleven, seemingly only loosely connected sections bearing the following titles:

1. Concept. General Effects of Spiritual Influences
2. Beauty as a Reflection of Health
3. Imagination
4. Will, Character, Indecisiveness, Moodiness, Absent-Mindedness
5. Reason, Education and Culture
6. Temperament, Passions
7. Understanding the Emotions
8. Oscillation
9. Hypochondria
10. Nature, Truth
11. Résumé

There is, in addition, a twelfth section introducing the whole work and entitled 'Zur Einleitung' (Introduction). Each section is, reflecting contemporary taste, headed by a kind of motto. Some of these eleven chapters are of a prescriptive nature, others more descriptive. Throughout the whole book there is a constant main theme, which is taken up and modulated in all manner of variations and modifications. This is, in essence, that the soul and the spirit have an unshakeable primacy over the body. In each person there lives the capacity not merely to recognize this primacy but also to take hold of it practical life to the extent that such a person becomes a master of his own existence. If he has the will to do this, the capacities with which he is inwardly endowed become available for him; and the *Diätetik* teaches him how to use them.

In the introduction Feuchtersleben indicates what real effectiveness and, hence, deep influence thoughts and feelings have. He says: 'If you [the public as opposed to physicians] are healed by trust, are you less healed than if iron or china had healed you? Is trust a real force? Is it a deception if one makes as good a use of it as of a physical force? Should one not be wanting to be able to awaken it within one?

In the opening section he first tries through reflection and example to demonstrate the power of the spirit over the body. In a very lively language full of courage and stimulation, the reader

3. ERNST, BARON VON FEUCHTERSLEBEN

feels himself to be personally addressed, cheered and enthused. He says,

> Any power which flows from the source of spiritual life enables the person who has given rise to this to give it artistic form. For art is a capacity which has been given form; and if he has come to the point where life itself has for him become art, why should he not be able to grow towards health, which is the life of life?

Feuchtersleben also tries in the first section to present a picture of the soul, characterizing it as follows:

> For the spirit appears to us on this planet only in so far as it manifests itself in man, hence in beings endowed with a physical body. In this connection with physical bodies, the spirit is in familiar linguistic usage called the *soul* and the physical vessel with which it is connected is called the *body*. Hence there should be no need for proofs that the soul works on the body, since we apprehend both only in the unity of their manifestation and it would need the highest degree of training to discover and clarify their difference.

He then leads the reader into the flood of soul-activities and asks him:

> In our soul there are always strongly developed images and ideas which evoke both happiness and misery. Is it really not possible to win power over their ups and downs? Should we not be able to acquire the insight that we unfortunately so often employ all conceivable care and astuteness to cast gloom over, thus taking the sparkle out of it?

And after referring to the instance of Goethe's having escaped from infection during a fever epidemic through his own will-power alone, he calls upon the reader: 'Inner activity is the condition for self-preservation; development of the spiritual in man is the condition of inner activity; and the greater the power of thought is in a person, the greater is his spontaneity; and the greater this is, the more he lives and is.'

However, the moment that these words have sounded, it is as though the picture arises of someone who was deprived of these qualities. This is the figure of the Youth from Goethe's *Fairy Tale,* who became so inactive, indecisive and introspective as a result of his love for the beautiful Lily. He walks beside the wife of the Old Man rather as Feuchtersleben's sensible thoughts try to guide the flaccid souls of his readers.

The second section is introduced by a motto from Friedrich Schlegel: 'Listen to your inner voice and proclaim that nature is alone worthy of reverence and health the only blessing.' There is much in these words to indicate the direction the author wants to take: he intends to show the reader a possible path of initiation.

First he speaks of the influence that a person can have on his surroundings; not only on the people around him but on everything — animals, plants and even the composition of the ground. He quotes Karl Leberecht Immermann's words: 'To be sure, one might well now express the idea as a hypothesis that a good person makes the ground and the air healthy whereas an evil act pollutes a place, so that a shudder comes over the virtuous person in such a place and a strong desire for what is forbidden over the weak person.'

Applying this idea to health, he cites Rahel Varnhagen's pronouncement: 'People such as ourselves will be able to be properly healthy only if they have the strongest loathing of illness, if they are filled with the idea that health is beautiful and highly desirable.' And Feuchtersleben adds: 'So we shall be imbued with it [health] if we consider that a person's physical form is an expression of his well-being.'

And now comes the further idea that it is a special attribute of the human mind that can bring this about: 'Thus we conclude that, if the mind possesses a power that can give form to the body, this same power will manifest itself both as beauty and as health.'

He is sharply critical of the *Freiluft-Apostel,* the open-air fanatics of that time and says,

> It is increasingly recognized that the weak state and, indeed, the illnesses of our contemporaries are rooted more in the moral than in the physical domain and are prevented, and, God willing, can be altogether eradicated, neither by washing in cold water nor by bare necks or by experiments in hardening children as promulgated by Rousseau and Salzmann but by a higher culture of a quite different kind which must first be developed in us ourselves.

This chapter concludes with a hymn-like call:

> So what is beauty other than the mind shining through the outer bodily sheath, and what is health other than beauty radiating through the functioning organs? Where the soul finds an instrument that is in tune with it, the ease with which it practises virtue blinds one to its true splendour; it shines as if cannot do otherwise. But where a chord has been wrested from dissonances, this can be experienced as a miracle. And just as in a moment of great solemnity the hidden beauty often shines forth from the countenance of a good person, so is the beautiful gift of health often won through a single, bold and intense resolve.

At this point, however, we meet another figure from Goethe's *Fairy Tale,* whose name is indicative of the power that works within her: the beautiful Lily. She bears the traits of that 'formative force' that proceeds from the intellect and has the capacity to work in a deeply transforming, and even also death-bringing way on its surroundings. As for the words of greeting which the Old Woman calls out to her, they do not recognize this tragic power of true beauty but praise only what she perceives: 'What a heaven does your presence spread around you.'

Thus in the first two chapters the two principal figures in the *Fairy Tale* are introduced to the reader as the two soul forces that correspond to the Youth and the beautiful Lily: the force of inner activity and that of harmony, which endows man with the highest beauty.

The third section, with which the description of specific soul forces begins, is about the imagination. For Feuchtersleben it is an all-encompassing faculty.

> If we pay attention to the processes going on within us, we shall be aware that neither thoughts nor desires have a direct physical origin within us but that they always come to manifestation solely through contact with the imagination. The imagination is the mediator, the nourisher, the motivating element of all the separate members of the mental organism. Without it all ideas stagnate, however great their richness may have been; concepts remain stiff and lifeless, feelings are coarse and sensual.

He then goes on to characterize imagination as an all-encompassing soul faculty:

> It is in us before we are who we have come to be and when we are no longer; and in all those remarkable situations in which free circumspection cones under the sway of a dark arbitrariness, in childhood, in slumber, in madness, in that poetic phase that is a mixture of all three of these, its spells exert their greatest influence. What the outer world with all its important influences signifies for the outer aspect of man's being, the imagination, this inner world of pictures that surrounds life's very core, means for the inner aspect.

Feuchtersleben is here quite clearly describing that broad field

3. ERNST, BARON VON FEUCHTERSLEBEN

of soul activity which was rediscovered in modern psychology and characterized as the subconscious. One should be mindful that this subconscious was so precisely described by a thinker such as Feuchtersleben in all its various aspects, from madness to the inspiration of the creative artist. He summons forth the power of the imagination in order to develop a healing influence within man, and adduces many positive and negative examples of its active and enduring power.

This quality of the imagination is none other than the Ferryman in Goethe's *Fairy Tale*. This Ferryman may carry people only from the bank on which the beautiful Lily dwells across to the opposite shore, but not back. Rudolf Steiner said,

> Unknown forces that we have no power over have brought us here. We know that certain forces have brought us from yonder world over the river that represents the border between the two worlds to this world. These are characterized by the Ferryman; but these forces working in the depths of unconscious nature cannot bring us back, for otherwise man would return exactly as he was when he arrived here to the world of the gods without any effort or involvement on his part.[12]

This is another way of characterizing what Feuchtersleben means by 'imagination.'

At the beginning of Chapter 3 Feuchtersleben goes on to describe the three basic soul forces. He says:

> We may divide ourselves into as many radii as can be imagined from the midpoint of our innermost being to the circumcircle of infinity; but there will eventually be three directions to which all others can approximately be traced back: those of the powers of thinking, those of sensation, where imagination and feeling belong, and those of the will. Collectively this is the inner man — his whole being, his whole tendency, what is philosophically

termed 'his whole thinking, all his thoughts and endeavours.' Thoughts are the nourishment, feelings the source of vitality and deeds of the will the strength-building forces of the life of the mind.

Here we meet in all clarity the figures of the three kings in Goethe's *Fairy Tale:* the Gold King, the Silver and the Bronze.

These three kings are then considered in turn in a chapter devoted specifically to each: the Bronze King in the fourth, the Gold King in the fifth and the Silver in the sixth. It would be delightful to describe all this in detail, for there are extensive characterizations of these three soul-forces in their heights but also in their depths, so that the fourth King also becomes visible from time to time. What Feuchtersleben says in this regard can only briefly be summarized here.

Regarding the will (Bronze King) he says:

> When I speak of the will, I do not mean in any sense the capacity for desires, whether of a debased or higher kind; rather do I have in view that inward, active energy of existence which develops out of all the other forces of our soul — as does the blossom from the leaves — in all areas of our life, a quality which is easier to feel and recognize in oneself than to define but which one could justifiably call the purely practical faculty in man.

This sounds like the cry of this King in the *Fairy Tale,* after the Youth has girded himself with the sword: 'The sword on the left, the right free!'

Then he has this to say about the power of reason (Gold King):

> Imagination wanders aimlessly in dreams, the will rushes into wild nothingness; the mind's task is to consecrate them. This is the highest theme of soul dialectics: to give the power of culture its place above the dark forces

of sense-perceptible nature; to express what intellectual culture can achieve for the establishing of the health of both individuals and whole communities, indeed of mankind in its entirety.

Thus in the *Fairy Tale* the Gold King speaks 'with a fatherly gesture of blessing' to the Youth: 'Understand what is highest!'

Regarding the Silver King, who features in the sixth section entitled 'Temperaments, Passions,' Feuchtersleben says: 'There are actually only two temperaments: active and inwardly withdrawn.' With these words he was anticipating the fundamental characterization which Rudolf Steiner subsequently gave of the world of feelings, namely, sympathy and antipathy. And he continues: 'Just as the character encompasses the totality of the fully cultivated will, so is the temperament none other than the sum of one's innate inclinations.' In the *Fairy Tale,* however, the silver King hands his sceptre to the Youth in order that he may know how to govern his temperament and passions and not act out of sympathy or antipathy alone. To this end he speaks: 'Feed the sheep.'

In the other sections of the *Diätetik* we meet with further soul forces. Thus the Giant of the *Fairy Tale* makes his appearance where Feuchtersleben writes about the emotions. In the chapter about hypochondria the Mixed King features in all his wretchedness. In the section about 'Nature, Truth' the old Man with the Lamp appears, that soul-force which Rudolf Steiner describes as devotion and religious veneration: 'The light of various different revelations is represented in the "Old Man" who has this light. Anyone who does not kindle his religious sensibilities with light from his inner being cannot be the vessel for the lamp of religion.'[13] Hence Feuchtersleben writes in this chapter:

> Nature conceives of many great thoughts, and those of man — once he has truly pondered them — become able to expand and develop a similarity to their natural

counterparts. The little ego learns to conceive of itself as an atom and, in contemplating infinity, becomes glad of its existence since it becomes aware of the harmony of the whole.

Finally, in the last section, in the 'Résumé,' the Green Snake herself is the object of our attention. Rudolf Steiner characterizes her as follows:

> If a person makes the effort to picture what he is able to experience in concepts, ideas and thought-structures not in a narrowly personal, abstract fashion but to observe these experiences in such a way that they become the guides and interpreters of the realities around him, he will be employing this soul-force as does the Green Snake. He can then fashion light and truth out of the purely abstract, out of pure concepts.

In this final section, as a parting note, Feuchtersleben addresses some words to the hypochondriac, that is, to the ill person, which penetrate right to one's heart:

> Amidst the glory of the ever-renewing and vibrant natural world, may the afflicted [the ill person] learn to find and furnish the balsam that is granted and given to all creatures; in the vast interplay between human individuals and their destinies, may he learn to evaluate the grounds for his own existence; and, if he has learnt to recognize this, may he strive for nothing more than being and remaining himself, purely and truly, as an unblemished pronouncement of God's word. *For health is none other than beauty, morality and truth.*

With these words the Temple of humanity is uplifted, just as in Goethe's *Fairy Tale* it rises to the surface from the depths of the earth. It is the same Temple that Rudolf Steiner wanted to bring to outward manifestation in the First Goetheanum in

Dornach. If Feuchtersleben refers to man as 'an unblemished pronouncement of God's word,' it is because he is conscious that this ideal will lead to the house of the word which is portrayed in the outwardly manifest Temple of the *Fairy Tale*.

Rudolf Steiner frequently indicated that the Goetheanum is the place where science, art and religion should again be united: morality being enacted in religion, beauty manifesting itself in art, and truth actively present in science. When the Goetheanum was opened on September 26, 1920, he gave the opening address on the theme of 'Art, Science and Religion.'

> There are three new powers that we would wish to bring creatively to manifestation out of spiritual sources: a visionary art, a recognition of the supersensible element in the rebirth of soul and spirit in that religion whose mood needs to be formed out of this art and this science ... so that we are able to bring into the various branches of human cultural life that which can nurture the life of humanity out of the new threefoldness of a visionary art, a spiritually comprehended science, a religion that experiences rebirth in the supersensible.[14]

Thus Feuchtersleben, who tried to renew the image of man in the dietetics of the soul, became a forerunner of all those endeavours which found an initial fulfilment in the Goetheanum. Both the *Diätetik* and the Goetheanum emerged from those sources whence Goethe's *Fairy Tale* arose. The call which human beings experienced through this book gradually died away in the course of the nineteenth century; but when on August 18, 1899 Rudolf Steiner published an article on Goethe's *Fairy Tale* in the *Magazin für Literatur,* this call began to sound forth once more. The *Diätetik der Seele* now took on a new, universal significance.

V

Feuchtersleben spent most of his life as a follower of Goethe. He felt intimately related to and connected with his life's work and knew everything by Goethe that had been published at the time; he lived with and out of his wisdom.

There is an essay by Feuchtersleben called 'Goethe and Schiller.' In it he tries to do justice to both, and says:

> No one should believe that Goethe and Schiller created the time they lived in. At the time when these great minds were in the ascendant the world was aspiring together with them. A countless number of sacrificial flames flared upwards, kindled from above by a common ray of light; but Goethe's flame leapt up higher than any other.

With these words he was referring intuitively to that spiritual event of which Rudolf Steiner was subsequently to speak and which irradiated that epoch as a 'common ray of light.' Feuchtersleben continues:

> Schiller worked amongst us somewhat as Lessing had done; but Goethe's spirit has worked on or, rather, continues to exert its influence now. From him sprang the source of the present, which roars around us; the sons of the mighty river have already recognized him as their father — he who released the primal wave of fresh life from its bondage and who himself knows no truer name than that of liberator. And to this extent one could say that his path was made for us; but the ever-living formative energies will eventually strip off even this skin and cause new outward forms to blossom.

Thus Feuchtersleben related Goethe directly to the time when he was writing these lines. He calls him the liberator and father of the 'sons of the mighty river.' There was no doubt that

3. ERNST, BARON VON FEUCHTERSLEBEN

he was referring to that movement which had begun to exert a liberating influence amongst the liberal middle class — that river of ever-strengthening power which sought to overwhelm the obstacles of Hapsburg centralism and the ties of a life based on censorship.

For Feuchtersleben, Goethe's spirit was the leader of the efforts at that time to gain state recognition. What spoke through him were the ideas of liberalism, of which Rudolf Steiner said the following: 'For those who listened to the speeches of the outstanding personalities of the middle class in the 1840s — and there many such people throughout the civilized world — indicating what innovations should be brought to mankind in every sphere, these years seemed to herald the dawning of a new popular movement.'[15]

This new popular movement which was in prospect was also Feuchtersleben's dream; he actively concerned himself with it, and tried to bring it about. Much that he undertook and sought to achieve was aimed at liberating the people; but he knew — since Goethe was his model — that this liberation had to come from the inner regions of the soul and that only if the individual becomes master of himself can the outward bondage of the state be dispensed with.

Thus the greatest commitment that Feuchtersleben imposed upon himself was to work as an educator — but as an educator who shouldered this role out of the broadest possible perspective of his vision as a physician. All people, be they children, adolescents or adults, were to be educated in such a way that their schooling could as they grew older gradually be transformed into self-education for each individual. The cultured existence that results from extending self-education to working constantly on perfecting oneself was Feuchtersleben's highest ideal.

So he worked as an educator when he was secretary of the Society of Physicians in Vienna; as a member of the teaching staff when he gave his lectures on a doctor's soul-science; as a teacher in the professorial group of which he was the Chairman;

and finally as Vice-Director of Medical Studies and as junior permanent secretary in the Ministry of Education.

After his enforced resignation from all these posts he began to work on two extensive projects. One was intended to become a 'History of Teaching,' the other an 'Outline of Lectures on Anthropology.' Both have been preserved only as fragments, but they show where Feuchtersleben's efforts were leading. He was trying to build up a new image of the human being in anthropology and to present this human image in the 'History of Teaching' as a learning being. Both, however, flowed from the universality of his medical vision. What is the *Diätetik der Seele* other than one of the most beautiful educational books that have ever been written? For it contains a new image of man which was engraved in the jewel of Goethe's *Fairy Tale* and, hence, bears within itself the highest formative forces flowing from the sources whence the guidance of humanity itself streams. These are the sources that give the old Man with the Lamp in the *Fairy Tale* the words which are the words for the inauguration of the new King: 'Love does not rule; but it trains, and that is more.'

On March 7, 1849 Feuchtersleben gave a lecture in the Imperial Academy of Sciences in Vienna, which had only just been founded. The title was 'On the Question of Humanism and Realism as an Educational Principle.' The closing words reveal the most intimate convictions of the speaker:

> The education of the human race in an expanded system of instruction, and the furtherance of the sciences in their free, many-facetted life in the sense of a true academic training, are a resource of great magnitude enabling those highest of human purposes to be striven for. May these resources be made available and used in both ways that I have indicated, and thus furnish mankind with that peace which hey, wearied of the endlessly recurring deceptions of political and social experiments, await with deep longing.

3. ERNST, BARON VON FEUCHTERSLEBEN

Seventy years later Rudolf Steiner tried to express this hope of Feuchtersleben's in an entirely new way: 'We need an art of education which in all its aspects educates and instructs children in a truly healthy way. It is this which makes health care a social question, *for the social question is essentially an educational question, and the educational question is essentially a medical question,* but a question only for an approach to medicine and health care which is fructified by spiritual science.'[16] [Emphasis added.]

Here, too, Feuchtersleben finds in the renewed Goetheanism of spiritual science the culmination of his endeavours. What he aspired to was seemingly a failure; for outwardly only little has remained of what he tried to inaugurate. As with many people of his time his will impulses were destroyed in the whirlpool of the approaching scientific agnosticism. Nevertheless, he was one of the pillars above which the bridge of the Green Snake stretching from Goethe to the Goetheanum was able to arch at the end of the nineteenth century.

Feuchtersleben's background was derived from the world of Viennese Romanticism. He bore this gift of a musical age over into the period leading up to the revolution of March 1848, raised it up to that sphere where Goethe's spirit was active and thereby tried to pass on a spiritual content to the next generation. His own efforts failed. Seven years after his death Sigmund Freud was born. Ten years after he passed away Darwin's book *On the Origin of Species by means of Natural Selection* and Marx's *Zur Kritik der politischen Ökonomie* appeared. With this the path of the descent was sealed.

However, Feuchtersleben will gradually rise again from oblivion in the memories of those who recognize that the renewal of all existence lies in the spirit alone. What he was trying to express as a poet in his most well-known song will also be understood:

> But you must understand me rightly,
> Yes, rightly!
> When people go their separate ways,

> They say: 'Till next we meet!'
> Yes, next we meet!

We need rightly to understand what he means by this: that death is not an end but a leave-taking, which opens up the hope for a spiritual and also an earthly future meeting. Feuchtersleben knew about this too, because he was a pupil of Goethe and a proclaimer of that same spirit as is represented in Goethe's poem, 'Die Geheimnisse' (the Mysteries) by Brother Mark.

4

Charles Darwin

Charles Robert Darwin (1809–82) was an English naturalist who sailed around the world on the famous voyage of HMS Beagle. *He proposed the theory of evolution by natural selection.*

I

The culmination of that great agnostic invasion which overwhelmed the cultural life of the nineteenth century came in the years 1858 and 1859. On November 17, 1858 Robert Owen died and on May 6, 1859 Alexander von Humboldt. As a result of their death the end of the age of Goethe and of the period prior to the revolution of March 1848 was clearly confirmed. At the same time (on January 20, 1859) Bettina von Arnim crossed the threshold and took with her the last lustre and fragrance of Romanticism. The gates were now open for the invasion of materialism.

In 1858 Virchow's *Cellular Pathology* appeared; in the following year Bunsen and Kirchhoff discovered spectral analysis, and around the same time Darwin published his two-volume work *On the Origin of Species by Means of Natural Selection*. Shortly before this (1857) Pasteur had been able to prove that bacteria only arise from bacteria, and hence refuted the idea of an on-going process of abiogenesis (spontaneous generation). Then Virchow was able to interpret the cell as the carrier of all diseases, Darwin to portray the unity of all organisms and their gradual emergence by means of natural selection; and through Bunsen's discovery the material structure and composition of the planets and fixed stars were demonstrated.

These fundamental discoveries, which came about in the two fateful years of 1858/59, were now conveyed to an attentive humanity and made an immediate, and lasting impression.

In the same period of time Karl Marx's fundamental book *A Contribution to the Critique of Political Economy* also appeared, seeking to inaugurate a new economic and social order. The die was now cast. The representatives of a humanity seeking to know itself in a new way had placed their demands on the table of history. It was an abrupt and self-conscious repudiation of wonder; it was a denial of all divine intervention into the destiny of the earth and a withdrawal of all concessions that were as yet still made to heavenly authorities.

A veil had come to overshadow people's thinking. For at that very time events were taking place in the supersensible worlds which had a far-reaching influence upon human souls at that time. The verse which Rudolf Steiner has given for the high summer week in the *Calendar of the Soul* describes the historical situation of that time with great clarity:

> Surrendered to the senses' revelation
> I lost my being's proper urge,
> And felt, in dreaming thoughts bemused,
> My selfhood stolen away.[1]

The advance guard of the agnostics was under the impression that mankind had now come of age and could take its destiny into its own hands. The truth was, however, that human souls had become the battleground of one of the greatest disputes in world history. A considerable amount of pride filled certain of these pioneers and led them into the greatest confusion, especially those who supported the spreading and popularizing of the new

4. CHARLES DARWIN

Charles Darwin

ideas. Thomas Huxley, Ernst Haeckel, Herbert Spencer and many others succumbed to their intellectual cult of the superman.

This particular time in the nineteenth century can be understood only if the events taking place in the background are taken into account, events which occurred between 1841 and 1879 beyond the threshold of the sense-world and were described at some length by Rudolf Steiner. He spoke towards the end of the First World War about that battle that took place in the supersensible regions of earth existence between the hosts of Michael and their opponents.

> You will form a correct idea about these matters if you think of a battle in the spiritual worlds which lasted for several decades, from the 1840s until the autumn of 1879. This battle ... can be described as a battle waged by spiritual beings belonging to the retinue of that being from the hierarchy of the Archangels who may be called Michael, thus as a struggle on the part of Michael and his followers, against certain Ahrimanic powers ... So this battle took place in the 1840s, 1850s, 1860s and 1870s; and its conclusion was that in the autumn of 1879 Michael and his hosts were victorious against certain Ahrimanic powers.[2]

This depicts the spiritual background lying behind the events of this time. It was precisely during this historical period that people's thoughts and feelings were more given over to the life of the senses than ever before. Because of this they had lost their last access to their spiritual nature, leading to a denial of their true origin. The 'holy kingdom' of their existence was no longer the world of the gods but, rather, the realm of nature that surrounded them and which they could perceive with their senses.

The years 1858 and 1859 were in the middle of that period when 'the war in heaven' was being waged, and the events of these two years had for this reason such an immediate and direct influence on people at that time.

4. CHARLES DARWIN

When *The Origin of Species* was published on November 14, 1858, it was at once a sensational success. Darwin wrote:

> It is no doubt the chief work of my life. It was from the first highly successful. The first small edition of 1250 copies was sold on the day of publication, and a second edition of 3000 copies soon afterwards. Sixteen thousand copies have now (1876) been sold in England ... It has been translated into almost every European tongue, even such languages as Spanish, Bohemian, Polish and Russian.[3]

The dam had now been breached, and the tide of agnostic science flowed into every realm of life at that time. Not only Darwin but also his friends and opponents were surprised by the decisive influence of this book. Hundreds of books, pamphlets and essays taking issue with 'Darwinism' in any shape or form began to appear every year. Darwin kept aloof from all discussions. He remained in his preferred environment of the solitude of his country house to the south-east of London and worked on further books and treatises. He left it to others to argue for and against him; he himself was so convinced about his work that he did not find it necessary to meet the 'unbelievers.' They would in the end gather round the flag of his prophecies.

II

How did this book, which exerted such a magical influence on thousands of its contemporaries, come into being? Was it the result of a suddenly conceived idea, or was it gradually prepared through long and serious research? Darwin himself gives a clear answer to this question. In the *Autobiography* which he wrote for his children at the end of his life he explains how this book came to be written.

In his youth, when he was still a student at Cambridge, he had the possibility of taking part as a naturalist in a voyage around the world lasting almost five years (1831–36). The vast quantity of material that he gathered during this journey, the observations that he was able to make and the breadth of horizon that he acquired thereby became the foundation of his later work. He had with him on the journey the newly published first volume of Charles Lyell's *Principles of Geology*. This was his first encounter with a theory of the earth's development based not on catastrophic change but on a continual process of evolution: all mountain ranges were the result of natural influences such as the weather, climate changes and forces that have re-shaped the ground. Darwin's own geological observations became for him a constant confirmation of Lyell's theories. Of particular interest to him was the phenomenon of variations in an individual animal or plant species that appeared in different regions of the earth. In this regard he made detailed studies on the various islands of the Galapagos archipelago and on the South American continent.

On returning home, he found that these phenomena of variation would not leave him alone, and he wrote in his *Autobiography:*

> After my return to England it appeared to me that by following the example of Lyell in Geology, and by collecting all facts which bore in any way on the variation of animals and plants under domestication and [in] nature, some light might perhaps be thrown on the whole subject. My first note-book was opened in July 1837. I worked on true Baconian principles, and without any theory collected facts on a wholesale scale, more especially with respect to domesticated productions ... I soon perceived that selection was the keystone of man's success in making useful races of animals and plants.

With this the first step was taken; and the second followed shortly afterwards.

4. CHARLES DARWIN

> In October 1838, that is, fifteen months after I had begun my systematic enquiry, I happened to read for amusement Malthus on *Population,* and being well prepared to appreciate the struggle for existence which everywhere goes on from long-continued observation of the habits of animals and plants, it at once struck me that under these circumstances favourable variations would tend to be preserved, and unfavourable ones to be destroyed. The result of this would be the formation of new species. Here, then, I had at last got a theory by which to work.[4]

Darwin initially refrained from formulating and publishing his new theory. He wrote it down briefly in 1842 and, in 1844, in a longer account as a kind of personal exercise. Hence at the time when the 'war in heaven' was beginning, the theory of 'natural selection through the struggle for existence' was crystallizing.

It needs to be pointed out repeatedly that the idea of a struggle for existence and the notion of natural selection which resulted from it were initially described in connection with human social circumstances. For Malthus described how increasing overpopulation leads to constant shortages of food, and how out of this a perpetual struggle for existence arises among human beings. A highly questionable human condition became for Darwin a principle that could be applied to the animal and plant kingdoms. The lowering of man's stature to the struggle for existence had been used to exemplify a mode of behaviour that was supposedly characteristic of the whole of the living world of nature.

Darwin worked in the following years on many other scientific questions; but his main preoccupation continued to be the collecting of further material for the theory of natural selection. In 1856 Lyell, with whom he had a steady friendship, asked him finally to write his ideas down and publish them. Darwin then wrote a manuscript which was 'three or four times as long as the ensuing book *On the Origin of Species.*'

In 1858 he was sent the essay of a younger naturalist, Alfred Russel Wallace, who was at the time on a research trip to Celebes Indonesia). In this essay, *On the Tendencies of Varieties to depart indefinitely from the Original Type,* Wallace described observations that he had made about animals and plants and arrived at conclusions which almost literally corresponded to Darwin's theory of natural selection.

This event was the final push for Darwin to complete the manuscript of his book. Wallace most generously respected Darwin's priority in this matter, so that there was no quarrel about it. A brief article by Darwin was published together with Wallace's presentation, in order to prove the independent nature of the discoveries that each had made.

However, this publication did not arouse any attention on the part of scientists at that time. It passed silently over the new theory. Only when Darwin's book appeared in the following year were the tumultuous applause and the cries of indignation generated which have not ceased to this day. The theory of natural selection in the context of the struggle for existence is an opinion that people continue to hold.

It took twenty-one years — from 1837 until 1859 — for this spirit-child to be born. For Darwin this period was full of illness, pain, solitude and unremitting work. He was pressurized by a transformation that was taking place within him. As a young man he had been a carefree, effervescent dare-devil. He was a good shot, a passionate hunter and a brilliant rider; and as such he was a typical young Englishman from a well-to-do family.

During his student days in Cambridge, he was always welcomed in his frequent visits to the houses of his professors as someone people liked to see. He described these three years as the happiest of his life, for 'I was then in excellent health, and almost always in high spirits.'

However, the moment when he received the invitation to participate in the research journey around the world, he became ill and his health declined. During the study trip his state of health improved, but he became poorly again as soon as he returned to England. Henceforth he was a man in poor health who nevertheless had ideas and insights of the greatest importance, for which he gathered together a mass of proof. *On the Origin of Species* emerged from pain and sorrow; and so the book was written not by a vigorous man who was coping with the struggle for existence but by a tormented and solitary individual whose sole inner support was the love of his wife and children.

III

The theory of evolution was not a beginning but the keystone of a long series of ideas which had been explored for a century, and by a great variety of thinkers and researchers. The Darwin family had played a particular part in this, since his paternal grandfather Erasmus Darwin was the author of a substantial volume on the classes and species of animals and plants which anticipated the later ideas of Lamarck. His book *Zoonomia* appeared in 1796 and bore the subtitle 'The Laws of Organic Life.' It is a speculative work which seeks to order not only all living beings but also diseases according to classes, species and families.

In 1809 Jean Lamarck's book *Philosophie Zoologique* appeared. Here, too, the attempt was made to present a comprehensive and at the same time organic system of the animal kingdom and to show how the higher forms have developed out of the lower. These transformations, it was said, arise mainly through the use or non-use of organs, through exercise and also through habit. Haeckel said of Lamarck: 'In the history of the theory of evolution he has pride of place alongside Darwin and Goethe. As the first to develop the theory of evolution as an independent scientific theory and as the philosophical foundation of the whole of biology, he has achieved immortal fame.'[5] Darwin was born in the same year, 1809, that the French researcher's book appeared.

It is strange that Goethe knew nothing of the existence of this theory of evolution. He knew only the younger naturalist whose work was based on that of Lamarck, Geoffroy Saint-Hilaire, who in 1831 held the famous disputation in the French Academy in Paris with an older man by name of Cuvier regarding the coming into being of organisms. Goethe was entirely on Saint-Hilaire's side and called out at the time: 'And I rejoice with justice that I can now finally experience the overall victory of a cause to which I have devoted my life and which is quite expressly also my own.'[6]

Goethe was deeply imbued with a clear perception of the oneness of all created things. What Kant hardly dared to postulate in the *Critique of Judgment* but nevertheless could see, that all living beings have originated from a common archetypal mother, had for Goethe already become clearly apparent. He saw the archetypal elements which lay at the foundation of the basic structure of animal forms, and what for Kant was still an 'adventure of reason' was manifested in Goethe's 'visionary power of judgment.'

Although the young and not very knowledgeable Saint-Hilaire was no equal to the famous and learned Cuvier, the victory of the evolutionary view over the old conception was assured. For at the same time Lyell completed his manuscript on the *Principles of Geology,* and on December 27 Darwin boarded the *Beagle* for the famous voyage. What had initially been conceived as a comprehensive idea of the oneness of all realms of life and of their common root was gradually condensed into a view of evolution unfolding in the physical domain.

In his book *Naturphilosophie,* Lorenz Oken was still able to express the following standpoint: 'When an animal becomes able to behold all its organs as objects — by contemplating the universe, by listening to the animal spread out in symbols — it beholds itself, appears to itself and is conscious of itself. For the animal is akin to the whole animal kingdom and to the universe. Man is the universal spirit.'[7] This means that the animal kingdom attains its perfection in man and at the same time has its root in him. Man is the synthesis of the entire animal system, while this system in all its rich abundance is the visible analysis of man.

This is a more speculative way of expressing what for Goethe came to manifestation more through sensory and moral experience. With Lyell, however, and then especially with Darwin the idea of a unified natural form pervading all living beings was lost. It was far more a question of structures with the potential to act and grow, developing in stages through adaptation, heredity, the selection of species and the struggle for existence. Behind this view there stand goal-oriented thoughts, but no longer any ideas. Nature is completely robbed of its plan of creation and development. The development of organisms results from a blind urge that is without any self-awareness, and which is actually meaningless. The truth is that this is no theory of descent but, far rather, a theory of ascent, since a many-facetted kingdom of organisms is supposed to have developed out of rudimentary beginnings without limbs or claims to perfection.

In the thinking of Darwin, Lamarck and the other researchers the question of the constancy or variability of a species was in the foreground. A species (tiger, lion, red deer, roe deer etc.) is that category in the system of animals which corresponds to the individual human personality, the 'I' or self. All tigers, all roe deer, all gazelles, all squirrels are a unity represented by an I; each of these species has a group soul.

As the former ways of understanding nature could still sense the I-character of a species, it held firmly to that constancy. With the idea of evolution, the discovery of extinct animal forms and the ever increasing extent of observations, the variability of species was recognized; but even today it has not yet been clarified whether this variability is real or only apparent. This is also connected to the frequently discussed question as to whether newly acquired qualities are indeed inheritable.

In the same year of 1858 as Darwin and Wallace launched the theory of evolution, a book appeared in America by Louis Agassiz called *An Essay on Classification*. In this book Agassiz, one of the leading naturalists of his time, tries to survey the categories of the animal and plant system and to outline a natural system of all living beings. He concerns himself particularly with the concept of a species and endeavours to understand it in its formative significance. This book was a last attempt to counteract the relative meaninglessness of the theory of evolution with an endeavour to give meaning to nature.

The book attracted no attention whatever at the time and was only rediscovered in the 1930s by certain authors, including Bernhard Steiner and Hedwig Conrad-Martius. The debate between Darwin and Agassiz therefore continues, although the Darwinists are convinced that their cause is already victorious. The voices of Darwin's opponents are very isolated; but their weight and their clarity are great and convincing.

What must be recognized is the direction in which Lyell, Wallace, Darwin and Huxley have guided the whole teaching of the evolution of organisms. They have not merely denied the acts of divine creation but have also eliminated the general idea which could lie at the foundation of the existence and development of organisms. For them there was no 'system of organisms' based on real categories and, hence, bearing the stamp of divine thinking. Species, families, races and tribes were abstractions which human beings had introduced for a better overview and understanding. Systematic thinking was alien to these researchers; experiment and interpretation of the facts alone had validity. They had inherited the mantle of the medieval nominalists.

IV

Only through Ernst Haeckel's fiery intervention was Darwin's theory filled with breath and life. Rudolf Steiner expressed himself very clearly about this, affirming

4. CHARLES DARWIN

> that Darwinism, which is directed solely towards the non-human aspect of the world and can never form the basis for anything but a utilitarian morality, was taken hold of a man so inherently Central European, not to say Prussian, in character, as Ernst Haeckel. With Haeckel, Darwinism does not remain what it was with Darwin himself. In Darwin we see the continuance of Bacon's mode of thought ... For him [Haeckel] there is no possibility of leaving religion untouched ...; he applies it [Darwinism] with a religious fervour to man himself, he makes a religion of it.'[8]

This happened when Haeckel, who was not yet thirty years old at the time, spoke in 1863 as the first lecturer at the annual great assembly of naturalists and physicians and advocated Darwinism in all its consequences. He said in this lecture:

> As far as we human beings are concerned, in order to be consistent we would — as the most highly evolved vertebrates — see our ancient common ancestors in ape-like mammals, then in kangaroo-like marsupials, then — reaching still further back to the so-called secondary period — in lizard-like reptiles and finally in still earlier times, in the primary period, in lowly organized fish.[9]

What Darwin had not initially dared to broach, namely, the place of man in the realm of living things, was now proclaimed by the young Haeckel. Only eight years later, in 1871, Darwin had reached the point of publishing his book *The Descent of Man*. He wrote about this in his *Autobiography:*

> As soon as I had become, in the year of 1837 or 1838, convinced that species were mutable productions, I could not avoid the belief that man must come under the same law. Accordingly I collected notes on the subject for

my own satisfaction, and not for a long time with any intention of publishing ...

But when I found that many naturalists fully accepted the doctrine of the evolution of species, it seemed to me advisable to work up such notes as I possessed and to publish a special treatise on the origin of man.[10]

Darwin devoted three full years to the composition of this work, 'but then as usual some of this time was lost by ill health.' He was never free from the afflictions of his body and suffered incessantly from anguish of soul.

This book also became an overwhelming success. The *Edinburgh Review* commented: 'On every side it is raising a storm of mingled wrath, wonder and admiration.' And in a letter of February 3, 1872 [to Dr Dohrn] Darwin wrote:

I did not know until reading your article, that my 'Descent of Man' had excited so much *furore* in Germany. It has had an immense circulation in this country and in America, but has met the approval of hardly any naturalists so far as I know. Therefore I suppose it was a mistake on my part to publish it; but, anyhow, it will pave the way for some better work.[11]

Self-confidence and modesty, reserve and arrogance were strangely combined in Darwin's nature. Since his return from his circumnavigation of the world the young and energetic hunter, rider and explorer had become a sickly, withdrawn person who shunned the world. 'My mind seems to have become a kind of machine for grinding general laws out of large collections of facts,' he said of himself, when he spoke of how all pleasure and joy in music, poetry and drama had disappeared for him. 'But now for many years I cannot endure to read a line of poetry: I have tried lately to read Shakespeare, and found it so intolerably dull that it nauseated me. I have also almost lost any taste for pictures or music.'[12]

4. CHARLES DARWIN

He was astonishingly honest to reveal this side of his existence so openly. Who would otherwise be so candid? But he was an Englishman, in his outward appearance tall and gaunt, with bushy eyebrows, a mighty bald head and a face somewhat weathered and at the same time difficult to penetrate, a figure that was bent forwards and deep-set eyes filled with melancholy and sorrow — a picture of a consciousness soul that has become empty.

In these years of constant research, collecting and experimenting, Darwin became a sceptic and agnostic. The chapter 'My Religious Belief,' which is at the heart of the *Autobiography,* describes his gradual and sorrow-filled rejection of Christianity. Initially it was the accounts of the Creation story, the building of the Tower of Babel and the appearance of the rainbow after the great Flood which caused him to doubt. Then came the contradictions in the Gospels and that they differ 'in many important details, far too important as it seemed to me to be admitted as the usual inaccuracies of eye-witnesses.'

And then he admitted that he had dreamt on several occasions that old letters had been found (in the course of possible excavations in Rome or Pompeii) which confirmed to him that Christ had nonetheless walked the earth. But he never received this proof.

> Thus disbelief crept over me at a very slow rate, but was at last complete. The rate was so slow that I felt no distress, and have never since doubted even for a single second that my conclusion was correct. I can indeed hardly see how anyone ought to wish Christianity to be true ...
>
> The mystery of the beginning of all things is insoluble by us, and I for one must be content to remain an Agnostic ... Nothing is more remarkable than the spread of scepticism or rationalism during the latter half of my life.[13]

The paragraph that begins with this sentence is annotated by Darwin with the words: 'Written in 1879.' This was in the same year that Michael was victorious over the hosts of his adversaries. But Darwin took no conscious part in this. Rather had he become the instrument of the adversaries' intentions and, hence, had fulfilled his historical task. He had poured all his vital forces into his work. His life, which ended in 1882, was a sacrificial path for which he had sacrificed his soul.

V

In the introductory lecture to the cycle on *The Fifth Gospel*, Rudolf Steiner deals at some length with the place of Darwinism in history. He indicates that a rightly understood Darwinism has a Christian destiny:

> Anyone who understands the doctrines of Darwin and Haeckel and can himself see that only as a Christian movement was the Darwinian movement possible (Haeckel had no notion of this, but Darwin was aware of many things), anyone who realizes this is led quite logically to the idea of reincarnation. And if he can call upon a certain clairvoyant power, he will be led quite naturally to a knowledge of the *spiritual* origin of the human race ... It is, of course, conceivable that someone may accept Darwinism in the form in which it is presented today and fail to grasp the life-principles inherent within it. In other words, if a person takes up Darwinism as an inner impulse and has no feeling for a deeper understanding of Christianity, such as does indeed lie in Darwinism, he may end up in the strange situation of understanding no more of Darwinism than he does of Christianity. The good spirit of Christianity and the good spirit of Darwinism may alike forsake him.

4. CHARLES DARWIN

> But if he has a grasp of the good spirit of Darwinism, then — however much of a materialist he may be — he will arrive in his survey of the history of the earth at the point where he recognizes that man did *not* evolve from lower animal forms, that he must have had a spiritual origin. He is led to the point where he beholds man as a spiritual being, as it were hovering over the earthly world.[14]

This interpretation contains a personal statement by Rudolf Steiner; for it describes the path that his own thoughts and perceptions were following around the turn of the century. This is reiterated in Chapter 30 of his autobiography:

> In Darwinism I saw a kind of thinking that approaches Goethe's thought, but remains behind it.
> All of this still remained at the level of ideas I had *worked out*. Not until later did I work it through to imaginative insight. The I understood that in primordial times, within the spiritual reality of the Earth, there were *beings* very different from the simple organisms. And I realized that the human spirit is older than all the other living beings; to attain our present physical form, we had to separate from the world being that encompasses us and all other organisms ... The human being was a macrocosmic being bearing the rest of the earthly world within; this then became a microcosmic being by casting off all the rest. I gained this spiritual insight only during the initial years of the new century.[15]

Only now does it become apparent how deep is the bond between Darwinism and anthroposophical spiritual science. Darwin had to carry the idea of evolution into the depths of materialism and agnosticism; and he accomplished this task, while losing himself.

Those who have since the beginning of the twentieth century

brought the theory of evolution ever more strongly into connection with the doctrine of heredity and made the game of mutations and the chemistry of chromosomes and genes the focus of their studies are following not the 'good' aspect of Darwinism but its 'evil' aspect.

Ernst Haeckel intervened at the point where Darwin left off. The younger man began to bring the element of ideas into what had hitherto been dry and matter-of-fact, and he was therefore able to pass on what he had received from Darwin to Rudolf Steiner, who carried the idea of evolution forward to its logical goal, recognizing the 'spirit-being of man as it were hovering over the earthly world' as the beginning of earthly evolution. But he transformed the evolution of species into the wider perspectives of reincarnation; for the physical evolution of organisms was carried further by him into a spiritual metamorphosis of the human self. Thus Darwin's destiny came to fulfilment in Rudolf Steiner by way of Haeckel, and so it became possible for thoughts of cosmic dimensions to enter once more into Darwinism.

5

Rudolf Wagner

Rudolf Wagner (1805–64) was a German anatomist and physiologist who made important investigations into ganglia, nerve-endings and the sympathetic nerves.

I

On May 13, 1864 Rudolf Wagner, who in his time had been a well-known physiologist and naturalist, died in Göttingen. Since 1840 he had held the chair there for physiology and comparative anatomy and was also the director of the physiological institute which he had founded. He had been asked to succeed the famous Blumenbach at Göttingen University when he was barely 35 years old. At the time he was an exceptionally gifted young naturalist, who had already written a large number of specialist works and comprehensive books.

To the general public, however, he first became known through a controversy about materialism which he had abruptly started. This happened as the result of a lecture that Wagner gave at the thirty-first assembly of the Society of German Naturalists and Physicians in Göttingen on September 18, 1854. In this paper, which appeared a few weeks later in the form of a pamphlet with the title *Menschenschöpfung und Seelensubstanz* (Man's Creation and the Substance of the Soul), he tried — with the support of his high reputation and academic position — to stand up against the encroaching wave of materialism. His fight was an unequal one; for the thought-forms of the time were not congenial to him, and his opponents — notably Carl Vogt — had the great majority on their side. Moreover, they were stronger, more quick-witted and younger than the elderly and ailing professor. Thus Wagner soon had to abandon the struggle, which was from the outset quite hopeless. He never recovered from this defeat. Illness and a declining reputation accompanied the last years of his earthly life. Like many others, he was overwhelmed by the engulfing tide of the materialistic world view.

II

A few weeks before the naturalists' assembly in Göttingen, on August 20, Schelling died in Bad Ragaz. With him the last of the great idealistic German philosophers of nature had passed away. A wholly new thinking about nature had taken its place. The great Johannes Müller was still teaching at Berlin University, and his most famous pupils, Hermann von Helmholtz, Ernst von Brücke, Emil du Bois-Reymond and Carl Ludwig, were working in their respective parts of Germany and Austria as standard bearers for the new view of nature. They were extremely successful in their endeavours to force an entry for a thinking based on physics and chemistry into the world of living things. They all belonged to a new and still youthfully vibrant generation. Most of them had — whether secretly or openly — subscribed to German liberalism and were full of the highest idealism.

They all had enthusiastic pupils and followers and were the advance guard of a more or less blatant materialism. But it was a materialism that was underpinned by ideals and which, in its energy and shining eloquence, had an effect upon all areas of life at that time. 'They [the thinkers with a materialistic orientation] attempted to oppose the idealistic world-picture of the first half

5. RUDOLF WAGNER

Rudolf Wagner

of the century with one that derives all explanation exclusively from the facts of nature. They had confidence only in a knowledge that could be gained from these facts.'[1]

This group of thinkers and researchers was opposed by another, older generation which still believed it had its roots in German idealism. Rudolf Wagner belonged to this generation. He saw in the insurgent materialism a process of denuding human beings of their souls and felt himself called to work against it. He tried — inadequately, to be sure — to preserve the old thought-forms, explaining that the new discoveries of the modern science of that time were not in contradiction with religious ideas.

He began his lecture — which subsequently became so famous — with the following words: 'It is only with reluctance that I have responded to the repeated request of my esteemed friend whom your confidence has called to be your secretary to give a lecture at this public assembly, which I would not otherwise have felt occasioned to do.'[2] This sentence was no empty cliché, for it really does seem to have been the case that Wagner resisted giving this lecture. He would have felt from the outset that his cause was a forlorn undertaking. This came clearly to expression a few days later when because of illness he did not appear at a public disputation with the physiologist Carl Ludwig which he had himself proposed. A detailed account of this embarrassing failure was preserved by a participant in the assembly.[3]

In his own lecture Wagner concerns himself with two cardinal questions of the view of nature current in his time. He goes back to the origins of the human race, and then goes to append to this some fundamental insights about the nature of the soul.

Basing his exposition on the research and descriptions of his predecessor Blumenbach, Wagner defends in seven brilliantly formulated sentences the thesis that the human race has a single, common origin. The differences between the races that are distributed throughout the earth 'are no greater than the differences that exist between animals and plants of one and the same species, for instance, between dogs or sheep ...' And then he expresses the following significant sentences: 'All human races, as with the breeds of many domestic animals, can be traced back to no race actually in existence now but to an ideal archetypal form, most closely resembling the Indo-European. The way that races have been formed is completely unknown. It occurred at a barely conceivable time inaccessible to research.' And with regard to the account in Genesis he adds: 'The possibility of descent from one pair cannot in any way be scientifically disputed for strict physiological reasons.' On the basis of these statements he makes the attempt to refrain from any investigation of the Biblical story of Adam and Eve. 'Neither positive proof nor evidence to the contrary can be given for the Biblical account. A scientific theology must proceed on the basis of this statement.'[4]

The second part of the lecture is concerned with the question of the immortality of the soul and its dependence on the organs of the body. Unfortunately, this was couched in terms of a pure polemic, without the support of real observations or intellectual foundations. Wagner launches into his theme as follows: 'Materialistic views have increasingly gained ground and general circulation among naturalists and especially physiologists, belief in a substantial soul is disappearing by degrees, and the attempt wholly to dissolve science into psychology is — for anyone who has learnt to decipher the signature of the times — the most probable course of the immediate future.'

It can be gleaned from the sentences that have been quoted that Wagner had taken up the fight full of resignation. He anticipated the inevitable victory of materialism, which he nevertheless opposed. What he was able to say by way of countering this new faith amounted merely to warnings and an appeal to his listeners' feelings.

Without naming him personally, he quoted the last remarks of Carl Vogt, who was with great clarity presenting his radical, materialistic standpoint: 'Free will does not exist, and so there is no *individual* responsibility and *individual* accountability, as morality and criminal law and God knows who else would impose on us. We are not for a moment masters of ourselves, of our spiritual powers, no more than we have power over whether our kidneys perform excretory functions or not.'

What is stated here with a crude clarity is that the old gods are no longer of any significance and that a new kind of thinking has been inaugurated. Wagner, however, was trying to defend himself against this. But his weapons had become blunt, and anyone using them would be full of uncertainty and despair. His arguments no longer had any validity.

Thus in spite of the warm applause that it received, his address made little impression. But the 3000 copies of the booklet that he published were sold out in a few weeks. As expected, Carl Vogt immediately launched an attack against Wagner, making some very harsh accusations, and a few weeks later Wagner published a defence entitled 'Concerning Knowledge and Belief, with Particular Reference to the Future of Souls.' But now all hell broke loose! This man who had formerly been so reserved used language at which one can only wonder. He had become infuriated and in a certain sense foolhardy. This was already apparent from the foreword:

> One should not always let it pass when this rabble [meaning Vogt, Büchner and many others] wants to deceive the nation regarding the most precious possessions that we have inherited from our fathers. [This rabble] shamelessly exhales its stinking breath at the people from the seething contents of its entrails, while trying to make them think that it's the most pleasant aroma imaginable.

Statements such as these were the basis for a general argument. Not that Vogt or the others concerned would have expressed themselves better or more objectively. They were equally furious and inflamed, and filled with a true *furor Teutonicus*. War broke out, and it lasted for quite a long time; then Haeckel became involved in the battle and crossed swords with Virchow, just as Vogt had with Wagner three decades previously.

Rudolf Steiner expressed his view of this dispute as it unfolded on the stage of world history:

> The controversy between Vogt and Wagner makes it perfectly clear that the materialists, as they fought their opponents, were not merely confronted with intellectual reasons but also with emotions. For in his Göttingen lecture Wagner had appealed to the moral necessity of being unable to endure the thought that 'mechanical machines walking about with two arms and legs' should finally be dissolved into indifferent material substances, without leaving us the hope that the good that they do should be rewarded and the evil punished. Vogt's answer was: 'The existence of an immortal soul is, for Herr Wagner, not the result of investigation and thought ... He needs an immortal soul in order to be able torture and punish it after a person's death.'[5]

In these words Rudolf Steiner goes to the heart of the whole controversy. Wagner was trying — amidst threats and highly emotional warnings — to continue calling upon the old gods. Vogt tore these graven images, which no longer had any real power or substance, to pieces.

However, the question arises: what does this controversy signify in the course of the nineteenth century? How did it come about that he was led with such great anger to the point of wanting wholly to destroy his opponent?

III

If one looks at the engravings and photographs that have been preserved of these two men, their contrasting nature becomes immediately apparent. Wagner's face is long and narrow, with a high forehead and a big nose. His eyes have a sharp and not altogether friendly aspect, but his expression is cultivated and tender. In contrast, Carl Vogt's, Jacob Moleschott's and Ludwig Büchner's countenances impress one as being those of big, powerful men. They are conscious of their mission and have the will to carry it out. One can have the feeling that a civilization in decline, represented by Wagner, is confronting a group of strong and youthful conquering figures. The Goths must probably have presented a similar aspect when they went to war against the Romans.

From a generational point of view there was likewise a vast difference. The young materialists had, without exception, all been born after 1815, the year of the Vienna Congress and the victory over Napoleon. The sequence of their birth gives an unambiguous picture:

1816	Carl Ludwig
1817	Carl Vogt
1818	Karl von Vierordt
1818	Emil du Bois-Reymond
1819	Ernst Brücke
1821	Rudolf Virchow
1821	Hermann von Helmholtz
1822	Jacob Moleschott
1824	Ludwig Büchner

Only the leading figures in the struggle for the breakthrough of the materialistic worldview are listed here. The generation that followed them approximately fifteen years later — including Ernst Haeckel (born 1834) and many others — ventured into the territory of the earth itself.

Wagner, on the other hand, was a child of the early years of the nineteenth century. He was born on June 30, 1805. This gave him an altogether different intellectual attitude and soul constitution. His direct contemporaries were Adalbert Stifter and Hans Christian Andersen, who came into the world in the same

5. RUDOLF WAGNER

year. Eduard Mörike had become a citizen of the earth a few months earlier (September 8, 1804) and the kind-hearted Baron von Feuchtersleben a short while later (April 29, 1806). Wagner forged a bond with this group of personalities. They were writers and aesthetes; they still inwardly carried the worldview of German idealism and lived within the thought-forms of the early Biedermeier world.

Wagner had a difficult youth.[6] He was the oldest of six sons; his father was a grammar-school teacher in Bayreuth, who was later transferred to Augsburg. The first-born came to Erlangen University at the age of sixteen and studied medicine there and in Würzburg. In 1826 he qualified with a study on 'the world-historical development of epidemics and contagious diseases and the laws of their dissemination.'

In 1827 he went to Paris, where — under the guidance of the great Georges Cuvier — he undertook research in comparative anatomy. From Paris he travelled to the Mediterranean for further studies, but — since he was entirely without means — he had to set up a medical practice in Augsburg. After a year he was asked to come as a professor to the University of Erlangen. This was the start of his career as a scientist. In 1832 he was appointed as a full professor to the Chair of Comparative Anatomy.

From this point he wrote a large number of books and treatises on anthropology, comparative anatomy and physiology, a textbook on zoology and much more. This intense period of creative work lasted for approximately fifteen years. His son wrote: 'Wagner's period of flowering lasted between the ages of 25 and 40, from 1830 until 1845.' And he characterizes his father's way of working as follows: 'Wagner's gift of quick observation, his intuitive eye and his easily excitable disposition may have led him somewhat too quickly to the premature ending of his labours. His tendency to refer to subsequent special projects which did not always come about — which can be explained equally by his intellectual gifts and, sadly, by his constantly precarious health — on more than one occasion gave his opponents grounds for

117

their attacks on him ... When he left a particular realm, Wagner always immediately turned his attention to working on another and for this reason exerted a highly stimulating influence both as an author and as a teacher.'

Wagner's character can well be imagined from this description: erratic, sanguine, probably often also depressed but also sensitive and gentle. His intellect was certainly outstanding, but he lacked the power of endurance.

The particular honour of his being offered a professorship at Göttingen University occurred in 1840 when he was 35. In 1845 he had a serious physical breakdown and went to Italy in a mortally ill state for a lengthy holiday. He remained there until his 42nd year (1847), when he returned to Göttingen strengthened and to a large extent restored to health. His interest in the visual arts awoke while he was in Italy; but while he was there he also carried out a lot of wok related to physiology.

On returning to Göttingen, he began his literary battle against materialism. 'For the enlightening of the public' he wrote his *Physiologische Briefe* (Letters on Physiology), which aroused the anger and furious opposition of Carl Vogt and others. This led in 1854, when he was 49, to the controversy about materialism and the ensuing battles. Thereafter he became more and more ill and could only occasionally — and with many interruptions — attend to his duties as a teacher and researcher.

An important element in the last years of his life was his detailed studies on the physiology and morphology of the brain and nerves. Wagner had probably become aware of the untenability of his theses on the nature of the soul and now tried to find the scientific foundations were necessary for them. He made some interesting discoveries, though without achieving a decisive breakthrough. Then in 1861, his 56th year, he devoted himself to some very detailed anthropological and ethnological studies; and questions as to the pre-history of mankind preoccupied him. Shortly afterwards he withdrew almost completely from his teaching position; he suffered a serious stroke, was paralysed and lost the power in his voice. However, he made a gradual recovery and to some extent regained his speech. A cold that he caught during a spring walk set him back, and he died on May 13, 1864.

With this a personality crossed the threshold who had got caught up in the darkness of that time, the wholly unique midpoint of the nineteenth century. The best of the people who passed through this time changed into inadequate reflections of themselves, who brought about the opposite of what they had striven for. Wagner was the victim of his own actions and behaviour. Consequently, he became an extraordinarily tragic figure who wanted much and accomplished much, but who nonetheless collapsed when he was still far from his goal.

The writers and dreamers of his generation — such as Stifter, Mörike and Andersen — were able to keep going through the characters and figures of their inner world. All the same, they were tragic figures, because the onset of the modern age left them in a solitary and abandoned state. Feuchtersleben died very early (1849), a genius whose untimely death can be put down to the misunderstanding of his contemporaries.

They all looked back; the pale reflection of German idealism and the romantic philosophy of nature lived in them, but it was no longer vigorous enough to be renewed in their souls. Although they were always quoting Goethe, they passed Goetheanism by. Thus they were overwhelmed and subsided into despair, mental derangement or resignation.

IV

One might ask with a certain degree of justice why Wagner's life unfolded in so tragic a way. Why did he not — as did his great contemporary Johannes Müller (1801–58) — become the founder of a whole school of naturalists and physiologists?

For both had their roots in German idealism. Both were gifted and had enthusiasm for their subject; both were hard-working and very skilful in the use of words. Each had a beginning that promised much. After a relatively short time of preparation they became famous university teachers, one in Göttingen and the other in Berlin. To be sure, Müller had a much stronger constitution. 'He is made of iron encased with bronze,' it was said of him.[7] Nevertheless he too sometimes had breakdowns and finally, when in such a state, took his own life.

There is probably only one answer to the question posed above: Müller was consistent; he obeyed the demands of his time and tried to establish a unified world-conception based on observation and experiment. Wagner, however, was inconsistent. He was unable to discard the ideas that were dear to him and therefore arrived at the same conclusion that Faraday also held, namely, that he closed the church door when he opened the door of the laboratory. Wagner openly confessed to a worldview of 'double bookkeeping.' 'I repeat,' he said, 'it is not physiology that makes it necessary for me to accept the idea of a soul but the conception of a moral world-order which is inherent within me and inseparable form me,' and he concluded this treatise with these words: 'In contrast to the erroneous views of spiritualism and materialism, the Bible puts forward the only foundation for a scientific physiology and anthropology that is also physiologically maintainable, in the true dualism of spirit and body united in a soul organism.'[8]

Here the difference between Müller and Wagner becomes even more clearly apparent. The one was a monist; he tried to develop a unified worldview. The other was a dualist, who — like Immanuel Kant — endeavoured 'to confine knowledge to create space for faith.' And Rudolf Steiner adds to this statement by Kant the observation that it was not of prime importance to this philosopher 'to establish the foundations of knowledge in an impartial, open-minded way but, rather, that he wanted above all to acquire a view of knowledge which allowed him to introduce certain religious dogmas through a little door into the intellectual life of human beings.'

These words appear in the obituary in which Rudolf Steiner commemorated Ludwig Büchner, who died on April 30, 1899. This article appeared on May 13, 1899 in the *Magazin für Literatur* which Rudolf Steiner edited at that time.[9] In the article, Büchner's formerly so celebrated and latterly so reviled book, *Kraft und Stoff,* is strongly defended against philosophical know-alls. With remarkably sharp words Rudolf Steiner castigates those 'philosophers who think they have ever higher sources of knowledge,' amongst whom are the 'timid naturalists who do not dare to draw *consistent* conclusions regarding the place of man and his intellectual faculties within nature from the observed facts' [emphasis added].

Here, too, there is a reference to the *consistency* which was so necessary for natural-history research at that time. This uncompromising consistency is what led Rudolf Steiner to defend Ernst Haeckel against his attackers and which also made him stand up for Ludwig Büchner.

> It cannot be denied, that Ludwig Büchner is a one-sided thinker and that one can, while fully agreeing with the scientific findings, also arrive at deeper ideas than was possible for the rough-hewn nature of his thinking. But it must be emphasized that the trends inherent in his thinking, together with the feelings that they bring in their wake, are much closer to a modern soul-life than the philosophical thought-structures that contrive artificially to rescue the outlived conceptions of earlier times with their higher sources of knowledge.'

Accordingly what mattered at the turn of the century was to throw all old ideas overboard in order that the threshold of this age could be crossed in the most rigorous and consistent clarity by each person as a 'single individual and his property.' 'Without an understanding of scientific results and of the methods through which these results have been achieved, no world-conception is possible today. And that Büchner recognized this, that on the basis of these methods and results he endeavoured to achieve a worldview, is his not inconsiderable service.'

Rudolf Steiner also spoke up in an equally significant and encouraging way for Vogt and Moleschott, characterizing the beliefs and convictions of these representatives of unalloyed materialism as follows:

> Quite a number of materialists were inspired by an esthetic enjoyment of the wonderful structure of organisms to a point where they felt that the soul must have its origin in the body. The magnificent structure of the human brain impressed them much more than the abstract concepts with which philosophy was concerned. How much more claim to be considered as the cause of the spirit, therefore, did the former seem to present than the latter.[10]

It is very clear from these quotations that it was indeed the case that at the end of the nineteenth century Rudolf Steiner saw to it that he spoke out in favour of materialism and monism. Already at that time he knew very well that the path to a science of the spirit went directly by way of modern materialistic science; that, moreover, a truly new Christianity had begun to manifest itself in what Haeckel and Darwin had presented.

In the introductory lecture to the cycle on *The Fifth Gospel,* Rudolf Steiner expressed this with the greatest clarity:

> Ernst Haeckel is inconceivable without the basis of Christian culture. And however hard modern science may try to promote opposition to Christianity, this natural science is itself an offspring of Christianity, a direct development of the Christian impulse. When modern science has got over the ailments of childhood,

men will perceive quite clearly that if followed to its *logical* conclusions, it leads to spiritual science; that there is an entirely *consistent* path from Haeckel to spiritual science. When that is grasped, it will also be realized that Haeckel is Christian through and through, although he himself has no notion of it.[11] [Emphasis added.]

Rudolf Steiner goes a significant step further here and tries to show how the ideas of Haeckel and Darwin, if developed logically, can lead to a view that begins to recognize the spiritual existence of man's being when the earth had its origin.

Anyone who understands the doctrines of Darwin and Haeckel and is himself convinced that only as a Christian movement was the Darwinian movement possible (Haeckel had no notion of this, but Darwin was aware of many things) — anyone who realizes this is led by an absolutely consistent path to the idea of reincarnation. And if he can call upon a certain power of clairvoyance, this same path will lead him to knowledge of the *spiritual* origin of the human race.

In these seminal words an altogether new possibility for judging materialism and the science of the nineteenth century based on observation and experiment is opened up to us. For they were the foundations of modern spiritual science and contained the germinal elements of a true Christianity. Those who fought against them — pastors and philosophers, who did so in the name of Christianity — were the true antagonists of a renewed Christianity. Thus Wagner, too, stood at the forefront of the opponents of Christ, because he paid tribute to an old dualism; whereas the new monism was already building the bridge that was to lead to the time of spiritual revelation.

V

In the important essay, *Reincarnation and Karma,* Rudolf Steiner juxtaposes the sentence: 'Everything living arises from the living' with another sentence: 'Everything of a soul-nature arises from the soul-element.' He goes on to show that the way that modern science unfolded in the second half of the nineteenth century led to the idea of reincarnation developing from it.

But we know, on the other hand, that this idea also began to stir within the minds of certain thinkers independently from scientific trends. Two of the most significant of these were Gustav Widenmann (1812–76) and Maximilian Drossbach (1810–84). Both were members of the generation (together with Richard Wagner and Otto Ludwig, both born in 1813) between the old representatives of a spirituality that was passing away and the new proclaimers of a modern science of nature.

Only this new science can create the phenomenological foundations for a spiritual-scientific knowledge of reincarnation and karma. What emerged again and again in the form of individual flashes of illumination — in Lessing in his old age, in Herder in his youth, in Goethe throughout his life — could be elevated to a modern scientific discipline only through Rudolf Steiner's research. And yet this rested on the foundations of those insights that Haeckel and Darwin communicated to us and were defended by Büchner, Vogt and Moleschott. A science that is *consistently* followed through leads naturally to the reality of reincarnation, which states that 'everything of a soul-nature arises from the element of soul.'

However, the rudiments of such a modern conception of the soul, in the light of the idea of reincarnation, can also be found in Rudolf Wagner. However awkward and dedicated to the old ideas — through his being dazzled by dualism — he may have been, the new world — albeit in an old outworn garb — was beginning to shine through him. Towards the end of his essay

5. RUDOLF WAGNER

Über Wissen und Glauben (On Knowledge and Belief) which has already been referred to are the following words:

> Why should the soul after death not have another existence in a nearby region, why should it not be able to leave the earth?
>
> Wherever this place may be where souls come together, from the standpoint of natural-history research we can well imagine that a migration to another spatial world can occur just as quickly and easily as the transmission of light from the sun to the earth. This translation of a human soul to a different world can of course only be conceived of if it is stripped of all visible physical matter.
>
> *It would be just as possible for a naturalist to imagine that such a soul could return and be provided with a new bodily garment formed of material substances which are similar to, or identical with, those that it has now.*
>
> Such a possibility has nothing against it and is just as conceivable as the manifestation of new animal forms and the sudden appearance of man in the more recent geological epochs. [Emphasis added.]

Here something is intuited which could at first live only in ideas and feelings had not been brought down to earth. The abyss of materialism had to be traversed in order that such premonitions could become a reality.

Rudolf Virchow

6

Rudolf Virchow

Rudolf Carl Virchow (1821–1902) was a German physician and politician, particularly concerned with the advancement of public health. He was one of the founders of social medicine.

I

Rudolf Virchow died at the age of nearly eighty-one on September 5, 1902, after a short illness. He had previously hardly ever been really ill, and as an eighty-year-old he could still astonish his younger colleagues by participating in the rambles organized at various conferences. He who tried to follow every illness into the innermost regions of its mechanism remained healthy until the end of his life.

At the beginning of 1902 he had fractured the neck of his femur as the result of a fall. It had healed well, and he was convalescing first in Teplitz in Bohemia (now Teplice) and then in Bad Harzburg in Lower Saxony. There he began to suffer from a serious loss of appetite, and Virchow sensed that this signified his end. He was brought back to Berlin and died peacefully soon afterwards.

His funeral resembled that of a ruling prince. His friend and pupil Wilhelm von Waldeyer wrote:

> The coffin lay in state in the great hall of the Berlin Rathaus [town hall]; colleagues, pupils, friends and admirers of Virchow assembled in large numbers from throughout Germany ... On all streets through which the funeral procession passed on its way to the cemetery, large numbers o people stood closely together, forming a dark line on each side, with a quiet dignity. One could see that these men and women had been drawn here not through curiosity but through the feeling that, by their participation, they were paying their last respects to their fellow citizen.[1]

A year before this, his eightieth birthday was celebrated throughout the world and above all in Berlin. Letters of thanks and messages of congratulation came from everywhere. A festive dinner was held with two hundred guests and, to conclude it, a celebratory gathering with over a thousand participants in the conference hall of the Prussian Parliament with the customary addresses and a letter from the Kaiser, which was read out. The entire scientific world took part in these festivities.

When towards the end of 1901 Virchow gave with much gratitude a description of these celebrations in the famous *Archiv für pathologische Anatomie und Physiologie und für klinische Medizin* (still known as *Virchow's Archives*) which he had founded and was subsequently named after him, he tried to pull together the threads of his life:

> The total number of telegrams amounted to nearly eight hundred. Their content was so varied that they constituted a reflection of my whole, restless life, for which reason they may seem confusing for anyone else. This is due to the fact that in the course of my life I have followed very different lines of research and activity, and that I have not merely changed my official residence but have visited the whole of Europe and important parts

of Africa and Asia on longer journeys ... Thus the path
of my research has not only brought the countries and
their inhabitants into the orbit of my presentations but I
have — in accordance with the individual circumstances
— made not only medicine and the natural sciences but
also anthropology and archaeology, occasionally also
literature, philosophy, politics and social conditions the
object of my studies.[2]

Thus his activity was on a really broad front. He was revered throughout the world as the uncrowned pope of medical science, and he was thoroughly conscious of this position; he demanded an awareness of this recognition from his colleagues and pupils. But members of the public also regarded him as a very helpful influence, for in addition to his intensive research-work he was equally active as a politician and social reformer. He was the founder in 1861 of the *Fortschrittspartei* or Progressive Party and through and through a representative of liberalism. He was full of ideas about bringing happiness to the people, and progress and freedom were his ideals. This came particularly to expression at the end of the account referred to above, where he recalled with the greatest devotion and particular sympathy the festival that the Berlin craftsmen's guild which he had founded many years ago prepared for him. The words with which he describes this are very touching and moving:

When I appeared recently at the festival put on for me,
when the old songs rang out, when once again I gave an
address, then everyone's hands stretched out towards
me, as did those of the children in the Schellingstrasse.
This is the gratitude of the people, and so I would say to
anyone: if you trust the people and work for them, you
will not lack your reward, even though the collapse of
countless institutions, the disappearance of many people
and the total transformation of public life bring thoughts

of the transient state of our lives closely to consciousness. This is my creed and I hope that it will suffice for me for as long as I live.

Hardly ever before had Virchow, who was a complete rationalist, spoken so deeply from his heart; for he was a man to whom any imagination or intuition, towards which — in whatever guise it might appear — he invariably adopted an antagonistic and disdainful attitude, had always seemed offensive.

II

Who was Virchow, who already in his youth was respected as the renewer of the medical thinking of his time and who seemingly without difficulty ascended the stairway of fame and recognition step by step? He was the only well-protected child of a very bourgeois family living in the Pomeranian town of Schivelbein (now Swidwin in Poland), where he was born in 1821. 'My early years flowed quietly by without any significant events which might have been of major importance for my later life; and so few or hardly any memories imprinted themselves on my memory.' Thus wrote the eighteen-year-old Virchow, who had written a curriculum vitae in the form of a report for his school-leaving examination. He attended the grammar school in Köslin (now Koszalin), where he was top of the class every year. In 1839 he became a student at the Pepinière in Berlin, the medical academy where the Prussian state trained its future medical officers. The course of study, which was for four years, lasted until 1843; and again he qualified with the best marks. At university he was a pupil of Dieffenbach, the surgeon, and Lukas Schönlein, the internist. But the deepest impressions were made on him by the lectures of Johannes Müller, the physiologist, who in 1856 resigned from his teaching

6. RUDOLF VIRCHOW

post in the Faculty of Pathological Anatomy in order that his celebrated pupil could take his place as professor.

In the funeral oration for his teacher, who died in 1858, Virchow said: 'It was his hand that guided the first steps of the medical apprentice, it was his words that awarded me my physician's degree; from this place from which his picture now looks down to us, I was able to look into his warm eyes when — during his time as dean — I gave my first public lecture as an unsalaried member of the university staff.'

Immediately after the end of his studies he became an assistant to the prosector* of the Charité Hospital in Berlin, and at the age of 24, in 1845, became interim prosector. His enthusiasm for work was indomitable. As a pupil of Johannes Müller, and as the moving force behind the modern scientific ideas that were becoming more and more strongly established, he began to renew the entire realm of pathological anatomy. He described leukaemia as a disease of the blood which was caused by a pathological increase of white blood cells (then called pus corpuscles). At the same time he pointed to the part played by the spleen in this affliction.

Soon afterwards he explained the origin and mechanism of thrombosis and embolism. Until then the connection between them was unknown, and no one had considered that the embolus might be part of the thrombus carried by the blood.

In 1846, when still an unknown, young prosector without means, he founded the great medical journal now known as Virchow's *Archive*. He so greatly fired the publisher Reimer's enthusiasm for this plan that the latter decided to take the risk. A year later the first issue appeared, and this important journal remains to this day one of the leading authorities in the realm of scientific medicine. Virchow edited this journal until his death and revised and reviewed every single contribution that was published in it. The most significant discoveries, experiments

---

★ The person in a medical school or hospital preparing a dissection for demonstration.

and descriptions of medical science of the second half of the nineteenth century were published there. Thus Virchow stood as a *pontifex maximus* of pathology, with a connection to all universities in the world; and it was an honour and a recognition of the highest degree for an author to have his work published in Virchow's *Archive*.

Virchow also began to publish many works of his own, for little by little his views about the nature of illness and its causes became more firmly established. The cell is the place that becomes the seat of a disease. The abnormal reaction of cells and tissues to pathological influences causes all symptoms and conditions which manifest themselves as signs of illness. Inflammation and tumour formation can be traced back to abnormal cell-formations and cell reactions. The young Virchow described carcinomas as cell growths already in the first volume of his *Archive*.

These were fundamentally new ideas; a hitherto unknown system of views and thoughts appeared and destroyed the outmoded vestiges of Hippocratic medicine with its youthful power. The theory of the humours was swept away within a few years. Illnesses were caused not by the wrong mixture of fluids but by the cellular organism itself, which lay at a much deeper level of the body.

The microscope became an indispensable tool of the pathologist and led his marvelling eye into hitherto unknown regions of the course of an illness. The young pathologist lectured and demonstrated, dissected and looked down the microscope, and each day brought new discoveries. His name became well-known, and old and young doctors attended his courses to let the fresh wind of these burgeoning spring-like ideas to waft around their ears.

III

Virchow's decisive experience was when in 1847 he was asked by the Prussian medical authorities to investigate the causes of the ever-recurring outbreaks of typhoid epidemics in Upper Silesia. Silesia was at the time a disaster area. In three weeks Virchow investigated the situation there and found that what appeared to be typhoid was a devastating typhus epidemic (spotted fever), which had its roots primarily in the wretched living conditions of the Upper Silesian working people Hunger, dirt and poverty were the causes. In contrast to previous commissioners, who had treated such 'studies' as periods of holiday and indulged themselves on the estates of Silesian barons, Virchow actually studied the social conditions in Breslau (now Wroclaw), Rybnik and Pless (Pszczyna). He wrote a report which lacked nothing in clarity, honesty and openness. He castigated with clear words the serious shortcomings that existed and demanded as a remedy the social renewal of people's living conditions there.

> All the world knows, that the working people of our time are affected to a considerable degree by the introduction and improvement of machines ... that human labour has lost all autonomy and has become part — albeit a living part but equivalent to a dead value — of the operation of machines. Human beings are regarded now only as hands. But should that be the significance of machines in the cultural history of nations?

This was followed by some fundamental arguments about working time and free time, about capital and the resultant social misery. Virchow became one of the principal advocates of the ideas which would in a few months lead to the March revolution in Berlin. He fought on the barricades and actively helped to found the Frankfurt national assembly. He also started to publish a new journal, *Medizinische Reform* (Medical Reform), where — together with other physicians and politicians — he tried to outline the social tasks of a new medical profession. He saw the position of the physician as central in the social life of the community; he wanted to train doctors to be educators of the people, in order that they might deal with general needs with their help:

> Physicians are the natural advocates of the poor, and the social question falls to a significant degree under their jurisdiction.
> It is wrong to substitute the Christian compassion of individuals for the fulfilment of a common duty.
> The ultimate task of medicine is that of setting society up on a physiological basis. Medicine is a social science, and *politics is nothing more than medicine on a larger scale.*[3]

These were indeed brave words. He saw the social question as one of education, for he continues: 'Our task [as physicians] is a pedagogical one; we must educate pugnacious men who fight the battles of humanism.' In these thoughts there glowed the fire of a newly awakened liberalism, which filled the best of the European middle class at that time. It was as though a new spirit of freedom was living in people and wanted to come to manifestation.

Rudolf Steiner once referred to this particular situation and clearly characterized it as follows: 'The 1840s were an important period; for the powers moving world evolution forward foresaw a kind of crisis at this time.'[4] And then he went on to say that at this time the developing proletariat was not yet ready to work constructively as a conscious element. 'For the most part, the bearer of the political life at that time was the middle class.' And into this middle class there streamed the 'impulse of the consciousness-soul age in the form of political views.' And he continued: 'For those who listened to the speeches of the outstanding personalities of the middle class in the 1840s ... indicating what innovations should be brought to mankind in every sphere ..., these years seemed to herald the dawning of a *new popular movement.*' [Emphasis added.]

There is no doubt that Virchow was one of those 'outstanding personalities.' This new popular movement which wanted to make medicine the bearer of the best social impulses lived in his words.

However, the middle class did not take hold of the task that was ascribed to it. It slept through this spiritual awakening, and Rudolf Steiner describes this omission as a 'great tragedy' for the unfolding of the nineteenth century. 'When at the time of the Archangel Michael's appearance as Time Spirit at the end of the 1870s the middle class had not understood the political impact of liberal ideas, the powers which became involved with mankind from this period started to obscure the nature of these ideas.'

This awakening and this process of obscuring can also clearly be followed in Rudolf Virchow's life. Indeed, without the indications given by Rudolf Steiner it would not be possible to understand that the young and the older Virchow were one and the same person. In all probability a common thread ran through the scientific studies of the great scholar; but the man himself became quite a different person, as one could see from the total transformation that had occurred by the fifth seven-year period of his life.

IV

In 1849 Virchow was dismissed from his position as prosector at the Charité Hospital in Berlin on account of his participation in the revolution and the on-going public conversation in which he engaged as a social policy maker; his lectureship at the university was taken away from him and the use of his office terminated. The Prussian state wanted to destroy the leaders of liberalism.

At the same time, however, Virchow received a summons to attend Würzburg University as a Professor of Pathological Anatomy and Physiology. During these years Würzburg was one of the leading German universities in the sphere of theoretical medicine; many well-known researchers worked there. As this university was in Bavaria, which for Prussians was 'abroad,'

Virchow made a quick decision and accepted the post. He remained in this beautiful town on the Main for seven years, until 1856. He married there and started a family. His institute became a famous place of learning, and he also concluded the preparatory work which then led to the composition of his basic book on *Cellular Pathology,* which appeared in 1858.

With this work, which came out a year before Darwin's *Origin of Species,* a completely new stage in the history of medicine began. The radical nature of this new beginning is clearly characterized by the fact that Diepgen structured his famous *Geschichte der Medizin* (History of Medicine) in such a way that the second part, which deals with modern times, is divided into two volumes: 'From the Medicine of the Enlightenment until the Founding of Cellular Pathology' (1740 to *c.* 1858) and 'Medicine from the beginnings of Cellular Pathology to the initial stages of the Modern Theory of the Constitution' (*c.* 1858 to 1900).

This division clearly identifies Virchow's place in medical history. He was the founder of cellular pathology; he built it up for the most part together with his pupils and, as he said of himself, 'medicine was [thereby] led from the realm of the philosophy of nature to that of natural science.' He was the founder of experimental and descriptive methods in the field of medicine. Knowing rather than healing was the essential principle for him.

Out of a social reformer who wanted to heal the entire nation there emerged a research scientist, who trusted only in experiment and appearances. Virchow increasingly distanced himself from the sphere of a true science of healing. He founded the Anthropological Society and developed stronger inclinations towards anthropology and ethnology. Acquiring knowledge and collecting were the principal themes of his life. With an indefatigable meticulousness he built up his museum, which with its 23,000 specimens became the largest collection of pathological organs and tissues. In addition there was an extensive gallery of human skeletons containing everything of particular interest: giants and dwarfs, abnormalities of all sorts; skeletons of all races and nations, ages and genders. Thus he gradually became the prisoner of his knowledge, his passion for collecting and his fame — an old man who no longer embodied himself but only his official position.

However, this transformation occurred only after his return to Berlin. In 1856 he was unanimously recalled by the senate of Berlin University and nominated Professor of Pathological Anatomy and Physiology. He built up a large research institute to which he linked the museum referred to above. Until his death, hence for 46 years, he was the undisputed *princeps* in the kingdom of scientific medicine. Through him the art of healing became a science and healing itself a questionable matter; whereas knowledge of the physical course of an illness was advanced by him to a quite extraordinary degree. The young man with a message became a grey, often cynical materialist and agnostic.

In his memoirs Carl Ludwig Schleich devotes an entire chapter to his meeting with Virchow. For some years he had been his assistant and pupil, and he describes his first meeting with the great old man in such a way that Virchow's appearance is clearly characterized:

> We stood before the almighty, bespectacled man with distinctively penetrating eyes, which were conspicuously lacking in eyelashes. His eyelids were paper-thin, like parchment. His nose was very finely chiselled, and expressed the pride of its bearer in its graciously curved nostrils which gently quivered as he spoke, as though conveying a note of scorn. His lips were thin and bloodless, and his grey beard was thin.[5]

This was in 1883, when Virchow was only 62 years old. At the time he said to Schleich, who was speaking with him about the possibility of a divine power: 'Leave all this theological twaddle out of the equation. Read what Kant had to say about so-called proofs for the existence of God.'

Virchow had made up his mind, he wanted to collect and

examine. He was convinced that there can never be any real knowledge of the purpose and roots of human existence. He no longer had an organ for anything of a metaphysical nature. But he fought against all those from whom a strong will to live, a real sense of conviction, sprang forth. People who acted out of their inner being and who were governed by their will rather than by logic, were his enemies. He persecuted them, often against his own better judgment.

V

There were two people with whom Virchow was perpetually aggrieved: Ernst Haeckel and Bismarck. He attacked both of them whenever he could, and it is truly incomprehensible that he, who had once been a liberal innovator, behaved towards Haeckel like an old, fossilized pastor. 'When I lie on my sofa,' he said to Schleich in a conversation about the theory of evolution, 'and spout forth the possibilities [of evolution] just as others puff the smoke of their cigars, I can no doubt follow such daydreams. But it doesn't hold any water. Haeckel is a fool. This will become perfectly obvious.'

In the essay on Haeckel and his opponents, Rudolf Steiner devotes several pages to this incomprehensible attitude on the part of Virchow, and clearly characterizes him as follows:

> More dangerous than all the damage that a 'religion of evolution' can cause in immature minds is the battle that Virchow has been waging for decades against the theory of evolution amidst the approval of theological and other reactionaries. It is made more difficult to have an objective argument with Virchow through his blunt rejection of the whole idea and his refusal to put forth any actual objections to the theory of evolution in general ... Virchow's battle against the theory of evolution is

indeed bewildering if one bears in mind that, at the beginning of his scientific career, this researcher was advocating the idea that all living activity has a mechanistic foundation before the publication of Darwin's *Origin of Species* in 1859.[6]

Virchow's opposition arose from his inability to acknowledge the personality of Haeckel, who had been his pupil in Würzburg. This upright, radiant and well-balanced individual made him feel uneasy. The endeavour to understand the whole of creation through the power of one great idea had become an unbearable prospect for Virchow.

His enmity towards Bismarck derived from the same root. The two men were always coming to blows with one another in the Prussian Parliament, of which Virchow was a member as the representative of the Progressive Party. Virchow, who had entirely lost his liberal fire and had become the narrow-minded embodiment of an abstract notion of progress, was not able to understand Bismarck the politician with his constantly changing ways. He objected to the latter's presence of mind, which was the match for any situation, and was constantly accusing him of weakness and of failing to stand his ground when he was actually being astute. Rudolf Steiner, in an essay from 1898 on Bismarck, has also referred to the hostility between these two men.

> At the session of the Prussian Parliament of June 2, 1865 Bismarck explained to Virchow, a fellow member of parliament who had reproached him, that he had no firm principles but allowed his political decisions to be governed by the way the wind was blowing. 'Virchow has complained that we turn the rudder to adapt to the changing wind. Now I ask what should anyone sailing a ship do other than turn the rudder in accordance with the wind, unless perhaps he intends to create his own wind' ... Bismarck never considered how the world

should be ... his concern was to act *powerfully* in response to the demands made by events.[7]

Virchow found such an attitude unbearable as well, for everything that was in a flowing process or state of flux — Bismarck the politician, or Haeckel, the intuitive naturalist –went against the grain as far as the aging Virchow was concerned. He could not bear people who acted out of the fullness of their individual being, who accepted their destiny without question and entered into life with a mighty 'yes.' He became the opponent of their thoughts and deeds — not because he was in conflict with them but because their advocates had become a nuisance to him. This was the same man who had demanded a far-reaching reform of medicine and fearlessly stood up for these revolutionary views. Since his Würzburg days he had become a different person. He now began to be resigned and to renounce the idea that the good, the great and the beautiful can become manifest on earth through human deeds.

VI

In Virchow's life the whole tragedy of people of the nineteenth century was revealed as if in an archetypal form. Many of them were heroes of the spirit who had set forth with flying banners to serve the cause of freedom in the age of the consciousness soul. They were born with extraordinary gifts; they grew up full of promise and courageously set about the tasks that they had dimly recognized in order to do them justice. But a dark mist began to descend over them; between 1850 and 1860 the horizon of intellectual and political Europe grew dark, and soon a thick layer of cloud obscured the view of the land of freedom. Liberalism became party politics, free knowledge turned into agnosticism, a therapeutic nihilism became widespread in medicine and technology began its triumphal march.

6. RUDOLF VIRCHOW

Virchow, too, fell prey to this tragedy. Born in 1821, he had his roots in the time of German idealism. Goethe, Schelling, Hegel, the Humboldt brothers and many others were still 'at work.' Their light radiated into the social and cultural realms of life at that time. Virchow as a child — even in Schivelbein — likewise received his portion of it. These faculties came to a over-hasty blossoming and maturity in his early Berlin years, when the young physician and prosector undertook to renew the whole of medicine.

The thoughts and ideas of a 'new popular movement' filled him; but this springtime of ideas was struck down by a sudden frost, which destroyed all blossoms in its icy breath. What remained was a science without presuppositions, which led one to believe in a paradise of progress and claimed to be able to achieve it through technical means.

Not even cellular pathology solved the riddle of illness and the mystery of life. It merely pushed them away onto another plane and had to be contented with the collecting and examining of facts. Resignation was its portion.

Resignation and cynicism were also the lot of its creator. He buried himself in his collections and tried to forget what had been a vital force within him before the middle of the century. Only at the end of his life, after his eightieth birthday, did his early memories rise up again, and he called to mind that springtide of intellectual impulses whose bearer and fulfiller he wanted to be.

Those who think that the reaction that set in after 1848, which suppressed and undermined anything that still ventured to speak of inner and outer freedom, was simply the consequence of political events are misjudging the history of that time. The middle class had not awakened to its real task; it remained imprisoned in mental sleep, and because of this powers antagonistic to freedom and the springtide of the mind entered into earthly existence. This battle was waged 'behind the scenes of outward history.' It was described by Rudolf Steiner as a battle which Michael fought with the dragon. But 'that ancient serpent, who is called the Devil and Satan, the deceiver of the whole world — he was thrown down to the earth, and his angels were thrown down with him' (Rev.12:9).

This came about at that time and it became the cause of the darkening cloud that spread over Europe and the whole of the western world in the second half of the nineteenth century. When it was too late, some individuals began at the end of the century to rub the sleep from their eyes. For what had previously still been possible could no longer be done. As Rudolf Steiner said in the lecture cited above: 'For afterwards nothing could any longer be achieved by following the path whereby these goals might have been attained in the period in question. Only through becoming completely awake to spiritual-scientific experiences could anything now be accomplished.'[8]

7

Carl Ludwig Schleich

Schleich (1859–1922) was a surgeon and writer. Born in Pomerania, he studied in Zurich and Berlin, and was an assistant to Rudolf Virchow. He is best remembered for his work on local anaesthesia.

I

Carl Ludwig Schleich was, like Goethe, born 'at noon on the stroke of twelve' on a Sunday 'in the old Oder town of Stettin' on July 19, 1859. The sun was not, as with Goethe, in the sign of the Virgo; it was at the end of its period in Cancer and in conjunction with the planet Mars. Saturn and Jupiter were at its side, Venus shone forth beside Jupiter and Saturn was accompanied by Mercury. It was a distinctive social gathering of all the planets, which gazed down upon the newly born earthly child from the zenith of this summer noon-tide.

It was at the hour of the highest development of light and warmth, with all planets in the sky by day, that Carl Ludwig Schleich passed through the gate of birth. The sun watched over his life in its fullest radiance, and when he surveyed his life at its end he could not but call it sunlit past *(Besonnte Vergangenheit)*. This title of his autobiography was not employed fortuitously; it describes the character of this earthly journey with inimitable precision.

Schleich's life was flooded by the sun. He was the third child and the eldest son of a father who was a popular physician in his home town, and a mother who still embodied traditional qualities of goodness and kindness. He grew up amidst a good crowd of cousins and other relatives who spent the summer together on the estate of his well-to-do maternal grandfather. His childhood was carefree, externally serious and wild, and full of music and security within his parental home. There were no cares and troubles but only gaiety and a cheerful affirmation of life such as only the maya of this time of the *Gründerjahre,* the economic boom of the mid-nineteenth century, was able to give.

When he was seven years old he experienced 'the devastating cholera epidemic ... that raged through Pomerania.' His father had no power to avert it, and in the evening in the family circle would tell of the many who had died while he was treating them. At that time Carl Ludwig received his first beating, because he lingered in the room of a woman who had just died of cholera against his father's orders. This punishment brought about the awakening of his faculty of memory, which had hitherto been conspicuously lacking. Schleich said:

> From this point my life took its course in so utterly conscious a way, and I have all its manifold moments so faithfully engraved in my memory that I could venture to describe them day by day in a fairly complete form ... If Goethe was right when he said so beautifully that memory is an affair of the heart, I must have had a highly impressionable heart; for my closest relatives have long forgotten many of our common experiences and recall theirs only when I ... fish them out again.[1]

Not many people can boast of a similar faculty of memory; but for Schleich, who had a powerful body, a strong voice that carried a long way and an almost irrepressible vitality, this phenomenal capacity for remembering was an intrinsic part of his constitution and way of life.

7. CARL LUDWIG SCHLEICH

Carl Ludwig Schleich

His father was a faithful support to him. Again and again he stood like a living voice of conscience before his son, who revered and acknowledged him as a true father until adulthood. He had good reason for this, for this man believed ever and again in his son's better self, however frequently it was overshadowed and befogged. His father was a child of the materialistic age. Born in 1822, he became a pupil of Johannes Müller and was a friend of Albrecht von Graefe, the great eye specialist, whose picture — alongside portraits of Helmholtz, Max Wilms and Virchow — hung above his desk. 'I spent my early youth,' says Schleich, 'happily under the eyes of these heroes.'

He spent his secondary-school years initially in Stettin (now Szczecin in Poland). This is what he says about them:

> Although my time at school felt like a series of more or less successful silly boyish pranks, ... I always had a certain interest in lessons, not so much in the dull subjects as in the personalities of the teachers, whose funny sides I had a particular skill in discerning, so that the class that I was part of always acquired the reputation of being a real collection of louts.

It was a strong and often very pagan sunlight that shone forth from this boy's heart. But then there soon came the second harsh intervention, which was again triggered by his father.

> The cause was that deep rupture in the happiness of my parents' marriage, which could not be healed ... Out of a severity of conviction which I could never quite understand, my father wrenched me out of my mother's arms, partly in order to wound her feelings and partly also probably with the honourable intention of distancing me from her all too indulgent love.

The boy was sent to the grammar school in Stralsund, where he spent several years, until he successfully passed his school-leaving examination.

7. CARL LUDWIG SCHLEICH

II

There now followed a strange interlude in Zurich. It must have been roughly between 1878 and 1880 (Schleich gives no precise dates) when he joined the university there as a medical student. He hardly did any studying. With the full extent of his hearty nature he enrolled in a student duelling society, and days went by in the service of this student group.

> High spirits verging on wildness, reeling on the brink of destruction, and yet this sense of security, of having the gift of life and of being a splendid fellow — all this was illusory to the point of absurdity, and yet it was a powerful and incomparable step towards the ideal of the highest human possibilities, towards brotherliness and a loving, enthusiastic community of blood.

He had wholly succumbed to these illusions. Then his voice, which must have had a mighty power and a pronounced musical quality at that time, added a further element. It brought him access to various choral societies and bolstered his pride to the point where he resolved to give up his studies and become an opera singer. He journeyed to Milan, underwent an examination at the conservatorium and was accepted there as a student with a scholarship. The following day his father, his faithful supporter, appeared and brought his son back to Zurich.

On his return he continued to drink and to sing, wasted his time and generally went to seed. But in the course of all this he had an encounter with his old drinking companion Gottfried Keller. They were often together, the old and the young, and it chanced that he asked Keller: 'How does one become a poet?' Gottfried Keller pondered for quite a while over his glass and then said quite softly and gently: 'When you discover what is extraordinary about yourself, then you are one.'

Schleich returned to his parental home in a state of severe depression, received guidance from his faithful supporter for the examination ending the pre-clinical stage and then got it over and done with. Immediately afterwards he went to Berlin, became a junior assistant in the surgical department in 1882, with Bernhard von Langenbeck and subsequently Ernst von Bergmann as his teachers. He worked for several years at the Institute of Pathology under Rudolf Virchow and for a long time was unable to make up his mind to sit his physician's degree.

Again his father had to intervene; he absented himself for half a year from his practice, went to see his son in Berlin and studied the handbooks and textbooks for examinations with him. It was 1888, and Schleich was nearly thirty years old. He passed all the examinations and finally qualified as a physician. The Kaiser, Friedrich III, died in the same summer, and with him the Bismarck period came to an end. The glow of the years of economic boom was transformed into the evening mood of the *fin de siècle,* and all events acquired a completely new shade.

Schleich was a child of the *Gründerzeit,* the boom when so many industrial firms were founded. He was intoxicated with this epoch of power and splendour. Man felt himself to be the master of the earth; he loved worldliness and gloried in the realm of technical achievements. Only few experienced with understanding and insight the far-reaching transformation that the year 1879 signified. Schleich, too, spent this time in a dissipated and intoxicated state.

When he returned from Zurich to Berlin, he continued to dream; although he was an assistant In surgery and pathological anatomy, and saw much and learnt much, life was nevertheless a game. His vitality was so great that only a little space remained for reflection. In conversations with friends this element began it enter in. Especially in his intimate friendship with Richard Dehmel, he became self-aware and began to ask questions about existence.

Again and again, however, Schleich would bubble over with creative energy. Since his youth he had been a 'writer.' He wrote volumes full of poems, a quantity of plays and dramas, stories and tales. He sang, composed, studied counterpoint and harmony and spent time with singers and actors. He had a number of new thoughts about all areas of knowledge, sudden ideas which flashed into his mind like inspirations. He studied 'the organ-playing-like technicalities of the brain,' and traced cancerous tumours back to 'cellular incest.' Later, he also embarked upon painting, and painted a lot and with a certain talent.

If one endeavours to comprehend all this, it is as if a constant spring was bubbling forth from within this man, producing ever new insights, ideas, pranks and pearls of wisdom. A portion of the sun's power seemed to be hidden within him that was in constant activity, creating, writing, speaking, writing poetry, painting, singing and making music.

In addition, he had an almost iron constitution which enabled him to work by day and spend the night drinking with friends and putting the world to rights in conversation.

III

Soon after the state examination Schleich married an old friend from Stettin, to whom he had already promised his love when they were still children. He established his 'own private surgical institute' in Berlin. 'So I didn't give a damn about becoming a professor or the highest honour of being able to drag around the violet finery of a rector from the alma mater in what's-its-name.' Not without resentment, he turned his back on the university and wanted to take his own responsibility for everything he did.

Soon after he had set up his practice a circle of artists formed with and around him which met in the evening in the Black Pig tavern. Schleich found much stimulation for his thought adventures and idea escapades amongst this company, and it was there that he received his intuition for local anaesthetic:

It was in 1890, when I was associating in lively fashion in the circle with Dehmel, Bierbaum, Hartleben and Ola Hansson and also came in contact with the Pole, Stanislaw Przybyszewski, whom we always called the bloody physiologist ... This poet who played Chopin enchantingly well had once showed me his marvellous notebooks of Waldeyer's lectures, which he had listened to, and I found there splendid details of ganglia structures. I looked through them ... I was as though immersed in the intimacy of this tiny miracle with which I had been entrusted. Suddenly I jumped up in the air.

'Stanislaw!' I shouted. 'Good gracious! The neuroglia is like the dampers of a piano! An electrical mute, a cut-out, an inhibitory regulator!'

I quickly explained to him the possibility that nerves could be deadened by the injection of fluids, that thinking might be phasic with the pulse, and that if this was so one would only need to inject deoxygenated blood between the nerve receptors in the skin in order to produce, artificially, a deadening of sensation or hypersensitivity at will.

Schleich rushed home at once to his clinic and injected himself with various saline solutions, which indeed brought about a pain-free condition. He subsequently added minimal quantities of cocaine, and as a result achieved a thoroughly usable local anaesthetic. Schleich undertook a large number of operations under local anaesthetic and reported about his experiences two years later at a surgical congress.

This tragic meeting, when Schleich infuriated the entire congress — under Bardeleben's chairmanship — through his effervescent carelessness and tactless behaviour, took place on April 11, 1892. He concluded his lecture with these words: 'So that with this innocuous means at hand, I do not think it is any longer permissible from an ideal, moral and legal standpoint to employ

7. CARL LUDWIG SCHLEICH

dangerous methods of narcosis where this means is adequate.' A storm of indignation followed, and the chairman 'rang the bell for a long time'; and he then put to the vote who was for and who against, and not a single hand was raised in Schleich's favour. The latter then left the room, followed by his father as his sole faithful follower. He was 33 years old at the time.

In his own account Schleich omits to mention the fact that he wrote Bardeleben a letter of apology shortly afterwards. It 'contained his regret that it had appeared that he wanted to claim the right to judge his colleagues, whereas he had only given his personal, subjective opinion.'[2]

The humiliation that was accorded to him at that time never left him. It showed itself in all his books and writings and became a bitter fruit that constantly wore him down and spoiled his pleasure in existence. He was still crying out as a sixty-year-old:

> Does a body which places so much higher a value on an alleged injury to its imagined dignity than upon a discovery which is recognized as a blessing to mankind — and which has in the meantime conquered the world — that it has gone to every length to ignore and suppress it, deserve the name of scientific society? Over and over again we see this same life-and-death struggle. No one must be allowed to lead the way; it's better to silence him utterly than allow him to get ahead of you!

He did not see, however, that it was he himself who had erected the hurdles that made it impossible for others with less power and grandeur of soul than he possessed to follow him.

In the year of this defeat a further event of similar significance, though of an altogether different nature, assailed him.

> It was at the beginning of the nineties [1892] when one day my colleague Dr Max Asch came into my study with someone I did not know.
>
> 'I have brought [August] Strindberg to see you.'

It felt really strange to me suddenly to see this man whom I had long revered standing before me and to be able to shake him warmly by the hand ... From the moment of our acquaintance onwards we probably spent some time together every day for a whole year ... mixing colours, devising chemical experiments, poring over the microscope, developing photographs, making music, painting, studying counterpoint and so forth.

Two people met one another who took pleasure and interest in all phenomena of nature and existence and were active in all spheres of human existence. Both were monists, but also mystics and dreamers, and at the same time agnostic fantasists. Nerves had to function electrically, but blood was influenced by the soul. They spoke of demons and goblins and meant substances and forces.

The whole world was interwoven with spirit and yet mechanical. Cell souls, crystal souls, an all-interweaving spirit, magnetically influenced and charged with soul — all this was buzzing around everywhere. That the earth was round was a fiction, because university lecturers believed it. And nevertheless there were questions and problems in plenty. In Strindberg's existence everything became coloured by tragic forms of life and soul conflicts. With Schleich there continued to be a sparkling, fascinating furnace of new thoughts and ideas.

IV

One must take one of Schleich's books into one's hands in order to be able to sense how many-sided and yet how much of a dilettante he was in everything that he thought and did. One of these collections of essays is called *Aus Asklepios Werkstatt* (From Asclepius's Workshop). Is there anything that it does not

7. CARL LUDWIG SCHLEICH

include? 'Friends and Enemies of Life,' 'Concerning the Rhythm of Epidemics,' 'Nutrition,' 'Of the Heart,' 'Self-poisoning,' 'The Problem of Cancer,' 'Care of Lunatics,' etc. And what assertions are made! A few quotations will enable some insight to be gained into Schleich's collection of curios:

> Thus experience brilliantly confirms the view that epileptic seizures are the result of periodic clotting processes of the brain fluids. Does this not offer a prospect of new ways of dealing with what one may term periodic madness? ...
> This [heart activity] works along the lines of true Marconi transmitters which every human being has [in various places] in the body and which are often far earlier — when the consciousness is able to grasp it — translated into mysterious vibrations; such is the solar plexus, the network of sympathetic nerves, which is the progenitor of the entire intellectual organization.
> [Regarding sleep] It is an electrical isolation mechanism which — like the turning of a crank — intervenes in the system of blood vessels in order to cover the receptors of the ganglia in the brain with little magic dampening hats. The fingers of the sun's rays bring about these electrical processes.

These quotations characterize this mixture of physics, mysticism and doggerel that came to manifestation in the colourful guise of the nomenclature of medical science. Nevertheless, there was much of practical value that came from all this phantasmagoria. It was extraordinary what Schleich managed to concoct! In his institute he produced a whole series of substances for body care — powders for wounds, pastes etc. — from beeswax dissolved in water, a process that he discovered. The whole problem of tuberculosis was to be immediately solved by applying Schleich's skin cream. 'A body deficient in wax [through constant use of ordinary soap] forgets how to dissolve the waxy shells of the tubercle bacillus and therefore becomes prone to tuberculosis.'

New anaesthetic mixtures were invented 'whose rapid recognition was of a long time obstructed by that undeserved failure at the surgical congress.' Again and again this spectre of the humiliation that he suffered reappears. New remedies for wounds were created. 'So there arose the paste made from blood-serum, peptone, gelatine and a preparation of formalin and gelatine which enables the body to disinfect itself in a natural manner.'

Then he invented marble soap, which was claimed to be the best therapeutic agent against all diseases of the heart. 'It is a vasomotor remedy of the first rank, a means of engendering elasticity in the blood vessels through — as it were — systematic microscopic gymnastic exercises generated by molecular electric currents in the skin — the only real way of preventing the calcifying of the arteries.' If this were not said in deadly seriousness, one might be tempted to see this tendency of leaping from one idea to another as akin to Morgenstern's nonsense *Gallows Songs*.

This imaginative quality in Schleich was unbounded, and because he not only had considerable knowledge but also a quite particularly kind and expansive heart, everything became not so much ridiculous as having the seriousness of Morgenstern's fictional creation of Palmström. In the introduction to the *Gallows' Songs*, which were written at the same time as Schleich was indulging in fantasies and performing operations in Berlin, the following words appear:

> Gallows poetry is part of a world conception. It
> is the unscrupulous freedom of the excluded, the
> dematerialized, which comes to expression in it. One
> knows what a mule is: the enviable intermediary stage
> between a school desk and university. Well then: a
> gallows brother is the enviable intermediary stage
> between man and the universe. Nothing more. The

7. CARL LUDWIG SCHLEICH

world looks different from the gallows, and other things are viewed as othernesses.

Schleich was a mule, or gallows brother, someone who lived at an intermediary stage between man and the cosmos. A childlike bubbly creativity lacking much in the way of correcting balance from the realm of thinking or conscience was characteristic of him. He lived and created and indulged in fantasies and was the friend of many hundreds of people.

V

In 1916 another book by Schleich appeared, *Vom Schaltwerk der Gedanken* (Regarding the Control Mechanism of Thoughts), which Rudolf Steiner spoke about in a lecture with warm recognition, even with enthusiasm. There he says: 'There is a remarkable chapter in this book which has the capacity to be epoch-making in our time, because what is written there indeed works from the one side in such a way that it must necessarily join forces with what spiritual science gives from the other side.'[3] Rudolf Steiner was speaking expressly about the chapter entitled 'Hysteria, a metaphysical problem,' where Schleich tries with the help of a number of observations to prove that thoughts have the capacity to bring forth illnesses and physical changes.

> A thought forcefully invades the preserve of the tissues, and with a direct mental hand creates a chaos of formations. Here we are well-nigh looking at the miraculous nature of the world, we can behold direct proof that ideas can work formatively, that a *nisus formativus* [formative energy] is working at the spinning-wheel of life's carpets, we have the intuition that Plato's belief that in the beginning was the idea, that it created matter ... that the marvellous Biblical words 'In the

beginning was meaning' (logos) are merely variations of the same certainty that a thought can breathe life into form.[4]

On the strength of Schleich's descriptions of the course of illnesses, Rudolf Steiner then says that it is not ordinary intellectual thoughts that give rise to interventions of this nature (such as the swelling of an eyelid, a hysterical pregnancy and even death on account of a harmless injury) but that a thought must become an imagination and then, when it manifests itself physically, brings about the pathological changes referred to.

Rudolf Steiner speaks with great enthusiasm about this attempt that Schleich makes to portray the power of ideas to mould organs. He takes up these endeavours with full positivity, because he sees in them one of the bridges across which a meeting between spiritual science and natural science could come about.

Schleich did not hear this call. He was too closely involved with his own web of thoughts to be able to take notice of anything brought by something as new as anthroposophy. Moreover, he had by then already become lonely, and the non-recognition which he constantly met with and his contemporaries' lack of understanding of his phantasmagoria made him bitter, but also vain and self-satisfied.

The chapter in *Besonnte Vergangenheit* where Schleich describes his memories of Dehmel is introduced with the following words: 'My life is becoming quite empty. I have reached the age from whose heights a person looks down upon his native village. Many buildings and huts of which I had happy memories are no longer there ... My father, Strindberg, Carl Prowe, Bindemann, Robert Langerhans, Bierbaum, Hartleben, etc. (what a sad etcetera!) are gone.' Hartleben had died in 1905, Schleich's father two years later. In 1910 Birnbaum had passed away, in 1911 his father's friend Reinhold Begas, the sculptor, and in 1912 his very intimate and inwardly cherished friend August Strindberg. They

7. CARL LUDWIG SCHLEICH

had all died and left him alone behind, until in 1920 his closest friend Richard Dehmel also parted from him. Then on March 7, 1922 he himself died; he followed them; he followed the friends without whom he could not live.

Schleich remained a child of the nineteenth century; he did not succeed in divesting himself of the thick and heavy coat of materialism. A taint of it continued to cling to him. For this reason he was also never able to gain recognition for his literary work and poetry. An aspect of the hollow sound as appears in the style of writers such as Felix Dahn and Emanuel Geibel pervaded his books. Hence even close friends such as Dehmel and Strindberg never took his creative work altogether seriously.

But what was it that — despite his well-nigh disastrous dilettantism — made him such a fascinating and generally loved personality? It must have been his bubbly temperament, his radiant affirmation of life and his never-ending readiness to help; but the stillness of simple insight was lacking, the first Christian involving pain and difficulty had not yet been made.

On September 7, 1924 Rudolf Steiner spoke once again about Schleich.[5] He described the sequence of his incarnations which had led him in close companionship with Strindberg from Egypt via Rome to Tyrol and finally to north Germany. Strindberg died ten years before him, but was ten years older. Both came to the world on the shores of the North Sea, the one in Stockholm, the other in Stettin. If through Rudolf Steiner's spiritual research one knows Schleich's previous earthly lives, they constantly radiate into his most recent one; and the impression arises that he was this time still completing what he had previously begun — as poet, writer, anatomist and surgeon. Everything remained pagan and pantheistic, it was a life full of exhilaration and richness.

On one occasion, however, his intuition led him onto a deeper level; this was when he was writing the conclusion of his book, *Vom Schaltwerk der Gedanken:*

However that may be, without the demonstrable cycle and the immortality of the living, and without the immortality of the soul that is ascertainable from this, this life remains a chaos divorced from reality, the earth a giant unfathomable grave and our birth in this same cradle a crime, for which the death penalty is prescribed. When it comes to understanding this from the highest perspective that humanity can muster, all this can only be referred to in the light of an endless evolution of nothing to matter, of matter to mind, of mind to the ensouled ego and the immortality of all these four great forecourts of eternity.

8

Justinus Kerner

Justinus Andreas Christian Kerner (1786-1862) was a German physician, poet and medical writer.

I

Anyone who surveys the Swabian countryside today from Waldenburg, the little town on the hill-tops, and sees the hills stretching into the far distance, with their meadows and woods, paths and streams, can form an impression of how this countryside must have looked over a century ago to Justinus Kerner. Its expanses were adequate for people living there; their lives were enveloped within the magic of its rugged beauty. The seasons flowed by in a constant process of change; they gave and took, threatened and bestowed, granted joy and loss.

The roads linked the little towns and villages, and many people wandered along them to visit friends and relatives, to rejoice about life or also to go about their business. Here were Mergentheim and Künzelsau, Schwäbisch Hall and Neckarsulm, Heilbronn and Weinsberg and many other settlements and hamlets.

In the distance lay Stuttgart and Ludwigsburg, where there were connections with the wider world. People came from there and from much further afield to Weinsberg, to visit the Kerner household: the friends of his youth, Ludwig Uhland, Gustav Schwab and Karl Mayer, the Hungarian poet Nikolaus Lenau, the faithful Varnhagen von Ense, and then also Freiligrath, the singer of freedom, came, as did the atheist David Friedrich Strauss. The parson Eduard Mörike sometimes came over with his sisters. Friedrich Theodor Vischer visited Kerner's home as a student, and people of high birth also often stopped there (then the word went round that 'Kerner's larking about with princes again'), for example Count Alexander of Württemberg, Duke Max and Prince Adalbert of Bavaria and many more. People journeyed from Sweden and Hungary, from France and Italy to see Kerner and to spend time in his immediate vicinity.

Many unhappy, suffering and forsaken souls sought Kerner's advice and help. But journeymen and travelling poets were also welcomed. The house was open to anyone who wished to enter it, and although it was not large it had room for all. Everyone was fed, and the children often had to withdraw from their so-called 'coffin room' in order to spend the night in a box bed in their father's study, so that the guests could use the beds.

The woman of the house, 'Rickele' (his pet name for Friederike) was never surly or cross on account of this bustling activity. She loved her Justinus and knew that the love that flowed incessantly from his heart was to be bestowed not only upon his family and patients but had to be available to a large circle of those burdened with hardship. Thus he also said of her,

> My wife did not give birth to me, but she did bear me.
> This was a heavier burden, as I well know.

And on their common gravestone he wrote to her (she died eight years before him):

> Friederike Kerner and her Justinus.

Nevertheless, she always placed herself in his shadow and served the sun that shone from his heart upon those around him.

8. JUSTINUS KERNER

Justinus Kerner

Kerner lived in his house in Weinsberg for forty years. It was the time that he spent in a state of beautiful perfection and harmony as a poet, doctor, philanthropist and seer. It was the settled part of his years of wandering on this earthly plane.

When he built the house in 1822, he was 36 years old and his years of teaching were over. He had been married for nine years and had come to Weinsberg as a medical officer from Welzheim by way of Gaildorf. Only there did he set up his practice and establish his home. The local authority gave him a piece of land, and as the senior medical officer he built his own house. His son Theobald wrote of this as follows:

> His house ... was initially only a small, unpretentious doctor's dwelling; it had a stable, a coach-house and a room on the ground floor, four more rooms up a flight of stairs and two store-rooms in the attic. In 1827 a Swiss house with a balcony was built, thus resulting in two additional rooms; and in the large garden opposite the house the little Alexander house also offered three cosy little rooms in which peaceful guests could spend the night. This extensive garden must have been a graveyard in times gone by; and the garden house — with the date 1600 over the entrance — had been a house for the dead and was therefore not free from the suspicion that it might harbour ghosts ... In the other garden surrounding the main house an ancient prison tower — known locally as the ghost tower — stood hard by the Weinsberg town wall. A Gothic room with recesses and round church windows had been furnished in a homely way in the thick walls. Beneath this room was the castle dungeon and above it a platform with a splendid view of the church, Weiberthreu and the Weinsberg valley.'[1]

This was the immediate environment in which Justinus Kerner spent the forty-year period of his creative work. An abandoned graveyard, a dungeon, all pointing towards the past —

and overlooking them a new house was built where guests and friends from all over the world would come and go.

This house and its vicinity are even today still imbued with the magic of Kerner's time. Many of the rooms have remained as they were formerly, full of household goods, medieval chests and chairs, tables and benches. Kerner's bookcase is still in the same place as it was, and his old desk, which he had himself made as a young joiner's apprentice, is still there. Many pictures of the Madonna and parts of painted church windows hang on the walls. Old church candelabra and holy figures stand around the room. From the balcony a large crucifix watches over the garden and reminds those spending time there of death and resurrection.

As one wanders through the rooms of Kerner's house one is little by little taken back into the time of the Middle Ages. The house must in its time have been a kind of cross between a castle and a monastery. A gentleman who was both a kind of monk and a seer lived there with his family and his servants. Later in his life Kerner was glad to bear the habit of a Franciscan and he was also buried in this garment. On his monument in Weinsberg are the words:

Justinus Kerner
1786–1862
Comforter of the Sick
And Terror of Ghosts
Pride of the Fatherland
Master of the Art of Poetry

II

Kerner was born in Ludwigsburg as the sixth child of his parents. His father was a senior civil servant. Three brothers and two sisters had already been born. Georg, the eldest, soon took an active part in the French Revolution and lived in Paris until

Napoleon came to power. Thus as a child Justinus was from an early age given a direct insight into current events through this brother whom he especially loved.

In his *Bilderbuch aus meiner Knabenzeit* (Picture Book from my Boyhood), published in 1849, he gives a detailed picture of this brother; and he describes Ludwigsburg as it was at that time with its rulers and servants with great poetic power.

When Justinus was nine years old, the family moved to Maulbronn, where he experienced a decisive turning point in his young life. He was gripped by a strange illness, which he describes as follows:

> My father had the idea of giving me an education in a larger town, but at this point my body was affected by an illness which with great stubbornness lasted for nearly a year. I was growing very quickly at that time, and it was probably because of a developmental illness that the nerves of my stomach became highly irritable, so that everything I ate and drank was brought up again, either at once or after an hour or so. The arts of many physicians foundered upon this obstinate scourge. I still cannot quite believe that I did not succumb to the often nonsensical remedies of these medical practitioners; it was perhaps only because their mixtures, powders, confections and pills were immediately rejected by my stomach that they were unable to perform their miracles in it through remaining there any longer.[2]

So things continued like this for a while, until the child was taken by his mother to a famous physician in Heilbronn, Weikardt. He was a Brunonian* and diagnosed the condition as 'extreme asthenia.' When Justinus found himself face to face with this gentleman, his heart started to pound. 'A sense of coldness rushed from my stomach up to my brow,' he relates in the

---

* A theory of medicine that regards disease as caused by defective or excessive excitation, developed by John Brown, a Scottish physician.

8. JUSTINUS KERNER

Bilderbuch; 'I saw all the people who were around me in the form of animals and immediately fell to the ground unconscious.'

This was the condition of this child, who needed only a slight shock to lose his waking consciousness.

At the same time, however, Justinus — under the strangest of circumstances, which he had just described and which were a mixture of jest and irony and of seriousness and horror — met the well-known mesmerist, Dr Eberhard Gmelin, who put the child in a sort of mesmeristic state of stupefaction. 'He led me into a little room ..., stared me in the face with his black eyes and began to stroke me with his outstretched hands from my head to the stomach region; he breathed several times on my heart region. I became quite sleepy and finally lost consciousness. I must have been asleep for a long time ...'

The same evening, when Justinus had been put to bed — and he was still very dazed — he looked through the window (which looked out upon Heilbronn market) at the beautiful old church. He could see its tower, on which there was an equestrian statue. He then describes the deep impression that it made on him:

> When the clouds had lifted, the moon appeared in the sky; and church and tower appeared before me with a beauty such as I have seen in a building. I looked at it for a long time, and my imagination played with the beautiful outlines of the tower, with its stone formations, grotesque heads of animals and hideous human faces which projected from it as the heads of drainpipes, and with its artificially installed spiral staircase which soared around it almost to its top where stood the form of the knight. Gradually all these images were overwhelmed in a tide of slumber and dream.

Justinus now dreamt that he was standing in front of the church and that the stone form of the knight on horseback began to move, descended the steps one foot at a time, walked through the church, opened the door and stood before the child. 'My brother Georg — still alive — stood before me and said: "Look at the clock, the bucks have banged together twelve times, the cock is crowing and the angel is blowing his trumpet — then my time was up".'

The dream continued; Justinus entered the church. 'It was brightly illumined by the moon, and the glass paintings of its windows were particularly radiant in a glory that I had never seen before.' Figures came towards him from the images of the windows, formed themselves into groups and then separated again. They were the forms of people whom he would meet only later in life. The child had a preview of his future earthly life.

> These images often came together, and I always saw myself amongst them in representations which constantly changed, and subsequently I recognized that these were scenes from my future life. On all the windows and in all the images I always saw one particular figure again and again amidst other figures of men and women, and it stood out clearly from all the others; and then it seemed to disappear, and a sense of anxiety came over me and I looked for it until I saw it again. Afterwards I recognized this figure that I had seen in my dream on this church window in my faithful life's companion.

Following this event the child's condition visibly improved, and in a short while Justinus was well again. But, as he said,

> the truth is that from this time onwards I have throughout my life had premonitory dreams which have been a real torment to me, a torment that I would not wish on anyone and which taught me in a very practical way to know what a misfortune it would be for man had not God's wise hand closed off the future from him. These dreams of future events come to me in the morning, especially when a sleepless night has allowed me to rest and fall asleep only towards morning.

8. JUSTINUS KERNER

The 'inner meaning' of this soul had been awakened. Henceforth the higher world was no longer wholly closed to it, and it was — out of its own experience — convinced of this higher world's existence.

This occurred in the same year in which Goethe wrote the *Fairy Tale* whose world of images derived from similar inspirations. *Wilhelm Meister's Apprenticeship* was also written then, and many of the Mignon songs speak of supersensible experiences that had become accessible to the people of that time in great numbers. Schiller composed the letters *On the Aesthetic Education of Man* and Novalis sealed his eternal bond with Sophie von Kühn. Justinus Kerner's dream was interwoven with these great events and defined his further life.

III

The age when Justinus Kerner experienced this decisive change is a significant phase of development in the life of every child. Novalis suffered something similar in the same period.

> Through a painful attack of dysentery in his ninth year he [who had formerly been dreamy and only learnt with difficulty] was as though transformed and thereafter showed talent and a great zeal for learning. A similar experience is related by Susanne von Klettenberg in the *Confessions of a Beautiful Soul,* and Obenauer sees in such a physical catharsis which brings the psyche into rapid development, a mark of mystical personalities.[3]

It is not so much the arousing of an accelerated development that is taking place here; for rather does the relationship between the individuality and its environment become one of a special and unique kind. Rudolf Steiner frequently indicated that before the ninth year is reached the child's psyche still feels itself as it were united with the world that surrounds it. 'Until this point the child distinguishes itself only to a small extent from its surroundings. Its feeling is that the world and it itself belong together.'4

When a serious illness occurs, the associated suffering and heightened catabolic activity in the physical body lead to an increased wakefulness in the realm of the soul. Under these circumstances the child becomes quite particularly attentive to its surroundings and perceives them in a new way. Rudolf Steiner said,

> The period after the end of the ninth year becomes particularly important, because ten, as at any significant turning point in life, questions spring up within the child — actually, whole mountains of them — which all arise from a new feeling of differentiation between itself and its surroundings and also from a feeling of separateness from the leader, from the person of the teacher.

Justinus as a child experienced this complete change with a quite particular vehemence, since his future life was revealed to him as in one great tableau. It was a death experience through which Kerner strode and which afterwards enabled him to be different from others and from how he had previously been himself.

On returning to Maulbronn, Justinus received further instruction from various individuals. By choice, however, he would spend time with his father in his large garden amidst flowers and trees. A strong sense for the riddles of nature now unfolded; Justinus collected beetles and butterflies, he observed animal life and laid out his own garden. He felt himself very intimately connected with the plant kingdom. When he was thirteen years old his father died, and this event became further, deep incision in Kerner's life. 'His funeral was arranged as he had ordered ... Accordingly, everything was deathly quiet in the house. I fled to my father's trees and to my flowers. My mother's sorrow made me even sadder; I avoided her.'5

8. JUSTINUS KERNER

His mother now returned to Ludwigsburg, and the growing boy received tuition in the classical languages and in everything else that could be learnt at that time. The poet Philipp Conz became in many respects his mentor and made him familiar with the works of Klopstock, Hölty, Matthisson, Schiller and Goethe.

The future poet began to proclaim himself in the growing boy. He wrote increasing quantities of poems, comedies, dramas and endeavoured to put what he had experienced into words. Many of these efforts were reproduced in the *Bilderbuch*. One of them is called 'In der Krankheit' (During Illness) and probably refers to the suffering that he had undergone:

> Sink, my feeble staff of life!
> Wilt, wilt my body! I want you no more.
> Stars, strew your pale gleaming
> On the grave of him who died young.
> Mother! What? A mourning band?
> Adorn with roses your grey hair;
> Those who die in the springtime of the year
> Soar upwards in the greatest purity.

After his confirmation in 1802 the youngest child's choice of profession was seriously discussed in the family and with his mother's friends. However, since after his father's death there were only very limited means, university study had to be shelved; and Justinus, who had in the meantime undertaken training in carpentry, came as an apprentice to the ducal cloth factory in Ludwigsburg. In spite of the gruelling and wholly inappropriate work, his poetry continued to flourish. His mother gradually recognized that Justinus would never become a proper man of business, and so she finally agreed that he should enter Tübingen University. He did not know what subject he should decide on, but he set off happily and made his way from Ludwigsburg to the south. Of one thing he was certain, that he would devote himself to natural sciences.

Exhausted by the long journey on foot he arrived in Tübingen by moonlight. Just before the town he lay down on a bench 'and slept beneath the rustling leaves of the nearby poplars.' He had a dream which from this time onwards continued to haunt him. 'I dreamt that I was sitting between a mountain of compendiums and manuscripts in a solitary little room, whose only window looked out onto a clearing in the forest.' Then 'a stag with stork's feet' came gliding out of the forest over the clearing, stood in front of the dreamer and in a mocking tone challenged him to place it — the stag with the peculiar feet — into Linnaeus's system However, neither its name, species or genus were to be found in the many compendiums, and the dreamer awoke 'in the sweat of his brow.' This was probably a clear exhortation not to devote himself to the natural sciences as they were usually taught at that time in the universities.

But as he got up from the bench, the wind blew a piece of paper before his feet.

> I grabbed hold of it with my hand: it was a doctor's prescription which the wind had blown out of the open window of the local hospice. Now then, I said to myself, this piece of paper has been sent to you as a sign of your future profession; you should become a physician! With these thoughts and this resolve I passed through the Lustnau Gate into this town of the muses which was as yet wholly unfamiliar to me.'

It was not Kerner who decided what he wanted to become. He took note of the sign proffered to him by destiny and felt that his innermost ideals were being satisfied and addressed.

The young student immersed himself in the life that the university offered him with the fullness of his heart. He, who had hitherto lived entirely within the warm embrace of his family and had — for all his dreams, poems, inner experiences and observations — remained solitary, now began to lead an active existence in the circle of many other people.

IV

Already in the first months of his stay in Tübingen Kerner became acquainted with the young Ludwig Uhland, and from then on an intimate friendship — which lasted until the end of their lives — united the two poets. Although they were so different, their relationship to one another was very close.

Kerner, who was devoted to the natural world and to its nocturnal aspect, was full of humour, disorderly and forgetful, cheerful and gregarious. Uhland, on the other hand, was withdrawn, serious, precise and — although he was a poet — also a scholar who carried out his research with great exactitude.

Thus the two friends outwardly complemented one another, whereas in their innermost nature they worked harmoniously together for the renewal of the spirit. The 'Swabian poets circle' found its focus in them. It was a group of friends who felt wholly related to and connected with romanticism. They called themselves 'The Knights of the Spirit,' and searched for riches among the people which were at that time again being collected and treasured in the form of sagas and fairy tales, legends and songs.

Rudolf Steiner referred to this Tübingen circle in his biographical portrait of Uhland:

> The times when Uhland was living in the circle of his university friends were such that he himself described them as 'beautiful and happy.' Justinus Kerner, the enthusiastic Swabian poet, Karl Mayer, Heinrich Köstlin, a physician, Georg Jäger, a naturalist, and Karl von Roser, Uhland's brother-in-law-to-be, belonged to the circle. In 1808 Karl August Varnhagen von Ense — who had a personal connection with a number of romantics and wholly shared their views — also joined it. Uhland's literary work at this time bore in many respects the stamp of the romantic spirit.[6]

However, this circle — despite its strongly romantic inclinations — was also a very combative association which directed its attacks against everything that represented the cause of enlightenment and classicism. They discerned the central organ of these tendencies to be the *Morgenblatt für gebildete Stände* (Morning Paper for the Educated Classes), which Cotta published in Tübingen. So they began to compose and produce a *Sonntagsblatt für ungebildete Stände* (Sunday Paper for Uneducated Classes), which they copied out by hand and distributed among their acquaintances. It appeared from January until May 1807 and contained some remarkable contributions, above all by Uhland and Kerner.

It is strange that one of the first patients who was entrusted to the student Kerner for care and investigation was Friedrich Hölderlin. In this mentally ill poet he encountered the 'nocturnal aspect' of all earthly existence, to which he had felt so closely connected since his serious illness.

However, he was also thoroughly at home in the everyday world, and for his doctoral dissertation he was working on investigations about the function of the organs of hearing. Varnhagen von Ense writes of this in his *Denkwürdigkeiten* (Memorable Events):

> His experiments are astute and meaningful, and he seeks to avoid all cruelty. All in all he has a very close relationship to nature and especially to its darker side. His eyes have something of a ghostly and pious quality. He can make his heart beat faster at will and likewise slow it down ... He lives in his room with cats, hens, geese, owls, squirrels, toads, lizards, mice and who knows what other animals quite happily together, and only has to take pains to secure doors and windows so that his guests do not escape; whether his books and clothes are in danger, whether an animal comes to sniff him while he is asleep or, if suddenly frightened, bites him does not bother him.[7]

8. JUSTINUS KERNER

These characteristics of Kerner's were particularly striking to Varnhagen, the elegant man of the world, for in his whole behaviour he must have represented the total opposite: elegant, smart, always fashionably dressed, well-read and — as an officer and diplomat — particularly skilful and courteous in his dealings with people. On February 14, 1809 he wrote to Rahel, his wife:

> Kerner has fully recovered from a minor throat inflammation, I see him daily, but I cannot say much to him, he doesn't know the German language sufficiently, because he is neither a philosopher nor a poet of the more refined world, never finishes a book; and I am accustomed to individualize what I say in all manner of different ways when I want to express my deepest and most intimate thoughts.[8]

The 'more refined world' was not in Kerner's line. He spoke the dialect of his native region and had no penchant for the subtle jargon of the German that was used in Berlin salons. As a student, Kerner was full of high spirits and wild audacity; a true child of nature. Moderation was alien to him, and Varnhagen will probably have observed correctly when he said of him:

> Everything of a magical or magnetic nature is manifested in him with particular strength. He himself has something of the somnambulist about him, a quality that accompanies him also when making jokes and laughing. He can be lost in thoughts and dreams and then suddenly flare up; and the fright that this arouses in others causes him to revert to jesting ... His poetry has the quality of wonder inherent in popular novels, the simple sound and rough power of folk songs; ... and if you now imagine the simplest, wholly neglected clothing, a total indifference towards things with which he comes into contact, a bent posture, an uneven, odd gait, a constant tendency to lean on things or lie down, where, for example, he prefers to

lie uncomfortably on a chair to sitting comfortably on it, and notwithstanding all this a thin, well-grown and quite nice-looking boy — you have a full picture of my Kerner.

This was Justinus the student. His body hung about him, big and powerful, but not penetrated by thinking and will. For his thoughts dwelt upon dreams and became rhythms in poems and songs. His will, on the other hand, was wholly imbued with feeling and pulsated with breath and heartbeat. Thus he could — as already mentioned — speed up the action of his heart at will. Kerner lived at that time — as a youth — predominantly out of the middle realm of his soul: 'Feeling is everything.'

At this time he also found the woman who had already appeared to him in a dream — in Heilbronn — as the central figure of his life. This meeting was so unique and so wonderful that it will be recounted here. On Uhland's twentieth birthday, on April 26, 1807, the friends went off on an excursion together with others. They visited the Achalm near Reutlingen, where there were many cheerful people making lots of noise. Among them stood a girl, looking sadly and silently into the distance. Kerner went up to her and spoke Goethe's lines:

> Why art thou sad, when all around
> So gay and bright appear?
> For plainly in thine eyes are seen
> The traces of thy tears.

Then she turned and, without hesitation, responded with the second verse:

> And if I wept in solitude
> The grief is mine alone
> And with the tears that sweetly streamed
> More light my heart has grown[9]

In this poem 'Comfort in Tears' two souls meet who are destined for one another. Friederike, or 'Rickele,' as he always

8. JUSTINUS KERNER

called her, was an orphan at that time and lived with an aunt near Tübingen. Both of them, Justinus and 'Rickele,' were in their twenty-first year when they had this first encounter. It was immediately obvious to both of them that they belonged to one another, although it would be some years before they could marry. They married only on February 28, 1813.

Hitherto it had been the period of Kerner's apprenticeship. In 1808 he qualified as a physician in Tübingen and then soon went on his travels in order to see the world as a doctor. First he visited his brother Georg in Hamburg. From there he travelled to Berlin and on to Nuremberg and at the end of November arrived in Vienna. He stayed there until the spring of 1810 and only then did he return home.

A strange book, *Die Reiseschatten* (The Shadows of a Journey) was the result of this journey. There he relates the most extraordinary things in a constant interplay of satire, Gothic novel, ghost stories and nature idylls. Something of Bonaventura's *Nightwatches* lives in this book, which has something thoroughly one-sided about it.

Kerner then became a medical officer in Wildbad in the northern part of the Black Forest. He remained there for two years and then went to Walzheim, where finally there was the opportunity to bring his Rickele home.

He stayed in Walzheim for a further two and a half years, zealously promoting the domestic flax industry and thereby relieving the poverty of the inhabitants. There he also met a blind man Melchior Lang, who still possessed natural healing powers, the possibilities and effects of which Kerner recognized full of admiration and astonishment.

In 1815 he transferred to Gailsdorf as a medical officer and from there, in January 1819, arrived in Weinsberg, where he would spend the largest part of his life. In 1822 his own house was finally ready, and a document bearing these words written by Kerner was placed in the foundation stone: 'This house was built with God's help by Justinus Kerner, the physician who also sang songs, and his wife Friederike in the year one thousand eight hundred twenty and two, at a time when the stars of heaven looked affectionately down on mountain and valley, but Europe's rulers, their eyes turned away from heaven, stood coldly by and beheld the devilish murder of Hellas.'

Kerner was in these stern and condemnatory words referring to the Greeks' struggle for freedom against Ottoman rule which had aroused the whole of Europe at that time. One can sense from this how seriously he took such signs of the time and how he must have felt himself to be in tune with the conscience of the age.

> But he also uttered this cry:
> What I barely saw in dreams
> Has truly found its form!
> Our little house stands friendlily
> 'Neath green trees, on the mount
> Of woman's faithfulness.
> And three beloved children
> Hop merrily in and out.

Now began the time in Weinsberg and the story of Kerner's house.

V

Some time before, Kerner had written a very strange work of fiction which was published in 1816 under the title *Der Wanderer zum Morgenrot* (The Wanderer at Dawn) and to which he later gave the name *Die Heimatlosen* (The Homeless Ones). Just as *Die Reiseschatten* is reminiscent of Bonaventura's *Nightwatch,* so can this story only be compared with Novalis's unfinished novel *Heinrich von Ofterdingen* and 'Klingsohr's Fairy Tale' which forms part of it. It is the story of a boy named Serpentin and a girl, Sililie, who find and lose themselves in a free fairy tale-like

8. JUSTINUS KERNER

fantasy and have the most remarkable experiences and encounters. Poems and stories are strewn about in profusion, and the whole work may well have a secret meaning which is, however, not disclosed to the reader. Serpentin's burial forms the conclusion — an event whose accompanying diction and content are reminiscent of Mignon's internment; the images employed give a real insight into Kerner's soul-world.

> The count let Serpentin be clothed in a light robe and placed in a coffin full of roses. His crystal flute, the only possession that he had on him apart from items of clothing, was laid at his side. A resting-place had been prepared for him in the choir of the old chapel. Four shepherd boys clad in white bore him away in the dawn accompanied by the count and Lambert. Many boys and girls from the region also followed his coffin clothed in white robes. The chapel was strewn with roses. The castle chaplain, a venerable old man with light silver hair, spoke a short prayer, consecrated the coffin with holy water and gave a sign to lower him into the vault with his head towards the morning light.
>
> At the self-same moment the fiery ball of the rising sun cast its light across the chapel, the stained glass windows with their images of saints burned in transfigured colours, and the chapel bedecked with roses glowed radiantly; and this fragrance and shimmering light enshrouded the coffin as it was being lowered. Amidst this radiant clarity the image of the Crucified One, before whom Serpentin had shortly before been kneeling with such a nobility of devotion, looked down with a friendly smile.

When Kerner sent the manuscript of this story to Uhland, the latter took a negative view of it and without much understanding. In a detailed letter Kerner turned to him once more and tried to express his innermost intentions to his friend. He wrote on November 26, 1812 from Welzheim:

I am sorry that you so much dislike the *Wanderer zum Morgenrot,* though this was not unexpected. I myself am not content with it (in terms of its poetry), it would have been better with a philosophical framework ... I cannot expect every reader — and perhaps I cannot expect any — to enter my concepts of illness (your pathological sensibility, as you call it) and death. I call death the most intimate union with the spirit of nature, illness is a striving towards this union. Death is the highest purification to which man comes in life. Magnetic sleep, epilepsy (this dreadful addiction to falling, as you may call it), cataplexy, ecstasy, madness (Pythia on three legs), sensitivity to metal (siderosis), then organic destruction in individual parts of the body, old scars which predict changes in the atmosphere — all these are conditions through which man comes closer to, becomes more befriended by, the spirit of nature, a universal life, the life of spirits and stars ...

In becoming intimately associated with nature one can be enabled to sense metals and water in deep places, look into future. In brief, to get to know everything that to the mind is covered by the barely self-subsisting hard, limited bulwark of the body (of health, the condition that is so wholly measured by earthly norms).[10]

In these words is revealed Kerner's view and interpretation of death and illness. He sees in them nothing wrong or abnormal, but rather a condition to be striven towards, because through them the wall that the healthy body erects between the earthly and spiritual worlds is broken through. Kerner then continues: 'Woman (to be a woman is an illness indeed) is more intimately connected than a man is with nature, and is therefore exposed to more illnesses and also hurries more rapidly than a man to the total union with nature, to death ...'

And finally, Kerner speaks once more of the picture which

8. JUSTINUS KERNER

constantly accompanied him and gave him the insights out of which he worked and acted:

> Before the slow-moving caterpillar, with an inner lightness, hangs in space, it becomes ill, sheds its skin and then falls into a magnetic sleep. In this sleep it feels the wings that will carry it over flowers grow, it receives presentiments of its future life, breaks open the sheath and floats off into this new life ...

In these indications Kerner is alluding to the magnetic sleep that he underwent in Heilbronn, when he was filled with presentiments of his subsequent life. Since that time he experienced his body as an obstacle that stood in the way of the free unfolding of his organs of life. And it was true that this body, however big it was, was little suited to becoming an earthly instrument. It bore Kerner's soul as the donkey carries its burden; it was a good 'brother ass' to its master. However, he was soon to meet someone whose physical organism had become so transparent and sensitive that it brought all the phenomena of which Kerner had knowledge to full experience.

As a doctor he devoted himself mainly to homeopathy, although he was not exclusively a homeopath. He had a deep understanding of human nature and of those relationships which are today called psychosomatic. He knew that it is not the remedy but the physician who brings about real healing. Thus it was his humanity that drew his patients. They came from far to see him and sought not merely the physician but the *human* Justinus Kerner.

He and his home, with his wife and children and all his guests and friends, were the medicine that he offered to so many. The deserving and the undeserving came to him, and he excluded no one. Among these many people a seriously ill woman came to Weinsberg in November 1826 to be treated by Kerner. She was 'a picture of death — wasted to a skeleton, and unable to rise or to lie down without assistance.'[11] This is how

Kerner described her condition. 'Every three or four minutes it was necessary to give her a spoonful of broth ... without it she fainted, or had spasms. She had many frightful symptoms, and fell into a magnetic trance every evening at seven o'clock.' This was a picture of the condition of that Friederike Hauffe, who later became known and famed as the seeress of Prevorst. She was 25 years old at the time and had since childhood had second sight experiences that had developed in their intensity until severe somnambulism associated with bodily illnesses became increasingly prominent.

Kerner initially tried to put her to rights by using reason. He told her that he 'was determined to take no notice of what she said in her sleep, nor would I be even informed of it; and that this somnambulistic state, which had caused her friends so much unhappiness, must come to an end.' This did not lessen her or anyone else's suffering. But soon the poet in the doctor learned to listen to the true nature of this sick woman. He allowed her to explain to him out of her semi-conscious state what needed to be done for her, and so he started with a magnetic stroking of her limbs, which immediately led to a certain improvement.

An intimate collaboration and mutual understanding between physician and patient began, which found expression in his notes about the seeress. Kerner described many exceptionally interesting details, which would need to be read in full. For example, he reports that she could not manage without an open window, even in the most severe cold. 'She also drew nourishment from the air.' This is a first premonition of the cosmic stream of nutrition to which Rudolf Steiner referred almost a century later.

> She was sensible of the spiritual essences of all things, of which we have no perception: especially of metals, plants, men, and animals. All imponderable matter, even the different colours of the prism, produced on her sensible effects. She was susceptible of electrical influences, of

which we are not conscious: and, what is most incredible, she had a preternatural feeling, or consciousness of human writing.

The physician made a number of investigations and experiments with his patient. She described to him exactly her feelings when she touched metals and stones, plants and animals. The influence of stone and moon on her condition was studied. When she looked at a person's right eye, she saw 'a picture of that person's inner-self' which also always corresponded to his character. In the left eye, on the other hand, 'whatever internal disease existed.'

'In the right eye of an animal, as a dog or a fowl, she saw a blue flame — doubtless its immortal part, or the soul.'

The seeress had contact with spiritual beings, with the dead, she had prophetic dreams and often saw herself outside her body. She also gave Kerner insights into the occult anatomy and physiology of her body, which were of a quite extraordinary nature. 'In a semi-conscious state,' she said once, 'I think only with my little brain, I feel nothing of the greater one, which must sleep. In this [latter] state I can think more with the soul, it thinks more radiantly than in a fully waking state, and the spirit also has more influence on it [the soul] than if I am awake, I always feel this spiritual influence from the region of the heart.'[12]

Although this woman had never received any higher schooling, she knew the parts of the body and its organs with an astonishing precision. She also described the organs and spheres of the higher worlds (e.g. the 'seven solar circles'), in which she appeared to participate directly. Although she had never heard of Swedenborg nor read any of his books, many of her descriptions precisely corresponded completely with his.

She once described man as follows: 'Through the body the nerve-spirit is linked with the world, through the soul the [intellectual] spirit is connected with the nerve-spirit and through the spirit the divine with the soul. Thus through constant interconnections a common bond runs from the lowest to the highest member.'

Translated into the language of spiritual science, one could formulate this statement as follows: 'Through the physical body the etheric body (nerve-spirit) is linked with the world, through the etheric body the astral body (soul) is linked with the body, through the astral body the thinking ego (intellectual spirit) is connected with the etheric body and through the ego the divine with the astral body.' The seeress had absolutely precise insights into occult physiology.

It is understandable that modern medicine manifests so little comprehension of phenomena such as that of the seeress of Prevorst and endeavours through persuasion of various kinds, with condescending smiles, to trivialize her experiences. Thus Leibbrand thinks that probably

> there was seldom a physician more strongly given over to the suggestive power of his own patient as was Kerner. She (Friederike Hauffe) had in a soul sense gone astray already as a child; on her wedding day ... she had entered into a kind of acute neurosis and after many futile physicians' visits had been healed from her 'chest spasms' by a peasant woman through the laying on of hands ... 1826 saw the beginning of magnetic treatment. And this Friederike Hauffe lived until 1829 in Kerner's home. Her companionship with Kerner should probably be viewed as the premise for the arising of a *folie en deux*.[13]

This mixture of psychoanalytical tendencies and intellectual arrogance distorts the picture of the truth that begins to be revealed behind Kerner's encounter with this special woman. The seeress stayed in Weinsberg until May 1829 and then returned to Löwenstein. There she died, after she had foreseen her impending death, on August 5 of that year. 'At ten o'clock her sister saw a tall bright form enter the chamber, and, at the same instant, the dying woman uttered a loud cry of joy; her spirit seemed then to be set free. After a a short interval, her soul also departed, leaving behind it a totally irrecognizable husk — not a single trace of her former features remaining.' And Kerner adds: 'In the night succeeding her death — of which I had not the least idea — I saw her in a dream, with two other female forms, and apparently perfectly recovered.'[14]

VI

Kerner was forty years old when he met Friederike Hauffe for the first time. They remained together for nearly three years; and this relationship between doctor and patient had something of the lustre of eternity about it. It was the high point of Kerner's life. Everything that preceded this living and working together must be viewed as a preparation, everything that followed as merely an after-echo.

At the time of this meeting Goethe was writing the second part of *Faust,* and it is strange that Kerner's earthly life and the composition of this work of literature were unfolding on almost parallel paths. What the concluding words of the *chorus mysticus* try to express is mirrored in Kerner's experience in his association with this woman. For he required that everything that is transient is but a semblance, and he had come to know through experience that the eternal feminine, which appeared to him in an almost perfect guise in the seeress, opens up the paths to higher existence. What was expressed in poetic form by Goethe was for Kerner a direct experience.

At approximately the same time, spiritual encounters between other remarkable men with women with visionary powers were also leading to miraculous results. The pastor Oberlin, from the Steintal (Ban-de-la-Roche) in Alsace, developed the capacity to follow the soul of his deceased wife on its paths through yonder world, and he received from this an exact knowledge of the 'geography' of the spirit-land. Somewhat later, around 1820, the poet Clemens Brentano met the nun Katharina von Emmerich and was able through her to gain some astonishing insights into the life and death of Christ Jesus, which were revealed to her over the course of several years.

At the same time Juliane von Krüdener was wandering throughout Europe. She met the leading lights of politics, but also formed a connection with the parson Fontaine and Maria Kummerin who told fortunes, became for several months the pupil of Jung-Stilling and visited Oberlin in the Steintal. She dissipated and spread abroad the powers that she had been given and finally lost her way in taking on new and greater challenges.

Through all these women a newly dawning spiritual revelation sought to come to expression. These were primarily women who had been chosen to become more or less worthy instruments of the coming epoch. With the death of the seeress of Prevorst, however, this period of direct revelations came to an end. It began with the religious crisis in Swedenborg's life, which occurred around 1740 and led to his inner calling in April 1745. Franz Anton Mesmer (1734), Frédéric Oberlin (1740), Matthias Claudius (1740), Jung-Stilling (1740) and Louis Claude de Saint-Martin (1743) were all born around this time. Pestalozzi, who came to the earth in 1746 as a kind of latecomer, belonged to the same circle. With these personalities a first stream of spiritual knowledge entered into humanity at a time when its attention was focussed on the enlightenment.

This rich spiritual ferment was set in motion for a second time when — as though under Goethe's patronage — Hegel, Schelling, Novalis, Clemens Brentano, Hölderlin, Friedrich Schlegel and many others were born thirty years later. They continued on a higher plane what the first group had begun.

Justinus Kerner came to earth in 1786 as a latecomer. But he, too, was together with a whole group who formed a kind of rearguard in order to carry forward what the individualities born in the 1770s had gone and brought to fulfilment. Amongst them were Jacob Grimm and Bettina von Arnim, who were both

8. JUSTINUS KERNER

born in 1785. Then in 1786, as Kerner's immediate companions, there followed Wilhelm Grimm and Carl Maria von Weber. In the following year Ludwig Uhland and Joseph Ennemoser, the last of those naturalists with a religious faith, were born, and in 1788 Friedrich Rückert and Freiherr von Eichendorff. Over all these figures shone the twilight of a day that was coming to an end, a day which had begun around 1740. After them — but also already in their time — the spiritual night of the later nineteenth century began to descend.

A year before the death of the seeress of Prevorst, Kaspar Hauser entered the stage of world history and in 1833 was forcibly removed. With him the last light of spiritual day was extinguished. Goethe and Hegel had also passed away, and only certain individual pillars of the past still bore the radiance of the former age into the middle of the century. Schelling lived on, Gotthilf Heinrich von Schubert, Carus and Alexander von Humboldt and a few others. Justinus Kerner was one of these.

In the years that remained to him he took the experiences that he had shared with the seeress further. Between 1831 and 1839 he published the *Blätter aus Prevorst* (Papers from Prevorst). They contain 'original documents and reading material for friends of the inner life.' From 1840 until 1852 the *Magikon* appeared, an 'archive for observations in the sphere of spiritual science and magnetic and magical life.' In these volumes an enormous number of observations and experiences relating to the inner life were brought together. Karl August von Eschenmayer, initially the senior medical officer in Kirchheim and then Professor of Philosophy in Tübingen, a pupil of Schelling, became Kerner's enthusiastic colleague. Many other important men of the time were represented with contributions in these papers and in the *Archiv*.

Thus Kerner's activity formed a central focus for contemporary Central European spiritualism. He regularly continued to correspond with a large number of friends, and hundreds visited him in his home. He remained a heart-like central point, whence a warming light radiated into the advancing night. Emil Bock was justified in entitling his beautiful study of Justinus Kerner, the 'Occultism of the Heart.'[15] It was the heart in Kerner that continued to beat even when the darkness became ever more impenetrable.

This growing darkness extended also to his eyes. His sight became worse, and around 1850 he had to request retirement on account of the onset of blindness. In a moving poem to his wife he expressed the approaching loss of his sight:

> Once I have wholly lost my sight,
> Night would still not overwhelm me
> So long as you, my radiant life,
> You, my sun, stay by my side.

But he was not spared from this night. On April 16, 1854 his 'Rickele' died, and on the same day he wrote to Sophie Schwab, whose husband, Justinus Kerner's friend, was also on the other side of the threshold: 'My Rickele is dead! Your unfortunate J. Kerner.'[16]

Prince Adalbert of Bavaria, whom he had befriended, said in a letter of condolence: 'Oh, could I only be with you now as I was before, when your dear departed wife was still alive, she who now hovers around you smiling as a transfigured spirit of light!'[16] The old poet also felt this, though nevertheless the loss of his faithful life's companion was to him of the deepest, lasting pain.

Kerner's life now began to grow quiet. The blindness of the old physician intensified, and his former friends continued to die year by year. And the approaching era was becoming incomprehensible. Three years before his death he wrote the following four-line poem:

> Fare onwards, O man, up to the heights,
> From steamer to a ship of the air.
> Fly with the eagle, fly with the lightning,
> You'll come no further than the grave.

8. JUSTINUS KERNER

His son Theobald reported,

> The last period of his life was made much harder for him through illness; he suffered especially through lack of sleep, and therefore resorted to artificial sleep-inducing drugs which, however, brought him into a state of 'nervous excitement.' Nevertheless in 1861 he published a quantity of poems in the morning paper ... At the beginning of 1862 the poet still felt relatively well. Then in mid-February he suffered a severe attack of influenza; his weakened body was no longer a match for it. On February 21, at half an hour before midnight, he was relieved from his suffering by a gentle death.[17]

Only a few people accompanied him to his final resting place, since in his will he had requested a quiet burial, without speeches or singing. Among them was Ludwig Uhland. Rudolf Steiner recounted the scene: 'The death of his old faithful friend Justinus Kerner was a source of deep sorrow to the poet. It is not improbable that he laid the foundations for his mortal illness through a cold caught at the funeral. He was unable to recover from this and died on November 13, 1862.'[18]

Thus the two friends crossed the threshold of death in the same year and remained united and connected. Kerner died thirty-three years after the passing of that soul who was so deeply connected with him — the seeress of Prevorst.

VII

The time of Kerner's death was probably one of the darkest periods in human history. Materialism and agnosticism had an immense power, and the expansion of power of a science that opposed the spirit had reached a high level. This science became the servant of a growing technology, and a barren faith in the material ascent of human beings had seized hold of people's souls.

A policy of colonialism imbued with purely economic thinking demanded the conquest of the earth in order to conjure forth an earthly paradise for the white man.

Darwin's research on *The Origin of Species* had appeared. Shortly afterwards Haeckel developed in his lectures on the 'natural history of creation' the general principle of evolution in the realm of organisms.

At the same time, spectral analysis was discovered by Kirchhoff and Bunsen, and proof could thereby be provided of the material composition of the planets and the sun.

Finally, however — and pre-eminently as a result of Kerner's activity — it was discovered that, alongside ordinary everyday consciousness, there are other states of consciousness which become manifest through the phenomena of hypnosis and somnambulism. This occurred before a modern science of the spirit based on thinking came into the world in the form of anthroposophy. When Kerner died, Rudolf Steiner had completed the first year of his life.

9

Josef Breuer

Josef Breuer (1842-1925) was an Austrian physician whose works led to the founding of psychoanalysis.

Medical beginnings

Breuer's autobiography begins with the following words:

> I was born on January 15, 1842 in Vienna. As I have lived since then in my native city for 81 years and have only left it for a few weeks of holiday, I can indeed consider myself to be a true Viennese. My father was a religion teacher for the Jewish cultural community in Vienna. I may be permitted to report something from the life of this man, to whom I owe everything. I venture this all the more since the development of the Jews in the first third of the nineteenth century is, I believe, of general cultural interest.

He goes on to relate how his father, who was born in 1791 in Burgenland, grew up fully dependent on his ghetto and received the customary instruction in the Jewish religion and way of life. At the age of thirteen he joined the Jewish seminary in Pressburg (now Bratislava in Slovakia), but left it after a short while and set off on foot to Prague with a school friend. There this Jew from the ghetto was gradually assimilated into European civilization and culture. He earned his keep initially as a home tutor and became what was called in Austria at that time a *Hofmeister*, a 'court tutor.' Breuer writes:

> My father was an excellent teacher and educator and practised the profession in Prague, Pest and Vienna; he finally gained a firm basis for his existence through his employment as the religion teacher of the newly-established Viennese congregation (1836). Then in 1840 he married a young, beautiful girl, my mother, whom I do not remember, since she died after the birth of her second son, my brother, 'in the flower of her youth and beauty' — as it says on her gravestone. After some time her mother, a brilliantly witty and amusing woman, came to our house and took over the housekeeping and the role of mother for the two motherless boys.

Breuer then goes on to say that he was enabled to grow up without any outward deprivation, for his father's income was adequate. He did not go to the local school but was educated at home by his father. 'By the age of four I could without any trouble read perfectly well.' In his eighth year he entered the very well regarded *Akademische Gymnasium* (grammar school) in Vienna and when he was sixteen passed his school-leaving examination. He continues,

> The intellectual level of my class was hardly much above the average; it was raised significantly when — I believe in the sixth class — Wilhelm Scherer joined it, and until the end of our schooldays he held on to first place without being challenged or envied. I do not recall any pupil who might subsequently have gained a position of excellence other than him.

After he had left grammar school, Breuer enrolled at Vienna University. 'Whereas some of my fellow pupils decided on their

9. JOSEF BREUER

Josef Breuer

choice of profession by counting coat buttons, I had long made up mind to become a physician.' Following his father's advice, he did not begin his medical studies immediately but enrolled for all the lectures that he could attend which interested him. Thus he heard some philosophy and a very lively presentation of political economy, which was given by Lorenz von Stein. 'The thin man, who always stood by the side of the chair with his left hand in his trouser pocket, spoke freely and was highly stimulating; making every effort to show that what we considered to be things are actually processes, he made considerable inroads into Hegel's world of thought.'

Only in 1859, when he was not yet eighteen, did he enter the medical faculty; and since the theoretical lectures were distributed over wide areas of the city he had to rush all over the place to attend the individual sessions. He studied anatomy with Hyrtl and physiology with Brücke.

> The highly inadequate background knowledge of a large proportion of the audience caused Brücke to preface his course of lectures with a six-week introduction on physics, which was not the least important and useful part of his lectures. The histological work in the laboratory laid the foundation for all knowledge of microscope work.

From this time onwards Breuer remained closely associated with his teacher Brücke and his laboratory. It was there that at the end of the seven years he met Freud. Later he also became Brücke's family doctor.

His clinical teacher was Škoda, and he studied pathological anatomy with Rokitansky. Thus as a student he was wholly part of the new materialistic, agnostic trend of the Viennese school. For at that time Rokitansky had relinquished his neo-Hippocratic views and had taken up Virchow's cellular pathology. Brücke himself was a direct representative of those views which sought to reduce all living things to physical and chemical processes.

Together with Ludwig, Helmholtz and du Bois-Reymond he formed the great quadrumvirate that governed physiology in Germany at that time (see Chapter 5).

'The ordinary path of studies led me in 1862 to the Oppolzer Clinic, and by a barely deserved stroke of fortune I was in 1867 made the assistant of this clinic. Oppolzer, who had hardly published anything ... was a sincerely well-meaning, fatherly friend and a favoured role model.' This man must have been a fascinating medical personality. He had hardly published any scientific or clinical work, but exerted an influence as a physician through his considerable human power and warmth. Billroth once wrote of him: 'With Škoda the diagnosis mostly seemed to be his exclusive goal, it was difficult to believe there was anything therapeutic about him. Oppolzer's therapy gave the future doctor a certain confidence. One admired Škoda for his solitary greatness, whereas one needed to warm to Oppolzer.'[1]

Schönbauer said of him: 'He was one of those doctors whose entry into the sick-room was enough to take away much of one' distress and pain. What was unique about him was, however, that he had the capacity to pass on this quality of "being a physician by the grace of God" — as it was once called — to a high degree to his students.'[2] It was of the greatest significance that this outstanding personality became Breuer's friend and teacher, for he awakened that therapeutic quality of acting out of love towards the sick person, which Breuer carried throughout his life.

Breuer then adds in a few brief words: 'After the death of my esteemed and beloved superintendent, Oppolzer, in 1871 I ceased working in a clinic and entered private practice.' This concluded his studies and his clinical preparation. Henceforth Breuer became one of Vienna's most sought-after family physicians, with many of the professors of the medical faculty asking him to be their family doctor.

As a young physician he had carried out some additional important physiological research which he writes about as follows:

> On November 5, 1868 I had the great honour that
> Ewald Hering, at that time professor at the Josephinum,
> lodged a treatise with the Academy of Sciences, 'The
> Self-Regulation of Breathing through the Vagus Nerve.'
> It was the report of an experimental investigation which
> Professor Hering had undertaken together with me in his
> laboratory. In this first scholarly work the greater part of
> the intellectual content should of course be ascribed to
> the teacher. It was a joyful and fruitful collaboration. The
> result of this work has, if I am not mistaken, been now
> for the most part generally accepted.

Another basic quality of Breuer's nature shines through these words: his extraordinary modesty. He never thrust himself into the foreground and never wanted to 'make a name for himself.' This is also why he gained the trust of thousands of his patients. His medical help and activity were far more important to him than his scientific career.

Around the middle of the 1870s he qualified as a university lecturer at the Faculty of Medicine:

> Shortly after my postdoctoral qualification I gave up
> an attempt to engage in activity as a lecturer; this was
> mainly because the *nisus docendi* (effort of teaching) was
> not sufficient to overcome the great difficulties that stand
> in the way of the activity of an internist lecturer. Hence
> when I heard that Billroth intended to propose me as an
> extraordinary professor to the professorial committee, I
> could do none other than cheerfully decline.

Not many physicians would have behaved similarly at this time and in this situation. What did the title of professor not signify under the social circumstances of that time? A doctor received from this a heightened standing, better fees and the possibility to have a significant influence in certain circles of society. For Breuer, however, the undisturbed functioning of his medical practice and the pursuit of certain scientific inclinations were more important than his outward reputation as a person.

The study of the function of the semicircular canals

In addition to his work as a medical practitioner, Breuer remained closely connected with Brücke's laboratory where, in the early 1870s, he began some extensive studies of the semicircular canals. He said of this in his modest and self-effacing way:

> When Goltz published some fundamental work about the function of the semicircular canals in the inner ear, a solution of the problem that differed from his seemed to me more probable, and I began to formulate it. I was almost ready with this when Professor Ernst Mach expressed virtually the same supposition, which Professor Crum Brown had also arrived at. In complete independence from one another we had developed almost the same line of thought which Mach formulated in his excellent book about sensations of movement. I presented the results of my work in the Viennese Medical Annuals of 1874 and 1875, and also in a series of treatises which appeared partly in minutes of the academy and partly in Pflüger's Archive for Physiology.

It was indeed the case that at the end of 1874 and the beginning of 1875 the three books or articles referred to appeared independently of one another and within the space of a few weeks, as often happens in the history of the sciences. This insight which came to expression simultaneously in three different places was one that was awaited by the spirit of the time. In this case, Mach, Breuer and Crum Brown were formulating a new theory of the sense of balance which has since then gained entry into the world of the physiology of the senses under the name of the Mach-Breuer theory (which is still adhered to).[3]

Breuer formulated the results of his findings at that time in the following way:

> When an annular tube filled with fluid begins its rotating motion, the fluid — as we have seen — makes, relatively speaking, a retrograde movement. As the rotating continues, the living power of this stream is gradually exhausted, naturally all the more quickly the narrower the tube is, and the fluid then moves in the same direction and with the same speed as the tube, thus bringing the system to a state of inner rest; the tube now suddenly pauses in its rotation, so the fluid still retains the living power of its movement; in accordance with the law of inertia, it will continue to flow in the direction of the former rotation of the annular tube until the living power of this ensuing movement is likewise consumed through adhesion.

Goltz was the first to express the view that the semicircular canals represent an organ independent of the cochlea and that only the latter transmit tone sensations, whereas the former are associated with sensations of movement.[4] He thought that the pressure of endolymph excites the ampullar nerves. Breuer, Mach and Crum Brown took up a position against this static conception. The above quotation makes it clear how Breuer wanted to oppose the static view with a dynamic explanation. He was of the opinion that it is the stream of fluid and not the pressure of fluid that brings about the stirring of sensation in the ampulla.

But it was also the case that all three authors, again independently of one another, arrived at the conclusion 'that the vestibular apparatus is made up of two sensory organs, one of which (the otoliths of the utricle and saccule) is responsible for the sensation of the position of the head or for progressive movements,

9. JOSEF BREUER

whereas the other organ (the three semicircular canals) transmits the sensation of the rotating movements of head and body.'[5]

With this, Breuer had laid the foundations for all later research on the labyrinth of the inner ear. His experiments with the semicircular canals of doves have made the familiar turning movements of the head understandable. Moreover, it was Breuer and not Robert Bárány who was the first to draw attention to nystagmus where there is irritation of the labyrinth.

For nearly twenty years Breuer worked diligently with these problems. At first, his experiments were questioned and their technique criticized. Later, however, it transpired that despite primitive research conditions all his results could be confirmed. When he was reproached in this respect he said: 'I am a practising physician, and my time for this work is late evening and the night, and my work-room is my home. I could work on doves there, but I couldn't carry out complex operations on mammals.'

Questions regarding the function of the labyrinth are still in a state of flux even to this day. What started in 1875 has become a far-reaching stream which has increasingly led to the mysteries of space and of spatial orientation. We are now confronted by the rich fullness of the questions and problems which at that time were not able to manifest themselves in their full magnitude and manifoldness. But it was Breuer who opened up the mysterious structure of the three semicircular canals; he was a man in whom the premonitions of a future age were dawning.

Perhaps he also experienced something of that being whom Rudolf Steiner once described and who appears as the spiritual archetype of the faculty of balance.

> This spiritual form was reminiscent of the physical world of the senses only in so far as it manifested something akin to three inter-penetrating circles; three circles standing at right angles to one another ... What flowed through these circles could be perceived, but it was not anything that reminded one of an impression of the

physical senses; it was, rather, reminiscent of something purely of a soul nature, only to be compared with the soul's sensations and feelings. But something streamed from this form which can only be described as like a reserved, intimate sorrow.[6]

This was the sorrow concerning its offspring, which had been banished to the human world. 'They have wrenched from me the last being which originated from me; they have taken him into their own realm and chained him to a rock-like structure after making him as small as possible.' And then this being adds: 'There in the physical world people refer to me as one of the senses, a very small sense organ. They call me the sense of balance, which has become quite small and consists of three incomplete circles which are bonded into the ear.'

Breuer's endeavour was to delve into the significance of this sense. He cleared a path to reveal a spring which will in future once more flow to this being.

The encounter with Sigmund Freud

The friendship between Breuer and Freud began towards the end of the 1870s (it must probably have been 1879). The two men met in Brücke's laboratory, and Breuer — who was fourteen years older than Freud — took much pleasure in the young twenty-three-year-old student. Freud was likewise deeply impressed by the older man's personality. He said: 'He was a man of outstanding intelligence; our relationship soon became more intimate, and he became my friend and helper in difficult life-situations. We had grown accustomed to sharing all our scientific interests with one another. Naturally, I was the main beneficiary in this relationship.'[7]

This is how the older friend appeared to the younger. Breuer gave Freud his constant and on-going support. He helped the

9. JOSEF BREUER

poor student with several loans; he enabled him to gain access to the professors and clinics of the Viennese faculty. He advised him in all possible life-decisions and was in every respect a fatherly friend.

Shortly after this first meeting a patient came to Breuer for medical treatment whom he found particularly interesting. He mentions this woman in his account of his life: 'In 1886 I had observed a sick woman who was suffering from severe hysteria and presented such strange progressive symptoms that I formed the conviction that I was here being offered an insight into deeper levels of psycho-pathological events.'

In his autobiography Freud wrote at length about this sick woman:

> The patient had been a young girl with an excellent education and unusual gifts who had become ill while caring for her beloved father. When Breuer took her on, she presented a confused picture of paralysis with contractions, inhibitions and states of psychic confusion. A fortuitous observation enabled the physician to recognize that she could be freed from such disturbances of consciousness if one caused her to give expression — in words of affective fantasy — to what was governing her. Through learning this Breuer acquired a method of treatment. He placed her in a state of deep hypnosis and let her speak on each occasion about what was affecting the way she was feeling. Once the attacks of depressive confusion had been overcome in this way, he used the same procedure for dealing with her inhibitions and physical disturbances ... Through this process Breuer succeeded through a long and labourious effort in freeing his patient from all her symptoms.

Only gradually did Breuer share his observations about this patient with his young friend. Although he thereby had some fundamental insights into the mechanism of psychic phenomena, a certain shyness probably held him back from engaging scientifically with the largely inscrutable depths of soul existence. It seemed as though he were standing with a great measure of reverence and apprehension before all that was resulting here from his insight: he recoiled from opening doors which — as he surmised — could only lead into the depths.

Hence Freud wrote, 'But the outcome of hypnosis was oppressed with a darkness that Breuer never illuminated; moreover, I could never understand why he had — it seemed to me — kept invaluable knowledge secret for so long instead of enriching science with it.' This was because Breuer, with his highly sensitive nature, could not so roughly grasp the phenomena that manifested themselves in his patients as could the much less considerate, and harsher Freud.

When Freud's psychologically oriented biographers, such as Ernest Jones, for example, want to make it seem as though Breuer stopped treating Bertha Pappenheim because he was suffering from countertransference and was sexually bound to his patient, this interpretation is rooted in the presuppositions of the worldview of psychoanalysis. It was not a suppressed bond that prevented Breuer from publishing his findings but his reserve in entering the 'realm of the Mothers.'

It seems to have been the case that only out of his friendship and affection for Freud did he finally decide to yield to his pressures and publish both studies together with him. The case of Anna O. (Bertha Pappenheim's medical history was recorded under this name) and the complications that resulted were made generally known through these studies. Thus in 1893 a shorter article, 'Regarding the Psychic Mechanism of Hysterical Phenomena,' appeared in the *Neurologische Zentralblatt,* and in 1895 the book based on it, *Studies in Hysteria.*

During this time, however, the friendship of these two men gradually came to an end. Freud became estranged from Breuer and started his intimate acquaintance with Wilhelm Fliess. A

9. JOSEF BREUER

number of references in Freud's letters show that his relationship with Breuer had by that time already greatly deteriorated. Thus he wrote in a letter of December 8, 1892 to Fliess: 'I am pleased to be able to tell you that our theory of hysteria (reminiscence, working off one's feelings etc.) can be read in the *Neurologische Zentralblatt,* and indeed in the form of a detailed, interim communication. Battles with my dear associate have cost me quite enough.'[8]

In a letter of May 25, 1895 Freud wrote: 'Breuer, on the other hand, is unrecognizable. One really has to like him without reservation ... he is making a great fuss about you in Vienna, as he has been totally converted to my theory of sexuality. This is an altogether different fellow from the one we've been used to.' It is clearly apparent from this context how hard Breuer was trying to maintain the human connection between the two friends, even at the cost of his own convictions. He approved of Freud's sexual theories, which in his heart he denied, only the sake of peace. Another letter gives very clear information about this. On November 8 of the same year Freud wrote to Fliess: 'Not long ago at the physicians' committee Breuer made me a great speech and introduced himself as a converted follower of sexual aetiology. When I thanked him for this privately he destroyed my pleasure by saying, "I don't believe in it at all." Can you understand this? I can't.'

Freud, a forceful person, could not understand this duality of views; battles of conscience of this kind were unknown to him. For Breuer, on the other hand, the beginning of psychoanalysis was a deep disappointment, a difficult decision which he had been constantly trying to postpone. He sensed that — out of loyalty to Freud — he had held out his hand to something that was repugnant and foreign to his whole being. The publication of the cathartic method that he had employed in the case of Bertha Pappenheim opened up perspectives which it would have been better to have left closed. And the interpretations which Freud gave to these phenomena led — as Breuer had to say to himself

–into subsensible realms through whose regions man was not yet strong enough to pass.

It does indeed seem to have been the case that Breuer initially yielded to the pressures of the more forceful Freud; but not only was their friendship ruptured through this but part of the mystery of the human soul was wrested from Breuer's weak hands, thus leading to the necessary, but nevertheless catastrophic consequences of psychoanalysis and the psychoanalytic movement.

The eternal physician

After this tragic interlude, which for Breuer was associated with so much pain and anguish, he again devoted himself to his research on the organs of balance and his medical practice. He must have been one of the most sought-after internal specialist in Vienna at this time. Among his patients were men such as Billroth, Brücke, Exner, Kaposi, Chrobak and other teachers of the Faculty of Medicine. Franz Brentano, the influential philosopher and psychologist, also went to him for medical consultations. It was apparently the case that everyone who was anybody in Vienna at that time looked to Breuer as a helping friend.

He embodied the ideal picture of the family physician, who was a man whom the whole family could trust. He was, however, not only a physician and researcher but had many worldwide interests. It was precisely this latter quality that would have made a decisive contribution to the conflict between him and Freud. He was single-mindedly utterly devoted to his work and his mission and altogether unapproachable as regards things that did not serve him or his research.

In Chapter 13 of Rudolf Steiner's autobiography there is a very perceptive characterization of Breuer. It stems from the time when Rudolf Steiner was living with the Specht family, roughly between the middle and the end of the 1880s:

9. JOSEF BREUER

Dr Breuer was a fascinating person. I admired him as a physician. But he also had a broad range of interests in other fields. He spoke with inspiration about Shakespeare. His profound medical knowledge added much to what he said about Ibsen or about Tolstoy's *Kreuzer Sonata*. I eagerly listened when he discussed subjects with my friend, the mother whose children I was educating. Psychoanalysis was not yet born, but the psychological problems were already there ... My friend and Dr Breuer had been friends since their youth. One fact gave me much to think about; in certain respects, her understanding of medicine was deeper than that of the distinguished physician. Once they discussed the case of a morphine addict Dr Breuer was treating. Referring to the conversation, she said to me, 'Just imagine what Dr Breuer did! He made the morphine addict promise on his word of honor not to touch morphine again. Dr Breuer actually expected results in this way and became indignant when the patient failed to keep his word. He said, "How can I treat someone who will not keep a promise?" Can you believe such a distinguished doctor would be that naïve? How can anyone think that something so deeply rooted in the man's nature could be cured by a promise?'[9]

Breuer, however, really did seem to have been as naïve as this. He must have had an unshakable trust in the effectiveness of the good in man, because everything evil and false was itself so utterly foreign to him. This was also what initially so aroused Freud's enthusiasm for him and later, once psychoanalysis had begun to develop, what repelled him from Breuer. He ceased to be able to tolerate his friend's perpetual goodness; it appeared to him like another form of bigotry, and his conscience pricked him and rebelled whenever he saw Breuer. He once said to Fliess that just the very sight of Breuer was sufficient to drive him away from Vienna. These malicious words only make sense if one compares the characters of these two personalities: Freud, who was inexorably in pursuit of his own self-fulfilment, and the modest Breuer, who was forever denying himself and was enshrouded in a mantle of goodness.

At the end of his autobiography he wrote some words that so comprehensively characterize his essential nature that they must be cited here:

> In an old Spanish story a king was searching in vain for the shirt of a happy man that would bring him happiness; and when someone was finally found who claimed to be happy, he was a beggar who had no shirt.
>
> If I now conclude this brief account of my life by saying that I have been and am thoroughly happy in my home, that my beloved wife has given me five capable, excellent children, that I have not lost any of them and have not had any serious worries, I can probably acknowledge myself to be a happy man (who even has a shirt).

When he wrote these words he was eight-one years old. He must indeed have been a happy man, for a quality of inner contentment and security streams from these sentences. They were written by someone who was truly wise.

If one were to ask, however, what was the nature of the grace that endowed this life with so much inner dignity and quietness, there can only be one answer: it was the grace of renunciation that made Breuer what he truly was — a man who was indeed wise.

When he had received the *Venia Legendi*, the qualification to lecture, he renounced this opportunity. He continued to devote himself to his patients.

When he learnt that Billroth wanted to propose him as a professor, he asked him to refrain. He did not want to come under the light of publicity.

When he could have been the father of a world movement, psychoanalysis, he withdrew. Through this he lost a dear friend to whom, nevertheless, he wanted to remain loyal. He must have sensed where being the father of psychoanalysis would lead him.

These three renunciations which happened within the space of a few years protected Breuer from the challenges and temptations of modern life. He remained someone who was strong in himself and who lived and worked at peace with himself. This was the source of his qualities as a physician. His deep conviction that he 'was happy through merit,' that he was aware of his good fortune and did not, as so many do, bear it as a burden protected him from the envy of the gods.

He died on June 20, 1925, three months after Rudolf Steiner's death. On St John's Day his mortal sheath was given over to the flames, and on June 30 the urn was interred in Döbling, one of the most beautiful cemeteries in Vienna.

This death has something deeply significant about it. Breuer was born in the depths of winter and died at the height of summer. These were the right times for birth and death. He entered the gate of birth in the darkness of winter. He left it again in summer's fullness of light and warmth. The spiritual powers guiding him gave him through this the mantle of justice which he bore throughout his life.

AT THE THRESHOLD OF THE MODERN AGE

Sigmund Freud

10

Sigmund Freud

Sigmund Schlomo Freud (1856–1939) was an Austrian neurologist who founded psychoanalysis.

Beginnings

Sigmund Freud was born on May 6 in Freiberg (now Pribor), a little town in northern Moravia close to the Silesian coal mines. He was the son of Jewish parents and the first child of his father's second marriage. Following the migrations of these years of economic boom, his parents moved with their children and relatives from the provinces to the imperial city of Vienna. At this time thousands of Jewish and non-Jewish citizens of the Austro-Hungarian Empire were streaming to the imperial city from many crown lands, from Bohemia and Hungary, Silesia and Galicia, from Carniola, and Moravia. They hoped not only to find better earning opportunities in this growing metropolis but also to gain a higher social position; they all wanted to be respected citizens.

Freud's parents were poor; they belonged to the lower middle-class. His father was a man of business, who had earned no regular income at any point in his life and was often reliant on the help of his relatives and friends. He particularly loved his eldest son Sigmund, who from a very early stage manifested outstanding intellectual capacities and was therefore sent 'to the grammar school.' The family was at the time living in Leopoldstadt, a part of Vienna inhabited mainly by Jews. This was no ghetto, but a unique district of lanes and alley-ways where Jewish people striving for emancipation had found their place. One family lived there like any other; they were all minor businessmen and tradesmen, employees or civil servants. They shared in common not only their outward life circumstances but also a kind of inner attitude, which gave them all the same inner mood of soul. They felt themselves to be Jews — albeit emancipated; nonetheless still Jews, who belonged to the chosen people and who in every respect felt themselves to be above all other people who were *goyim,* Gentiles. The Jews were distinguished by a quite particular pride. They were not merely proud of their Jewishness but also that each family was developing its own particular arrogance. There were the Freuds and the Freunds, the Roths and the Blaus, the Bettelheims and the Reschovskys, the Pollaks and Poppers, and each of these special types regarded the bearers of another name with a greater or lesser degree of scorn. A similar haughtiness based on the blood of the family can be found among the Scottish clans.

Nevertheless, they were all harmless citizens, full of good will, no more or less selfish than most other people of the time. The rapid growth of technology at that time, the industrialization and materialization that were extending to every corner of life were imposing their stamp upon this epoch.

Sigmund Freud quickly and without difficulty completed his secondary education and in 1873, in his seventeenth year, entered university. He had already decided to study medicine. He himself describes how he arrived at this decision:

> Under the powerful influence of a school friendship with a boy rather my senior who grew up to be a well-known politician I developed a wish to study law like him and to engage in social activities. At the same time, the theories

of Darwin, which were then of topical interest, strongly attracted me, for they held out hopes of an extraordinary advance in our understanding of the world; and it was hearing Goethe's beautiful essay on Nature read aloud at a popular lecture by Professor Carl Brühl just before I left school that made me decide to become a medical student.[1]

Thus the choice of medicine came not from an impulse to want to heal and help but from the need to understand the world and man better. This is also evident from many of Freud's later statements. He did not like treating patients or working as a physician. Hence Margarete Susman is quite wrong when she says, 'For in his discoveries he lifted the veil from a gloomy reality that heavily oppresses human beings. He was motivated not by the seductive power of curiosity or solely out of a great researcher's hunger for knowledge but originally and primarily by a wish to heal people.'[2] This was absolutely not so! Freud was neither a physician nor someone endeavouring to bring healing. His pupils and friends were aware of this. Thus Theodor Reik, for example, wrote:

> Freud told us [his pupils] many times — and he repeated it in his writings — that he had no great liking for the profession of physician. The therapeutic ambition, the need to help sick people, was not strongly developed in him .. He considered himself first and last a psychologist, not a physician, and here is the line of demarcation which separates many psychoanalysts from the founder of their science, to whom they pay lip service and little else.'[3]

Many similar statements could be added to this one.

In order to understand Freud as a human being it is necessary to know that he had no medical inclinations. He had, in addition, a total indolence with regard to music. He could not bear people making music near him. In characterizing him, it is important to note that he was from the outset an inartistic person.

The lecture where he heard Goethe's hymn, *To Nature,* that led to his choice of study, had to do with comparative anatomy and opened up to him the magnitude and breadth of the idea of evolution. The mighty opening up of the past of the earth and of humanity that was being accomplished through natural-history research at that time was the gate through which Freud entered the world of knowledge.

Thus to begin with he studied above all zoology and only incidentally anatomy in the context of medicine. In addition, he loved listening to the philosopher Franz Brentano and attended his seminar on Aristotelian logic.[4] He made a particular, and detailed, study of Aristotle's writings. He conducted his first scientific research in the recently established research station in Trieste, where he worked with eels on the histological description and interpretation of certain organs. It is in a sense a symbol of his later research that the object of his studies was the gonads of those creatures of the night and the depths of the ocean.

Once Freud had completed his preliminary studies at the university, he devoted himself to physiology and in 1876 joined Ernst Brücke's laboratory as a research assistant. He soon came under the influence of this man whom he greatly revered and whose pupil he remained for six years.

Ernst Brücke was one of the most famous physiologists of his time and was one of the quadrumvirate which consisted, in addition to him, of Emil du Bois-Reymond, Hermann Helmholtz and Carl Ludwig. All four were pupils of the founder of modern physiology, the great teacher Johannes Müller. As young assistants they had firmly resolved to arrange their life and work in such a way that they would produce proof that all life-processes are none other than complicated physical and chemical procedures. The battle against the idea of a specific life-force was inscribed on their banner; they made their way into the world as proclaimers of an extreme materialism. They initially formed a private club, which later developed into the Berlin Physics Society. In the space of 25 years these four men had taken over the leadership of scientific physiology. What they accomplished in this field was a unique triumph of materialism. Its four journeymen shared a common destiny, in that they came and went through birth and death in accordance with a mysterious arrangement which can be discerned from the dates of their birth and death.

        Carl Ludwig   1816–95
        Emil du Bois-Reymond 1818–96
        Ernst Brücke   1819–92
        Hermann Helmholtz   1821–94

They were born in the brief span of five years, and died within the space of four years; and one of them was Freud's scientific father. Freud himself wrote:

> At length, in Ernst Brücke's physiological laboratory, I found rest and satisfaction — and men, too, whom I could respect and take as my models: the great Brücke himself, and his assistants Sigmund Exner and Ernst von Fleischl-Marxow. With the last of these, a brilliant man, I was privileged to be upon terms of friendship.[5]

Under Brücke's guidance, Freud devoted himself to the histological study of nerve tissue, and the results that he obtained were helpful in creating the foundation for the 'neurone theory' which von Waldeyer and others subsequently established. The young student published a whole series of important contributions which testify to his scientific industry and his abilities.[6] Held up by working on these studies, Freud sat his examinations for qualifying as a physician only in 1881 — a delay of three years, because it was not medicine but scientific research which held all his affections.

In the same year he left Brücke's laboratory, since Brücke advised him against a scientific career. His poor material situation was the reason for the advice that his teacher gave him. At that time only a person of independent means could take up the profession of a theoretician. Thus the young physician went from research into practice and worked for several years as an assistant at various departments of the General Hospital in Vienna. In addition, however, he continued his work at the brain anatomy institute under Meynert and carried out many important studies — for instance, about the course of certain bundles of nerves. Moreover, he studied the whole area of nervous illnesses, and in 1885 he was finally able to qualify as a non-salaried lecturer for neuropathology at Vienna University.

By taking this step Freud had reached the first stage of the scientifically successful career possible for a Viennese physician. Despite poverty and being Jewish he was able to prove that he was courageous and intelligent enough to have at the age of 29 gained accreditation to teach at Vienna University.

The pride that he had imbibed in his parental home accompanied him throughout his life. But he was also full of ambition and sensitivity; and in his autobiography it becomes apparent again and again how often he felt humiliated and wounded and how his pride rebelled against this. He writes as follows of his university years:

> Above all, I found that I was expected to feel myself inferior and an alien because I was a Jew. I refused absolutely to do the first of these things. I have never been able to see why I should feel ashamed of my descent or, as people were beginning to say, of my race ... These first impressions at the university, however, had one consequence which was afterwards to prove important; for at an early age I was made familiar with the fate of being in the opposition and of being put under the ban of the 'compact majority.' The foundations were thus laid for a certain degree of independence of judgment.

The inner attitude of the writer is very clear from these lines. He felt himself to be not only someone who had been expelled but also a 'special person,' a 'chosen one,' someone who had quite definite and important tasks to fulfil. In many a letter to his fiancée he speaks of how his future biographers would write about him; he was conscious of his mission. This was a feeling that reached back into his earliest childhood and was based on various, somewhat mysterious prophecies which were kept secret as family traditions concerning this 'special' child.

After he became a lecturer and had almost completed his thirtieth year, he took the first steps leading to the consolidation of his life. His path of destiny began to emerge. Between 1885 and 1900 he met three men who would be of particular importance for his further development: Charcot in Paris, Breuer in Vienna and Fliess in Berlin. He liked to remember only the first two, although his personal animosity towards Breuer became ever stronger; yet he did not disown him. Fliess, on the other hand, he would have been very happy to wipe altogether from his memories; he represented a dark period of his existence.

These three meetings, which took place in close succession and ensured that these men had an equal role as godparents at the cradle of psychoanalysis, were probably the hardest trials that Sigmund Freud was subjected to. They were tests that he had to pass before embarking upon the road to the Mothers, the origins of the soul.

The three tests

In the autumn of 1885 the young lecturer went to Paris in order to gain further insights into the domain of neuro-pathology under Charcot at the Salpêtrière Hospital. He financed this study trip with a stipend that was allotted to him through the support of his old teacher at Vienna University, Brücke. In Paris he initially felt overwhelmed by the atmosphere of the cosmopolitan city, and he wrote full of homesickness to his fiancée in Hamburg. As his command of French was somewhat shaky, he felt lonely, solitary and withdrawn even at the Salpêtrière. He had no prior connection with the great Charcot and was merely one of many foreign visiting students — a position that he did not relish.

Jean-Martin Charcot was at that time at the height of his fame. He was one of the most well-known neurologists of his time, who tried to permeate his particular area with modern scientific ideas. At the time when Freud was attending his lectures and clinical demonstrations, Charcot was concerning himself with the realm of hysteria. Freud gives his own account in his autobiography:

> What impressed me most of all while I was with Charcot were his latest investigations upon hysteria, some of which were carried out under my own eyes. He had proved, for instance, the genuineness of hysterical phenomena and their conformity to laws, the frequent occurrence of hysteria in men, the production of hysterical paralyses and contractures by hypnotic suggestion and the fact that such artificial products showed, down to their smallest details, the same features as spontaneous attacks, which were often brought on traumatically.

This was how Freud summarized his new experience of this realm. However, he not only became familiar with hysteria but also gained some understanding of the power of hypnosis and hypnotic suggestion in treating nervous disorders.

The whole area of hypnosis was first discovered by science at this time. Through the travelling hypnotist Carl Hansen the attention of many thousands was drawn to hypnotic phenomena around the middle of the nineteenth century, and a little later they were introduced in France into the therapy of nervous disorders through Charcot, Pierre Janet and Hippolyte Bernheim.

The power of hypnosis is an ancient possession of humanity which has been cultivated for millennia in various mystery schools. However, it has been handed on only to a few chosen people. Around the turn of the eighteenth to nineteenth centuries, reflecting the course of the evolution of consciousness, it gained entry through Mesmer — under the name of animal magnetism — into official and semi-official medicine. Freud initially became aware of it through a public demonstration by Hansen and he then followed the effect of hypnosis on sick people in Paris. Here he encountered phenomena that were initially wholly incomprehensible to the scientific understanding of that time. For forces were coming into play whose existence was not denied but the understanding of which lay beyond the scope of all current conceptions. Charcot was endeavouring to prove that hypnotic effects could be achieved only with people with a hysterical disposition, and, hence, tried to shift what could not be interpreted to the wide domain of hysteria.

Freud was confronted by this threshold phenomenon of the human soul and deeply struck by it. Through his ambitious nature he also found the opportunity to come into personal contact with Charcot in the last months of his stay in Paris and was entrusted with the task of translating Charcot's works. 'Charcot accepted the offer [to translate his lectures into German], I was admitted to the circle of his personal acquaintances, and from that time forward I took a full part in all that went on at the hospital.'

After a few months Freud returned to Vienna and presented a paper on his impressions of Paris to the Society of Physicians. He writes in this connection:

> I met with a bad reception. Persons of authority, such as the chairman (Bamberger, the physician), declared that what I said was incredible. Meynert urged me to find some cases in Vienna similar to those which I had described and to present them before the Society. I tried to do so; but the senior physicians in whose departments I found cases refused to allow me to observe them or to work at them ... As I was shortly afterwards excluded from the laboratory of cerebral anatomy and for a whole session had nowhere to deliver my lectures, I withdrew from academic life and ceased to attend the learned societies. It is a whole generation since I have visited the Society of Medicine.

Although the transcripts of the meeting in question do not indicate any suggestion of the hostile attitude of which Freud writes, and he was never actually barred from the laboratory of cerebral anatomy, Freud's over-sensitivity and also his embitterment can be detected from these sentences. It is true that studies about hysteria and hypnotism were received with a large measure of scepticism at the time. Materialism had triumphed in German medicine, and everything that did not fit within its framework was regarded as non-existent or unscientific.

It was through hypnosis and hysteria that Freud's rejection of orthodox medicine became complete. The phenomena of the abnormal and inexplicable now became his sphere of research, and this meant that he had to tread a solitary path. Nevertheless he did not abandon his agnosticism, but continued to be a pupil of Brücke and an adherent of his views. He was trying to grasp new phenomena with old ideas.

He wrote to his betrothed about Charcot from Paris in tones of the highest recognition. This is worthy of comment because his criticism of people and conditions in these letters was quite particularly sharp and far-reaching; hardly any person or situation escaped his intellectual condemnation. He said of Charcot: 'He engrosses me: when I go away from him I have no more wish to work at my own simple things. My brain is sated as after an evening at the theatre. Whether the seed will ever bring forth fruit I do not know; but what I certainly know is that no other human being has ever affected me in such a way.'[7] This was Sigmund Freud's first significant meeting.

The second involved an individual who was probably one of the most remarkable people in Vienna at that time: Dr Josef Breuer. He was around fourteen years older than Freud and was, like him, a lecturer at the university. He had declined a professorship offered to him by the famous Professor Nothnagel, in order to be able to work in his medical practice independently of academic pressure. He was one of Vienna's most well-known family physicians, treated many influential people and a large

10. SIGMUND FREUD

number of the university professors. He was friendly with an astonishingly large number of people, and his advice and his recognition were sought by many hundreds. In addition he was a very discerning research scientist, who had made important discoveries already as a young man. His interests were world-wide and his extensive knowledge of the most diverse realms of life was astonishing for his time.

There is a characterization of Breuer in the first of two lectures that Rudolf Steiner gave on psychoanalysis:

> What one calls psychoanalysis today derives from a case that a Viennese physician, Dr Breuer, had observed back in the 1880s. Dr Breuer — whom I myself knew — had a remarkably subtle mind in addition to being a physician. He was interested to a very high degree in all manner of aesthetic and general human questions. Because of the very thorough way in which he engaged with cases of illness, it was understandable that he found a particular case which he had in the 1880s quite especially interesting.[8]

Rudolf Steiner then goes on to describe at some length that famous young woman, Bertha Pappenheim, who had been one of the well-known patients of the nineteenth century. From her hysterical symptoms and the way that Breuer treated them, there developed the medical and human interest in the 'unfathomable.' This young woman was also one of those significant somnambulists who, like the seeress of Prevorst whose destiny Justinus Kerner has described, or Gottliebin Dittus of Pastor Blumhardt, released great waves of healings. When Breuer began to treat Bertha Pappenheim in December 1880 she was in her twenty-first year. (She was born on February 27, 1859 and died on May 28, 1936.) The treatment, which was largely of a hypnotic nature, lasted for approximately two years; in 1882 Breuer gave it up, for he was so taken up by this one patient that he was having to neglect his other patients and his family. Moreover, the connection between physician and patient had become so strong and far-reaching that it seemed necessary to break it off. Bertha Pappenheim subsequently recovered; at the age of thirty she became one of Germany's first social welfare workers and founded some model educational establishments where social workers and welfare were trained under her leadership.[9] This destiny was a very typical aspect of human history from the end of the nineteenth century.

Breuer and Freud met one another for the first time around 1879 in Brücke's laboratory. From then on a friendship developed which was of the greatest significance particularly for Freud. The older colleague helped the young student in many respects. He also supported him financially in an extremely generous way, and to a large extent Freud was Breuer's spiritual son. In a letter of June 6, 1883 he wrote about this to his betrothed: 'To talk with Breuer is like sitting in the sun; he radiates light and warmth. He is such a sunny person, and I don't know what he sees in me to be so kind ... One does not adequately characterize him by only saying good things about him; one has also to emphasize the absence of so much badness.'

Breuer must have appeared thus to many other people, for in later years he was almost a legendary figure in certain social circles in Vienna.

After his return from Paris Freud took up his connection with Breuer again, and the latter helped him to obtain medical positions in various hospitals. At this time Freud also started his private practice as a neurologist, and Breuer sent him many patients, especially those suffering from hysterical and neurasthenic conditions. In these decisive years between 1887 and 1895 Freud came to the first fundamental observations and insights through which the foundations of psychoanalysis were laid. In particular, Freud based his ideas on what Breuer had learnt through treating Bertha Pappenheim. He wrote regarding this:

> I ... began to repeat Breuer's investigations with my own patients and eventually, especially after my visit to

10. SIGMUND FREUD

> Bernheim in 1889 had taught me the limits of hypnotic suggestion, I worked at nothing else. After observing for several years that his findings were invariably confirmed in every case of hysteria that was accessible to such treatment ... I proposed to him that we should issue a joint publication. At first he objected vehemently ... In 1893 we issued a preliminary paper, *On the Psychical Mechanism of Hysterical Phenomena,* and in 1895 there followed our book, *Studies in Hysteria.*

With the publication of this book the friendship of the two men broke down; for Freud could not understand why Breuer fought against publishing their findings.

Even though psychoanalytical interpreters would seek to interpret the conflict between Breuer and Freud by claiming that Breuer's strong sexual connection with his patient led to the interruption of the treatment and that he therefore never spoke further about its outcome, there was most probably another reason behind this event. Breuer's method was to put his patient in a state of hypnotic sleep, thereby exposing the foundations of her hysterical symptoms in this semi-conscious state so that she was enabled to speak about them. Her subconscious revealed what her conscious mind was unable to discern. However, Breuer recoiled from having to express anything definite about the night aspect of human existence. It is also likely that his masonic connections sought to prevent him from revealing the deeper aspect of hypnotism through scientific publications.

Freud, in contrast, had no notion of such matters. He was a bear in his robustness of soul, and as soon as there was any question of occult problems he played the agnostic who wanted ruthlessly to illumine the depths of human existence with the torch of an 'enlightened' and sharp intellect. Breuer, on the other hand, rebelled against this, especially at the moment when his younger friend began to place sexual patterns of behaviour in the foreground as the virtually exclusive cause of hysterical symptoms.

219

Their common work and their friendship now rapidly broke asunder. Freud developed a pronounced antipathy to Breuer and wrote in a letter of February 6, 1896 that just the sight of Breuer could cause him to emigrate. These were spiteful words to utter about someone who had for almost twenty years been his true helper and inspirer. But Freud was unrelenting in his rejection of others and, repudiating his older friend and brother, now went on his way into the darkness alone. Rudolf Steiner spoke some very significant words about this: 'To put it hypothetically, one could well believe that if Breuer had obtained a professorship and had been able to pursue this problem, it would perhaps have acquired a completely different form. Now it was primarily Dr Freud who concerned himself with this matter.'[10]

This expresses that his destiny could have taken different paths. Breuer drew back, perhaps he also had to withdraw altogether. Freud took his place. This is an important nodal point of the destiny that was unfolding at the time when Rudolf Steiner's *Philosophy of Freedom* appeared in 1894. The original German bears the subtitle 'Some Results of Introspective Observation Following the Methods of Natural Science.' On several occasions Freud sought to characterize his line of research with almost identical words. However, he took precisely the opposite path to that of Rudolf Steiner; the point of departure was the same, but the directions they took were poles apart. Rudolf Steiner's endeavour was to investigate the spiritual nature of the soul; Freud, on the other hand, was led to uncover the soul's animal aspect. Between the two stood Josef Breuer, who was unable to decide for one or the other.

Thus it was also the case that the emergence of psychoanalysis as a movement was in many respects a shadow of the path taken by the anthroposophical movement. This could be considered at greater length later. Josef Breuer, the mediating figure, died at an advanced age in 1925, the year of Rudolf Steiner's death.

During Freud's growing estrangement from Breuer, he began a new friendship with Wilhelm Fliess. Freud had come to know him through Breuer at the end of the 1880s. Fliess was at the time in Vienna for purposes of study, and he and Freud soon took to one another. A first correspondence developed, which became more intense from 1893 and reached its culmination at the end of the century. Unfortunately, only Freud's letters to Fliess have been preserved; these were saved for posterity in an adventurous manner through the energetic intervention of Princess Marie Bonaparte. The princess, who had been Freud's pupil and friend for many years, acquired them from the estate of Fliess's wife and on several occasions, in Vienna and also in Paris, snatched them from the hands of the Gestapo. When she told Freud of this, he wanted this correspondence to be destroyed, for he had long before got rid of Fliess's letters to him. The deep hatred that lingered as a residue of this so intimate friendship was for Freud unbounded and Old-Testament-like. Fliess had been obliterated from his life and memory.

A substantial number of these letters have now been published, and they reveal a very interesting portion of the history of the time.[11] For Freud goes in his letters into full detail about his developing views of psychoanalysis as it was then emerging. He regarded Fliess, his friend who was two years younger than himself, as a mentor to whom he put forward his ideas and asked him to subject them to his scrutiny.

Fliess had a magnetic personality. He was a nose and ear specialist in Berlin and was working at that time on the biological and pathological relationships which, he supposed, existed between the nose and the sexual organs. Moreover, he was beginning his research on the periodicity of all organic events and believed — from female menstruation — that he had discovered a generally effective periodicity of 28 days as a female rhythm, and of 23 days as a masculine rhythm. Since Fliess was, however, convinced of the androgynous nature of every human being, he also sought and found both rhythms in a man and also in a woman. Thus it was that ancient mystery knowledge shed the light of spirit into the modern age.

It is very important that these ideas of Fliess — for they could hardly be called discoveries — stood as godparents at the cradle of psychoanalysis; for this is further evidence of Freud's tendencies towards irrationality. His constant longing was to investigate the deeper connections of life and to penetrate to where the nineteenth century was not able to venture. His friendship with Fliess was a clear symptom of events that were going on behind the scenes of everyday happenings around the turn of the century, for 1899 was the end of that epoch of five thousand years referred to by mystery teachings as the Kali Yuga. This period of spiritual darkness came to an end at that time, and many lesser and greater beacons of an awakening spirituality were making this turning point manifest. Fliess's ideas were one such symptom; for he set about investigating the rhythms of life in a far-reaching way and bringing the androgynous, double nature of man's being to people's consciousness.

Because of his intimate participation in his friend's work, Freud also became acquainted with Swoboda, one of Fliess's pupils, and through him also with his friend Otto Weininger, the author of the famous book *Geschlecht und Charakter* (Gender and Character). Strange threads of destiny can be discerned here. Hermann Swoboda became Freud's patient, but his meeting with Otto Weininger was perhaps fleeting.

Freud was at this time directly involved with starting to implement psychoanalytical methods. Whereas previously he had used Breuer's 'cathartic' means of treatment, he gradually changed these into those of interrogation. He tried — without hypnosis — to sound his patients out to the point where they could gradually make their repressed complexes conscious. This questioning was later replaced by the methodology of free association.

At this same time Freud himself took what was probably the most decisive step of his life. He set about submitting to a self-analysis. In the course of this, the great significance of dream life disclosed itself to him as a revelation of subconscious soul-processes when he studied his own dream experiences thoroughly.

10. SIGMUND FREUD

He found the unconscious causes of such phenomena as forgetfulness, making slips of the tongue and other similar shortcomings. Through these experiences a further process of loneliness started for Freud, which eventually led to the break with Fliess.

The editor of Fliess's letters, Ernst Kris, writes of this as follows:

> After the beginning of Freud's self-analysis in 1897 Fliess's influence could only hinder this development. His attempts to attribute mental events to periodic intoxications or to biologize the theory of repression could only have the effect of alien bodies. Fliess's allegations that psychoanalysis was incapable of yielding scientific results, that Freud's interpretations were only 'projections' of himself, were all the more painful to Freud because of the crucial advances in technique he had made during the years of their closest intellectual contact.

The two men had their final meeting in 1900. After this there continued to be an even more perfunctory correspondence, which lasted until 1902 and then altogether ceased. The whole story had an unpleasant aftermath, for Fliess subsequently accused Swoboda, Weininger and Freud of plagiarism and did so in a very hateful manner. Weininger was already dead by then, whereas Swoboda retaliated in a nasty way. Freud alone behaved nobly and kept himself aloof. But he never forgave his lost friend's trespass. At the same time Freud could not forgive Fliess for the fact that Freud could not but recognize himself in him.

These were the three fateful meetings that Freud had to deal with on the path that led him to psychoanalysis. After he returned from being with Charcot in Paris he fell out with the medical world of his time in his quest for solitude. A few years later he also abandoned Breuer and the warmth that enveloped him from this friendship. With this he denied himself a human contact which would have brought a little light and radiance from the wider world into his solitude. Finally he also withdrew from Fliess, for the latter was for him associated with those feelings that he experienced when he had for the first time heard and read Goethe's hymn *To Nature*. This pantheistic feeling that pervades all Fliess's books, that somewhat oppressive and also bombastic 'living and breathing' quality which enters in there in a dreamy way was, as it were, forbidden territory for Freud.

With these tree steps he had renounced his connection to science, to a free lifestyle and to the last residues of true humanism. With self-analysis he had started to show himself for what he really was, and so, abandoned by all and everyone and driven by a dark impulse, he strove towards a goal which was unknown to him and whose outlines were wreathed in mist.

The mission

Thus Freud became one possessed by a mission. This awareness of a mission had filled him since his earliest youth. Each of his biographers has testified to this, and it was utterly clear from many of his conversations and also between the lines of his *Autobiography*. He believed that he was 'destined for something higher.' From this he derived his pride and his profound contempt for humanity, which was associated with a complete lack of religious feeling. Thus he became lonely, hard and uncompromising in his work; a person who was constantly on the defensive, even when he was not under attack.

He lived in the circle of his family (he had six children and a wife who was deeply devoted to him) as if on a distant isle. One of his pupils, Hanns Sachs, said of this: '[Freud's] household gave an impression of exterritoriality, like an island that is easily accessible from the mainland, but still an island.'[12]

His daily rhythm was strictly ordered. From 9 am until 12 noon patients were analysed. After lunch he would have a short, rapid walk and then resumed the analysing of his patients between 3 and 7 pm. In the evening he withdrew into his study and worked through what he had learnt in the hours of analysis. In preparation for Sunday, however, he played cards every Saturday evening with a circle of acquaintances (the game concerned was tarot, which was very popular in Vienna at that time).

This was the dry, self-imposed and monotonous life of this lonely man. He lived for almost forty years in the same dwelling, and although he loathed Vienna he left it only when his existence was threatened by National Socialism. A deeply rooted conservatism filled Freud's personal life, despite being revered by so many as a pioneer of a new world.

He often spoke bitterly about his loneliness, without acknowledging that it was his own self-imposed fault, and that there was something self-destructive about it. He reflected as follows about his lonely state: 'For more than ten years after my separation from Breuer I had no followers. I was completely isolated. In Vienna I was shunned; abroad no notice was taken of me.'

Thus he often also became negative towards others. A harsh destiny pursued this man who was making ever greater claims to be able to fathom the depths of the human soul. This task gave him an unrelenting quality, causing him to be afflicted with a blindness that closed up the other side of his human nature, with the result that he could only mock anything that ventured to indicate its existence. One of his first admirers, who — although he never became his pupil — nevertheless greatly appreciated him, Ludwig Binswanger, reported from a conversation that he had with him in 1927 — a time when Freud was at the height of his fame. The Swiss psychiatrist was trying to point out that there was something 'religious' in each person. Freud's answer was: 'Religion arises out of the child's and young person's anxiety and need for help, there's nothing you can do about that.' And Binswanger then added:

> Freud led me to the door. His last words — accompanied by a wise, slightly ironic smile — were: 'I unfortunately

cannot satisfy your religious needs.' Never was parting from the revered friend and great man made more difficult that at this moment, when, in full consciousness of the 'big idea' with which his gigantic struggle was imbued and which became the destiny of his genius, he held out his hand to me.[13]

At about the same time Freud met the well-known German clinician Viktor von Weizsäcker, who describes this meeting at some length in his memoirs.[14] When the conversation had already come to an end, there was the following dialogue which Weizsäcker relates:

> I said somewhat abruptly that it seemed to me to be a remarkable coincidence that my visit to him happened to fall on All Souls' Day. The unexpected upshot of this remark was that Freud asked with astonished, 'Why?'
> I felt somewhat confused and tried to explain that I was 'probably also a mystic in my spare time.'
> On hearing this he turned quickly towards me and said with an utterly horrified look, 'That is really terrible.'
> Trying to make amends I said, 'What I mean to say is that there are things that we do not know,' whereupon he said, 'Oh — I've got the edge on you there!'
> His tormented tone and quick changing of the subject did, I believe, prove that he was on this occasion being deadly serious. He must have said something about the inviolable nature of the power of reason; but I either did not hear or have forgotten.

In this one scene the whole ascetic tendency that Freud had imposed upon himself is made clearly apparent. He sensed things that he forbade himself to know. He asserted something which, he was convinced, was not the whole truth, but he was serving the work which he had established without being able wholly to identify himself with it. This happened, to be sure, only in his old age. For in the same discussion he replied to

Weizsäcker's question as to whether he regarded the psychoanalysis of a patient as a finite or infinite process 'softly and hesitantly: "I think infinite".'

For the most part he was astonishingly untouched by and bereft of feeling for human affairs and relationships. Thus Sachs reports in one particular context: 'I saw him when the news came that someone with whom he had been on friendly terms for years had committed suicide. I found him strangely unmoved by such a tragic event.'[15] The same pupil reports that weeks after one of the closest colleagues (Karl Abraham in Berlin) had died, Freud asked after him and only then — as though suddenly realizing and apologizing — said, 'I still cannot believe that he has died.' People meant little to him; the task and he himself as the one who carried it out were the only values which had significance for him and for his existence. Hanns Sachs also relates:

> I have no doubt that Freud too thought of himself as not being one of common men. He never said anything which could be taken as a hint of his high opinion of himself, but neither did he ever modestly disclaim his superiority ... I simply could not believe that he was made of the same clay as others. Some special substance had been infused into him and gave the finished product a higher grade of perfection. This meant a gulf between us which I did not try to cross.

Many people must have probably experienced a similar measure of distance when they met Freud. He was a solitary, isolated person but for that very reason also outstanding and commanding. This special position was never challenged in his circle. Indeed, it gradually led to the psychoanalytical movement acquiring a thoroughly sectarian stamp and becoming a religious substitute for its adherents; Freud himself appeared to them in the role of a god-like prophet who as far as his disciples were concerned had become inviolable. Only Lenin and, more recently, Stalin, Hitler and Mussolini have in certain facets of their existence achieved a similar veneration on the part of the people surrounding them. This feature of Freud's life must be clearly considered, while not detracting from his essential nature; for he did much himself to contribute to the fact that it was able to develop to such an extent. But this was one of the underlying reasons why psychoanalysis became so widespread in the western world. For wherever religious tradition has been replaced by a stultifying belief in scientific progress, the appearance of a religion emanating from science is greeted with particular favour. Whether it is called Christian Science or psychoanalysis is not so important. That, however, it has a prophet, that it keeps people together in lodge-like associations and, moreover, gives them the possibility of carrying out charitable work by helping others are basic characteristics that are the key to success for such efforts in America and England. Through his behaviour Freud laid the foundations for this aberration; it was not his teachings but far rather his personality that became the focal point of the psychoanalytical movement.

In his memoirs Weizsäcker mentions something else which casts a significant light on Freud's destiny and his personality: 'I still remember the whole array of classical statuettes, bronzes and terracottas on the desk in the spacious consulting room itself. Thus the professor's eye encompassed these satyrs and goddesses whenever he looked up. They show him as a collector of precious pagan objects.'[16]

Freud allowed himself this one extravagance. He built up this collection over many decades, and seldom returned from his summer holidays — which often took him to Italy and Greece — without new acquisitions. Jones writes in his biography: 'Freud's fondness for collecting Greek, Assyrian and Egyptian antiquities played an important part in his emotional life and afforded him great pleasure and interest.'[17] Two of the pictures included in Jones's book show Freud's treatment room and also his study. The desk in each room is thickly covered with statuettes of Egyptian and Near Eastern gods and animal gods in copper and clay. One needs to try to imagine how the thoughts of this

10. SIGMUND FREUD

man could hardly ever escape from the sight of these statues of Hermes and other gods. Osiris and Isis, Aphrodite and Hermes, Ishtar and Horus were watching him more or less constantly. Were they reminding him of times when he thought differently about the soul to the way he did now, where in the exile of this incarnation he had trodden the path of death? Or was it the one sole unconscious memory that he granted himself in order not to be wholly absorbed in the night-phase of his existence?

If one had the capacity to hear the dialogue that Freud's soul had with the images of gods that accompanied him, one could have a better understanding of the true background of psychoanalysis. The innermost longings of this man were revealed in this special addiction which he allowed himself. His inner vision journeyed to Egypt and Babylonia; for in former times there had been a mystery-wisdom in those places which recognized man's androgynous nature in his spiritual structure and where Isis was not only the mother but also the wife and sister of the husband, son and brother Osiris.

But insight into mystery wisdom has been obscured, and the beginning of the age of light affected Freud in such a way that he tried to penetrate with the power of intellect into areas that are barred to ordinary thinking. If, however, someone approaches this shore who has not been called, everything that he perceives becomes a figment of his imagination; semblance mingles with true existence. This destiny of a great transgression was the lot of the researcher who was Sigmund Freud.

Loss of direction and downfall

In his formative years Freud had rebelled against all those powers which had formed and fashioned his epoch. These forces came towards him in the figures of Charcot, Breuer and Fliess; he made use of them, but only so far as they were of service to him, at which point he soon turned his back on them. He did not lovingly overcome them but proudly and dismissively distanced himself from them.

The result was his inner and outer solitude: that cloak of being different which enveloped him throughout his life and which signified to him both a protection but also a constant torment. It was with this self-imposed mask that he set about freeing the soul from its enchantment and unveiled certain realms of its existence which had hitherto remained hidden. Because he so relentlessly and single-mindedly began to gain insight into certain regions of his own life of feelings and impulses, and encountered similar phenomena residing in his patients, he gradually ceased to be aware of the many other areas of the soul out of which every human being lives and acts. He became as one possessed by his own particular sphere of research.

He was like someone who had set off for a walk in the morning when the sun was shining brightly and then found the entrance to a mysterious cave, entered it against all the warnings of his inner voice and — having got into it — began to assert that the world of day whence he had come had been nothing but an illusion, a pipe-dream of those who live in this cave.

The discoveries that he brought to light out of the unconscious were so fascinating that individuals on a path of discovery gradually found themselves inspired by them and began to research in a similar way. In comparison to the ideas of association psychology which were dominant at that time, Freud's results were stimulating and enlightening. They brought illumination to hitherto obscure realms of human modes of behaviour.

For Freud, however, those realms had become the only province of the soul which existed. He was sufficiently blind to believe that a natural-scientific method applied to the domain of the soul must necessarily arrive at purely zoological results. Many of the phenomena investigated by him wholly corresponded to reality, but the manner of his interpretations gave rise to a Darwinistic psychology on neurological foundations.

Thus he linked materialism together with agnosticism and

Darwinism, and stood at the gateway to the twentieth century proclaiming its truth by brandishing his scourge. Many of those who rose up against the Victorian epoch but did not have the courage to seek the spirit were attracted by him. Those who with justice rebelled against the old but nevertheless continued to devote themselves to agnostic ideas became his pupils. Prominent among them were educated and superficially educated people who had a similar Jewish background to Freud himself. They formed the advance guard to which the rest of the army of the psychoanalytical movement was linked in the course of the following decades.

Freud must quite likely have often felt himself to be like Moses: as one who likewise was leading a chosen people, which was made up of those who had come to know the 'true' nature of man, out of the land of Egypt. They, his pupils, saw themselves as chosen ones, who proudly and with hostility looked down upon the 'uncircumcised,' that is, those who had not been analysed, the *goyim*.

It is no mere chance that at the same time as the psychoanalytical movement arose, the wave of extreme nationalism represented by Zionism was stirring people in Europe. Both mass aberrations sprang from the same root, and both are a result of a Judaism subconsciously preparing for its downfall. This historical factor should not be overlooked if a true understanding of the mass psychosis of psychoanalysis and of Zionism is to be gained.

In no other place is the twilight nature of the psychoanalytic movement so apparent as in the story of the seven rings. In his collection of classical works of art Freud also possessed a large quantity of old engraved gems. From these he let his particularly faithful pupils make a ring. In the end there were seven such rings, and their bearers were Rank, Abraham, Eitingon, Ferenczi, Sachs, Jones and Freud himself. During the Psychological Congress in The Hague in 1920 Freud called the 'ring bearers' together and formed a kind of 'inner circle.' Sachs writes very revealingly about this event:

> Henceforward we would form a coordinated, but strictly anonymous group. The future of psychoanalysis should not be left to chance nor exposed to partisanship or personal ambition. It would be our duty to direct the ever widening movement by joining together and acting according to preconcerted plans. We ought to use for these ends our personal influence and our solidarity, but not rely on the authority given by office and title. To enable us to do our work unmolested, the fact of our organization had to be kept secret. Our circle was to be considered as completed, once for all, without further cooperation by other members.[18]

This core group held together for five years. Then Rank became an apostate, Abraham died, and the others felt themselves to be released from their obligations. Whether intentionally or unintentionally, Freud had in this case used an element of the old style of occult leadership. He united the individual pupils with himself initially by giving them a special sign — the ring; after this preparation he forged the group together into a ring whose gemstone he himself was. But he left the 'people,' the 'uninitiated,' in the dark as to who was actually leading them. He made them into a herd, while ensuring thereby that he would soon be in great demand.

Thus the outer entanglements gradually continued and an inner loss of direction followed; for in the course of his further research Freud entered increasingly into the realm of far-reaching speculation. The attempt to order man's various motivating forces led him to distinguish two principal spheres of the soul: Eros and Thanatos, or the instinct for self-preservation and the death-instinct. Margarete Susman describes them thus:

> Whereas the libidinal instincts, the instincts for self-preservation, restlessly seek immortality, another, opposite tendency of life which comes to expression

in the inorganic, seeks the opposite: a return to rest, to ossification. This battle between two opposite powers — of which the second, that which restlessly thrusts forward and has broken free from the maternal womb of eternal rest in order to be challenged by it in higher forms to ever mightier battles — breaks out in every primitive form of organic life ... And the primal hostile force that is opposed to life's urge towards immortality and hinders its unlimited realization, setting it boundaries and causing it to turn and change course, is death.'[19]

In this description one finds that watered-down mythology, that bombastic pantheism which was so formlessly proliferating in the work of Bölsche and Fliess, in Prentice Mulford and others. This mixture of half-baked mythology with sexual mysticism and psychology also appears in Freud's later writings. He was trying to apprehend the nature of the ego and began to identify the ego-instincts partly with the death-instinct and partly with the libidinal instincts. Through this he became embroiled in a whole network of entanglements.[20] Both the 'ego' and the 'id' eluded his insight and could be found neither in the realm of Eros nor in the domain of Thanatos.

It soon, however, becomes clear to anyone with a discerning eye that, with the name Eros, Freud was characterizing the working of Lucifer and, with the word Thanatos, the sphere of Ahriman. And when Margarete Susman fabricates the notion that out of the death-instinct in the soul a kind of awakening arises and describes this in such a way that it 'frees us from every warming and sheltering sheath of life, from every protective illusion' and thrusts us 'into the rarefied, ice-cold air of truth,' she is not describing the realm of truth but the land of the icy, death-like wasteland of Ahriman — that land to which Freud had to bring the tribute of his existence.

Because he gave himself up to the great bringer of solitude, Ahriman, part of Lucifer's activity was revealed to him. And since he accepted that the instincts for self-preservation and death were alone worth taking into account, he was unable to grasp that these two are merely the aberrations of a middle sphere of existence where He who said of Himself: 'I am the way, the truth and the life' is active. Freud was totally blind to this sphere of existence; his pupils and followers accordingly formed a front which necessarily behaved in an anti-Christian way. Hence Egon Friedell also calls psychoanalysis 'a new revolt against the Gospel which encompasses the whole earth.'[21]

In the final years of his life, when he had come to suffer constantly from a malignant tumour in the region of the mouth, Freud wrote his last book, *Moses and Monotheism*. There he tried to engage in a dispute with Christianity and did so on the strength of Darwinistic errors and psychoanalytical illusions.

He suffered under the idea that primal humanity developed in hordes and that the strongest 'male' made himself the leader of the horde:

> There rose before me ... the following hypothesis, or, I would rather say, vision. The father of the primal horde, since he was an unlimited despot, had seized all the women for himself ... One day, however, the sons came together and united to overwhelm, kill, and devour their father, who had been their enemy but also their ideal ... The totem feast was the commemoration of the fearful deed from which sprang man's sense of guilt.[22]

From this Satanic perspective Freud proceeded to an interpretation of Christianity. He regarded the Last Supper as a meal for the dead which recalls the murdering of the Father, and then wrote as follows about the arising of Christianity:

> It seems that a growing feeling of guiltiness had seized the Jewish people — and perhaps the whole of civilization of that time — as a precursor of the return of the repressed material. This went on until a member

of the Jewish people, in the guise of a political-religious agitator, founded a doctrine which — together with another one, the Christian religion — separated from the Jewish one. Paul, a Roman Jew from Tarsus, seized upon this feeling of guilt and correctly traced it back to its primaeval source [the murder of the Father]. This he called original sin; it was a crime against God that could be expiated only through death. In reality, this crime, deserving of death, had been the murder of the Father who later was deified. The murderous deed itself, however, was not remembered; in its place stood the phantasy of expiation and that is why this phantasy could be welcomed in the form of a gospel of salvation (Evangel).[23]

With such wishful illusions did Freud try to justify the sacrifice of his life. He knew in his own 'id,' his higher self, that all this was only a false path; but he had to continue on his way until the bitter end. He could free himself from the blood community of the Jewish people neither in his thoughts nor in his actions and thereby fell back again and again into old ideas which were no longer of any relevance for his time.

What Freud presents in the above passage needs to be contrasted with the following words of Rudolf Steiner if the truth of the matter is to be discerned:

> When Paul appeared with his interpretation of Christianity there was a fundamental break with the principle whereby human knowledge was determined by the blood ... For Paul was the first to declare that neither blood nor racial identity nor any factor by which human knowledge had been determined in pre-Christian times could continue to prevail, but that man must himself establish his relationship to knowledge through inner initiative; that there must be a community of those

> whom Paul designated as Christians, a community to which one professes allegiance in spirit and soul and to which one belongs not through blood-ties but because one has chosen to do so. Paul was well aware of the need to establish this spiritual community on earth, because the time was approaching when man's knowledge of outward, earthly realities would necessarily become utterly materialistic ... People had to learn to understand that that aspect of man's being which can be discerned here on earth through sense-perception alone may indeed perish and disintegrate, but that there is within him an essence not immediately perceptible in this physical frame which belongs to the spiritual world. Thus in future what would bind people together in this community of Christians was not to be dependent on the blood.[24]

However, Freud wanted to hold on to this blood community, because he found in the blood all those powers and forces that he had set out to research. Thus he also ultimately had to regard Christianity as springing from this root, because he accepted that the ground of all existence was to be found here. This was the last confusion into which he fell.

He died several weeks after the outbreak of the Second World War — on September 23, 1939 — in exile in London. He could not but see how the same demons of the blood which he, too, had served were now leading to the unleashing of the new war. In spite of the great fame by which he was surrounded, he stood abandoned and alone in the world. Sachs reports about this time:

> I saw Freud himself often, but always only for a short time. I found that the pain in his mouth hardly ever permitted him to sleep at night ... He looked very ill and incredibly old. It was evident that he pronounced every word at the cost of an enormous effort which nearly went

> beyond his strength ... Then came the hour of parting.
> [As I was going to America], he said: 'I know that I have
> at least *one* friend in America.'[25]

While he was feeling so abandoned that he spoke of having only one friend, whole brigades of psychoanalysts had begun to be active in America. After he had passed away his memory was honoured as something sacred, and his followers carried his picture around with them as a precious mummy. He himself ascended to other fields of activity, freed from what he had been compelled to do on earth.

Those words which Emil Bock wrote could serve as an epitaph for him:

> In the heights of the spirit the world of clear, pure,
> creative and healthy archetypes holds sway over man. If
> this world is forgotten, dark, pathological counter-images
> will all too easily be engendered in the depths of man's
> subconsciousness. In an individual human being the
> supersensible world which has been forgotten gives rise
> to illness, but within the compass of a whole age it leads
> to dramatic apocalyptic catastrophes.[26]

These words can be read as an interpretation of Sigmund Freud's own destiny. He created these counter-images because he had forgotten the archetypes; and the community that he founded was chosen through the fact that it appeared a the shadow of those events which were being proclaimed as a shimmering light in the dawn of the new age.

This was Freud's tragedy: that he went out to search for truth, whereas his path to the Mothers, to the depths of the soul, was deceptive and actually led him to Satanic illusions. It was a path, as Mephistopheles says to Faust, 'into an untrodden domain which none can enter, a path into what has not been asked for, and which none would request.'

Adalbert Stifter

11

Adalbert Stifter

Stifter (1805–68) was an Austrian writer, poet, painter and pedagogue. He has long been popular in German-speaking countries, but almost unknown to English readers.

Adalbert Stifter and death

During the night of June 24–25, 1867, the night after St John's Day, Stifter wrote the following letter to his wife seven months before his death:

> My Dearest Wife,
> It is well-nigh midnight on June 24. I woke at half past eleven full of anxiety, turmoil and dizziness. I could not endure being in bed any longer. I got up and dressed. Lest an accident befall me while I am here, separated from you, I am writing you these few lines to thank you for all the love and kindness which you have shown me in this life. This loving kindness has been greater than I have deserved. If I should now or at some future time be called away from you, you ought not to burden your heart with any great sorrow and spend the days that are still allotted to you in a mood of resignation and with fond memories of me. If I were with you, you would

comfort me; and your loving words would make it easier for me to get over my agitation. I really shall never go away from you. It is probably only a symptom of the kind I had twice in Karlsbad; but while it is lasting I always think that something immense is imminent. When will these nerves improve?[1]

The letter continues, but this passage is characteristic of Stifter's state in the last years of his life. A fear of dying and of death itself lived in his soul; they tormented and tortured him, and so he sought a hold and a support in this earthly world which nevertheless brought him only trouble and pain. Hence he reached out with both hands to his wife as his anchor. Even though he found her unbearable at times — which is why he would escape from her and wish that he had a different life — he was forever trying to get back to her, on the grounds that she was his salvation, like a capsized boat is to a drowning man.

Stifter was constantly travelling between Kirchschlag and Linz. The village meant 'fresh air' to him in every respect. 'The wonderful holy peace that emanates from these heights never fails to have restful and beneficial effect on my mood,' he writes from there. But since he bore the mark of death and kept on encountering it again and again, Stifter could not bear solitude. So he would return to Linz, to his warm dwelling, his nest with his niece, his wife Amalie, the cook, the cacti, the tiled stove and the comfortable bed. And then all his torments would begin anew: his body bothered and tormented him and gave him pain, and he again renewed his break for freedom.

This troubled existence came to a climax when he visited his beloved Lackenhäuser. This estate and lodging house lying at the foot of the Dreisesselberg had latterly become a preferred residence for Stifter. In this particular autumn he fled from Linz out of fear of cholera and had initially spent some beautiful and peaceful days in this place together with his niece. It was a warm and clear October, and Stifter was able to work on a picture that he was painting and enjoy the inner and outer peace. But then at the beginning of November it began to snow, and the way back to Linz was blocked. In addition, he received the news that Amalie was ill, and now he spent days and nights in painful anguish. He wrote to his wife every day; he spent significant sums so that a path would be cleared for him in order that a carriage could bring him to the road. But the snowstorm resumed every day, and this white element which for Stifter signified grace but also demonic power kept him imprisoned in this utterly lonely region far from those he loved. At the end of the month he broke the spell and walked — in the company of two local people — through storm and snow to the nearest little market town. On November 28 he finally arrived in Linz, but the following day he raced back again and on November 30 wrote from Kirchschlag to his 'most dearly beloved wife.' It became a remorseful letter about his so speedy flight.

Although these states became increasingly prominent towards the end of his life, the same torment and anguish had been exhibited in Stifter for several decades. Just as a pregnant woman hopes for and awaits with anxiety as well as joy the hour of birth from the beginning of her confinement, so was this writer constantly haunted by death's measured tread — although he was filled far more with anxiety and fear than hopeful anticipation.

Much of the wonderful harmony that flows from his tales and stories is an attempt to evade death and his fear.

The distinctive undercurrent of his existence was that he was seeking to escape death. In the entirety of *Indian Summer,* which in its conception and execution can be regarded as the high point of Stifter's creative work, death does not appear at all in its full power and magnitude. Even destruction and injustice are as it were banned from this book. It reveals a world which encompasses the life of nature and human beings in a state of unbridled harmony. There are young and old people, women and men, people of high and low birth, all of whom live and work together and are also connected through their destiny. But not a single one of them is summoned by death. It is a world that is immune to injustice, finality and parting. Thus the carriers of the action are also masters of their emotions; tears of emotion but not of grief are wept. There are smiles of joy but no laughter from high spirits. Man has not merely become the measure of all things but he has assigned himself a measure that enables him to achieve perfect moderation. If at any time an outlandish person prone to excess strays into this world, he has special abilities such as the zither player, who is always appearing and disappearing, and Roland, the brother of Eustach, who is also an artist, who comes and goes and demonstrates capacities which go far beyond the ordinary. The zither player and Roland could still die; but the others? Is it conceivable that Mathilde or even Natalie, or Heinrich's parents would be ill and succumb to death? This is the miraculous fairy-tale-like quality of *Indian Summer,* that one enters a realm where death has no power. Once the iron gates leading to the rose-house have opened and the owner, Freiherr von Risach, has admitted the guest, he has entered a world of eternal life. This life knows and recognizes growth and decay, it admires the richness of an ever-changing nature, its metamorphoses and transcriptions; but man, as a spiritual being, has an unchanging, ever-remaining existence.

After all, how can he pass away, since he is himself the measure and midpoint of all natural growth and all creaturely creation? No, his existence is deathless, without death. This is what Stifter wants to prove, this is what he begs for himself and for people in general, this is why he endlessly makes up and creates stories in which this paradise is made manifest.

At the end of many of his works one could simply say: 'And as they did not die, they are still alive today' — and it would be correct. For they do still live today and, moreover, in everyone: Witiko and Mathilde, Natalie and the confirmed bachelor, the two children from *Rock Crystal* and the three little ones from *Muscovite.* Likewise Margarita and her father, the colonel, the physician and Thomas, Johanna and Klarissa from *Hochwald,* and it is just as it says at the end of *Narrenburg:* 'Old Rupert is still alive. He sits forever on the sandy slope in the sun, smiling as he twiddles his stick with his fingers and tells stories that no one understands.'

Hence Walther Rehm also calls *Indian Summer* an idyll in the style of Schiller.[2] 'This was a poetic depiction of an innocent, happy humanity, this was man in a state of harmony and peace with himself and with the outer world ... the concept of a fully resolved struggle both in the individual and in society, of a free union of inclinations with the law and of the highest moral worth of a purified nature.'

It is, however, not the idyll of paradise, as Schiller understands it and Rehm interprets that is meant by Stifter. Not the paradise before the Fall but a premonition of the Eternal Jerusalem which can arise through the overcoming of sin — this is what Stifter longs for. Hence Rehm also quotes that very important letter of May 12, 1858 to Stifter's publisher and friend Gustav Heckenast:

> I soon came to master the initial outpouring of grief over my mother's death through my powers of reason, and, I may say, through my religious feeling, which I have developed to a significant intensity through my contact with nature and my experiences of human life. Grief of this kind jumps out at one like a snake, and I was ... virtually defenceless against it. But I plucked up my courage and overcame it. What came afterwards was almost worse. I spoke, I visited people, I joked and even laughed; but I was in a dismal state of emptiness and in a mood of desolation that even became oppressive and which I could do nothing about, because it arose from a shifting of a network of intimate and complex relationships to which I had long been accustomed, whose new nature could be placed on a sound and lasting footing only with time.

Here the 'snake' that 'jumps out' at Stifter out of the depths of his soul emerges into the light of day. What has taken place here is a 'shifting' or 'displacement'; something within him had thereby been displaced, driven insane, and he was confronted with death. Immediately afterwards he demands that 'a sound and lasting footing' is re-established, in order that the image of death can disappear again into the depths whence it came.

He longs to experience an 'Indian summer' himself in the way that Freiherr von Risach eternally enjoys it. 'For I want to die very late,' he wrote to Heckenast, and subsequently added: 'A home in Vienna, a charming but simple house in the country, some beautiful pictures and a life such as one can have amongst the flowers of the field. If fortune were not blind, something indescribably wonderful would be possible.'

Fortune, however, is always blind, but destiny has a visionary power. For death cannot be ignored or outwitted. The 'eternal within man' exists, though not as an earthly rose-house but as a heavenly dwelling. And so Stifter had to become restless and suffer, had to struggle through torment and anguish until he — who spent his life mulling over it — had to stand before the sight of death, of spirit-birth. But even then he could not endure it. In order to escape death, he took hold of a weapon and inflicted a mortal wound to his neck. It was the inexpressible, indescribable fear of death that led him to use the knife. He gave himself the gift of death in order to escape dying. He wanted a sacrifice, as in classical antiquity a lamb or a bull was sacrificed, in order to achieve eternity. He died three days later, without regaining consciousness; although shortly before his death, on the morning of January 28, 1868, he opened his eyes once more and they filled with tears.

These were the last greetings that he bequeathed to his beloved earth; what he had constantly and repeatedly tried to avoid — the dark gate into a radiant kingdom — he had to pass through as one making a sacrifice. It might well be supposed that he could decipher the inscription that can be read on the archway of the gate. It says, *In Christo morimur.*

Adalbert Stifter and life

The character of Roland from *Indian Summer,* who has already been mentioned, is one of those fleeting figures who appear again and again in Stifter's writings. For the most part they are on the fringe of both the story and the action and only occasionally, at particularly important moments, do they take a decisive part in events.

Thus the strange, dark-haired girl who appears completely out of nowhere and then accompanies the whole story called *Muscovite* is one of those fringe figures who are, nevertheless, of the greatest significance.

Roland, who moves with his paintbrush and his crayons from place to place, draws old churches and buildings and brings the results of his studies and work back to the rose-house, is likewise one of these. He is a fringe figure who lacks proper dimensions but makes an effort and gradually acquires them. Moreover, he is a painter.

So too is Friedrich, the young man from the story *Nachkommenschaften.* But as he comes from a race of stubbers (people engaged in land clearance) he has a strange hereditary characteristic, for 'each of his race was thoroughly imbued with the unceasing nature of his striving until it came to an end.' Thus Friedrich is completely devoted to his painting and knows nothing other than this. From morning until evening he stands at his easel completing a painting which is to correspond faithfully to reality. He gives everything to this task; his strength, his time, himself. But in the end he casts everything aside, destroys the almost completed picture and all the sketches belonging to it and begins a wholly new life through marriage, the state of matrimony and conjugal love.

As a result he tears himself away from the qualities that had been passed on to him, however noble they may be, and begins what for Stifter is 'a heavenly existence on earth': leading a life devoted to art and the study of nature on a country estate at his wife's side, surrounded by future offspring. The time that he had previously spent was only preparation; it still lay beyond the gate leading to the rose-house and through which only the selected few can go. However, a painter reaches such a state of existence only rarely. For by painter and graphic artist Stifter means, and is describing, himself; that part in him which creates pictures and which has constantly to struggle with the writer in himself. For the painter in Stifter comes out of his innate disposition and gifts; he brings the colours and the joy in using them with him. But the writer is the late and gradually achieved result of his existence.

Stifter knows his 'Roland' and his 'Friedrich,' as he is them himself at a certain level of his existence. He carries them with him in the blood as that force of nature which, in man, is the life that can toss him about hither and thither. It is the power which — rooted in the stream of inheritance — rules the body, determines destiny, brings about misfortune and causes passions. It is the creaturely power that each person carries within him but which he has gradually to overcome. Thus someone like Freiherr von Risach must spend the greater part of his life in solitude and mental anguish in order to make a sacrificial tribute for having secretly loved Mathilde and for not having told her parents about this love.

That power seems to Stifter to be symbolically identified with the art of painting and with the person who practises this art, the painter.

The figure of the 'painter' appears already in *Kondor,* his first story, unbridled and unbounded and unable to achieve a degree of moderation; hence at the end of the story it is said of him: 'And far, far in the ancient mountains of the Cordilleras there roams an unknown, strong, scornful man in order that he may seek there a new heaven for his turbulent, creative, thirsting, still innocent heart.'

In *Field Flowers* the diary of the 'painter' tells of his experiences and feelings, and again it is the as yet unbridled, natural and often mightily tempestuous aspect that appears there and comes to manifestation.

There can also be an intensification in the direction of the demonic and aberrational; thus already before the appearance of the strange girl in *Muscovite,* the grandmother tells the children the story of the Hagenbuch farmer who, as he was walking through the forest, suddenly hears a voice calling out to him: "'Yoke-bearer, yoke-bearer, tell the Sture Mure that the brindled cow is dead." The farmer looked among the trees, couldn't see or catch sight of anything, so he fled, setting off as quickly as he could, and arrived home with the sweat dripping from his brow.'

Here Stifter is describing the undercurrent of what 'the painter in us' is. The demonic power of the creative urge that holds sway throughout the whole of nature lives at te periphery of man's being but often penetrates deeper into it with both good and harmful effects and influences. Old people know these forces; whether it be the grandmother or the old farm labourer, the white-haired person or the grandfather — they are on account of their wisdom protected from the dangers of these demons. Thus children in their innocence also have an affinity with these outlandish forces. The 'painter,' however, as an adult standing in the midst of life, must find his refuge where those demons are compelled to be silent: in the ordered framework of the family. It creates a holy place which is magically safeguarded and protects the 'painter in us' from false steps and errors.

These demonic forces in nature and in our inheritance as human beings were the reason for the transformation that Stifter underwent between his 28th and 35th years; during this time he changed in every respect from being a painter to being a writer. He began to understand that his impetuous and unbridled nature as a painter could make itself useful perhaps also as a lyricist; but that the writer of epics, he who must describe, relate and devise, can be trained for this only through constant inner transformation.

The termination of his ill-starred relationship with Fanny

Greipl was by no means only externally imposed; he himself withdrew from this potential source of happiness, because he sensed that, even were it to come to fulfilment, this relationship would not lead to the awakening of his higher self. Renouncing Fanny was at the same time a relinquishing of painting. The painter was transformed into the writer; and if Stifter had the hope that in his marriage with Amalie Mohaupt he could create that magical domain where he felt protected and secure, his hope was indeed fulfilled.

However, he did not know that the other aspect of human existence would then begin to come to prominence in the form of his fear of death. Stifter discovered this only gradually. He escaped from his birth and from everything that was for him connected with it — the powerful driving forces, the painter's faculty of expression, the unbounded and also untameable powers of the Sture Mure. The further he distanced himself from these, so much the more threateningly and directly did the fear of death stare him in the face and, with it, the ever-growing dread of eternal extinction. 'No, I do not want to die, I cannot believe that annihilation is part of human existence.' This resounded in Stifter's heart, pounded at his breast and throbbed in his blood. In order to moderate and overcome these fears he devised the fairy-tale-like images of his characters, which brought him peace and inner equilibrium.

Stifter continued throughout his life to be a soul struggling between 'life' and 'death.' He fled from demonically inspired life and dreaded the inexorable nature of death. As a painter he battled with the forces of nature that hold sway over man; as a writer he practised the art of overcoming death, but for him himself it became an increasingly fruitless pursuit.

He was stretched between these two millstones of earthly existence and, with an unremitting intensity and a constantly renewed faith, he endeavoured to achieve this transformation.

The greater and wider the range of his literary work became, culminating in *Indian Summer* and the last stories, so much the less did he forget that the painter in him also demanded his rights. Thus he continued to paint constantly, and meticulously kept a book where he recorded how many hours he devoted to it. Between 1854 and 1868, when he met with death, he worked simultaneously on several pictures and endeavoured to portray what he felt in his landscapes. He called the pictures: *The Past, Roman Ruins; Merriment, Greek Temple Ruins; Solitude, Ruins with a Rising Moon* — and many more. Thus he devoted many hours to curbing the painter in himself, measuring the time he spent on it and thereby bringing it into a properly ordered structure.

He made the attempt to transform the painter so that life and germinal power were brought into order and the superfluity of existence became fused with law; he succeeded only in part; for at the end of his life the painter picked up the weapon and inflicted a bloody wound on his neck. Fear of death broke through the thicket which had been his means of exorcizing his violent impulses. This earthly life ended crushed between birth-forces and fears of death, but the soul was released, redeemed from this unremitting struggle.

In his literary works Stifter constantly transformed the leering ghost of destruction; he was able to restrain the demonic, blood-oriented power of his birth- and life-forces in the ordered garden of his marriage; but he could not transform it sufficiently. This beast tore the chain asunder and constantly wreaked havoc with his life. On one occasion he tried to describe this:

> Far back in the empty void something akin to ecstasy and delight powerfully took hold of my being with an almost destructive urgency which was like nothing I have ever experienced since. The distinguishing features that I recall are that there was radiance, a turbulent motion and something of a subterranean aspect. This must have been very early, for it strikes me that there is a high, wide obscurity of nothingness around the whole phenomenon.

Those violent forces which Stifter was forever holding in

check rose up out of this void, this darkness. There at the gate of birth, as one enters into life, one's family and one's race, there lie those aptitudes, gifts and qualities that make us into fringe figures and which so often cause the straight path of life to become crooked and confused. A little magic sometimes helps here, as for example the *Kuss von Sentze,* which has the capacity to establish peace and also love. But often no help is available, and yet nevertheless a fullness of life, an overwhelming power and a holy passion stream from this gate of birth, which releases the stream of life. Ever and again Adalbert Stifter had an experience of the knowledge which is inscribed on the archway of this gate: *Ex Deo nascimur.*

The Snow and the Roses

Stifter once reported the following about his childhood: 'I was told that at my birth it was very stormy and snowed heavily, and that I had immediately cried vigorously when I was only a few minutes old.' So it must have been an early winter which came on very abruptly in 1805 for it to have snowed already on October 23. This was in Oberplan (now Horni Planá), a little place in the southern Bohemian forest at the source of the Moldau (Vltava).

After his death, however, it was related that the children went ahead of the coffin in a long train on the morning of January 30 at 10 o'clock and attended the writer's funeral. As the procession was approaching the walls of the cemetery it began to snow gently, then the flakes fell more and more thickly and bier, tree and shrub were veiled in a pure whiteness. This was in Linz, and the children followed the supervisor of schools as he was borne to his grave.

Thus snow was whirling impetuously through the world when this man's birth took place, and covered this body's coffin in the gentle light of the winter morning, falling softly down

11. ADALBERT STIFTER

to the earth from the sky. Snow was Stifter's companion at the beginning and end of his life.

In his living world of pictures and symbols, snow is frequently a prominent theme. It appears in quite definite and specific places in the stories and is only part of a whole thematic sequence which includes hail and also ice and wintry light.

When Heinrich's descent of the mountain in winter time is described in *Indian Summer,* the snow plays a very special role. This element of nature is described in its grandeur and beauty in ever different ways, and the young man says to himself in retrospect:

> I was completely filled with what I had seen and found up there [in the mountains]. The deep feeling that had always been in my heart and which had given me the impulse to seek the tops of the mountains in winter had not disappointed me. A sublime feeling had entered my soul, almost as sublime as my love for Natalie. Yes, this love was further elevated and ennobled, and I fell asleep with reverence for the Lord our God, who has created so much beauty and made us so happy, when I returned to my bed in the homely room of the alpenhouse.

Thus here the snow is brought into a close connection with the sublime feelings of the human soul with respect to the creative greatness of the Father God. The snow that is the cause of everything in the story *Rock Crystal* has a similar quality. It begins to fall on Christmas Eve, 'to the delight of the children,' when they are returning home. More and more snow falls from the sky, covering the forest and the paths, and little brother and sister become completely lost in this whitish grey light, in the snow's enveloping security. 'But nothing was around them other than the dazzling whiteness, everywhere whiteness, but which itself surrounded them in an ever diminishing circle and was then changed into descending shafts of mist, consuming and obscuring everything beyond it in the insatiably falling snow.'

Here snow begins to manifest its night aspect, its insatiability and uniformity which enshrouds everything and makes it all the same. In *Rock Crystal* it is called 'one single white darkness.'

At the end of the story it stops snowing and the elemental power of the snow yields lovingly and protectively to the two innocent children. Sanna and Konrad reach their native climes again.

However, snow becomes particularly threatening and all-destructive when it develops a hardening quality and congeals into ice. This is described in *Mappe meines Urgrossvaters,* where in the icy forest the snow becomes the destroyer of all trees:

> The rushing sound which we had previously heard in the air we now knew at close hand; it was not in the air but was now beside us. It continued without interruption in the depths of the forest as branches and boughs cracked and fell to the earth. It was all the more frightening since everything was motionless; not a branch or needle stirred amidst the gleaming and glittering light, except when one looked again after a while at a tree that was bent over and saw that it was drawn down lower by the icicles.

Thus the destructive power of the ice into which the snow has turned becomes clearly manifest.

There is another theme in Stifter's work, that of redness and the rose, which strongly contrasts with this 'theme of whiteness.' As the sun rises again after the icy cold of Christmas night and summons the two children in *Rock Crystal* to break out of their shelter, there is the following description: 'At this moment the sun rose. A giant red disc rose into the sky above the snow and, as it did so, the snow around the children acquired a reddish hue, as though it were strewn with millions of roses.'

Heinrich in *Indian Summer* describes the approaching morning in the mountains in a similar way:

> As we were standing there and speaking, the mist in the East began to brighten in one region, the snowfields were

tinged with a more beautiful and appealing colour than the leaden grey that had previously covered them, and in the lighter region of the mist a point began to glow that became ever bigger and finally stood hovering the size of a plate dull red in colour but inwardly glowing like the fieriest of rubies. The sun had climbed above the lower mountains and broken through the mist.

The magical breath of day and the sun wafts over the white, cold snow, and the whiteness is thereby transmuted into redness and the red appears as 'millions of roses' that are strewn over it. Here where it simply brings the warming touch, the red is the fulfilment of what is demanded by the 'white darkness.' But it can also become stronger and hotter, as for example in *Mappe meines Urgrossvaters,* when the physician is suddenly struck by the pain of jealousy:

> Up where the red ochre stones reach up into the sky I passed by the Rothberg range, making a detour past the stones and beneath the pine trees towards evening, until I came out on the edge of the willow marshes. From there I walked to the Eschenwald, where I had seen the will o' the wisp, and from there I went on to the Haghaus. I had washed the blood from my hands in the Rotbach and dried them with a towel.

This is almost a painting, bathed in red, and describes the inner upheaval in the physician's heart. In *Field Flowers* the painter tells of 'the rosy cheeks that began to bloom through her movement,' and of the dancing girls who 'go hunting with wild fiery cheeks, ugly with their severe red faces' to the sound of the 'red incandescence of the dance music, which vibrated outside in jubilant sensual pleasure.'

Thus red can be an image of passion and sensual intoxication, of a superfluity of blood, but also of the soft and gentle effect portrayed in the image of the 'millions of roses' strewn over the snow. This theme is brought most fully to expression in *Indian*

Summer, where a wall of Freiherr von Risach's property is completely overgrown with roses. Here everything red is raised to a new dignity. No longer does it represent passion, or even the shame that sometimes breaks through in old age as a memory of youthful impetuosity. (Hence it is described with such forcefulness how Risach blushes 'as deeply and at the same time as beautifully as I had ever seen him do' when Heinrich asks him why he had not married Margarethe in old age.) Here the roses become something entirely new; something that is not merely the red of passion but also the white of snow and ice is uplifted above them. When Heinrich sees the roses blossoming on the wall for the first time, he describes it as follows:

> One day thousands of flowers had opened up beneath the clearest, most beautiful and deepest blue of the sky; it seemed that not a single bud lagged behind and remained closed. They covered the surface in their manifold colours ranging from the purest white to yellowish white, yellow, pale red, fiery red, crimson, violet-red and deep red, so that in looking alertly at them one wanted to admit that those country folk who almost revered roses and crowned themselves with these flowers at festivals and times of rejoicing were right.

Here the rose appears in its manifold variety of colours from white to deep red, combining snow and blood but also transforming one into the other; both reach up into a higher and nobler existence 'beneath the clearest, most beautiful and deepest blue of the sky.' The red of the blood that is active in the painter and the white of the snow — death and dying — which confronts the writer as a benevolent but also destructive force, are for Stifter the two poles of all creaturely existence. But there is a third element, a transformation which occurs when the human soul begins to resign itself to the 'law of gentleness': 'An entire life full of justice, simplicity, self-control, rationality, effectiveness in one's own circle and calm aspiration I consider to be truly worthy.' This is what Stifter writes in his famous foreword to *Coloured Stones*. But this is none other than what Rudolf Steiner formulated and what is spoken by many thousands of children throughout the world, beginning,

> To wonder at beauty,
> Stand guard over truth,
> Look up to the noble,
> Resolve on the good ...

In these words there comes to expression what Stifter sought to convey symbolically by roses. And when he lets Heinrich refer to the veneration that the country folk of olden times have for the rose, he is pointing to the mystery character of his symbol. In Eleusis the pupils appeared at festivals adorned with roses. Thus they manifested outwardly what had been fulfilled within them, in the soul realm: the law of transformation. They had to overcome both death and life within themselves; to transform both the painter and the writer in such a way that both life and death could develop towards spirit-birth. They then came to experience what Rudolf Steiner once expressed in mantric form:

> In light-and-air of spirit-land
> There grow the roses of the soul.
> And their raying red, downpouring
> Into the weight of Earth
> Fashions the heart of man.
> It rays again in the force of blood —
> The rose-red of the Earth —
> Forth into the spirit-fields.[3]

These spirit-fields are re-enlivened by that which human individuals who have transformed themselves are able to ray back as the rose-red of the earth into the snowy landscapes of the spirit-world. A foretaste of this can be found in Adalbert Stifter's work. When Rudolf Steiner — probably on the only occasion — said something about the writer, he spoke as follows:

Adalbert Stifter's grandmother said to the boy, 'Child, what is the redness of the sunset sky? Child, when this reddish glow appears, Mother Mary is hanging out her clothes, for she has so many clothes to hang out every evening in the vault of heaven.'

These are words on which the gods can draw for the further development of the world! Modern science tries as best it can to grasp conceptually how things are now. But this will never grow into the future; it is of the present. Adalbert Stifter's grandmother, who still retained much of what lived in people in former times, said something about which a modern scientist could only smile. He might perhaps find it rather nice; but it would not occur to him that it is of far greater significance for the cosmos than all his science when Adalbert Stifter's grandmother tells the child that the redness of the evening sky consists of the clothes that Mother Mary has hung out. For divine-spiritual forces have created it in order that what is now present in the cosmos may be developed further into the future.[4]

This is an indication of the seed out of which the tree of Stifter's work as a writer grew. It was the red glow of the evening sky and the image of Mother Mary that his grandmother gave him. She lovingly accompanied his first steps and sowed a seed in the child's heart which has yielded manifold fruit, the seeds of which are able to bring forth still more fruit in thousands of human hearts. These are roses of the soul which spring forth from his writings, which help the law of gentleness to come into its own in human souls and lead the ice and the glow within us to the Indian summer-like freedom of 'self-overcoming.'

Behind this, however, appears the sign of the cross surrounded by roses, that image which shines before Brother Mark in Goethe's poem, 'Die Geheimnisse' (The Mysteries) and teaches him:

11. ADALBERT STIFTER

> A person who overcomes himself is liberated
> From the power that binds all beings together.

This was the innermost melody of Stifter's existence. It was the sound of the bell that rang out for him ever and again and which, as the blue bell of heaven, protects and blesses the blooming of roses of all colours. On the rim of this bell these words can be inscribed: *Per Spiritum Sanctum reviviscimus*.

Adalbert Stifter and the nineteenth century

Schiller died in May 1805, and Stifter was born the following October. A few weeks after his birth the Battle of Austerlitz was fought in the same region, bringing a decisive victory for Napoleon. This was the historical background of Stifter's earthly beginnings.

His birthplace was Oberplan (now Horni Planá), a little place in southern Bohemia at the foot of the Bohemian Forest and in the region where the Moldau (Vltava) has its source. The Moldau, which becomes the main river of Bohemia, rises in this magical valley surrounded by forests of tall, dark conifers and towering mountains. The whole Bohemian countryside in its fullness is oriented around this river.

However, Stifter did not follow this river; had he done so, his life would have taken him northwards following the Moldau through Bohemia to the Elbe. Instead he turned towards the East and South; instead of making for Germany he went to Austria. He received his basic education as a boy at the famous Benedictine foundation of Kremsmünster, and his inner life was thereby formed by the liberal Catholicism of that time. From there he went to Vienna University, where he studied physics, mathematics and the natural sciences in order to prepare for the teaching profession.

It was the Danube and not the Moldau that became his

destiny. When he arrived in Vienna in 1826 Beethoven and Schubert were still alive, and the last radiance of the fading Biedermeier period surrounded the students. Little by little this last beautiful flowering of a life in which all humanity could share faded and was overwhelmed by the approaching night of the age of technology.

At this decisive turning point between 1828 and 1835 there also took place Stifter's gradual change from painting to literature. Some highly important events happened in these few years. Charles Darwin made his voyage round the world in the *Beagle* and assembled the basic elements of the theory of evolution. There was the dispute between Cuvier and Geoffroy Saint-Hilaire at the Paris Academy which led to the decisive victory of evolutionary theory. Karl Ernst von Baer, the great natural scientist, identified mammals as a group and described in detail the embryological development of the young chick. Urea, an organic substance, was artificially manufactured in the laboratory, and with Haeckel's birth in 1834 the agnostic scientist and technical expert made his entry into the earthly domain.

At the same time Hegel (1831) and Goethe (1832) died, but H.P. Blavatsky, too, was born (1831). Just at this time Kaspar Hauser appeared on the stage of European history; but his influence was prevented through his murder.

Whether Stifter consciously participated in, or was aware of, all these events is barely known. Nevertheless, he was their contemporary and participated on a soul level. His dealings with many significant people in Vienna at that time brought him many points of contact in the form of books and conversations where these events were reflected.

The education that he received in the Kremsmünster monastery led him to become affiliated with the liberalism that was stirring at that time. He belonged to the higher class of citizen — the teachers and professors and lower nobility, the physicians and artists — who were gradually developing liberal ideas. Stifter belonged in every respect to this historical vanguard, and

11. ADALBERT STIFTER

therefore also shared in many of the modern scientific abstractions and could no longer fully find the bridge between God and nature. This was the historical conflict in which he stood.

In the seven-year period from 1827 until 1834 the modern agnostic way of thinking overwhelmed the disintegrating bastion of the romantic philosophy of nature. Goethe's attempts at interpreting nature also succumbed to the advance of materialism. Stifter was at heart a Goetheanist, but he did not have the possibility of developing himself as such in the field of physics and mathematics. There was a gulf here which he was able to bridge through literature and painting but could not heal. In this way he outwardly became a sacrifice to agnosticism.

Rudolf Steiner has indicated how the 1840s were of world-historical significance, since it was at this time that liberal ideas began to develop. He said in a lecture of October 25, 1918:

> In the 1840s it seemed as if the impulse of the consciousness-soul age might stream into the political domain of the civilized world in the form of political views ... In the main, the carriers of the political life at that time were members of the middle class ... Mankind was given until the end of the 1870s ... One needs to be quite clear that it was in these decades — beginning from the 1840s — that what one calls liberal ideas flowed in an abstract form into human evolution, and that mankind was given until the end of the 1870s to grasp these ideas and relate them to the realities of the time. But the bearers of these ideas — the members of the middle class — missed their opportunity. There is something utterly tragic about the evolution of the nineteenth century. For those who listened to the speeches of the outstanding personalities of the middle class in the 1840s indicating what innovations should be brought to mankind in every sphere, these years seemed to herald the dawning of a popular movement! But ... the middle class missed their

opportunity. By the end of the 1870s, the bourgeoisie had failed to understand liberal ideas.[5]

Adalbert Stifter had not only shared in this missed opportunity but bore part of the responsibility for it and paid the penalty. The uprisings of the year 1848 left a deep impression on him. In his poetic heart he sensed the approaching darkness of the century's end and the middle class's obliviousness towards what was going on spiritually behind the veil of outward events. In *Kondor* a new period is announced. This introductory story to the *Studien* is at the same time the beginning of Stifter's path as a writer. The description of the balloon journey, which in an almost direct way makes this rising above the earth an experience, is like a proclamation of what will begin at the end of the century in the form of the age of light. One can recognize Stifter as completely a man of his time and as one who, together with others, went ahead of this epoch. But then his innermost ideal was overwhelmed, alienated, and he had to bring about what could no longer be achieved outwardly in the realm of the soul. He withdrew from active participation, became a school supervisor in Linz and tried to hold on to what was old and conservative so that the dark floods of the advancing waves of destruction would not be able to invade too quickly and directly. He stood there as a drowning man in the floods, but he was able to struggle inwardly for perfection rather than help to bring about a new order outwardly.

Stifter was part of this middle class which had missed an opportunity. He was aware of his guilt and his inability to defend himself against the rising flood. Only one thing was left to him: the inner path. He followed this path full of courage and devotion, but also with all the limitations that the bodily configuration of the nineteenth century brought with it. In this helpless and yet heroic tragedy Stifter was a brother and destiny-companion to Karl Julius Schröer, who was two decades younger. They had much in common in the ups and downs of their respective lives.

When Stifter died, materialism had reached its culmination.

11. ADALBERT STIFTER

In the same winter Ernst Haeckel gave his famous lectures on the Natural History of Creation in Jena, and Karl Marx published the first volume of his seminal studies, *Das Kapital*.

In the year of Stifter's death Rudolf Steiner was seven years old. With courage and a mighty cognitive power, the latter opposed agnostic science with a new science of the spirit. It was not long before he, too, went to Vienna as a student, where in 1879 he met Karl Julius Schröer and, at his behest, was entrusted with the task of renewing the Goethean conception of the world. What was not yet achievable for Stifter and Schröer was inaugurated by Rudolf Steiner.

Initially, however, darkness extended everywhere, and Stifter's death was wholly veiled in obscurity; it was a downfall, a defeat in a completely spirit-forsaken epoch. Shortly after his death Johannes Brahms composed the 'German Requiem.' It is as though the divine order of the world was celebrating the death of a hero of the soul through this choral work. Perhaps it was indeed the case that this requiem was the answer of the cosmos to the demise of the human being Adalbert Stifter.

Wilhelm Dilthey

12

Wilhelm Dilthey

Dilthey (1833–1911) was a German historian, psychologist and philosopher.

Dilthey's Life

Wilhelm Dilthey was born on November 19, 1833. The last, almost already disappearing reflection of the great classical and romantic period surrounded his entry into earthly existence. Goethe had died in the previous year and Hegel had been stricken by cholera two years earlier. Many living witnesses of the past were still alive, however; Schelling, who would be appointed to Hegel's chair in Berlin, Clemens Brentano and his sister Bettina von Arnim were still there. Mörike was writing poetry and Hölderlin was dreaming his life's dream in the Tübingen tower room. The great naturalists Carus, Alexander von Humboldt and Gotthilf Heinrich von Schubert carried the spirit of the previous period forward as forgotten heroes of a forgotten epoch. At the end of this year 1833 Kaspar Hauser was stabbed in Ansbach and died on December 17, as a result of this misdeed. It was the concluding phase of a great period; the night of the nineteenth century was beginning.

Johannes Brahms was Dilthey's exact contemporary. Born in 1833, he also lived in the evening phase of a great past. All who were born shortly before or around 1833 — Karl Julius Schröer, Hermann Grimm, Josef Joachim, Ralph Waldo Emerson and many more — had a similarity in this respect. They formed a bridge spanning the period until the end of the century which fostered a connection with a science of a different kind — the new science of the spirit.

Dilthey came from an old Protestant family of pastors. His grandfather and great-grandfather had been pastors, and his father was active as a member of the ecclesiastical council in Mosbach-Biebrich on the Rhine. He 'belonged to the rationalist school. With his warm affection for nature he sensed the proximity of the Godhead in nature and admired the Creator in his works.' The inflexible sermonizing which was totally overcome in the son was already beginning to disappear in him.

Wilhelm was born in Mosbach as his parents' eldest son. Three more children followed, two sisters and a brother, with whom he grew up in his parental home. It must have been a carefree and happy childhood and youth. He learnt with ease and passed his school-leaving examination on April 1, 1852 with the best marks of the school, and as valedictorian had to give a farewell speech. His theme was 'The Influence of Greek Antiquity on Young People.'

In accordance with the family tradition he was, as the eldest son, intended for the priesthood, and he therefore initially studied at the Theological Faculty in Heidelberg. He remained there for the first three semesters, and later transferred to Berlin. His father was not altogether happy with that, but Wilhelm did his best to persuade him to go along with it. He wrote to him in the summer of 1853 while still in Heidelberg:

> It is of the greatest value for every person's views to have lived once in a big city, and I shall never get an opportunity later. One can learn to understand life on a grand scale and experience all-round activity only in a largish city. And if I tell you that I have a greater need

12. WILHELM DILTHEY

than most people of the kind of flexibility and having one's corners rubbed off that Berlin specializes in, you will surely not raise any objections.[1]

He goes on to point out that he needs to see works of art and go to the theatre, and then continues: 'As for the marvellous music in Berlin I shall turn to my mother, who knows that there are few pleasures in the world to be compared with listening to a Beethoven symphony.' And then he defends himself against the ecclesiastical councillor by adding: 'Luther and Schleiermacher, our two greatest theologians, have understood that music is the closest sister to religion and that listening to music — if it is true music — is a religious act.' His father agrees, and the son is now allowed to go to Berlin, where, with brief interruptions, he was to spend the rest of his life.

The young student was extraordinarily industrious. He liked studying, and the more aspects it had the better. Although he was enrolled in the theological faculty, he attended many lectures of the other faculties. What he liked most of all was studying in his room, isolated and undisturbed from outside. He delved into the writings of the Church Fathers, concerned himself intensively with the Gnostics and made a thorough study of church history. In addition he read a very wide section of European literature, attended the big concerts, the theatre and shared in intimate reading circles where Plato, Shakespeare and many other writers were studied.

The future classical philologist Hermann Usener, who also became his brother-in-law, and the philosopher and ethnologist Moritz Lazarus were among his most intimate friends. It was a group of people who were very awake and sensitive to the approach of a new cultural epoch and also wanted to help to bring the future age about. Their endeavour was to encourage an exact scientific discipline within the humanities.

> I have embarked upon the path of critical, historical research and I am serious about it, so that it would make

me unhappy if I were to give it up for good and all on the grounds that I can barely see where it is leading. For these things can never be studied retrospectively, because one never retains the interest in these minutiae that one has while being one of those searching for truth.

Thus wrote a young man who was not yet twenty-one and knew nothing of his ultimate goal but nevertheless believed that he had found the path. A year later he writes: 'There can be no richer and more wonderful subject than church history with which I am now wholly preoccupied.' Theology, philosophy, music, literature — they were all intermingling, beginning to associate with one another and form the first general perspectives of past epochs. An imaginative power was beginning to be active in Dilthey.

For the sake of his father he took his state examination in theology, and soon afterwards (in November 1856) sat the state examination for a teaching qualification. He then immediately joined the Joachimsthal grammar school as a teacher in order to gain some teaching practice and experience of education. What he really quite single-mindedly wanted was to qualify as a university lecturer. This aim, which had achieved certainty in his mind shortly after he arrived in Berlin, now began to be realized. In a short outline of his path of studies which he wrote in 1870 for Wilhelm Scherer he put it very clearly: 'Thus I arrived at university, where very soon I formed a plan to link church history and the history of dogma to the study of the Christian worldview in the West and to pursue a university career.' This makes it plain that his inner aim was to present an account of 'the history of the Christian worldview in the West.'

He did not remain a school-teacher for long. He taught Latin, German, Hebrew, religion and history until the autumn of 1857. Then he left his post as a teacher and thereafter lived entirely from his studies, initially becoming a private tutor. What he had previously begun he now pursued more intensely. He focussed mainly on Schleiermacher. 'At Jonas's* fortuitous suggestion,' Dilthey reports, '... it chanced that I became involved with Schleiermacher's estate.' And he thought that 'here what people in olden times had necessarily to divine could be made transparently clear from adequate sources.' Thus it turned out that after Jonas's death he continued to work on Schleiermacher's unpublished writings and edited his correspondence with Friedrich Schlegel.

In addition, he worked on a prize essay for the Schleiermacher foundation on 'The Relationship of Schleiermacher's Hermeneutics to the History of Interpretation in Philosophy and Theology.' For this he received not the ordinary prize but double the amount 'in recognition of the extensive study and the thoroughness of the research.' Dilthey wrote of the ensuing period:

> From the treatise, which had not yet been printed, there arose the intention of a life of Schleiermacher. But my medieval studies had the first claim on my attention. At the same time I attended Ranke's seminar in order to learn his methods. In addition, I entered strongly into political history, read the three great Greek historians and now stood between history ... and philosophy.

Only in 1864, thus seven years after he had stepped back from teaching, did he gain his doctorate with, as he said himself, a 'very superficial work on Schleiermacher's ethics,' and a few months later he qualified as a university lecturer at Berlin University with an essay, 'Attempt at an Analysis of Moral Consciousness.'

Two years later he responded to a call to go to the university in Basle, went to Kiel after two years as a Professor of Philosophy and again after some time from there to Breslau. At the age of forty-nine he returned to Berlin. Now, in 1882, he was teaching in the same place where Fichte, Hegel and Schelling had been before him.

---

* Ludwig Jonas was executor of Schleiermacher's literary estate.

Until this point he had tried to draw history and philosophy closer together. He described Schleiermacher's life and published individual studies of German historians. In his inaugural address when he was nominated a member of the Berlin Academy of Sciences in 1887 he said emphatically: 'I have come here from history. When I was studying here, the school of history was still surrounding me.'[2]

Only after his resumption in Berlin did he try to formulate the foundations that he sought to lay to philosophy as a science. In 1883 the first volume of the *Einleitung in die Geisteswissenschaften* (Introduction to the Humanities) appeared. By revising the concepts of 'understanding' and 'experience' he developed a renewal of hermeneutics. He applied this to the most diverse materials and areas of intellectual history, political and legal history. His attempt to include as much as possible in the sphere of his observation and philosophical consideration also led him to write basic treatises on psychology and pedagogy.

The general account that he had envisaged of a 'history of the Christian worldview in the West,' which would have gone far beyond his capacity, did not come to fruition. Hence his daughter wrote to him:

> When in former times I used to accompany my father on his walks in the Grunewald, he often spoke to me of how all his creative work had really been no more than carrying out the thinking and planning of his youth. It was the tragedy of his life that he had reckoned with spans of time that are not granted to a man, and so ever increasing quantities of uncompleted projects piled up around him, which made him severely depressed and did not allow him to sleep at night.[3]

Out of this mood of failure he put together a further collection of essays in 1911 under the title *Die geistige Welt. Einleitung in die Philosophie des Lebens* (The World of the Mind: Introduction to the Philosophy of Life). In the foreword he tried to sketch the path of his intellectual development. But this foreword, too, was not completed. He died unexpectedly on October 1, 1911, aged 78, in his beloved Seis, on the slopes of the Schlern in South Tyrol.

Dilthey's ideas

Even if one of those who knew Dilthey best, his pupil and son-in-law Georg Misch, was of the view that the *oeuvre* of this philosopher does not have anything of a fragmentary nature but is a self-contained whole, this assumption should probably be understood as deriving solely from a love and reverence for Dilthey. For in comparison to what he had sought to achieve it was no more than a torso. Misch wrote in this connection about Dilthey's individual explorations: 'They are investigations that draw ever wider circles from a constant focus where each part has its background, in which they all cohere and which was elaborated to a far greater extent than most of his unfinished essays would lead one to suppose.'[4]

We shall now try to discover this 'focus' and also the 'background' of Dilthey's thought. It seems to me to be the case that Dilthey himself did not all that often say anything about either of these elements. On two occasions, however, he did: in his inaugural address for his professorship in Basle and many years later in an address that he gave in Berlin on the occasion of his seventieth birthday festivities. The former points more towards the source of his aspirations, the latter represented an attempt to describe his own historical position.

He spoke with remarkable clarity in the Basle address. It had to do with the 'poetic and philosophical movement in Germany' between the years 1770 and 1800. He declared his full commitment to modernism and saw himself by no means as conservative but as an innovator: 'Philosophy, too, has joined the circle of the empirical sciences, which focus on the right relationship of phenomena.

It works in tandem with the other sciences on the great problem of establishing an empirical science of mental phenomena, and I consider this to be the primal task of our generation.'

He then shows himself to be a modern researcher, who must necessarily reject the absolute validity of philosophical systems but who endeavours to understand their historical place and the need for their having arisen. 'Historical study seems to me to open up a viewpoint through which the universal significance of systems can be truly evaluated, however openly and unconditionally their logical and metaphorical basis has to be rejected. We understand what the nation found so persuasive about them, and rightly so.'[5]

A new focus of attention was introduced into the humanities: the idea of evolution. Darwin's book *On the Origin of Species* had appeared eight years before this address, and in the winter semester of the year of the Basle address, 1867, Ernst Haeckel began his lectures on the Natural History of Creation at Jena University.

In both instances the same intention, the same will, was seeking to break through: to understand both nature and history, the manifoldness of the forms of natural creation and also the great variety of the results of human intellectual endeavour, out of the concept of evolution.

Just as Haeckel endeavoured to track down the laws of organic form, so Dilthey tried to decipher the laws of intellectual development over the course of human evolution. He saw the same impulses in both poets and philosophers. Indeed, he linked the two forms of expression together when he said: 'The systems of Schelling, Hegel and Schleiermacher are merely the logical and metaphysical formulations of this view of life and the world developed by Lessing, Schiller and Goethe.'

> This is the eternal oneness,
> Revealing itself in manifold ways;
> The great in small things, the small in great,
> Everything in its own fashion.

12. WILHELM DILTHEY

In these lines by Goethe there comes to expression this general law that Dilthey also followed. What had been prepared since the beginning of the century by Lamarck and Goethe, Geoffroy Saint-Hilaire and Meckel in the scientific domain, and then came to be considered with ever greater intensity by people in general, was extended by Dilthey to an area which had not hitherto been included in the compass of the idea of evolution.

Dilthey describes in his Basle address how the 'view of life and the world' of this period between 1770 and 1800 came to expression in three generations. The path went from Lessing through Goethe and Schiller to Hegel, Schelling and Schleiermacher. He concluded his address by stating: 'The need to understand the meaning of the world is eternal. But I well know that we all — whether consciously or unconsciously — participate in it, we feel somewhere at home in it in our deepest souls — and that it does not satisfy the claims of the feelings and convictions of a completely different generation.' He knows himself to be a representative of this different generation, and he writes in his diary ' ...that the urgency of the times and their seething inner aspirations are something we wholly identify with. It was present in the colourful activities in Weimar; it lived in the serious librarian in Wolfenbüttel; and it is a theme that leads us to burn our midnight oil.' He feels himself to be linked to the stream of the history of ideas; he feels at one with Goethe and Lessing. But despite this knowledge of being at one with the great figures of the German past he has to opt for the modern path and pursue philosophy historically rather than systematically.

Here lay the focus for all his research. But he himself was a living, self-evolving element of the context that he describes. With each of his endeavours he grew and underwent a transformation. Hence he was an opponent of systems of any kind. He wanted to continue his development and remain inwardly active, in order that he might do justice to the times, people, epochs and streams that he was describing in their own terms. This was his life's philosophy: 'to seek to understand life as it really is.'

In his 1875 treatise on the 'Study of the History of the Sciences of Man, Society and the State,' he states quite paradigmatically:

> Man's task is not to be but to act; the value of his work is measured not in accordance with what it means to his individuality as a whole but in terms of its significance to the evolutionary process of which it is part. And what can be said of its worth can also be said of how it arises. For a person does not simply have ideas that work creatively within him *but is taken hold of by them*. And the impulses of the distinctive form of his activity develop to an overwhelming extent out of the circumstances of the circle in which he is working. [Emphasis added.]

A person finds his true worth in doing and accomplishing, as part of his time and of the ideas and impulses with which it is imbued. He is an active participant who engages with the stream of events. The task of philosophy is to describe and recognize this stream of historical becoming. No longer is it objective knowledge but a description and, as such, part of what has been experienced. Dilthey dethrones philosophy by drawing it into the fields of other scientific disciplines. One must also reject the notion of a ruling power of reason, and Hegel's system should be regarded as an expression of its time rather than an eternal truth. 'The rational structure of the world has turned out to be an illusion in nature and history,' he wrote in his note-book.

Thus deeds rather than reason become the central driving-force of all that arises in the course of the evolution of mankind. This is the source of the way that Dilthey looked at things.

However, the background to the development of what he put forward lay in a particular situation that arose around the middle of the nineteenth century in Berlin. Dilthey was in this respect

12. WILHELM DILTHEY

conscious of his destiny and described it in the address on the occasion of his seventieth birthday. The first sentence already makes reference to it: 'When I came to Berlin at the beginning of the 1850s ..., the great movement leading to the definitive constitution of history — and, hence, the humanities as a whole — as a science was at its height.' Then he mentions all those whom he met at that time or had something to do with: Wilhelm von Humboldt, Savigny, Grimm, Bopp, 'the founder of comparative linguistics,' Trendelenburg, 'whose dominant position has been lost sight of today,' Niebuhr, Böckh, Mommsen and many others. At the end he speaks of Ritter and Ranke with much reverence and then says: 'I owe the orientation of my mind to these great impressions. I have tried to write the history of literary and philosophical movements in the light of this universal conception of history. I undertook to investigate the nature and conditions of historical consciousness — a critique of historical reason.'[6]

And then come the statements which are perhaps the most important for understanding his intellectual aspirations and with which he concluded this confessional address:

> The finiteness of every historical phenomenon, whether it be a religion or an ideal or philosophical system, consequently the relativity [here he gets to the point!] of every kind of human conception of the connection between things is the last word of the historical world-conception, everything flowing, nothing constant. And on the other hand there looms the need of thinking and the aspiration of philosophy for a knowledge that is universally applicable.

This becomes for him the greatest question, for he recognizes what the threat is here:

> but where are the means to overcome the anarchy of convictions that threatens to take hold?' And he

concludes: 'I have worked throughout my life on solving the problems which ensue. I can see the goal. When I fall by the wayside, I hope that my young companions on the journey, my pupils, will follow the path to the end.

All 'universally applicable knowledge' could be made available for him against the background of the universal history of his youth. Nevertheless, it had to be sought, for somewhere — but where? — it too must have its place. Here we find Dilthey's innermost need, which was never fulfilled.

In a letter to his brother Karl written from Basle on July 7, 1868, he mentioned the fact that he had heard a physiological lecture and was 'doing physiology.' The previous year he had studied the physiology of the senses with the anatomist Wilhelm His, because he anticipated receiving significant help for his efforts concerning aesthetics. This need for natural-scientific insights lay at the foundation of his endeavours to attain objectively valid knowledge.

His attempts to sketch the basic outlines of a psychology went in the same direction. Firstly, in 1888, he devoted a whole chapter of a treatise entitled 'Concerning the Possibility of a Universally Applicable Pedagogical Science' to the 'qualities of soul-life which make possible a system of rules for education.' Hence the starting-point here is a 'universally applicable' rather than a relative pedagogy, as was to find its foundation in psychology. If one reads this proposal, one recognizes the extent to which Dilthey was imprisoned in the natural-scientific mode of thinking of that time: 'We view every sentient, mobile creature as living in a manner appropriate to the maintenance and, indeed, the enhancement of its own existence and the existence of its species. The actions that convey this character we call expedient.'[7] All the same there is much in this treatise which — despite its theological thrust — contains new impulses. There is a glimmer of the threefold picture of soul-functioning in thinking, feeling and will.

12. WILHELM DILTHEY

The 1894 essay, 'Ideas Regarding a Descriptive and Analytical Psychology,' was considerably more far-reaching. Of particular significance here is the attempt to establish a universal psychology in threefold form. A 'structural connection in developed soul-life' needs to be found through which 'intelligence, impulses and feelings and also acts of the will are combined ... into an ordered whole.' This would be a kind of architecture of the soul. Then a second principle results, 'which works as it were in a longitudinal direction: that of evolution.' Dilthey sees this above all as a purpose-led influence. As a third element he identifies 'the change of conditions of consciousness.'

> Only by understanding this overall situation, according to which each individual act is in its manifestation and character determined by the totality of the soul-relationships which have been acquired, does one find the true connections between the teachings of the restrictions of consciousness, the unity of this same consciousness and the differences of our inner states.

In this endeavour to define the three regions of psychology and to be a teaching of the human soul, a principle shines forth which found a first fulfilment in three series of lectures that were given in 1909, 1910 and 1911 entitled Anthroposophy, Psychosophy and Pneumatosophy.[8] In these lectures Rudolf Steiner comprehensively describes the structure or architecture of the soul, its functioning in change and development and the way that various spheres of consciousness work through it.

With Dilthey it remained only an attempt to approach the real roots of a 'generally valid knowledge.' Neither the natural science nor the psychology of his time could furnish him with the necessary foundations.

Again and again he set about finding the general laws of spiritual existence and — as he called it — the 'world of the mind.' Even at the age of 74 he wrote a lengthy treatise on 'The Nature of Philosophy,' in order to establish the core of all knowledge.

He tries to approach this essential core in stages through a series of carefully and circumspectly constructed circles, but he does not succeed; because the power of is thinking is not able to reach beyond itself: 'It is not possible to gain a deeper understanding of the world that is given to our experience, the knowledge of which is the task of the various sciences, through a metaphysical method differentiated by its processes.' And he again tries to establish some clarity for himself out of an analysis of soul-life. But he only gets sufficiently far to be able to say: 'At each point of this process (which brings forth the various experiences of life and the world) impulses and feelings are at work. In these can be found the focus of our soul-structure; all the depths of our being derive their motivation from this source.'

What he then manages to achieve is an overview of the various philosophical systems in accordance with the soul-sphere out of which they have arisen. It makes a difference whether it is observation and thinking, or feeling, or 'the behaviour of the will,' that determines a world-conception.

If, however, one reads this late treatise with the question in the background as to what Dilthey was really hoping to find in this inspired piece of research, even though he was unable to understand it, it suddenly becomes clear that he means and describes — but nevertheless cannot name — the working of the human I. He knows that man as an individuality is the source of all development. However, he cannot conceive of the I as a spiritual reality, although he describes its aspects and effects. For this 'insatiable need for an ultimate awareness of being, reason, value and purpose and their relationship in a world-conception' which Dilthey calls philosophy is in its essential reality man's higher self.

Dilthey did not succeed in recognizing this, for his knowledge did not extend to such a point. He acted and felt and wrote out of this ego and had the capacity to empathise in an inspired way with thinkers, writers and musicians. His 'philosophy of life' was an expression of this higher ego actively engaged within him. His

12. WILHELM DILTHEY

portraits of Lessing, Hölderlin, Novalis and many others were only possible out of a highly developed sense of I. Nevertheless, he was blind to the instrument out of which he worked and lived.

Dilthey's destiny

Towards the end of his book *The Riddles of Philosophy* Rudolf Steiner gives a detailed presentation of two modern thinkers, Dilthey and Eucken. He describes both in the chapter 'Modern Man and his World Conception' and mentions their names several times in the course of the final chapter, 'A Brief Outline of an Approach to Anthroposophy.'

As a conclusion to the description of the great thinker W.H. Preuss, thus before Dilthey himself is considered, Rudolf Steiner says: 'The way towards the riddles of the world in modern philosophy must go through an investigation of the human entity manifested in the self-conscious ego. This becomes apparent through the development of this philosophy.'[9] And then Dilthey is discussed in such a way that a certain aspect of his thinking, which endeavours to comprehend the reality of the external world, is referred to. In this sphere the efforts through which Dilthey arrived at the insight that certainty regarding a real external world would never be gained through sense-perceptions and thinking remain no more than an illusion. The cause for the certainty of our feeling that we live in a reality lies, by contrast, in the realm of the will, where man encounters the resistance of the world. Rudolf Steiner goes on to explain why this problem is in any sense a question for Dilthey and other modern thinkers. 'The "ego" that had ... separated itself from the world, strives to find its way back into the world from what appears in its own consciousness as a state of loneliness.'

What is under consideration here is a renewed understanding of the human ego, which in the course of modern history has become increasingly separate from the surrounding world because of the development of ego consciousness and is now trying to regain its access to this world. Dilthey's endeavours stand in the stream of this development, for the whole of philosophy shares this concern of rediscovering the reality of this ego. Rudolf Steiner, citing some words of Franz Brentano, puts it thus: 'What is essential, however, is the fact that philosophy arrived at reflections of this kind on its way ... to "gain certainty for the hopes of Plato and Aristotle concerning the continued life of our better part after the dissolution of our body".'

Even though they did not yield fruit, Dilthey's efforts were concerned with recognizing this. Steiner says of him:

> He is intent on finding an element *within* the soul that does not *spring from the soul* but belongs to an independent realm. He would like to prove that the world enters the experience of the soul ... In this manner he is led to recognize the spiritual life as something of a higher significance than the mere natural existence ... as a counterbalance to his recognition of natural development, he insists on the independent existence of a spiritual world.

This clearly indicates the fundamental contradiction in Dilthey's thinking and existence: that he extended the law of natural evolution into the sphere of mankind's intellectual development but did not comprehend man as an individuality. The personality is part of the streams that become active through it. That the individuality itself dwells in an actual world of spirit whence it receives its impulses is a closed book to Dilthey. He even has to deny the possibility of such knowledge, because — not going beyond Kant — he rejects all metaphysical knowledge.

In the introductory sentences to the last chapter of *The Riddles of Philosophy* Rudolf Steiner continues:

12. WILHELM DILTHEY

> what [these thinkers] have to say often appears as if driven by hidden forces, which they are unwilling to acknowledge and from which they recoil. Forces of this kind live in the thought worlds of Dilthey, Eucken and Cohen. They are led by cognitive powers by which they are unconsciously dominated but that do not find a conscious development within their thought structures.

These words give a clear indication of the conflict that we found in Dilthey; for he was indeed dominated by forces that he cannot master and, hence, was unable to develop. But what is the nature of these powers? Is it at all possible to gain an understanding of them?

The three philosophers referred to by Steiner were born quite closely together. Dilthey saw the light of day in 1833, Cohen in 1842 and Eucken in 1846. (Meanwhile, Nietzsche had been born in 1844.) These years introduced a period of world evolution which was of the greatest significance for the spiritual life of mankind. Rudolf Steiner has referred to this from various points of view. It was the time of a battle which took place in the spiritual worlds:

> And so one can observe that the years from the 1840s until the year 1879 were the time of a major battle in that super earthly domain which borders directly upon our earthly world. This was a hard, arduous battle which that spiritual being who may be called the Archangel Michael had to fight against certain opposing spirits.'[10]

In another context Rudolf Steiner spoke about this as follows:

> Thus those people who were born in the 1840s beheld the beginning of the spiritual battle as souls before their birth. If one bears this in mind, one will be enabled to have considerable understanding for the outer and inner

destiny-experiences of such people ... So this battle took place in the 1840s, 1850s, 1860s and 1870s; and its conclusion was that in the autumn of 1879 Michael and his hosts were victorious against certain Ahrimanic powers.'[11]

Dilthey lived out his childhood and youth under the impression of these experiences. He, together with many other leading contemporaries, perceived this approaching battle and were later overshadowed by it. The last ray of light from the time of Goethe still surrounded him and his exact contemporary Johannes Brahms. Because of this he was endowed with the breadth of the sense of ego with which he was able to interpret the great figures of the past through reflective experience. Eucken and Cohen no longer had this possibility. For them philosophy had become an abstraction, because it was under the same dark cloud as Dilthey's attempt to find a generally valid knowledge.

When — three years after 1879 — he became Professor of Philosophy in Berlin and, as it were, became the successor to Hegel and Schelling, his relativism and his rejection of metaphysics prevented him from having insights into the living world of spirit. But he was honest; he forbade himself to believe something that he could not know, and therefore escaped the temptation to which Eucken was subject: of speaking about the spirit while denying the true spirit.

The knowledge of his youth that the impulse of the new is also accessible by 'burning one's midnight oil,' the fire that blazed from his address in Basle, was the reflection of that light which he had unconsciously beheld: the light which radiated from the hosts of Michael into the souls of human beings. At the same time, however, the darkness of the opposing powers was also exerting its influence and veiling the ego with a shadow that his striving for knowledge could no longer penetrate. Hence his endeavours remained unfulfilled, and what he left behind was merely a noble fragment. Rudolf Steiner said,

12. WILHELM DILTHEY

> Several philosophers, such as Dilthey, Eucken and others, direct philosophical investigation toward the self-observation of the soul. But what they observe are those experiences of the soul that form the basis for the self-conscious ego. Thus, they do not penetrate to the sources in which the experiences of the soul originate.[12]

One would suppose that this probably happened for these thinkers only after they had passed through the gate of death. It is striking to find that on the day of Dilthey's death (October 1, 1911), a Sunday shortly after Michaelmas, Rudolf Steiner gave the lecture in Basle on 'The Etherization of the Blood.'[13] This was one of those instances when he spoke about the appearance of the etheric Christ and described the soul's nature in waking and sleeping and in its relationship with the spiritual world.

13

Karl Eugen Neumann

Neumann (1865-1915), an Austrian linguist, was the first translator of the Pali Canon of Buddhist scriptures into a European language.

The times of Neumann

In not too long a time an account of history tracing the evolution of the human spirit on earth will state with regard to the time of the turn of the nineteenth to twentieth century, that, as though emerging from the dim recesses of the times, some distinctive writers and poets were appearing. The bore the mantle of prophecy, but only a few of their contemporaries understood the stammering and the fiery intensity of their linguistic expression. They went around like rhapsodes who were seemingly immersed in a state of consciousness that did not belong to their time. Their poems, epics and songs had a psalm-like quality; there was something great and profound about them. But what was their purpose?

This is a point made by Dominic Jost, who worked on the biography of one of these men.[1] He wrote in the foreword: 'Around 1870 some German writers and poets were born who embodied the type of the *poeta vates,* poet bard, with a degree of purity such as was seldom the case even in the earlier history of poetry.'

13. KARL EUGEN NEUMANN

He names Ludwig Derleth, Theodor Däubler, Alfred Mombert and Karl Wolfskehl. But many others belong to this group, pre-eminently Stefan George, also Hugo von Hofmannsthal, although he locked himself up in a mussel-like way in his Austrianness, the archaeologist Alfred Schuler, who belonged to the *Kosmiker,* the Cosmic Circle around the pseudo-philosopher Ludwig Klages. Even Gerhart Hauptmann can only really be understood if one singles out this rhapsodic nature of his being; he was always easily carried away. I myself still remember the figure of the painter Fidus (Hugo Höppener) walking through the streets of Vienna, with long hair, his beard blowing in the wind, in sandals and a brown monk's habit. My heart longingly rejoiced whenever I saw him; 'I shall be like that when I am older,' I thought.

Each of these men created his own circle. Often there were only a few, but sometimes many and very influential people, who surrounded them. In themselves, however, they were the great solitary ones. Like King Lear they stood forsaken on the barren moors and wastelands of the world of their time. They tried to take hold of something that constantly eluded them. Their endeavour was to achieve mastery of something radiant that they were dimly aware of but which they were unable to bring to manifestation. So they went about the world like unknown bards and druids, as strangers to their time and to their contemporaries.

No literary historian has been able to categorize and evaluate them, because they are not regarded as 'literature.' They belong to a group of people who intuitively sensed the spirit-light that was soon to be dawning but which they were not able to take hold of. Hence they tried to interject what they wanted to say in sibylline voices from the depths of their souls; each one of them was convinced of the importance of this own mission. George wanted to renew the whole of culture, Derleth to establish a world government, Schuler longed for the end of the world which Däubler and Mombert prophetically foresaw.

They were being engulfed by the radiance of the dawn which

was beginning to shine forth in the early years of this century. Kali Yuga, the dark age, which had lasted for five thousand years, had run its course in 1899. A new spiritual light was appearing on the horizon. Young people, too, began to notice it. They joined together in the *Wandervogel* movement, which gathered momentum as it embraced the dawning light of the spirit. These young people bore the stammering verses of these bards on their lips.

Only few of them, however, stood firm and fulfilled what they promised. Some fell in the battlefields of the First World War, others were forced into a bourgeois way of life, still others subscribed to the ideologies and utopias of power-hungry false prophets and seducers.

On the other hand, those who felt themselves to be teachers and proclaimers, without knowing whom and what they should impart, stood in the light of this dawning of a new morning for humanity. They felt that they had a task; new mysteries were beginning to be disclosed to human beings. Like witnesses of a long lost epoch, when speaking in tongues and psalm-singing was still appropriate, when the gods still imparted their message to human beings through dreams and trances, these seers stammered their verses and sayings and exhibited pictures to an unheeding humanity.

It was the time when — also following a higher inspiration — Anton Bruckner created his symphonic works, Fercher von Steinwand wrote the *Kosmischen Chöre* and J.J. Bachofen drew back the curtains of the time that preceded the advent of man. Here, too, the approaching spiritual dawn was revealed.

One of these solitary pioneers, who only lived in retrospect and was single-mindedly devoted to his work and task — that of a translator and writer with the greatest gift for language — was the Austrian, Karl Eugen Neumann. He has remained almost entirely unknown, and I doubt whether he is remembered anywhere in the world.

Neumann's life and translations

Not only Neumann's name but also his life has remained a matter of deep secrecy. We possess no biography of him, and only a small number of his letters have hitherto been published. One of the few people who could give some information about him shrouds himself in secrecy.* It has, nevertheless, been possible to furnish an approximate outline of this remarkable man's life from the few documents and statements that are available.

Neumann was born on October 18, 1865 in Vienna; his father was a well-known stage director and singer of that time, Angelo Neumann (1838–1910). The latter had a glowing admiration for Wagner and in 1882 founded a Wagner theatre, with which he travelled through Europe and performed the operas of his master. From 1885 he took over the leadership of the German Theatre in Prague.

Thus the child grew up in an atmosphere impregnated with the spirit of Richard Wagner. Neumann also mentions in one of his later letters a 'banquet with Richard Wagner' where he was present. This must have been in his youth, since Wagner died at the beginning of 1883.

Neumann wrote about his childhood in another letter to his life-long friend Guiseppe de Lorenzo: 'I am hoping to share some bits and pieces of my personal wretchedness, about my

---

* This is the scholar E.R. who lived in London, and who was entrusted with the publication of Neumann's works. He knew Neumann personally and was close to him. I have visited Mr E.R. on two occasions. He assured me that what was needed was not so much to portray Neumann's life as to make his translation work more widely known. Neumann, he said, was a 'genius', and so the particular circumstances of his life could be more confusing than enlightening. A biography was therefore not thought desirable.

We now know that the Mysterious 'E.R.' was the actor and Buddhist Ernst Reinhold whose real name was actually Ernst Hirsch (1886–1964). He was was the son of a Jewish merchant from Budapest and had been a friend of Neumann. In February 1939, a few months after König, Reinhold fled from Vienna to London, also living in British exile. From there he edited 19 volumes of Neumann's translations as 'E.R.' Since König wrote this note in 1965 two biographies have appeared in German, Hecker's in 1986 and Zotz's in 2000. *(Editor)*

youth, which by the age of 20 had taught me more knowledge of the world than many have at 40, and about listening to a whole variety of different moments, both merry and sad, such as the lion's roar of the carpenter in the mechanicals' scene in the last act of *A Midsummer Night's Dream.*'[2]

We may suppose that the child accompanied his parents on many journeys and as a result had such a 'colourful education.' On completing his school education, he seems to have been involved as an apprentice in a bank.

However, his inner call soon came. He wrote to Lorenzo about this on August 27, 1897:

> The five years that lay between my first acquaintance with and my marriage to my wife were the strangest, most delightful and most flourishing of my life. I spent these years living entirely for myself. At that time, that is in 1884, a sun rose who shone also over you, my dear friend. I was so deeply captivated that I broke, inwardly broke with the whole of my life hitherto. The romantic enthusiasm of youth melted like lead on the sacrificial dish. I sought after Indian translations, and although by day I was completely absorbed in my professional duties, I immersed myself often until 3 o'clock in the morning and even later in philosophical studies. Eventually I also made an outward breakthrough. I returned to formal studies, left the bank and entered a school for mature students, and then after completing two wonderful years there went on to university, to Berlin, in the summer of 1887. Two years later, naturally still as a 'student,' I got married. Since then my kaleidoscopic life has changed little: its constellation has been constant for a while. But at times I think of my delightful, youthful good fortune of utter solitude, and if I become 90 years old perhaps when I am 91 I shall be a wandering Capuchin friar, though no Christophorus.

We have learnt much from this letter. Around the age of nineteen — roughly at the end of the first moon-node period of his life — the young man was led to the literature of ancient India through reading Schopenhauer.[3] He took hold of this inner call with great resolution and left everything that had preceded it behind him. His mind was filled with exciting new ideas. A further letter of May 2, 1899 indicates what this time meant for him: 'I became acquainted with Buddhism for the first time in the spring of 1884 from Spence Hardy's *Eastern Monachism,* on Schopenhauer's recommendation. I still think today of that incomparably moving time. It was the flowering of my entire life, full of jasmine fragrance and warm moonlight and the singing of nightingales; I was discovering and pondering those teachings for the first time in such an environment.'

It was in the spring of 1884 (the exact time of his first moon node), in the intoxicating abundance of the month of May, that Neumann encountered his life's destiny. From this point onwards he set about his task: the translation of all the Buddha's addresses from the Pali Canon, which had been found a few decades previously in Ceylon (Sri Lanka).

He immersed himself in the religions and languages of ancient India and must have acquired a degree of mastery in a very short time.

Already in 1892 he published a *Buddhistische Anthologie* in his own, albeit incomplete translation. He wrote in the foreword: 'The present anthology will be welcome to those who want to acquaint themselves with true Buddhism from its own documents; for complete extracts have, with the greatest care, been translated for the first time out of the original texts.'

In the same foreword Neumann makes his first profession of belief: the Buddhist religion is a great, a mighty work of art and needs to be recognized and understood as such. 'A work of art rays forth in eternal youthfulness, a science becomes older day by day, and the previous one — even if it was regarded in its time as superb — is obsolete.'

He worked at all his further translations on this basis. They became an ever-growing new creation of the words of Gautama Buddha.

In 1892 he translated the collection of verses known as the Dhammapadam, which was published in 1893. He wrote in the foreword:

> The present adaptation is a faithful reflection of the text. Nevertheless, or perhaps because it reproduces the original metres, it fully approximates to the original even to the extent of the wording, almost comparable to a plaster cast of a classical work of art ... The great German nation to whom I dedicate it may come and be refreshed by it.'[4]

The author wanted to draw the attention of 'the great German nation' to Buddha and his teachings in its native language.

The following verse from the chapter on the saints, verse 96, may serve as an example of how beautiful the translations had already become and how harmonious the Pali text sounded in German:

> *Gestillt ist seines Herzens Sinn,*
> *Gestillt das Wort, gestillt die That*
> *Des weisheitsklar Vollendeten,*
> *Des friedestillen Heiligen.*

> Stilled is the feeling of his heart,
> Stilled the word, stilled the deed
> Of the perfected one radiant in wisdom,
> Of the saint swathed in peace.

This is not simply a professional translation, but a new creation complete in itself.

In 1894 Neumann visited India for a few months, and repeatedly returned for this pilgrimage. On August 2, 1899 he wrote: 'Five years ago today I went sailing on the Indian ocean, off

Madras in the direction of Calcutta ... a wonderful morning, a clear starry night. Seagulls circled around, countless silver flying fish leapt up again and again beside the ship ...'

And on July 3, 1902 he wrote: 'Eight years ago today I arrived in Anuradhapura; in a mail van at half past five in the evening; twilight, utter desolation, vast wasteland of ruins, parched forest as black as night ...; first quarter of the moon, walk to the Bodhi tree which Asoko's son planted there.'

After his return from India he lived for a time in London, where he began to translate the addresses of the *Majjhima Nikaya,* the *Collection of Middle-Length Discourses.* He worked on these for six years, until 1901; he spent most of the time in Vienna, with short journeys to Prague to his father and to Naples to his friend de Lorenzo.

On one occasion he wrote to him: 'Can you believe that I would have translated a single line without previously knowing it by heart, *de coro,* and without turning it constantly in all directions until it finally acquired a suitable form? Thus I have on occasion tirelessly worked for two or three full days on no more than four lines, lying on the sofa, going for walks, in the tram, everywhere; there was no other way of managing it ...'[5]

So year after year more and more new translations came about. It became increasingly difficult for him to find a publisher for them; his outward existence became ever more wretched and impoverished. Neumann lived in a Vienna suburb, on Gentzstrasse, a big, noisy, dusty street. But he continued his work tirelessly, single-mindedly and obsessed by his task.

He translated the greater part of the Pali canon: the *Longer Collection* of the addresses, the 'Songs of Monks and Nuns,' 'The Last Days of Gautama Buddha,' the 'Collection of Fragments.' The language became increasingly poetic, and word and line, addresses and song spoke ever more directly to the reader and listener.

The following extract from the collection of fragments (from the chapter 'The Rich Farmer') may serve to illustrate Neumann's artistry of language:

DER REICHE LANDWIRT:
Der Reis ist gar gekocht, der Rahm ist abgeschöpft,
Am Flusse weil' ich in der Au gemeinsam hier,
Ein Dach bedeck mich, Feuer flammt am Herd:
Wohlan, o Wolke, riesle, regne recht.
DER HERR:
Der Reiz ist gar gekocht, der Gram ist abgeschöpft,
Am Flusse weil' ich in der Au alleinsam hier,
Kein Dach bedeckt mich, Feuer flammt nicht mehr:
Wohlan, o Wolke, riesle, regne recht.

THE RICH FARMER:
The rice is barely cooked, the cream has been skimmed off,
I am here in the meadow by the river with my companions,
I have a roof over my head, a fire burns in the hearth:
Come now, O cloud, let the rain come trickling, pouring down.
THE LORD:
The charms are superficial, the sorrow has been siphoned off,
I am here in the meadow by the river all alone,
I have no roof over my head, the fire has gone out:
Come now, O cloud, let the rain come trickling, pouring down.

Could anyone juxtapose these contrasting words *Reis* and *Reiz, Rahm* and *Gram, gemeinsam* and *alleinsam* more beautifully, expressively and simply?

Neumann's translations amount to over two thousand pages. In addition there are many hundreds of pages of important notes, where his extensive knowledge becomes clearly evident. He was at home in many languages; he spoke English, Italian and French. He had extensive knowledge of great world literature and quoted it constantly. He was familiar with Greek and Latin, and his awareness of philosophy was also unusually broad. But was he really a Buddhist? He loved Buddha and his addresses. He revered the great master, 'the Sublime One' as he called him. But he himself was very much a person of his time, that is, of the transition from the nineteenth to the twentieth century.

From his letters there is evidence of pride, anger, contempt for humanity, but then also of compassion and a striving for that boundless love shown by his master, the Buddha.

Karl Eugen Neumann died on his fiftieth birthday, October 18, 1915, in the middle of the First World War. His fame began to spread only after his death, in the early 1920s. An inexpensive edition of the addresses in both collections, the 'Path of Truth' and the 'Songs of Monks and Nuns,' conveyed Buddha's words in Neumann's versions to many German hearts. Well-known and also famous writers and authors such as Gerhart Hauptmann, Stefan Zweig and Hofmannsthal bore witness to him. They acknowledged what had been created here with full admiration. Zweig wrote,

> From time to time, the miracle occurs that a new rhythm comes to birth in a language, the possibility of development opens up fruitfully from a new source, all of a sudden an as yet unborn sensibility is impelled to create new forms. The translations of K.E. Neumann present an example of this phenomenon.

However, this wave was engulfed by the tide of advancing nationalism. The teachings of suffering and the overcoming of suffering, together with guidance for the eight-fold path, were forcibly silenced, for Germany had chosen the opposite path of self-annihilation. It preferred the option of violent self-destruction.

Wagner and the inner Orient

The destiny that guided Neumann's life is clear; but it can be understood only if it is interpreted with the help of the indications that Rudolf Steiner has given for an understanding of the history of the nineteenth century. As a child and youth the future translator of the Buddha's addresses lived in the sphere of influence of Richard Wagner, whose work strongly impressed themselves upon him. Wagner, however, was himself under the influence of Schopenhauer's philosophy. In 1854 — exactly thirty years before the similarly drastic event that brought about the change in Neumann's life — Wagner came to know of Schopenhauer's conception of life.

In his biographical study of Schopenhauer written around 1893, Rudolf Steiner said: 'It was these ideas about music that made that man who opened up new paths to music, Richard Wagner, one of Schopenhauer's most ardent admirers. These ideas worked upon him like a new gospel.'[6]

However, Schopenhauer's so-called pessimism, which had developed wholly under the influence of Indian philosophy and of Buddhism in particular, also had an effect on Wagner. A short while afterwards Wagner learnt about Buddha's life from a French book that he was reading. His immediate impulse was to write the libretto for a future musical drama. He subsequently wrote about this:

> Apart from the profound beauty of the material I was immediately guided in my choice by its particular relationship to the musical processes that had been developing within me. For the past life in former births of every being whom he encounters lies open to the spirit of the Buddha no less than does the present itself. Ordinary history acquires its significance only through this past life of the suffering principal figures that plays into the new phase of life as an immediate present. I

recognized at once that this double life can only be fully accessible to the feelings through an ever-present quality of reminiscence, and this made me resolve to give myself up to the task of composing this work with a particular love.[7]

The sketch of this draft for a drama entitled *Der Sieger* (The Conqueror) was written on May 16, 1856. It was never performed. But many features of the material experienced a kind of resurrection in *Parsifal,* where the idea of reincarnation breaks through and is connected with the mysteries of Christianity.

Wagner's creative work on *Tristan* was also strongly influenced by Schopenhauer. This musical drama is full of the spirit of Buddhism, of suffering, love and the overcoming of suffering. It was performed for the first time in Munich on June 10, 1865. A few months later Karl Eugen Neumann was born.

A direct destiny connection leads from Schopenhauer through Wagner to Neumann. But why is the influence of karmic laws so clearly discernible in them? Rudolf Steiner gives the answer.

In the introductory lecture to the course on *The Gospel of St Mark* he says the following:

> What happened in the nineteenth century — and this is little appreciated or understood today — is that the East exerted an influence on the culture of the West, indeed very intensely so. This intervention of Oriental influence in a quite distinctive way is what we need to bear in mind when considering the transformation that occurred in the cultural fabric of the nineteenth century. This deep involvement of the East cast light and shade upon everything that gradually flowed into European culture and will increasingly do so, thus requiring a new understanding of certain matters which humanity had hitherto viewed in a quite different way ... An inner Orient entered into the cultural life of Europe in

ways that external history is at first completely unable to fathom ... One needs only to recall the name of one single person who caused a great stir around the middle of the nineteenth century, and this will immediately make it clear that something came to Europe from the East on mysterious paths. One needs merely to mention the name of Schopenhauer.[8]

In another context, however, Rudolf Steiner indicates that there was as yet nothing of this 'inner Orient' in Goethe. The culture of the Renaissance and of Christianity appeared in him in a 'glorious union.'[9] Earlier on in the same lecture there had been a description of how a stream gained access to European culture which Rudolf Steiner defines as the Mercury influence. He was referring here to that 'inner Orient' which began to take hold of the hearts and souls of Europeans in the nineteenth century. He then continues:

> Having studied Goethe as we have been doing for years we can easily recognize that these elements [of the Renaissance and Christianity] did indeed flow together in his soul. But we should also ... expect that there would as yet be no evidence of the Mercury influence in Goethe's soul; we should expect it to appear as something new only after his time. And here it is interesting to note that Goethe's pupil, Schopenhauer, already reveals signs of this new influence. I have already said that Schopenhauer's philosophy contains elements of Eastern wisdom, particularly in the form of Buddhism. Since Mercury may be regarded as the symbol of Buddhism, you may see that ... after the age of Goethe there was a revival of the Buddha influence.

In the winter of 1813/14 Schopenhauer became Goethe's pupil in Weimar . He received from him a personal introduction to the fundamental laws of colour theory, which the younger man later developed in Dresden into an extensive treatise *On Vision and Colours.* Finally, in 1817/18, his principal work, *The World as Will and Representation,* appeared, which already bore the mark of the 'inner Orient.'

Around the same time ancient Indian wisdom was beginning to make its mark in Europe. The Vedas became known and were translated, above all the *Bhagavadgita,* which soon became part of every educated person's cultural world. The stream of the Mercury-Buddha influence had taken hold of Europe and began to spread pre-eminently in the German-speaking world.

Wagner was gripped by this influence; and it was the idea of reincarnation that became prominent at this time and impressed him so deeply. For he recognized that in the formulating of a musical motif he enables the eternal individuality of a person to sound forth and so has the possibility of letting 'the past lives of the suffering principal figures' play into the dramatic events 'as an immediate present.' One of the archetypal endeavours of Wagner's music can be found here. They also re-appear in the text in the figure of Kundry. Klingsor calls her 'she-devil, rose of hell, you were Herodias and what else besides?'

Rudolf Steiner has indicated that it was in the moment when the idea of karma and reincarnation was born — in Lessing and others — out of the cultural life of Central Europe that the Oriental Mercury influence began to stream in, bringing in its wake the Eastern forms of the teaching of reincarnation. Until the time of Goethe European humanity knew only the history of the previous three thousand years. Then the curtain was torn aside, and earlier epochs of human evolution began to be revealed to people's marvelling souls.

> Through the idea of reincarnation arising in modern souls, a bridge was formed which extended across the three thousand years of which we have been speaking; for during these years the doctrine of reincarnation had not been central in people's thinking.

This is one aspect of what came about in nineteenth century Europe through the 'inner Orient.' Another thing to be considered is what happened as a result of this transformation. Rudolf Steiner characterizes this as follows:

> If one wishes to form a more exact conception of what was going on, one needs to see that there was a general convergence of peoples and their folk cultures and beliefs, so that adherents of entirely different creeds in the nineteenth century began to understand each other in quite remarkable way.[10]

Thus two different things were going on. The curtain that for three thousand years had veiled the previous existence of mankind was pulled aside through the dissemination of the cultural treasures of the Orient and enabled the idea of karma and reincarnation, which had already emerged, to blossom anew. This was the preparation for the end of the Kali Yuga, which came in 1899.

The second was a process of a mutual understanding of peoples which began to develop and sought to bridge the frontiers that had been erected. This was the preparatory measure for the year 1879, when the Archangel Michael rose to become a spirit ruling over humanity. The most disparate peoples wanted to meet up and learn to understand one another under his rulership.

The ideas of Buddhism united with these new impulses which were emerging, arrived in Europe and impressed themselves upon Schopenhauer and Richard Wagner, together with many of their other contemporaries including Karl Eugen Neumann. He embraced them with the totality of his being; he became the exclusive servant of the Buddha, he became the mouthpiece and tongue for the addresses of the enlightened one and formed them into a new part of German literature. By this means he carried the torch of the Mercury influence into Central Europe. His translations were not merely a great work of art, not merely a great religious call but a necessary service to the German people which corresponded to those supersensible events that were taking place at this time in the realms of spirit.[11]

However, we should not view Neumann's life's work as an attempt to revive Buddhism. Where this has happened, a bitter injustice is being done to this destiny. There was no question here of a renewal of pre-Christian Buddhism, nor the restoration of an old reflection of a still older wisdom! The addresses and parables of the sublime Buddha were rightly added to the German language as a gift and treasure. They should begin to live in this realm and from there reach the soul of the people in order to guide this nation on the paths that are right and appropriate for it. This was the real motive ascribed to the world destiny of Karl Eugen Neumann: to make Buddha's words part of the language of the German people. That this was misunderstood, scorned and ignored was a cause of the catastrophe that befell Central Europe.

For it is not the pre-Christian Buddha who should be renewed but, rather, the Buddha who is active today. Rudolf Steiner was referring to this when he said:

> We look to the Buddha who has moved onwards and from spiritual heights exercises an enduring influence on human culture ... We contemplate the Buddha at the further stage of his development in the realm of the spirit, proclaiming from there truths of fundamental importance for our time.[12]

The Buddha has become the servant of the Christ impulse 'in the realm of the spirit' and is working there, in the light of the Risen One, for the future of mankind.

Neumann clearly had a feeling for this, even if only an intuitive one. In a letter of April 26, 1901 he wrote about the 'smiling Buddha' and thought that it was difficult to understand this but that it would nevertheless need to be researched. And he adds:

> The other aspect [he means the smiling mood in contrast to the serious, sombre one] is that of San Francesco; and that is definitely the most important. After all, this is that San Francesco who said: 'Anyone who sees Minorites [Franciscans] on their wanderings will praise God' — that is, be happy for having seen happy people.

St Francis had, however, been a pupil of the Buddha as he was developing further on his path; he ascended through earthly suffering to bliss and joy in beholding the Risen One.[13] This transfiguration of the Buddha should not be forgotten if the 'inner Orient' is to find its rightful place of influence in Europe. The 'Sublime One' should not be leading us back to the past but, rather, forward into the future.

Then those mumbling prophetic voices referred to at the outset will be able to find their fulfilment. Rather than rhapsodes, solitary and far removed from ordinary life, disciples of Christ will need to emerge striding humbly and yet upright into the dawn of the spirit, speaking a language in which Buddha's addresses in Neumann's re-creations will also sound forth. Then words such as these about love from the Collection of Fragments, which are beyond all religions, will be spoken for all people!

> *Liebe soll durchleuchten so die ganze Welt,*
> *Unbegrenzbar einbegreifen in der Brust:*
> *Oben, unten, mitten quer hindurch*
> *Unermesslich strahlen, ohne Grimm und Groll.*

> Love shall so irradiate the whole world,
> Limitlessly encompassing the breast:
> Above, below, streaming right through the middle
> Beyond measure, without fury and rancour.

14

Marie Eugenie Delle Grazie

Delle Grazie (1864–1931) was an Austrian novelist, playwright and poet.

The year of birth, 1864

Nearly forty years ago [in 1924] the art historian Wilhelm Pinder wrote a book in which he tried to prove that the history of human art and culture proceeds in generational leaps.[1] He spoke there about the 'entelechies of the generations' and meant by this that at particular times groups of artists are born who develop certain stylistic elements together and at the same time. 'There are ... indeed groupings of particularly significant births.' Through the discovery of these laws it is possible to discern very real evidence of a ruling time spirit who chooses specific personalities to be its bearers. 'With succeeding generations basic moods, basic feelings are born which express themselves in problems of unity. A unity-problem as a formula for a generation-community includes rather than excludes tension and contrasts of the strongest kind, and even requires the possibility of their existence.'

The first chapter of the recently revised book by Soergel is introduced by similar thoughts: 'The modern literature of Germany begins with so-called naturalism. Under this category a generation began to stir who felt themselves at variance with

AT THE THRESHOLD OF THE MODERN AGE

the past and wanted something new. The birth-years of the new generation were the 1860s; the most significant figure of this trend was Gerhart Hauptmann, born in 1862.'[2] This generation whose birth sequence began with Hauptmann also included Eugenie Delle Grazie.

A listing of the dates of birth of the 'new generation' who found their way into the public eye around 1890 yields an impressive array of writers and poets, playwrights, painters and composers who were born between 1862 and 1866. It is like a swelling chord of births which reached its culmination in 1864. Here is a sample of dates:

1862	May 15	Arthur Schnitzler
	June 21	Johannes Schlaf
	July 12	Hermann Conradi
	July 14	Gustav Klimt
	August 22	Claude Debussy
	August 29	Maurice Maeterlinck
	November 15	Gerhart Hauptmann
1863	March 12	Gabriele D'Annunzio
	April 3	Henry van de Velde
	April 26	Arno Holz
	July 19	Hermann Bahr
	November 18	Richard Dehmel
	December 18	Edvard Munch
1864	February 16	Hermann Stehr
	March 17	Karl Henckell
	May 12	Cäsar Flaischlen
	June 3	Otto Erich Hartleben
	June 11	Richard Strauss
	June 21	Heinrich Wölfflin
	July 18	Ricarda Huch
	July 24	Frank Wedekind
	August 14	Marie Eugenie Delle Grazie
	November 24	Henry de Toulouse-Lautrec

14. MARIE EUGENIE DELLE GRAZIE

1865	June 11	William Butler Yeats
	June 28	Otto Julius Bierbaum
	August 14	Dmitri Merezhkovsky
	October 4	Max Halbe
	December 8	Jan Sibelius
1866	January 29	Romain Rolland
	March 7	Paul Ernst
	July 11	Richard Beer-Hofmann
	August 29	Hermann Löns
	November 12	Sun Yat-sen
	December 4	Wassily Kandinsky

This is an impressive list of significant personalities who without doubt had a deep and far-reaching influence on the end of the nineteenth century and the beginning of the modern age leading up to the outbreak of the First World War. They became the bearers of a new spirit of the age which brought about the breakthrough of a new feeling for social relationships, a new sense of style and the awakening of a radical view of the world and of life. What we generally categorize with words such as 'naturalism,' *fin de siècle* or *Jugendstil* are only the individual waves that arose out of the sea of this epoch-making transformation that was coming about at that time amongst mankind.

The generation of those born at the beginning of the 1860s opened the gates through which those who carried the banners of expressionism and of the Brücke, the Blaue Reiter and the Bauhaus brought about an artistic revolution in the early decades of the twentieth century. All of them, Marc and Macke, Paul Klee and Georg Heym, Wilhelm Klemm, René Schickele, Ernst Stadler and many others, were born between 1880 and 1890. They broke up the forms which the previous generation from the 1860s had more or less preserved and used as they had inherited them from the past.

It was this distinction which gave this group, of which Gerhart

Marie Eugenie Delle Grazie

Hauptmann was the oldest, most versatile and most significant member, its particular position. The scope of Hauptmann's work ranges from *Before Dawn* through *Drayman Henschel*, *Rose Bernd* and *The Weavers* to *Indipohdi* and *The Sunken Bell*, *Henry of Auë* and the Atride Tetralogy. No other member of his generation — with the possible exception of Richard Strauss and Hermann Bahr — attained the breadth of this horizon. The others represented only parts of his manifoldness and richness. They were naturalists or mystics, lyrical impressionists, sensitive writers of epics, poetic social reformers. It was a generation that unearthed the memory of the past as a mighty block of stone and, as it were, picked it up and hurled it at the gates of the future so as to break them open.

Pinder characterized this epoch:

> If one casts a comparative eye over noticeably older and noticeably younger people one senses instinctively from their physiognomy, even before any analysis, that there is something in common at this age, which in most cases is manifested as an urge towards a chaste form ... here and there as classicism, in others as a dreamy quality, but always as an instinctive (*inborn*) retrospective relationship to the Feuerbach generation, as something refined and distant in mood: such is the generation of the 1860s.[3]

This characterization fitted no one better than it did Delle Grazie. One could always feel in her that artificial and yet inadvertent classicism which appeared in Feuerbach, and yet she bore the social and ideological destiny of her time with a consuming fervour and with constant self-dedication.

The breadth of her horizon and the richness of her forms can only be compared with the diversity of Gerhart Hauptmann's work. He did indeed speak the language of the new generation; but she put the new wine in old bottles, which is why she has been forgotten today — even though she will in future times be granted a return to her people's consciousness. Adalbert Stifter also remained forgotten for decades, likewise Hölderlin and Hamerling. A new generation will come to remember Delle Grazie once more.

The Vienna circle around Delle Grazie

How distant is the time when a real gregariousness still led people together! They had common inclinations and interests, and there was still enough inner tranquillity to come together of an afternoon and to discuss not only 'everyday' and 'essential' matters but to be amongst other people in a truly social context.

These *jours* were cultivated in many Viennese citizens' homes and also in the houses of the nobility. People met in these places, got to know one another, and discussed the events of life. Destiny had a free rein and did not have to expend all its forces in offices, lecture halls and machine-shops.

Every Saturday, in the late afternoon and evening, a group of people met for such a *jour* at the house of the priest and Professor of Philosophy Laurenz Müllner. This was in a suburb of Vienna, in Döbling, in the Coloredogasse. 'There was something almost magical about these Saturday gatherings. After dark the red shade of the ceiling lamp spread a festive light over everyone.'[4]

Eugenie Delle Grazie, who was barely twenty years old at the time, was the focal point of these social gatherings. She lived in the same house as Laurenz Müllner, who was her teacher and whom she deeply revered. She recited her poems in the Saturday circle, and we are indebted to Fritz Lemmermeyer, who was one of the visitors, for a lively description of these meetings:

> I can still see the painted picture clearly before me in every detail after many decades: the youthful, blonde poetess standing in the red salon, thin, erect and donned with a festive, gaily coloured dress made from red silk

beside a cast of the beautiful bust of Apollo Belvedere, reading with a solemn pathos.[5]

Delle Grazie was at that time working on the great epic *Robespierre,* from which she would choose new parts to recite. 'We listened to scenes of great poetic ardor, but fundamentally pessimistic and richly coloured by naturalism; it depicted life in its most shattering aspects. Great men, utterly deceived by fate, rose before our imagination and sank away in a deeply stirring tragedy. This was my impression' — this is how Rudolf Steiner wrote in recollection of these evenings. And he continues:

> The poet ... read from her poems and spoke in the spirit of her worldview with assured emphasis, and she illuminated life with those ideas. It was not the illumination of the Sun, — indeed, it was always sombre moonlight, with threatening, overcast skies. But in that dusky gloom flames arose from human hopes, carrying high the passions and illusions consume humanity. Yet all this was also humanly touching, always enthralling, and the bitterness was softened by the noble magic of a truly inspired personality.[6]

Here was this young woman who was little more than a girl — she was studying at the time at a teacher training establishment for ladies called St Anna — proclaiming in enchanting and destructive words the blind working of nature in man.

> *Mit ehernen Banden hält*
> *Und kettet an Staub und Verwesung*
> *Natur, Deine Zeug'rin, Dich fest;*
> *Natur, das lockende Ungeheuer,*
> *Bald lächelnd und sonnengoldig*
> *Zu wütender Daseinfreude Dich spornend, bald*

Entsetzen und Not gebärend
Mit der Rute des Jammers Dich peitschend,
Doch immer vernichtend und rätselhaft, immer
Medusa und Sphinx zugleich.

Nature, thy procreator, holds thee
Firmly with iron bands
And chains thee to dust and decomposition;
Nature, the alluring immensity,
Now spurring thee with smiles and golden sun's rays
To a raging joy in existence,
Now engendering horror and anguish,
Whipping thee with the rod of misery,
Always devastating and mysterious,
At once Medusa and Sphinx.

This was the mood that lived in Delle Grazie's heart. She was a pessimist, but not exclusively so. She had also identified herself with the scientific world-conception of that time, was an ardent admirer of Ernst Haeckel and was full of the ethical ideals of Bartholomäus Carneri. Her highest authorities were the views of Darwin and Lyell, which had at that time achieved their triumphant ascendancy..

At the same time, however, this girl was the centre of a circle of important people who lived and thought in accordance with a completely different set of convictions. The friends and colleagues of her mentor Laurenz Müllner visited every Saturday and surrounded the intellectual games of this poetess with their traditional Catholic theology: the church historian and biographer of Thomas Aquinas, Karl Werner, the learned and virtually omniscient Professor and Father Wilhelm Neumann and the aesthete Vincenz Knauer. They were all Cistercians and were full of the thought-forms of scholasticism, which was being revived at the time. Many other people turned up there: the musician Alfred Stross, the psychologist Adolph Stöhr, the author Emilie Mataja (who wrote under the pseudonym of

14. MARIE EUGENIE DELLE GRAZIE

Emil Marriot) and, among several others, the young Rudolf Steiner.

A strange mixture of the greatest variety of people came together there, and yet they must all have been led there by a common destiny: philosophers, theologians and that impetuous young woman who had such devastating thoughts and feelings in her tempestuously excited soul.

> Delle Grazie's house was a place where pessimism revealed itself with the direct force of life. It was a place of anti-Goetheanism. When I spoke of Goethe they listened, but Laurenz Müllner thought that what I attributed to Goethe had fundamentally very little to do with the actual minister of Grand Duke Karl August. Nevertheless, for me every visit to this home (where I know I was welcome) was immensely fruitful; I truly benefitted from the cultural atmosphere.[7]

These are Rudolf Steiner's words. He was at home in this circle; he felt accepted and accorded a place there. There were people there who — although they were unable to share his views — were nevertheless related and closely affiliated to him. His views were in stark contrast to those of the brilliant young poetess who was roughly the same age, and the older members of the circle organized themselves around the two poles represented by these two young people.

It was the time when Vienna was experiencing immense transformation as a city. The old fortifications that were still preserved around the inner heart of the city had been demolished, and a splendid new road, the Ringstrasse, created in its place. Huge buildings in imitative styles — Renaissance, Gothic, etc. — were being erected, and the whole of the city was thereby acquiring a new aspect. Out of a small central area and many suburban regions one of the great metropolises of the time was now emerging. A great statue of Pallas Athene in the Greek style was put up in front of the Parliament building, and it gave a particular touch to the architectural impulse. Was it by chance that the tall figure of the goddess, with her helmet and spear, could be seen from afar? Did a Greek spirit not waft through the city in those years? Had not Athens arisen once more in a Central European guise, conjuring up a reflection of the world of Pericles before the eyes of the living? Did a Greek, pagan element full of beauty, devotion and an intense quest for ideas and knowledge permeate those gatherings in the villa of the philosopher Laurenz Müllner? However diverse the guests may have been, the spirit of Vienna as it was then held them together and evoked within them a feeling of primal companionship.

Childhood and youth

Eugenie Delle Grazie was born in one of those German enclaves in southern Hungary which still preserved much of their independent culture at that time. The place was called Weisskirchen (Bella-Crkva) on the Danube; it lies approximately 100 km (60 miles) east of Belgrade and is today part of Yugoslavia (now Serbia). Her father was the director of a mine; he came from an old Venetian family. Her mother had grown up in Weisskirchen but on her father's side had north German, and on her mother's side French-Alsatian, ancestors. A virtually European mixture of northern, southern and western blood flowed together in this distinctive family. Eugenie was the first-born; she was followed by a brother, who grew up with her. Her father must have been a remarkably kind person; late in life he married a much younger, beautiful wife and was completely devoted to her and the children. The child was surrounded with wealth, a beautiful natural environment and a peaceful parental home, all of which formed her earliest impressions; and a whole variety of different languages — Hungarian, German, Rumanian and Italian — jostled for supremacy in the future poetess's hearing.

14. MARIE EUGENIE DELLE GRAZIE

Her first verses came very early to consciousness from her soul's inner experiences.

When she was about eight years old, her father died and left her mother and the two children not very well provided for. Her father's brother was appointed guardian; he lived in Vienna and cannot have been a very reliable man. He wasted his money and that of his wards instead of protecting and increasing it.

Her mother, who had through her wealth become inactive and somewhat feckless, left Weisskirchen and moved with her children to Vienna. Eugenie was then eleven years old, and she describes this journey from southern Hungary to the imperial capital in an inimitable way. Shortly before they reached Vienna, in Marchegg, the child got out of the train in order to fetch something to eat for her little brother, and at the station buffet a young priest helped her to make her purchases. This became the destiny meeting of her life. His eyes rested upon her — 'the look in his eyes was as radiant and as kindly as I had only ever seen in the eyes of my father.'[8]

The arrival in Vienna was sad, for her uncle did not come to the station as he had promised; and the family lodged in a hotel. In the night the child had a strange dream. She saw a room that she did not recognize where the priest from Marchegg station was sitting and holding a letter in his hand — 'a big, big letter which was still closed with a large red seal ... And then he sat and read and read, while the reddish light of the lamp fell on his delicate pale features ... She saw all this with great precision and in minute detail, as in a picture that one looks at with the certainty that one will never be able to forget it.' Then the priest in this dream picture got up, turned to her, 'and as he held out the letter to her — as though something was concealed in its lines which in some mysterious way had a connection with her destiny — he uttered a word loudly and clearly which was like a flash of lightning in her soul: Vienna!' Then the child awoke.

It subsequently transpired that shortly afterwards the young chaplain — it was her future teacher Laurenz Müllner — received this big white letter from his protector, Cardinal Rauscher, who was at the time Archbishop of Vienna, summoning him from the provinces to the capital. He was appointed parish priest at the church whose school Eugenie attended. Thus it came about that through her religion teacher she was soon led to the young priest. They recognized one another again, and Müllner now took over the spiritual guidance of the young girl. A radiant magic of noble humanity surrounded the friendship which united this child and the priest sixteen years older than herself.

From now on this precocious girl found security and protection. Outward circumstances became more and more difficult, since her mother was incapable of any kind of work; her uncle, a playboy, wasted his money. Gradually one item after another from her father's possessions had to be sold in order to cover their daily needs. The houses where they lived became increasingly modest, and the growing girl who had formerly had so protected a childhood personally experienced hunger and social deprivation.

Inwardly, however, many poems were beginning to take shape, lines and images stirred within her, and one day she started to write down these early experiences of youthful creativity. In the early years of her creative life she had not dared to fix what was germinating within her. Müllner, however, encouraged her to write down one poem after another and to overcome her shyness. One of the first that she showed him — she had written it when she was eleven — runs as follows:

> *Bei Blumenduft und Mondenschein*
> *Sprachst du zuerst das süsse Wort:*
> *'Ich liebe dich.'*
> *Da zog es in mein Herz hinein,*
> *Wie Blumenduft und Mondenschein —*
> *Doch zog draus Ruh und Frieden fort,*
> *Als ich auch sprach das süsse Wort:*
> *'Ich liebe dich.'*

14. MARIE EUGENIE DELLE GRAZIE

> Midst scent of flowers and light of moon
> You first spoke the sweet words,
> 'I love you.'
> Then into my heart there flowed,
> Like scent of flowers and light of moon —
> There flowed tranquillity and peace,
> When I too spoke the sweet words,
> 'I love you.'

A similar kind of perfection as is to be found only in the poems of Hugo von Hofmannsthal when he was a grammar-school pupil comes to expression in the verses of this child. A distant memory of the past and of past experience which only now, after re-birth, seems to have found its expression wells up from the depths of existence.

This is a further example of a child's poem:

> *Es liegt in weisser Hülle*
> *Begraben Berg und Tal,*
> *Der Blumen holde Fülle*
> *Entschwunden allzumal*
> *In ihren dunklen Räumen*
> *Birgt sie die Erde warm*
> *Und selig sie hier träumen,*
> *Vergessen allen Harm.*
> *Auch ich möcht' gerne träumen,*
> *Mein Herz, es ist so schwer —*
> *Willst du noch lange säumen*
> *Mit deiner Wiederkehr?*

> Mountain and valley lie buried
> In a white shroud,
> The fair abundance of flowers
> Have disappeared in a trice;
> In their dark expanses

> The Earth warmly shelters them
> And they blissfully dream here,
> Forgetting all distress.
> I too would like to dream,
> My heart, it is so hard —
> Will you tarry longer
> Delaying your return?

Before Delle Grazie was seventeen years old her first book of poems appeared and was greeted with enthusiasm by the great names of her time. A new poetess seemed to have emerged, and much more was expected of her. Hamerling, Bodenstedt and Martin Greif wrote at length about these verses. And Rudolf Steiner wrote about her in 1886:

> A mighty phenomenon has appeared before us here. Delle Grazie is original in the way that only a mind that has been nurtured from the inexhaustible sources of the German spirit can be; her characterization is powerful and profound, as is possible only for the German mind with its loving involvement with the human heart and soul.[9]

She was beginning to gain appreciation and recognition.

The maturing writer

Shortly after her first volume of poems there appeared the epic, *Hermann,* a drama, *Saul,* and the story, *Die Zigeunerin* (The Gypsy Woman). A few years later, these were followed by a further volume of poems, *Italienische Vignetten* (1892), the stories *Der Rebell* and *Bozi* and in 1894 the two-volume epic *Robespierre*. In over a thousand pages, the history of the French Revolution is presented there in images full of tragic grandeur and fierce scorn for all humanity. It is a work that portrays man's loneliness, his weak greed and the mighty power of an all-destructive nature. Carneri wrote at the time in his letter to Haeckel of February 7, 1895: 'I am living at present wholly in Delle Grazie's *Robespierre,* which reads exemplarily; despite having a few excesses here and there it is a masterpiece which I am currently mentally reviewing and will perhaps also do so in writing.'

Haeckel answered on February 20:

> I am — when time permits! — studying *Robespierre* in the evenings ... I have read the twelfth song, 'The Mysteries of Humanity,' with the greatest pleasure. Our thoughts will often be meeting there! I admire the bold and wide-ranging spirit of the poetess almost even more than her great and rare poetic talent. She must be a quite *extraordinary* example of the *rare* species Homo sapiens. If writing were not so difficult for you, I would almost beg you to share with me something about the development of this wonderful creature.

Carneri's reply to this letter is interesting, in that her refers to the life-circumstances of the now thirty-year-old Delle Grazie:

> Her father, whom she lost early, must have been a most unusual man ... Her uncle and [then her] guardian took her in ... Now she cares for his household and can, in her turn, live freely for her art. Her former guardian is no less than the present rector magnificus (Professor Laurenz Müllner) of Vienna University, who is also a Catholic priest .... He sees the 'best people' at his home every week, and the poetess does the honours. Dr Müllner has an absolute confidence in her genius. He crosses her in nothing; however, she would in any case not let herself be crossed. The young woman is barely thirty years old, a veritable phenomenon, who, one hopes, will manage to get rid of some excesses in her behaviour.'[10]

Haeckel describes a visit to Vienna on April 28, 1897 as 'a very happy afternoon with our worthy friends, Professor Müllner and E. Delle Grazie' (letter to Carneri dated May 10, 1897).

In the same year a satirical poem, *Moralische Walpurgisnacht* (Moral Walpurgis Night) appeared, and around the turn of the century there followed three plays: *Schlagende Wetter* (Firedamp), *Der Schatten* (The Shadow) and *Goldener*. The first of these was performed in the Volkstheater of Vienna. It is a social indictment in the style of Hauptmann's *Die Weber* (The Weavers), full of deeply distressing drama and power. The play *Der Schatten* was put on in the Hofburgtheater, the Imperial Court Theatre, with Josef Kainz in the leading role. A poet and dramatist at that time could have no higher recognition than this. In 1902 the ten-volume edition of her collected works appeared. The poetess was in her 38th year at the height of her fame. The first biographical appraisal of her life and work also appeared at this time.

Rudolf Steiner likewise did not tire of writing about her. On September 15 and 22, 1900 he published a more extensive essay about Delle Grazie in the *Magazin für Literatur*. Here he characterizes the greatness of her art and the force of her individuality.

> There is probably no other personality who has so deeply and with such distress experienced the pain of the collision between an old world of ideals and a new world of knowledge as has Marie Eugenie Delle Grazie ... Anyone who is unable to have a sense for the greatness of these poems must lack one of the feelings that have entered so deeply into the hearts of people today. Either such a person has never inwardly felt the great longing that the mighty ideals of mankind, the urge towards yonder world and belief in the gods have engendered and have kept vitally alive as a matter of personal destiny, or else the modern world-conception which has engulfed our cultural life like an earthquake of immense power must have more or less passed him by without leaving any trace.[11]

14. MARIE EUGENIE DELLE GRAZIE

With these words the heart of the struggle in Delle Grazie's soul is clearly depicted; it is the same nodal point which could be found in all creative spirits of her generation. But Rudolf Steiner was one of the few who knew more; he saw what could grow from this germinal essence and which, in Delle Grazie's case, did not as yet come to light. He continues:

> I do not doubt that this modern world-conception conceals within itself the seeds for higher spiritual spheres, more beautiful, more sublime than all the old ideals; but I do not believe that joys will ever fully triumph over sorrows; I do not believe that hope will ever conquer renunciation. It seems to me just as certain as light is born out of darkness that the radiant fulfilment of the quest for knowledge must spring from the deepest pain of existence. And the vital nerve in Delle Grazie's art is the great pain underlying existence.

These words illumine this germinal nature and its possibilities. But Delle Grazie did not ask for the fulfilment that would correspond to the expectations that people had for her — or only in a quite particular way. Hardly any of her contemporaries succeeded in reaching those 'higher spiritual spheres' which can develop out of the germinal nature of monism. Hermann Bahr remained a windbag, whether in a Catholic or pantheistic guise. Otto Erich Hartleben became an alcoholic and died as a result. Hermann Stehr, Frank Wedekind, Ricarda Huch and many others all knocked at the gate of the spirit, sometimes loudly, sometimes softly, but never strongly enough for the doors to open and grant them access to a new realm. Eugenie Delle Grazie also failed in this respect.

She wrote further stories, novellas and novels such as *Heilige und Menschen* (Saints and Men, 1909), *Vor dem Sturm* (Before the Storm, 1909), the play *Ver Sacrum* (1906), many essays and literary articles, but none of this went beyond her early work and carried it forward to some kind of fulfilment. Her poetic power seemed to be in the ascendant, until an event intervened which brought new ideals to her life and her creative work.

The great conversion

The decisive turning point came in 1912. It was the year when, through the sinking of the *Titanic* on April 14, an awakening call went out to a humanity that was intoxicated with a mad drive towards progress and affluence. The few who became truly attentive sensed the approaching catastrophe.

Shortly before, on November 28, 1911, Delle Grazie's teacher and friend, Laurenz Müllner, died aged 63. In a lecture of December 27, 1911 Rudolf Steiner said of him:

> He was too great a man to stop short at a mere dogmatic Catholicism, but on the other hand Catholicism was too preponderant in him for him to be able to rise to a spiritual-scientific grasp of reality. It is extraordinarily interesting to observe such a person who has come to the point where one can actually study what man needs in order to approach reality. For of course this astute man saw quite clearly that he was unable to approach reality with his thinking.[12]

Müllner remained a Catholic believer until his dying day. He taught Christian philosophy at Vienna University and was a member of the philosophy — and not the theology — faculty. Despite his deep faith, which was in total contrast to Delle Grazie's aggressive monism, teacher and pupil continued to be linked by an intimate friendship. For Müllner was enough of a sceptic to recognize the limits of his thinking, and Delle Grazie was so generous and magnanimous that she never lost her ideals. She sought the eternal in the past and had an intuitive knowl-

14. MARIE EUGENIE DELLE GRAZIE

edge of the spirit that works in all living things. But the step that Rudolf Steiner took was one that was not possible for her or her teacher. She did not manage to make the breakthrough from the scientific view of the world to a science of the spirit.

In an 'open letter to the writer of *Hermann,* which he called 'Nature and Our Ideals,' Rudolf Steiner had in 1886 given a preliminary outline of this step:

> Now, we really ought to admit that a being that knows itself *cannot* be unfree! ...Laws [of nature] are changed into ideals, which in their turn become laws. We should really admit that God, whom a weary humanity imagined to be in the clouds, dwells in our heart, in our mind. He has flowed forth fully into humanity in complete self-renunciation. He did not want to keep anything for Himself; for He wanted a human race that could freely rule over itself. He has become fully part of the world. The will of human beings is His will, the aims of human beings are His aims. By implanting His whole being in human individuals, He has given up His own existence.[13]

In these words lies the essence of everything which was subsequently brought to the clearest expression in *The Philosophy of Freedom.* Delle Grazie published her epic *Robespierre,* in the same year — 1894 — that this book appeared. Here, and especially in the great song *Die Mysterien der Menschheit,* she brings her pessimism to the most eloquent form of expression. Nature is again described as the all-devouring and all-begetting being that constantly gives birth to and destroys the whole creation out of greed and power, out of creative passion and lust for death.

A future historical account that endeavours to focus upon the true phenomena of human evolution will regard these two works of the human spirit as being the seeds of what subsequently led both into the depths and into the heights. In *Robespierre* the apocalyptic events of the twentieth century — in so far as they led to the results of the national totalitarianism which became ever more widely disseminated — are described as a kind of foreboding. In *The Philosophy of Freedom,* on the other hand, human souls are enjoined to conduct themselves in such a way that they form communities in which the individual can become free.

Eighteen years later — in 1912 — Rudolf Steiner was preparing for the founding of the first Anthroposophical Society. In the same year Delle Grazie returned to the fold of the Catholic Church.

It is said that her conversion occurred under the impression of Laurenz Müllner's death and the great event of the Eucharist Congress that was meeting at the time in Vienna. This return to the fold had a defining effect on Delle Grazie's further life. She was 48 years old, a woman maturing in years whose teacher and companion in life had left her. She set forth from Vienna, moved into the country in Styria and seemed from then on 'to be lost to the world.' Her later years were veiled in solitude and desolation, until she died in 1931.

The First World War brought its catastrophes and the collapse of the great imperial monarchy, all of which had a profound influence on the poetess's soul. Delle Grazie tried to engage with the legacy of the war (*Homo. Der Roman einer Zeit,* 1919). However, the principal theme of her novellas and novels is the great song of conversion, the return to the Catholic faith. She tried to present this soul-transformation — the inner Eucharist — to her readers in a variety of different forms and guises. However fascinating many of these stories are, they lack formative power and linguistic vigour. Hence they have a belletristic quality and are of value mainly for entertainment and light reading.

In many places the fire of poetry flares up once more, as in the two autobiographical novels *Donaukind* (Child of the Danube, 1916) and *Eines Lebens Sterne* (Stars of a Life, 1919). But the great artistic discipline that pervades the totality of a work does not return. Delle Grazie had become a 'Catholic writer.'

One of her last books, *Die Empörung der Seele* (The Soul's Outrage), which even becomes an exciting crime novel, has on the other hand features relating to an overcoming of a one-sided

14. MARIE EUGENIE DELLE GRAZIE

Catholicism. One can dimly sense the glimmering of a higher Christianity which wants to embrace all religions. A 'world Pentecost' is longed for, encompassing Christians and Jews, monists and Muslims, Indians and apostates. It is as if the sign of the Rose Cross were appearing in the gloaming of a future dawn of consciousness.

The last verses of the epic *Robespierre* likewise contain a strange hint (the emphasis are hers) which contains the premonition of future knowledge. Robespierre is standing before the guillotine, ready for execution. He sees the head of his friend Couthon fall; then in the light of the rising sun there appears to him the countenance of his deceased comrade-in-arms Saint Just:

> *Mit einem Blick umfasst er Tod und Leben*
> *Noch einmal von der Höh' der Guillotine;*
> *Dann lächelt er, und lächelnd winkt den Freund er*
> *Zu sich empor, wie einer, dem nachfolgen*
> *Nicht sterben, sondern* wiederkommen *heist!*
> *Das Fallbeil knirscht ...*
> *In seines Blutes Spuren*
> *Tritt rasch und sich'ren Schrittes Robespierre!*

> With a glance he encompasses death and life
> Once more from the heights of the guillotine;
> Then he smiles, and smiling, beckons his friend
> Up to him, as one person calls to him that follows
> Not to die but to *come again*!
> The guillotine crunches ...
> Robespierre moves quickly and with sure step
> On the trail of his blood!

These are the last words of the great epic. Do they not sound like the morning call which so many of that generation could no longer hear — which Delle Grazie likewise slept through and, hence, did not take the step that all her efforts were aiming to achieve?

She neglected, squandered and wasted much, and yet she was great and immensely powerful in her destiny. One can often sense an almost Trojan destiny in her and her life, her writings and her poems. She was great in the mood of downfall and destruction. Thus one can make sense of the words that Rudolf Steiner wrote about her at the end of his great essay: 'It will seldom happen that one can so admire a writer whose feelings and views one does not share as is the case with the works of Delle Grazie. For even where one has to say "no," one is aware of saying "no" to something great.'[14]

15

Grant, Hildebrand, Dohrn, Marées

Charles Grant (1841–89) was a rather pathetic figure, aspiring Scottish poet and literary critic. Adolf von Hildebrand (1847–1921) was a leading German sculptor of his time. Felix Anton Dohrn (1840–1909), a German Darwinist, was founder and first director of the Stazione Zoologica in Naples. Hans von Marées (1837–87) was a German painter. These four were together in Naples at the founding of the Stazione Zoologica.

The Circle of Friends

The history of the nineteenth century is still waiting to be properly written. It will be a long time before the Homer appears who will write the epic of this special time; for it was a time which — like the epoch of the Trojan War — had to destroy the old in order to allow the new to come into being. A generation of heroes wended its way through the decades of this century; and technology became the Trojan horse that achieved the breakthrough into Ilium in order to destroy the citadel of the old ideas.

The cries of Cassandra came constantly to the ears of the warriors. Achilles and Hector fought hundreds of battles in the souls of individual people, the old and the new struggled not only outwardly but also inwardly for supremacy. Then Agamemnon and Ajax, Patroclus and Odysseus appeared in ever new forms conquering the past, but there, too, stood Priam with his trusty band defending the old.

In the nineteenth century, however, there were no armies waging these battles in solid groups. Each individual hero was a solitary human being; self-reliant, thrown back on his own resources and sufficient unto himself. After the first third of the nineteenth century there were no longer any circles of friends. What had still existed in the circle of the romantics quite naturally and as a matter of course disappeared and faded into oblivion. Neither the Nazarene movement nor the pre-Raphaelites could bring back what had been lost. Only at the beginning of the new century did groups and circles arise such as the pupils around Stefan George, the guild of the Blaue Reiter and others of a similar nature.

The nineteenth century itself was a valley of solitary people. Figures like Ibsen, Richard Wagner, Cardinal Newman, C.F. Meyer clearly embodied this type of person. They took their lonely path through life and met others only as tangents to their own circles. Johannes Müller, the great physiologist, still had a group of students that he kept together. After he died, they all lived for themselves: Brücke, Haeckel, Helmholtz, du Bois-Reymond and others. And a similar situation prevailed in each individual destiny: to be alone, escaping from one's friend, fleeing from one's brother.

Thus Nietzsche lamented his former friend Wagner; Liszt and Chopin went their separate ways, Brahms did not venture a connection with Clara Schumann and withered away in his solitude. Gottfried Keller endured a similar destiny, and none of the great and strong spirits could do more than keep going and die honourably.

They were confined to themselves and entangled in their individual destinies. The 'I' as a personality was so distinct a phenomenon that the particular sound of its *per-sonare* tried to overwhelm all other tones. Those who became older and were still able to be active in old age became their own memorial. The young stood in front of them and admired them, but could no longer gain access to them, because it was hardly possible to converse with a memorial (except as a stone guest).

At the same time materialism became the dominant view of the world. This was the ultimate result of that separation which had started to come into effect in the previous centuries, that separation which cut human beings off from the knowledge and inspirational guidance of the heavenly world. What had begun as a process in the minds of a few individuals from the sixteenth century onwards sank gradually down ever deeper into people's souls, until by the nineteenth century it had taken hold of the hearts and hands of many. As yet the sky was still blue, but the colour was devoid of any reality. It was an illusion that arose within the bodily organism. Behind the blue colours was nothing but the infinite space that encompassed the planets which, supported by gravity, orbited the sun, and much further beyond were other stars — but where they came from was hardly any longer questioned. Only classical professors continued to speak about the 'moral law within me' when they looked up to the starry sky. But they were not being serious and only meant it euphemistically.

Even though everything was no longer real, on the earth the trumpets of the ruling politicians were extolling the mania of progress. Material happiness and a prosperity that could be attained by many people were among these aims. Trade and change were to be extended, knowledge became power and forces of nature were to be enslaved by man. Knowledge lost all wisdom, and nature forces withdrew from man and left him with their corpse. Out of this he created electricity and nuclear power. In this respect our twentieth century has become the fulfiller of its predecessor.

This breakdown which is happening even now, and whose

children we all are, already lay like a mighty shadow over the deeds of the generation of our ancestors who had to follow their destiny a hundred years ago. They did not want to admit that this burden was a heavy weight for their backs to carry. They believed in their illusions or tried to numb themselves with this faith. Nevertheless they were unhappy people, because their hearts were filled with delusions and impending doom.

This solitude and isolation of the individual was the underlying theme in the destiny-symphony of the nineteenth century. A group of people who have already almost been forgotten carried this theme as the central melody of their lives: the painter Hans von Marées, the sculptor Adolf von Hildebrand, the zoologist Anton Dohrn and the Scottish layabout Charles Grant. Something will be said about them in what follows.

At the beginning of the 1870s, soon after the end of the Franco-Prussian War, a start was made with the building of a handsome house in Naples. It was to stand in one of the most beautiful places in the city, the Villa Reale, the royal promenade on the shore of the magnificent bay. The senate had made the land available for building under certain conditions, although the client was himself a foreigner (he was German). This young man had the curious idea of establishing the house as a scientific research station, where researchers from all over the world could pursue their questions and problems.

The maintenance of this enterprise was to be guaranteed through the establishing of a large aquarium which could be visited by the public. Thus it was a kind of show booth — so many people said — which would contribute a good pension for the architect. When the city councillors granted approval for the building, they probably also thought that it was one of the many business enterprises that were appearing everywhere at that time.

15. GRANT, HILDEBRAND, DOHRN, MARÉES

Dohrn had himself made the architectural sketch for the building, and when it became a reality his young friend Hildebrand came to Naples and helped to ensure that the building's forms were harmonious and noble.

Dohrn, a pupil and friend of Ernst Haeckel and an admirer of the master Darwin, wanted to bring into being a biological research station where the great theses of Darwin could finally be proved through observation and experiment. This idea had come to him like a dream, and immediately after it had been revealed to him he had to devote himself to it. He was a young zoology lecturer at Jena University when on January 4, 1870 he was jolting from Apolda to Jena by mail-coach. He wrote subsequently:

> As I sat there lost in thought and the coach moved slowly up the gently ascending road to the summit, the idea suddenly came to me that the zoological station could come about if one were to establish a large aquarium on the Mediterranean, Europe's richest sea, and with the income derived from it at the same time cover the costs of the small laboratory! I immediately felt the full consequences of this idea, not only in general terms but also for my current situation, and I was so excited by this that I asked the coachman to halt and let me jump down. I wanted to go to Jena on foot, for I needed physical exertion in order to contain the excitement that was increasingly overwhelming me and at the same time also time and solitude so as to withstand the thoughts that were raging in my mind and bring some kind of order to them ... Incited by my vivid and energetic imagination, I did not doubt for a moment that I had found a way of dealing with a big task and also with the whole problem of my life.

Once he had reached Jena he immediately summoned his two closest friends, Nikolaus Kleinenberg and Ernst Abbe, who was later to become well-known as the creator and founder of Zeiss, and elaborated the plan. Both agreed with enthusiasm. 'We were all in the happy state of paradisal innocence, which helps to form the foundation for a faith that can move mountains.'[1]

With this the idea of the Deutsche Zoologische Station* in Naples, which was to become so famous, was born. Its architect was just 29 years old. Thus Saturn had almost completed an orbit since Dohrn's birth. It was at this moment that this insight which would completely determine his further life was revealed to him.

Dohrn then soon began his negotiations in Naples, but with the outbreak of the Franco-Prussian War he was summoned to Germany for military service. Only in 1872, with Hildebrand's help, did the construction of the future station begin. On August 19, 1872 the young sculptor wrote to his friend Marées:

> Your brief words gave me much pleasure. I received them in Naples, where I have been spending a few weeks and making my services available for Dohrn's façade. For part of the time we have been in hammocks and partly very happily in the water, and living on fruit. Grant is, of course, here too; the world is once again as open for him as the Bay of Naples.[2]

The following year Marées and Hildebrand were together in Naples, for Dohrn had asked them to take over the decoration of the central hall of the station that had been built. Marées had previously been for some time in Dresden; Dohrn had met him there and requested this work of him. Marées set to work, although he knew that he would not receive any financial remuneration from Dohrn. But the task attracted him, and a workfever suddenly and unexpectedly seized hold of him and made it possible to complete the whole project in a few months. What he had set aside two years to complete he was able to manage

---

* The research institute is now known as the Stazione Zoologica Anton Dohrn.

in one summer and autumn. Thus the whole work formed an integrated whole. On September 8, 1873 Hildebrand wrote to the great patron Conrad Fiedler, who made it possible for the two artists to live and work in Italy: 'What I have long wanted to share with you is my delight with Marées's pictures. They go far beyond my expectations and I can barely express how unique and appropriate they are. If one considers how quickly they were done, it seems quite incredible.'

This was astonishing, for Marées had for many years been as though paralysed. Fiedler had built him his own studio in Dresden, but nothing came of it, because Marées was always starting something new and then again discarded what he had begun. But in Naples his productive power suddenly broke forth from him like a fire that had long been contained, and the great artist emerged before his friends' eyes. Fiedler noted that same autumn in his diary: 'From my previous experiences with Marées I had indeed not considered this possible and had been fairly certain that the enterprise would be a failure.' He had also warned Dohrn about Marées, but Dohrn had not agreed and so the great project came into being.

On November 15 Hildebrand reported about the completion of the task. 'The hall is virtually finished, tomorrow the last of the scaffolding will come down, and then there'll be some touching up. The last picture is the best of all; I can hardly tell you how surprised and delighted I am.'

The last picture is like the signature that an artist adds to the work that he has completed. It is the fresco on the eastern front wall of the hall and depicts the karmic situation in whose light and shadow the whole project arose. All the other frescoes describe life in and around Naples: the sea, the fishermen on the beach and in their boats, the orange pickers in the coastal groves. Thus the life of the landscape reappeared in this internal space, which Dohrn wanted to be the focus of a truly convivial meeting-place of scholars and researchers from all over the world. There they would meet one another, have conversations,

Hans von Marées, Fresco on the east wall of the Stazione Zoologica Anton Dohrn in Naples.

15. GRANT, HILDEBRAND, DOHRN, MARÉES

listen to music together and exchange information about their innermost thoughts in lectures.

This space was conceived of as the heart of the station, but it did not become what Dohrn had initially dreamed. But what does this last picture, the fresco on the eastern wall portray?

The picture tries to catch those evening hours when the friends are sitting together after the day's work in a little *trattoria* at Posilipp, drinking, looking across the sea into the distance and sometimes also saying a few words. The little inn stands adjoining the ruins of the Palazzo di Donna Anna, and in the shadow of a pergola is the solitary table around which Marées, Grant, Hildebrand, Kleinenberg and Dohrn are gathered. A particular magic must have pervaded these gatherings, for it still streams towards the onlooker from the picture.

The midpoint of the fresco is the flight of steps leading from the forecourt of the *trattoria* to its entrance. The balustrades of its steps form a little wall, and above and behind it rise the ruins of the old *palazzo*. The evening sky glows red, and the light of the setting sun awakens the magic play of colours on the ruins of the bare columns and arches. The right side of the picture shows nothing but the featureless wall of the inn; in the bottom corner, however, an old woman sits amidst the shimmering play of colour of her rags and baskets, in which she offers for sale oysters and other *frutti di mare*.

On the left side of the picture, beyond and beneath the little wall bordering the flight of steps, stands the friends' table in the pergola; this is where they have assembled. But they appear somewhat in the background, for the central focus of the picture is the *padrona* [patroness of the inn] sitting on the wall of the flight of steps. She sits there casually enthroned, awaiting the shout of the drinking men: a dark, serious woman, her arms resting on her left thigh, with a green robe and a white cape over it that reaches from her shoulders to her knees. She is looking straight ahead, on the right stands her house, above her are the ruins and the sky, on the left the group of friends. At the foot of the wall, directly beneath the woman, a little dog stands listening.

The figures of the friends themselves are arranged in such a way that Charles Grant has a central position. He sits on the long side of the table, a large black hat on his head, his face framed by a dark beard, and his left hand supporting his head. He is staring directly ahead. On his left (on the right from the observer's standpoint) sit Hildebrand and Marées. The young sculptor, seen in profile, is looking away across the friends' table in an upwards direction. Behind his form, and half obscured by it, are the face and upper body of Marées. He appears as a dark background to his young, more radiant friend. Opposite Hildebrand, on the left narrow side of the table, sits Dohrn. He seems to have just sat down, tired from work, still holding his hat in his hand. His half stern, half good-natured face, with a long brown beard, high forehead and deep-set eyes, is tense and troubled. Behind him, still standing, his assistant Kleinenberg is portrayed.

Thus the five are beautifully balanced. On the one side are the two artists; opposite them the two scientists. Between them, as a focal point, is the writer, alcoholic and idler Grant. The group is merely one section of the overall impression of the big fresco, at whose focal point is the *padrona*.

'Seriousness, restraint and even a feeling of reserve has taken hold of the figures, as if a shudder of transitoriness had wafted over them.' Thus writes Ludwig Grote as he gives his overall impression of the pergola fresco.[3]

> 'Mysterious in the light of day' — this is how the fresco of the eastern front wall appears to the beholder ... An everyday scene, and yet one is presented with a riddle. Nothing is going on in the picture. A mood of stillness pervades it ... The unflattering European baggy suits of the men at the table, the rags of the fishwife scare away all thoughts of any intended festivity.

15. GRANT, HILDEBRAND, DOHRN, MARÉES

> Nevertheless, there is no suggestion of any intimacy with the people in the picture. One perceives them as though in another world, they have been enchanted into a strange cosmos ... An extraordinary power of perception has brought forth a heightened sense of reality out of the every-day. This power is initially disturbing, but when the observer submits to it he is blessed and gratified by the revelation of the depths of the visible which has been granted to him.

Thus writes one of Marées's few biographers.[4] What is revealed in this fresco which — despite its being a kind of genre-picture — people find so striking? Do not the mood and the background of the nineteenth century appear before us here?

The world has grown old. The old palaces are in ruins, and the inn of everyday existence, which is still part of our lives, is surrounded by bare walls. The world has become poor and empty. The evening sky casts the beautiful colours of transience over the situation which has thus emerged; but this only enhances the melancholy of what we see.

The friends sit at the bottom of the picture, as though thrown together by chance. None of them seems to know how and why he has ended up here. No one looks at the others, their eyes either look ahead, upwards or downwards; but they do not look at one another. It is a collection of separate people rather than a group. This is the source of the infinite sadness that radiates from the fresco. There they sit, five men chosen by fate, with a common task which they have — and have been able — to accomplish. But they look past one another, each of them is totally alone, focussed on his own work and destiny.

Grant is absorbed in his thoughts and eccentricities, and in a decade he would be wandering through Styria and Carinthia as a drunkard in total solitude and dying an unhappy death in a hospice in Graz.

Kleinenberg was to fall out with Dohrn within a couple of

years, because he could not keep up with his work. Embittered, he parted company with the research station.

Marées would initially share his life with Hildebrand in Florence. Soon, however, a misunderstanding would cause them to fall out with one another, and hatred and enmity stirred between them. Marées would die unfulfilled in his fiftieth year, leaving behind many uncompleted works.

Hildebrand and Dohrn alone would climb the ladder of outward success. All the honours that their age could bestow were accorded to both the sculptor and the scientist. They became friends of kings and ruling princes; recognition encouraged them, and they continued to be active in their work into old age.

Both lived into the early years of the new century. Dohrn died shortly before, Hildebrand shortly after the First World War. He still experienced the collapse of Europe, which for so long they did not want to admit.

This future destiny of the five men weaves through the mood of the picture as a premonition. The old fishwife, however, sits like a sibyl in the bottom corner; she gazes into her own past, filled with the tears of what has been. But the other sibyl looks ahead into the future: this is the *padrona* sitting on the little wall. An impending destiny is reflected in her eyes. She has the look of one of the Parcae or Three Fates, and perhaps she is thinking of the old song spoken by Iphigenia beginning with the words:

> Oh, fear the immortals,
> Ye children of men!

and then:

> If contest ariseth;
> The guests are hurl'd headlong,
> Disgrac'd and dishonour'd,
> And fetter'd in darkness,
> Await with vain longing,
> A juster decree.[5]

'Fetter'd in darkness' — this is how the five appear in the pergola fresco, and the *padrona* silently proclaims to us their fate. They were all lovers of the gods; gifted and much sought-after, full of hope and joy at the beginning of their working life. But the thick mists of the age of progress, of materialism and Darwinism had an increasingly paralysing effect on their souls and darkened their spirits.

A true race of new Tantaluses seems to have taken shape in them. They were all men from northern Europe. Dohrn came from Pomerania, Kleinenberg was a Balt (from what is now Latvia), Grant grew up in Scotland, and Marées and Hildebrand came from Central Germany. They sought and found one another in Italy, where an old historical destiny had summoned them. There they came together for a few weeks; the miracle of the frescoes came about, and as soon as the work was finished they parted company.

On December 6, 1873 Hildebrand wrote to Fiedler: 'On the last evening in Naples we had a farewell meal and peace celebration, so that all bad moods were outlawed; and we left Naples with beautiful memories.'[6]

Marées wrote three days later to Dohrn, with whom he had again been having disputes though now, having arrived in Florence, looking back happily and joyfully on the past months: 'It will be hard, and quite probably impossible, to find a circle of similarly ambitious and industrious men of a similar age (also a necessary requirement) as we found in Naples, and it is my sincere wish that it does not fall apart because of distance.'

This wish was not fulfilled. But Marées had sensed what he had brought to expression in the pergola fresco: a group of people who, united for a common task, nevertheless did not find ways of overcoming the solitude of the individual and of meeting one another in the realm of the self. The darkness of the age and the blindness of the epoch had kept their spiritual eyes closed.

Germany and Italy

In one of his early lectures Rudolf Steiner gives an illuminating indication. He speaks of how the speed with which historical events run their course becomes ever quicker, and gives a very arresting example. 'The period from Charlemagne to Frederick the Great,' he says, 'corresponds to the period of the nineteenth century. This should be understood in such a way that all events during the long time identified correspond in their number and significance with respect to evolution to the period of a hundred years.' And he adds: 'In times to come we shall evolve even more quickly.'[7] We can experience this with great clarity already in this twentieth century.

If one looks from this standpoint at the destinies that unfolded in the nineteenth century, many events appear in a completely new light. Their extraordinary richness and many-sidedness become more understandable, and many features are revealed as a reflection of the past millennium.

European history between the eighth and the eighteenth centuries can be seen as a conflict between two opposite history-forming impulses. The one tendency is that historical force that endeavours to dominate the second millennium out of the early history that preceded it, above all Graeco-Roman culture. This is an impulse that wants to preserve a hierarchical order in the life of nations. This tendency conflicts with the other force of history which, heralding the future, flows out of the sources of the awakening consciousness soul. This counter-stream has a democratic orientation, it has its point of departure in isolation and seeks the humanizing of the whole of humanity and the individualizing of the human individual.

Viewed geographically this conflict manifests itself in that the south of Europe — which represents the old tendencies — lives in a state of perpetual conflict with the northern regions. In the millennium that extends between the reigns of Charlemagne and Frederick the Great, the centre of the aspirations promoting the past was, without doubt, Rome. In this city and its surroundings those historical and religious impulses that sought to preserve the cultural life of the fourth post-Atlantean period were particularly intensified. Rome therefore became the centre of gravity of European history at that time. It united within its walls those tendencies that looked backwards and approved of a Renaissance but not a Reformation.

The opposite pole cannot be so clearly defined, because, depending on the period, it moved from one city to other cities. At the time of Charlemagne it was Aachen, later Mainz and Speyer, then Braunschweig, Florence and, in the fourteenth century, Prague. Nuremberg, Augsburg and then Vienna followed in succession, until at the end of the eighteenth century Berlin entered upon the scene of history in order to become a historical star of the first magnitude.

The 'Holy Roman Empire of the German Nation,' as it is called in German, was the one-thousand-year attempt to bridge this conflict between north and south, between the historical past and the historical future. In this epoch the effort was made to enable the past and future elements to form a kind of synthesis in a constantly self-renewing present. What was founded by Charlemagne had to be brought to an end by Frederick the Great. In the Seven Years' War (1756–63) this empire was destroyed from within and subsequently totally broken up by the Napoleonic campaigns.

What had hitherto been a history-forging tendency came in the nineteenth century to be a driving force within individual souls. People from northern Europe went to the south in order there to forge a relationship as individuals with the past, while at the same time preparing the future. Goethe's journey to Italy marks this turning point from outer to inner history. When on September 3, 1786 he started out from Karlsbad (now Karlovy Vary), he was drawing the consequence from Frederick's campaigns. Two weeks previously, on August 17, Frederick the Great had died in Potsdam. Shortly afterwards the French Revolution began.

AT THE THRESHOLD OF THE MODERN AGE

Goethe expected a number of things from this journey. Above all he wanted to penetrate beyond the veil of the northern natural environment in order to get onto the track of the archetypal picture of beings and phenomena in general. In a clear and matter-of-fact way he endeavoured to train his perception in such a manner that he could discern the active, creative element in the forms of nature. He wanted to 'observe everything with a quiet, discerning eye.'[8] A few days before (on September 24) he had written: 'I am keeping to a strict diet and conducting myself calmly, so that objects do not meet with a heightened inner state but can put the soul on a higher level. In the latter case one is far less subject to error than in the former.' Thus it became a pilgrimage of the soul, in order that the spirit of things and their creative power might be revealed to the seeking human being. Goethe was therefore able to confess much later (on October 9, 1828) to Eckermann: 'I may say that I experienced in Rome only what I really am as a human being. I never again found this intensity, this sheer happiness of feeling.'

The efforts to establish an outward synthesis between the European north and south were brought to an end by Frederick the Great. By crushing the Austrian supremacy he cut the old Holy Roman Empire to the quick.

The conflict between the northern future and the southern past now had to be shifted to the inner regions of the human soul. From the north journeys to Italy began apace; artists and poets, historians and archaeologists, students and craftsmen traversed the Alps in order to 'wake up' in Italy. They did not only seek the blue sky and the light of the ever-radiating sun. Their expectation was to inspire their souls and spirits with the magic of the landscape, the freedom of the way of life and the constant encounter with antiquity. Each person had the longing to find there — in Rome and Florence, in Naples and Pisa — his inner Iphigenia. They experienced themselves in the north as if they were with the Scythians, and, like Iphigenia, their souls uttered the words:

> ... For the sea
> Doth sever me, alas! from those I love,
> And day by day upon the shore I stand,
> My soul still seeking for the land of Greece.[9]

This is the historical karmic background which determined the longing for Italy in the nineteenth century. The battle between worldly and spiritual power, the conflict between princes and bishops, emperors and popes had shifted its scene from the domain of history to the inner world of the soul. The individual human being had to accomplish his Canossa within himself.

Charles Grant

During a visit to Jena Rudolf Steiner once drew a sketch in a circle of his pupils which indicated that in Ernst Haeckel's time this town had been the opposite pole to Rome. In Jena at that time there was a confluence of anti-Roman sentiment.

It was also around the time of Haeckel that the life paths of those men — with the exception of Hans von Marées — who later sat together around the table of the pergola at Posilipp met in this same place. As in Marées's fresco Grant was in the centre, with Anton Dohrn and Adolf Hildebrand flanking him on either side. This was how they met at that time in Jena.

Charles Grant, born in 1841, grew up in northern Scotland, in good, even well-to-do circumstances. His father had large properties in the Gambia in West Africa; he died when his son was in his childhood, and because of disputes over the inheritance the fortune was lost. Even before this the young Grant wanted to go to Germany to learn the language and to be able to read the great authors in the original. Thus while he was himself not fully grown he took a position as an English teacher at a private educational establishment (the Stoysche Institute) in Jena. There

Charles Grant and Adolf von Hildebrand (detail of Marées's fresco)

15. GRANT, HILDEBRAND, DOHRN, MARÉES

in 1861 the boy Hildebrand became his pupil. In the same year Ernst Haeckel joined Jena University as a lecturer.

In his reminiscences of his youth Hildebrand writes: 'We had English lessons with Mr Grant, a Scot ... Brought up a rich man, he suddenly had to sustain himself through a profession, with the result that he started using opium to help him cope with the pressure ... I soon developed a special relationship with him.'[10]

Grant became Hildebrand's friend. Together they roamed through the landscape of Central Germany. The Scottish teacher became a frequent guest in Hildebrand's parental home, where he met the young zoologist Anton Dohrn, who was a pupil and friend of Haeckel. Grant and Dohrn liked one another. They were almost the same age, Dohrn being a year older than Grant. 'Dohrn made great efforts to care for this man slightly younger than himself, moving heaven and earth in order to establish connections around the quiet, not exactly worldly individual and finally linking this other person's destiny completely with his own.'[11]

After Hildebrand had had his first and very stormy meeting in Rome with Hans von Marées and then followed him to Berlin, Grant also joined them. Marées, too, was very taken by the appearance of this fascinating person, and there is a picture from this time in which he tried to grasp the nature of the two friends. The bright, youthful Hildebrand is sitting at a table and behind him, as though appearing out of the darkness of the space, appears Grant's bearded countenance. The one has too much day and too much light, the other too much night and darkness.

Grant spent his entire life between Dohrn and Hildebrand. He was the first whom Dohrn summoned to Naples to help him with the building and establishing of the Stazione Zoologica.

> Without ever having a specific function or position, he was available, helped out, reported to the frequently travelling Dohrn about this and that, entering into the bustle of Neapolitan life with a certain passion, an attentive, silent observer, full of tact and kindness; he

became a mediator in countless little affairs and difficulties which the day brought and soon, actually, well-nigh indispensable.

Later he went again to Hildebrand, who had settled in Florence. From this time we have a very characteristic description of his appearance by Isolde Kurz, who often met him there:

> His face is a brownish-red copper colour, as though Etna's fire were radiating from it, beard and hair are black, his dark eyes roll and flame ... Many believed he had Negro blood in his veins. The ardour of his temperament was balanced by the most sensitive tenderness of feeling, and an element of humour — which flooded his whole being — sorted out arguments. He was a brilliant conversationalist, whose wit and imagination sparkled as many hundred coloured lights ... He had a good knowledge of Shakespeare and Goethe, as he was equally at home in German literature from its beginnings until our own day as in his own and, moreover, spoke German fluently and with complete personal mastery ... However, his deepest instincts drew him to Dante.[12]

He tried being a writer. For a while he was a correspondent for English newspapers; he wrote poems and stories from the popular life of Naples; he translated Kleist into English and attempted this and that. 'But life was too hard on him or too unattractive; in the end he completely turned his back on it — it was a slow suicidal path from which no friendly hand could divert him, in that he sought the destiny that he had missed in the glass of oblivion.' He died in 1889.

This strange and self-willed personality bore the past millennium of the figures of Dante, Shakespeare and Goethe in his soul. These were the three great writers who, from Florence, London and Weimar, tried to overcome the past represented by

Rome. Grant's eternal being kept faithful to this and made ever renewed efforts to draw strength and uprightness from it.

He stood between Dohrn and Hildebrand. The zoologist often became deeply immersed in his melancholy. The sculptor became lost in his constant cheerfulness and lightness. Grant, who was in a process of disintegration and addicted to drink and poison, was too weak to keep the balance around the other two. Because he suffered a breakdown the other two went their own ways and soon lost contact with one another. Grant had been their focal point and mediator. When he disappeared, they fell apart.

Adolf von Hildebrand

Adolf Hildebrand was the youngest of this group, Hans von Marées the oldest. The other three were born between 1837 and 1847, the years of birth of these two — Dohrn in 1840, Grant in 1841 and Kirchenberg in 1842. They were all rooted in the first half of their century and were moulded by this epoch. They still lived as successors to Goethe. This provided the prevailing mood of their destiny.

Hildebrand came into the world in Marburg. 'I still see the monastery beneath the castle,' he wrote later. 'We lived close by, and a long garden with a summer-house belonged to us; from there we could look down into the valley.'[13] This romantic landscape surrounded his early childhood.

Shortly afterwards he came to Zurich to his father, who had had to flee there after the revolution of 1848. They lived in the same house as the Herweghs, whose little daughter became his friend and play-mate. 'The human body interested me from a very early age and I remember that at the age of five I could spend time contemplating the forms of my bare bones and pursued this with interest and delight. I also undressed my four-year-old friend and was not satisfied with simply looking at her, so I also kissed her from top to toe.'

Adolf von Hildebrand

15. GRANT, HILDEBRAND, DOHRN, MARÉES

Somewhat later the child was so struck by the jumps and climbing arts of a little monkey when visiting a zoo that he took his clothes off, climbed up a tree and played at being a monkey. The magic of human and animal muscular movements had an overwhelming fascination for this individuality from his earliest childhood.

The Hildebrand family later moved to Bern, where his father had been appointed Professor of Political Science. There the child — he must have been in his tenth year or so — had a decisive experience. 'One day,' writes Hildebrand, 'I just happened to be walking in front of a collection of statues from classical antiquity. The impression was quite overwhelming, I had never dreamed that there was anything like it ... It was for me a completely new event in my life. As the room was always locked and we boys were not allowed access to the university, I do not recall going there again; but nonetheless I can still see the figures — above all the statue of Achilles.' In this moment of destiny what became the *gestalt* movement was revealed to the boy. He discerned the archetype of all sculpture in the Grecian apparel.

The impetuous boy found all learning difficult. The world of writing and reading was one that he could barely master. 'It took me many years to become familiar with these things,' Hildebrand confesses. 'Why the A looks as it does I could not understand. For me it was a visible, living world; and abusing it by employing a mere symbol was to me contrary to nature.'

Some years later, at the Stoysche Institute in Jena, all learning was nothing but a pain and torment. There was only one exception to this, and that was geometry. He wrote in his reminiscences of his youth:

> Finally I acquired some substance whereby one can consider and develop everything *ab ovo*. I was now in my element and could not keep to the usual prescribed tempo but was always hurrying onwards. However, the greatest event was algebra, when all the consequences

of the simple *a* and *b* lit up for me. This liberation from matter was like a flash of illumination, one of my great experiences. I radiated happiness. I had never been so inwardly enthralled since seeing the Greek statues.

The disposition and gifts of this personality can be assessed from these few memories. Already as a child Hildebrand lived mainly in the sphere of the sense of movement and balance. His joy in his own mobility and his delight in directly experiencing its laws and forms in thinking as geometry and algebra created the preconditions for the future sculptor.

While he was still a young man — and without being conscious of the process — Hildebrand became a complete master of his art almost without hindrances and with only the slightest measure of guidance. He must have been a radiant human being throughout his life. This is how Isolde Kurz describes him:

> Irrepressible cheerfulness was the element in which Hildebrand's life and work ran their course. Moreover, the rule that nothing is more difficult to bear than constant sunshine found its exception in him. Such a long sequence of good days as fortune had blessed him with would have made anyone else slack and apathetic; but his capacity for pleasure and freshness in his work never deserted him .... He seemed to me to be the happiest of men and capable of transmitting this happiness — even if only briefly — to others. The air became light and free wherever he appeared, and it was good to be near him. It was like seeing the first human being in a world that was as yet unconscious ... When Hildebrand spoke, it was as though the Sacred Grove of Dodona had rustled.[14]

Hence it was not surprising that, on meeting Marées in Rome in 1869, this eternal youth was immediately acknowledged by this taciturn, introverted and proud man and taken on as a pupil.

15. GRANT, HILDEBRAND, DOHRN, MARÉES

Marées's studio, a sanctuary which was closed even to his best friends, opened up to the young Hildebrand. Moreover, it would not be easy to say whether the older painter followed the young sculptor or the pupil followed the teacher when they moved from Rome to Berlin a year later.

They remained together and, as a team, created the frescos in the Zoological Research Station in Naples. Marées painted the pictures, but Hildebrand framed them with painted decorative friezes and panels and surrounded them with painted columns and arches. Thus a *Gesamtkunstwerk* (total work of art) of the first rank came into being in that beautiful hall and its loggia.

In autumn 1873 the two friends moved to Florence, where they acquired an old monastery called San Francesco di Paola and gradually furnished and organized it as a studio and as a place to live. But they stayed together for only two years. The solitary, self-preoccupied Marées became such a taciturn and embittered living companion that even the ever-joyful Hildebrand could no longer bear him. In September 1875 Marées moved out and went to Rome. This was made possible through the mediation of the ever faithful Conrad Fiedler, who was standing by as a friend and patron of both Marées and Hildebrand. Nevertheless, the breakdown of this relationship was a catastrophe. It signified Marées's deterioration and decline. He struggled on in Rome in complete solitude for a further twelve years creating perfect paintings in the style of classical antiquity. However great his desire, he did not achieve his aim. When he was fifty years old, unknown and surrounded by a handful of pupils, he died as the result of a physical crisis which he was inwardly unable to master.

Hildebrand lived on in the light of his joy and mastery. At Christmas 1890 he was appointed professor at the Munich Academy of Arts. Titles and honours were heaped upon him in the ensuing thirty years, until on January 18, 1921 he crossed the threshold of death after a lengthy period of illness.

He passed through his times as a stranger — a happy, ever-cheerful and pagan man who was somewhat out of place in the cultural environment of the nineteenth century. His works have an immediate power and sense of reality. His portrait busts speak, laugh and contemplate as though the person depicted in them was actually present, albeit in a state of enchantment.

Anything that Hildebrand took hold of — whether spatula or slate-pencil, brush or pencil — was used in a masterly way to create perfect likenesses which conveyed the breath of the living soul's reality.

He himself, on the other hand — the person who created them — never wholly came forth out of himself; he never became 'real.' His cheerfulness was enlivening, but it did not bring warmth. His joy radiated out, but it did not know the brightness of love. Marées withered at his side, Fiedler committed suicide, Grant succumbed to drink, and Dohrn became no more than a rare guest in later years.

It would be presumptuous to assume any suggestion here of blame or error. It was the century itself which disowned the would-be lover of the gods. It had no place for such figures. It wanted personalities who were crushed, lost and brought to ruin by it.

Anton Dohrn

Anton Dohrn was a typical scholarly figure of the nineteenth century. A photograph from his later years shows him with a big slouch hat and a cigar in his hand; a greying beard hides the lower part of his strong face; his eyes are hiding behind spectacles and a hat covers his brow. Thus both head and countenance are covered up and veiled.

Behind these layers, however, there lived a restless, constantly active soul devoted to its work and task. An existence without ceaseless activity, without a task and something to do would have

Anton Dohrn

been unbearable for Dohrn. He battled and spoke, gave lectures, wrote petitions, drafts, scientific treatises and books. He carried out experiments, looked at things under the microscope, settled disputes between his colleagues, soothed ill-natured craftsmen and received dignitaries and notabilities who came to visit the Zoological Institute in Naples. He knew everyone; ambassadors and scholars, ministers and princes were his friends and acquaintances. He dealt with ministries and research institutes and corresponded with most of the universities of that time.

His foundation had become a centre for biological research and he was the focal point of this centre. This incessant activity confirmed him as a person. He needed this constant affirmation of himself and the on-going reassurance that he was somebody who had brought something about. For how else could he justify his life?

Dohrn came from Stettin in Pomerania (now Szczecin in Poland). Born in 1840 as the third son of very well-to-do parents, he grew up in a patrician house near Stettin. Theodor Heuss described his father, Carl August Dohrn, as being 'in every respect a remarkable figure, a late child of the romantic age, with some flashes of brilliance but also certain droll characteristics, gifted in many things ... a dilettante but one on a grand scale.'[15] He was also a strict master. Father and son had a difficult relationship even into old age. The old man had a distinct antipathy towards his youngest son, for he wanted to see him as Professor of Zoology at a German university. But the young man went to Naples in order to establish a zoological exhibition there. He had no money for such fooleries. Thus he took away the fortune which his son was entitled to, and the son would have to manage for himself.

Nevertheless, the father had a determining influence on his sons' development. The old man became, as though fortuitously, a member of the Entomological Society in Stettin and later its Chairman. He took this position very seriously and gradually became a respected entomologist. He published the

15. GRANT, HILDEBRAND, DOHRN, MARÉES

Entomologische Zeitung, and it was partly as an honour to him and his society that the annual conference of German Naturalists and Physicians in 1863 took place in Stettin. It was at this gathering that the young Ernst Haeckel gave his first seminal lecture *Über die Entwicklungstheorie Darwins* (On Darwin's Theory of Evolution). This was heard by Anton Dohrn, 'who saw a radical change emerging in the formulation of questions and the methods of zoological research.'

Dohrn had by this time already been Haeckel's pupil in Jena for a year. The two men became friends, and during a serious, almost life-threatening illness that afflicted the student it was touching to note how Haeckel cared for him and gave him medical treatment. He reported to Stettin about his patient's progress and, according to Dohrn's own testimony, saved his life.

However, the intimate connection between teacher and pupil, which had begun with such a sparkle and such promise, soon broke down. Dohrn indicated later that he no longer wanted to go along with Haeckel's pseudo-philosophical tendencies and his drive to popularize science. But there must have been far deeper-rooted feelings which soon led to the development of a disregard and a hostility between the two of them. This process of estrangement began when in 1866 Dohrn became Haeckel's assistant in Jena. At the very outset Dohrn wrote in a letter: 'He has within the limits of his nature granted me an extreme degree of friendship, and I have the duty to reciprocate this ... And as I feel myself to have ... the upper hand in our relationship, I shall also find ways and means not to give this wonderful but limited man the right to draw me into ingratitude of the worst kind.'

In the same year Dohrn came to know a book that moved him deeply: Friedrich Albert Lange's *Geschichte des Materialism* (History of Materialism). He wrote enthusiastic letters to the author and later on visited him in Winterthur. The break with Haeckel became complete through his study of this book. The 'intellectual self-examination' that this kindled, Heuss considers, gave him ... a sense of confidence, if not exactly superiority, towards some of the scientists and particularly Haeckel, and, hence, an intellectual breadth and freedom, and furnished him with a foundation for his faculty — in the age of scientific 'overdrive' for which his own work later shared responsibility — to see the limits of, and to remain protected from, the hubris of a self-confident analysis of the world's riddles.

Here the intellectual opposition which unfolded between Dohrn and Haeckel is clearly presented. Rudolf Steiner referred even more clearly to this conflict. He devoted an extensive section to Lange in his *Riddles of Philosophy*. At the end of this exposition he writes:

Thus, two currents of a distinctly natural scientific character can be distinguished as abruptly opposing each other in the development of modern world-conception; the monistic current in which Haeckel's mode of conception moved, and a dualistic one, the most forceful and consistent defender of which was Friedrich Albert Lange. Monism considers the world that man can observe to be a true reality and has no doubt that a thinking process that depends on observation can also obtain knowledge of essential significance concerning this reality ... The dualistic conception of Lange divides the world into a known and an unknown part. It treats the first part in the same fashion as monism, following the lead of observation and reflective thought, but it believes that nothing at all can be known concerning the true essential core of the world through this observation and through this thought ...

For monism, true knowledge represents a supreme spiritual value, which, because of its truth, grants man also the purest moral and religious pathos. To dualism, knowledge cannot represent such a satisfaction. Dualism must measure the value of life by other things, no by the truth it might yield.[16]

Haeckel, the monist, remained in Germany and fought a hard battle for his world-conception; whereas Dohrn, the dualist, went to Italy, even further south than Rome to Naples, where he spent the rest of his rich, work-filled, successful and yet so impoverished life.

His marriage with a friend from his youth, a Polish woman called Marie Baranovska who had grown up in Italy, was only initially successful and later led to a temporary separation. The children — with one exception — turned away from him. Around the turn of the century, however, the Stazione Zoologica had become a firmly rooted part of German science in foreign lands and of international biology. Its founder was revered and respected and acquired an esteemed position in the academic world. He still pursued his scientific research, without ever really being able to bring it to a conclusion. The daily cares and tasks associated with the Stazione occupied his interests and inclinations.

A serious heart condition developed, and during a visit to Munich — after he had given up his post as Director of the Station — he died on September 26, 1909.

A new age had dawned. The spiritual world had begun to manifest itself, and the bearers of the destiny that prevailed in the nineteenth century were replaced by others. The spiritual darkness, be it monism or dualism, that had surrounded human beings was now beginning to brighten. The tension was no longer between north and south, between Germany and Italy; a new field of conflict was now manifesting itself. The east was consolidating itself as a growing world power and standing against the west. The destiny of the twentieth century was directed — in a way that Dohrn and Hildebrand could not understand — towards those who, as we all are, have been the prisoners of their time.

Hans von Marées

Hans von Marées

In his poem *Reiselied* (Song of a Journey) the poet Hugo von Hofmannsthal has given a lasting expression of the immense tension that exists between the German north and the Italian south:

> Water rushes to engulf us,
> The rock rolls to strike us,
> Birds flock on powerful wings
> To carry us away.
>
> But below there lies a land
> With endless fruits reflected
> In the ageless lakes.
>
> Marble brow and fountain rim
> Arise from the flowery landscape
> And soft winds blow.

In the first verse there is a reference to the experience of the threefold danger that threatens anyone who is crossing the Alps: the rushing waters, the rolling rocks and the mighty wings of great birds. Fearlessness is the shield that gives protection against these attacks. Anyone who lacks courage will succumb. He will be engulfed, struck and carried away. Thus Dante was likewise in a thicket of the dark forest of riddles when the three beasts — pardal (leopard), lion and wolf — approached him and he had to seek the way out. Only Virgil could deliver him from his predicament.

Once the wanderer has crossed the Alps, the miracle of the south stretches out before him: a dream land, 'with endless fruits reflected in the ageless lakes.' A new, unknown realm is revealed in his soul; it has found its homeland.

Marées will have felt something similar when in 1864, at the age of 27, he came to Rome for the first time. He had previously lived in Berlin and then for a longer period in Munich, where he also sometimes worked, and then went to Italy on behalf of Count Schack. His companion was Lenbach; he was by no means a Virgil but he guided his first steps through Rome and Florence. The Count wanted copies of old masters for his gallery in Munich; Marées and Lenbach were to provide them for him, and for this he treated them to a stay in Italy — a good offer for two young and gifted painters. To begin with Marées copied very industriously; but the more he was overpowered by the richness of the Italian air and landscape, the greatness of the old masters and the over-abundance of impressions the less active he became, and he spent his time studying, making sketches, thinking and reflecting. Conrad Fiedler, his faithful patron and first biographer, writes about this time:

> In this period Marées had moments of sublime perception interspersed with deep depression. Many a drop of bitterness intermingled with the joy of experiencing an inner artistic rebirth. He was under the spell of the time in which he was born; only too clearly was he reminded at every step that he stood alone with his own innate aspirations. He himself had an overwhelming hunger for renewal and, since he had not as yet discovered a new foundation on which he could gain a firm foothold, he was subject to a tormenting uncertainty.[17]

Here in Italy what had already occurred in Berlin and Munich became all the more apparent. The young artist initially tried his best, left all his companions far behind in skill and insight, but suddenly could not go any further. He came to a halt, became subject to alternations between low and high spirits, to despair and also drunkenness, because he did not wholly succeed in his aspirations. What was it that he demanded of himself, of his art and abilities? Did he know what he wanted, or was it only pressure and anguish that tore the brush from his hand?

Fiedler says that a great gulf opened up in Marées between his wishes and his abilities.

> When he had opposed the resistance of the world with
> the consciousness of a higher insight, the power to break
> this resistance was denied him. He exhausted himself in
> the battle against the shortcomings of his own gifts, and
> where the battle would — once directed outwards —
> have been able to have a liberating effect, he saw himself
> thrust back on himself ... This inner conflict governed his
> life from that time when he first became fully conscious
> in Italy of his profession as an artist right until the end of
> his life.

For the correct, faithful, but in many respects limited Fiedler, this seemed to be the solution to the riddle. He saw in Marées an artist who hoped more of himself than he could fulfil. Much, however, would contradict this insight, for from the outset Marées was very capable. Already as a child and later as a young man he had no technical difficulties with painting. He was to begin with a pupil of Steffeck in Berlin and continued to develop further on his own in Munich, because no one could guide him beyond this point. The horses and soldiers, scenes of war and camps, that he painted were technically outstanding, his portraits — schooled in Rembrandt's style — were both expressive and enigmatic. What he did not initially find was a thematic content that was equal to his abilities. What were landscapes — and the people who appeared in them as mere accessories — to him? This was not art but mere copying, of which he had a dim view.

One day, suddenly and quite unexpectedly, a theme opened up to him like a vision: Diana in the bath.

> A German Corot emerges ... The first true Marées.
> The theme occurred to him ... in the park of
> Schleissheim Castle ... A wholly soft, tender sensuality
> is in the atmosphere; the theme for the first time
> introduces a naked figure, a Goddess. She grows

forth from the shadow of the wood as does the body of the beloved from the thoughts of a young man who has fallen in love for the first time, like a beautiful fairy tale.[18]

This was truly a new beginning, for suddenly a content had emerged which he had sought for so long. Not reality but dream and myth appear here in earthly form and illuminated by a higher reality. A world of supersensible transparency had made itself known. But it subsided again and the vessel through which it had begun to manifest itself was left empty and abandoned. Marées did not have the energy to endow the magical fragrance of this vision of Diana with that perfection of expression that belongs to great art. It was not ability that he lacked — it was the theme, the inner image, the imaginative vision that he sought and failed to find.

Already as a young boy Marées had learnt to reproduce 'what could be seen' with crayon and paint. He once wrote to Fiedler:

> I remember more or less exactly how the world appeared in my fifth year, and how I have also tried to give a résumé of this impression pictorially. From this point onwards the distractions also began. For hardly has my attentiveness been awakened than an influence enters in which — even though well-meant — in the majority of cases places a wall between the individual and the revelation.[19]

At that time the child had visions; when he tried to take hold of them his parents intervened and took pains to show him how to draw 'correctly.' 'But the visions disappeared with the well-intentioned cultivation of his talent. They no longer appeared to him, and there was no way in which he could invoke them. Only a memory remained and engendered an infinite longing for the paradise of childhood.'[20]

15. GRANT, HILDEBRAND, DOHRN, MARÉES

The idealized theme, the imaginations that revealed themselves to the child, disappeared and faded away. The boy learnt the craft and hoped for new inspirations. They came sometimes, suddenly and unexpected as in dreams, and imbued him with a new strength; and he was consumed by them like a flaming torch. This is how his vision of 'Diana' came to birth in Schleissheim. Similarly, he painted — suddenly and directly out of inspiration — the colour-radiant picture of *Philip and the Treasurer,* which records a scene from the Acts of the Apostles. The *Evening Forest Scene* is also such a picture. In the foreground, on the edge of the dark forest, a naked man is sitting at a simple wooden table with a scantily clothed woman opposite him. His back is turned to the observer; she is looking to the front. A horse, led by a child, comes into the picture; a clothed man is on the horse. Clouds cover the sky, which lights up the clearing in the forest. The whole scene is free of tension and eroticism. All is form, colour and harmony, which show the human being in the most beautiful light.

These radiant fairy tales of eternal truth were only rarely — mostly at an interval of a few years — conceived and created by Marées. In between was emptiness, despair, fruitless questing and an unprofitable squandering of his gifts.

Then in 1873 the possibility arose to paint the big central hall of the Stazione Zoologica, and in this work of art, which came about in a few months with Adolf von Hildebrand's help, inspiration and vision were again prominent.

After this, night again descended, until around 1879 the last, decisive ardour of creativity took hold of the painter and was sustained until his death. The reality of his thematic material broke through his pictures in an ever fuller way. It released his technique; he changed from oil paint to tempera painting. Supersensible figures appeared before him in human form which he tried to record in triptychs. In a twofold burst of energy he endeavoured to capture the richness that was streaming into him, first at the beginning and then at the end of the 1880s. The themes were: *The Hesperides, The Holy Riders, The Judgment of Paris, The Courtship,* and *Praise of Modesty.* In the meantime coloured sketches, designs and drawings came into being, all of which were imbued with the same formative will. The world of the senses was overcome. It had become transparent and translucent. Pictures and figures came into view which seemed to rise out of the primal depths of human evolution. They were not mythical figures but transformations of the human form for which there are as yet no names. These figures look upon us in such a way as if the eternal formative forces of the world creators were appearing before our eyes. Despite their contorted attitude, they have a harmonious effect because their movements speak and sound. The feelings that stream forth from these works are at once stern and relaxed, serious and yet merry, cautionary and healing. Youths, children and virgins, men and old people stand, sit and lie with grace and dignity in a natural environment which has been transfigured into a spirit-landscape

Clothed and unclothed figures can exist alongside one another without creating any disturbance, for purity and greatness permeate them with unmitigated power. They are not human beings, nor are they gods and angels. They rise up before the astonished eye like the geniuses of a new race which has emerged from the slough of earthly entanglements.

This is an archetypal picture of human existence: not the Luciferically ambivalent form of the superman dreamed up by Nietzsche, nor the form of the human predecessor sought by Huxley and Haeckel; the eternal likeness of God begins to be revealed between the human form wrested from the animal and the crazy idea of the self-sufficient superman who rejects the past.

In the earlier pictures, however beautiful they may be, the animal is still prominent. Horses and dogs (for example in the

Diana's Bath) enliven the scene. Man, although elevated and refined, is still part of nature. Only in the last pictures is man as such the actual, and sole, theme. He appears as the gesture of his soul capacities and as the expression of his spirit-being.

Only in the triptych of the three holy riders does the animal appear again in the form of the horse. Here, however, man is no longer the companion of animals but their redeemer. Hence the central picture also represents St Hubert. He kneels before the deer, in whose antlers the vision of the Crucified One appears. The two dogs in the foreground begin to have a presentiment of the event, and the horse without a rider touchingly lowers its head, as if it wanted to kneel before its Lord. Paul's words regarding the longing of all creation in its hope for redemption pervade this picture. Both side panels tell of the power of the human heart: St Martin shares his cloak with the beggar; St George overcomes the dragon. Compassion and courage rise above the animal in man.

Thus Marées's last creative work stood in the light of a future spiritual knowledge. When the child's imaginative perceptions disappeared in 1842, the growing boy began to search for them. Until 1879 he had to be a wanderer, fighter and homeless person. Only then did the revelations of his early childhood return to him in a transformed fashion. Between 1842 and 1879, however, the mighty 'War in Heaven' was taking place behind the scenes of the outer world.[21] 'Now war arose in heaven, Michael and his angels fighting against the dragon; and the dragon and his angels fought, but they were defeated and there was no longer any place for them in heaven' (Rev.12:7f).

In Marées's soul there was a reflection of this battle, which was waged in heaven amongst spiritual beings. A solitary human being who left behind any kind of earthly temptation became the reflection of this cosmic event. His work is the ash of that spiritual fire which consumed him.

Hans von Marées was born on Christmas night 1837 in Elberfeld. His father came from an old, Central European family, his mother, Frederike, was Jewish, daughter of the banker Sussmann from Halberstadt. Thus a reverberation of a romantic destiny (reminiscent of Dorothea Schlegel and Rahel Varnhagen) surrounded Hans von Marées's childhood and youth. 'Such parents, to whom a free, independent attitude — even if not the creation of beauty — was natural and whose house was open to all good spirits, could hardly give their son a harmful dowry to take with him on his way.'[22] But the child remained lonely; he was the youngest of four brothers. The other three grew up as most boys do. None of the three later managed to cope with outer life. The youngest resembled them in this, but instead of succumbing became a hero of the spirit.

His youth was already a struggle. He suffered hunger in Berlin, served out his time in the forces and then went to Munich, remaining there in solitude. None of the painters who were around him came close to him or so much as became his friend. He must have had something dismissive and attention-seeking about him which the others could not put up with. Fiedler wrote in his diary after the Spanish trip on which Marées accompanied him: 'Marées is the purest mirror in which one can observe oneself. If one does not always see what one would like, that is not exactly his fault. As a matter of fact, I know no other person with regard to whom one would be so little capable of self-deception.'

He was and remained different from others, isolated, thrown back on his surroundings, concerned with his own affairs and understood by few people. What was he to identify with at this time — the historical staffages of Kaulbach and Piloty or Makart's bombastic marionettes? Moreover, he had no connection with the French impressionists, and he does seem to have known anything about Cezanne.

He formed a brief friendship with Böcklin and Feuerbach, who were living in Rome at the time, but Böcklin was too extroverted for him and did not appreciate his pictures. Feuerbach was closer to him as regards his convictions; but he was often disturbed by the painter's immoderate over-estimation of his abilities, bearing in mind his limited skills. He saw in everyone the barriers that they themselves put up and saw through their shortcomings, but they felt themselves acknowledged and let him alone.

Thus there were only two people who accompanied him throughout his life, although even with them he was only intimately attached and befriended at the outset. Subsequently, after the break with Hildebrand and his departure from Florence this connection was also sundered as regards everyday life. Nevertheless, the three men remained closely linked and associated with one another in a spiritual sense: the bright, cheerful, eternally youthful Adolf von Hildebrand and the serious, melancholic Conrad Fiedler, who was enshrouded by the shadow of his father's madness. They met one another for the first time in the winter of 1866/67 in Rome. From then on Fiedler became Marées's generous patron and remained so — despite their subsequent estrangement — until the end of the painter's life. He demanded no pictures of him or other proofs of gratitude. He had probably lost faith in the artistic capacities and perfections of Marées, and he feared this solitary fighter whose constant struggles with himself he could no longer understand. Nevertheless, he remained faithful to him, although — oscillating between contempt and sympathy — he no longer took him seriously.

Hildebrand initially stuck devotedly and lovingly to his older friend. He revered the teacher that he had in him and grew into a great sculptor under Marées's guidance. They combined forces in their work on the frescoes in Naples. Then they moved together into the old monastery near Florence; but Marées soon forced himself to give up his friend. Life around him was too everyday, too bourgeois, too friendly and too unproblematic. The fighter's ever-wakeful conscience could no longer put up with this beautiful illusion with which the younger man surrounded himself.

His eye sought the imaginations which could provide themes for his pictures.

The separation from Hildebrand was an immense sacrifice. With him he also lost Fiedler, for the two men had found a deep friendship in their lack of understanding for Marées. The painter returned to Rome. Hildebrand remained in Florence, and Fiedler, who married soon after the catastrophe, went every year with his wife to his friend in Florence, where they spent many months in one another's company.

Marées remained alone; he tried his hand as a suitor when a Viennese schoolgirl, Melanie Tauber, came for a visit to Rome. (She is one of the two girls who are sitting chatting on the bench in the orange grove depicted in the Naples frescoes.) But she, too, left him, because he was not able to keep her. After they had taken leave of one another, he continued to write her despairing love-letters; but he did not himself any longer believe in a connection. A further sacrifice had to be made; the most difficult, which freed him from all earthly ties.

Then came the last years. The visions began to overshadow him, and he followed their call. He painted, covered up what he had achieved, added layer upon layer to what he had already completed and was never satisfied with his work. A few pupils again gathered around him; they helped him to bear the last difficult years of hardship and illness. After a serious feverish sepsis on June 5, 1887, when the sun was rising and the nearly full moon was setting in the west, Hans von Marées crossed the threshold of death. He had struggled to fulfil his destiny until his last day. Under his pillow lay a Bible, and it was open at the Book of Job; he remained faithful to the spirit. In one of his last letters to Fiedler he wrote:

> The calm awareness of always, despite my many errors, having striven for what seemed to me to be necessary gives me an inner lack of concern which either helps me to overcome all difficulties or enables me to bear

the inevitable in the right way. The only good attitude of mind is one that grants value to a person's deeds and existence; it has a necessary and continuing influence, and anyone who manages to transmit such an attitude to other individuals can be sure that his better part will not die.[23]

A true Job speaks through these words. Marées died with this same conviction. He was certain of his continuing existence; not only in his works, whose unfinished nature he recognized. He himself, as an eternal individuality, wanted to strive onwards, to grow and develop. This is what he had struggled for. The torso of his pictures is merely the beautiful and wonderful sheath that the eternal part of him has left for us.

At the time of Marées's death his name was virtually unknown. His few friends and pupils knew of his aspirations, but even they were barely aware of the true greatness of his creative work. Approximately a year after the painter's decease Fiedler published the little commemorative book in which he tried to explain Marées's art and to justify his friend's behaviour. It appeared as a private publication intended for a small circle of acquaintances. In 1891 a first exhibition of Marées's work, arranged and financed by Fiedler, took place in the Munich Glaspalast. It drew little attention, and the pictures and drawings that Fiedler had given to the state of Bavaria were placed not in the Pinakothek but after a fashion in Schleissheim Castle. Only through Julius Meier-Graefe's dedication in writing his large, three-volume book about Marées and putting on the two exhibitions in Berlin and Munich in 1909 did the painter become known and also, an ideal for young people in Germany at that time. Simultaneously with Marées two German poets who had almost completely been forgotten were rediscovered: Friedrich Hölderlin and Novalis, the proclaimer of magical idealism. At this time a dream of reawakening was pervading a Germany that was experiencing a renewal of youthful forces and becoming more self-aware, a dream of poets and painters, students and the young. A new generation seemed to be awakening, and for them Marées began to live and come to life again in his paintings. This youthful wave of true Germanism that was so full of promise was destroyed by tanks and machine-guns on the battlefields of France. Karl Thylmann, Franz Marc, Norbert von Hellingrath, Otto Braun, August Macke, Bernhard von der Marwitz, August Stramm and Georg Trakl are only some names of this great legion of the German rebirth.

Subsequently, at the time of the Third Reich, Marées's work was banished from museums, because his mother had been Jewish. Since the end of the Second World War it has again — very gradually — begun to win the hearts of some people. But who is still willing to understand him?

The picture of the five friends looks down at us from the dim twilight of the great hall in Naples. They are gathered around the table of the *trattoria* and gaze at us; only Marées's face and form are almost hidden. All around his frescoes can be seen. On the north wall are the four upright figures of the rowers. They pull the great oars, and the boat glides onwards. Behind them stands the *padrona* and looks down at the young woman sitting in the boat. She gazes into the water, her head inclined forwards, dreamily engaged with the play of the waves. Behind her appears a boy, like a genius. This is the boat of life that carries us all. We think we are like the *padrona,* and yet we are merely dreamers, guided by the genius of our eternal self.

On the opposite wall two frescoes shine forth. Chatting girls are sitting in an orange grove, and beside them a youth is picking fruits, an old man digs the soil and a boy lies playing in the grass. This, too, is life! In these figures there is already an anticipation of the figures in the later triptychs.

Between the frescoes of the north wall stand the busts of Charles Darwin and Karl Ernst von Baer. Both were great naturalists; the one came from the west, the other from the east of Europe. Von Baer still held to the story of the Creation and remained to the last the pupil of his great teacher Cuvier. Darwin, on the other hand, rejected the idea of creation and mechanized the idea of evolution. His shadow, which was regarded as light, grew more and more and became bigger and more powerful. He filled people's thinking with darkness, and they thought that he was illuminating it. Through him the last residues of the true image of man were obliterated. This began to happen around the year 1860.

In a lecture where Rudolf Steiner refers to this year, he says that today

> the time is ripe for people to understand that every human being who does indeed have a body, soul and spirit and is present before us has come down from the spiritual world, and in such a way that he has previously passed through a pre-earthly life. He himself seeks the blood through which he would incarnate on the earth ... The time is now coming when the perception of man as a spiritual being who has undergone a development between death and a new birth will become a living feeling, where one needs to conceive of the idea of the super-earthly significance of human souls. For without this idea all earthly culture will die.[24]

Here Marées's true mission becomes clearly visible. In his particular domain of form and colour he was prepared to allow the renewed image of man's eternal being to reawaken. This became a 'living feeling' in his soul, and so — once the year 1879 had been reached and Michael had ascended to the rank of Time Spirit — he was able to paint the great panels where the redeemed image of man begins to appear again.

In another lecture Rudolf Steiner spoke about the supersensible sources of the arts. This is what he says about painting:

> There is a world of spirit, the world through which we pass between going to sleep and waking up. It is this world, which we bring with us out of sleep, which really inspires us when we paint ... Painting becomes — for anyone able to apprehend it correctly — a revelation of the spiritual world which surrounds us in space and thence also permeates us. This is the world in which we find ourselves between falling asleep and awakening.[25]

It was in this world that — unknown to himself — Marées experienced the mighty imaginations that became his themes. He brought them with him out of this spirit-world and tried to give form to them. And there was always one particular theme around which his ideas unfolded: the rescuing of the eternal image of man. Iphigenia's call must have often rung out in his soul when he was standing in despair and despondency before his unfinished efforts:

> Save me.
> And save your image in my soul!

One of his last drawings portrays an Iphigenia who bears the same features of super-earthly beauty that belong to his late images of women. His life was a sacrifice to Iphigenia; it kept a distance from outward events, in order that in the silence 'certain elements of our intellectual culture could be purified and offered up to the higher gods in a priest-like, religious way, so that this outward intellectual culture does not cause the heart and souls of human beings to wither away.'[26]

In the world without, life hurtled on its way in Darwin's shadow. Dohrn had become his servant, and Hildebrand had not been able to elude him. Through his marital connection with Mary Meyer, his friend Fiedler was drawn into the whole Bayreuth business. Kleinenberg and Grant escaped into an early death. Marées alone remained steadfast. He was the true antipode of Darwin, solitary and unrecognized.

That he left Germany in order to live and create in Italy was a Canossa journey of destiny. His homeland, for which he longed, gave him nothing; there was no place for him there. But likewise in Rome he remained homeless; he died and only long after his death did he return to Germany through his work. He deserves to be called a servant and bearer of the Folk Spirit of the German nation. Born on Christmas Day, he was throughout his life surrounded by the words of the angels who spoke to the shepherds of peace on earth and of good will to the hearts of men.

When he died in Rome, the young Rudolf Steiner had begun editing Goethe's scientific writings and published his *Goethe's Theory of Knowledge*. What with Marées had still to remain a beautiful appearance was now transmuted into spiritual reality and truth. The rescued image of man was brought into the twentieth century.

Gustav Mahler

16

Gustav Mahler

Mahler (1860–1911) was an Austrian late-romantic composer and one of the leading conductors of his generation.[1]

Mahler's nature: a summons

'That's Mahler!' You could hear the words whispered whenever he entered a restaurant or coffee shop in Vienna, Munich, New York or Hamburg. You could feel in these words all kinds of soul elements: admiration and envy, devotion and fear, abhorrence and, last not least, the atmosphere, when a truly great man, commanding and masterful, suddenly appears in a group of people: revolt and rejection.

That's Mahler!' You could hear the words spoken joyfully by children as they saw him pass in the streets of Munich in September 1910. They were eager to take his hand when he was on his way to the rehearsals of the first performance of his Eighth Symphony; he was always so kind to them and joked with them.

This was Mahler: from 1897 to 1907 director of the Vienna Court Opera House which position made him ruler of the kingdom of music in those days. He was well known all over the world: by the singers and the orchestras of all great cities, by high society, by rich and poor alike. He never made a show of himself; he almost never had time for parties and socializing, occupied as he was by the onrush of his work. Yet most of his important contemporaries or those believing themselves important, knew of his existence. Some had shaken his hand, some had spoken to him, many had seen him conducting in the large concert halls and experienced his powerful firmness when he kept a tight rein on the world-famous Vienna Philharmonic at the beginning of an opera performance.

His biographer, Richard Specht, said of him:

> What is so tremendously powerful in Mahler's personality and in his work, is quite something different from what we feel when we admire the creations of other geniuses ... the storms of his soul; his greatness and exuberance, the highly strung will to achieve the ultimate and extreme, the boundless yearning of a restless soul, the grim determination of one continually on a quest.[2]

It is these features we meet in Mahler. An undying fire burned within him, which he served because it would not leave him. It consumed him, it drove him and it was ever present around and within him.

Everywhere he went he became the centre of attention without, however, desiring to be. His word dominated everyone around him, but so did his silence. They were afraid of his ill-humour and were happy, when he was kind. Often a certain awe spread before him, forcing open the way which his will compelled him to take. He was a direct personality, always himself. Unrelenting as he was in all what he expected from his colleagues as well as from his friends, he was never rude or malicious. He was strong and clear-cut and there were no limits to what he demanded if it seemed right and necessary: he did not easily suffer human shortcomings. Bruno Walter said of him:

> His life and his work were driven by impulse; thus he had to struggle again and again, for all achievements. Therefore, life, art and human relationships became

new to him every day; but he lacked the advantages of systematic progression and mastering and applying what had been achieved. Every day he had to start anew and every day he had to waste himself in struggle and devotion.[3]

However, the torch of his existence was able to burn calmly and quietly also. At such times it radiated warmth and peace, lost itself in an intimate devotion to others, to the suffering and illusions of existence, to the needs and troubles of his fellow human beings.

This powerful flame within him was constantly metamorphosed into music. It resounded in him and he formed and moulded it so that other people too were permitted to listen to it. This music was indomitable, yet formed measure of the man Mahler; it was his yearning, his suffering, his love, his struggle, his desperation, his devotion. This music became both path and challenge. It shook human souls, calling upon them to follow.

The abundance of his forms of expression was as inexhaustible as the volume of his orchestra. He made use of everything that produced sound: harps and bells, kettledrums and cymbals, bundles of sticks. He let another orchestra sound from backstage, and called on the human voice that it too could express in words what in music conveyed in sounds. Wherever, shining in light, the human word arose from the fiery sound, everything became intimate, solemn, but also merry, or powerfully redeeming.

Here, Mahler was entirely himself, the human being. He was eager to console where consolation was needed, to heal where he had wounded, to bring balm where he had struck the weak or had scourged the unworthy.

Often he said to his friends, 'My time will come.' On the one hand, he lived in and for the future, while on the other hand he was a part of his own epoch, like everybody else. He belonged to his epoch as the epoch belonged to him; he was constantly a challenger, never resting amid the tempest of his life.

All who met him experienced the unrelenting quest of his nature. No one could resist his challenge. It was not so much the spoken word, but his very presence which had this effect; many felt it as a summons to appear before Judgment Day. But then they confused Mahler the man, with his higher being, thinking that he was overbearing and wished to judge them. However, he was the inspired bearer of this summons, he was not the summons itself. He sounded the trumpet, not for judgment, but because he felt his mission to summon.

These were the mighty sounds of the trombones und trumpets in the last movement of the Second, the *Resurrection Symphony*, which let the enthralled listener experience the vision of Judgment Day. This spell fell on people, when Gustav Mahler approached them with, as it were, his trombone summons. This was not always true, for he was a human being. Nevertheless, it sounded whenever his *daimon*, his higher being, shone through him.

Mahler's work: a summons

The short man with his lively movements approached the podium; immediately there was absolute silence. He greeted the musicians with his clear, friendly voice, and as though in a spell they followed his directing will the instant he raised his baton. His features showed a deep earnestness, a holy zeal; his shining eyes seemed to radiate light, appearing entranced whenever the orchestra came to mystical places in the score; his powerful chin spoke of a strong will. Concentrated, entirely the master, he moved about freely, sometimes even in a grotesque manner, nervously twitching and stamping his foot.[4]

He had been conducting from his early youth. Almost without interruption he was active, first as a conductor, and later as a director of greater and ever greater opera houses. He began at the age of 19 in a small, third class summer theatre in the Austrian resort of Bad Hall; from there he went to Ljubliana (now in Slovenia) and later to Olmütz (now Olomouc the Czech Republic, though in Mahler's time both were part of the Austro-Hungarian Empire). From there he went to Kassel in Germany, and at the age of 25 he became principal conductor at the Prague Opera House. There the great disciple of Wagner rehearsed *Rheingold* and *Walküre* and on a Sunday morning, February 21, 1886, he conducted the Ninth Symphony by Beethoven.

From Prague he moved to Leipzig and after having been active there for two years, he was made general director of the Budapest Opera House. For a 28 year-old Jewish musician, an ever-unruly fellow, obsessed by his work, unfamiliar with the work, it was quite an accomplishment to be appointed general director of this Royal Opera House. The latter had been built only a few years before, an achievement of the well-known Hungarian national pride. There he drew an annual salary of 10 000 florins and, with this income and his position, he became a member of the high society. A great number of revivals of operas and first performances are put on under his baton. He was not only the conductor but was stage director as well, forging the orchestra, the chorus and soloists together in such a way that all became a single unit, devoted to a common task. There were no stars who came and went as they liked, but an impassionate group of people, in which every individual was striving to achieve his best.

Owing to his uncompromising firmness and vigour, his activities there soon came to an end. He took his leave and went to Hamburg, where he remained for the next six years. Many who experienced him there, tell of this time. Paul Stefan wrote:

> All soloists were almost afraid of his rehearsals, but they realised that these rehearsals were an advanced school in the musical-dramatic field. His unbending strictness and the all-consuming zeal by which he was obsessed, required the highest degree of exactness in the rhythm of the music which originated for him exclusively in the rhythm of the drama on the stage.[5]

It was in Hamburg where for the first time, he met Bruno Walter, his junior by sixteen years. Walter had been at the opera house as a young singer's coach, and it was then that the life-long friendship of the two great men began. Walter recalls those times:

> It was extremely valuable for my musical growth to serve professionally a genius with such an overwhelming musical gift and such a powerful personality, to be allowed to work at an institution whose very life was centred around a clear-burning and power-radiating figure, and where the enemies of true art, indolence and cynicism, were never able to gain a firm footing.[6]

Again and again the fiery will power of the conductor and stage director was mentioned. Everyone was caught in his spell; each one of his performances, both in the opera house and in the concert hall, became a festival for both musicians and listeners. He took the souls of his audience with him into the kingdom of sound; he raised them aloft into the world of music and the waters of life and the mysteries of destiny flowed around the people thus united. What before had been *show business* and a means of entertainment, was now metamorphosed into a holy deed. What Richard Wagner had attempted at the end of his life, to make the opera a mystery drama, was achieved again and again by Gustav Mahler wherever he was active. Everything around him became important, was filled with a new meaning. In his presence there was no room for incompleteness, for coquetry, for superficiality. His entire personality was filled with an all-pervading earnestness.

In the year of Wagner's death Mahler experienced a performance of *Parsifal* for the first time in Bayreuth. He spoke of this event in a letter: 'when I left the Festival Hall, not able to utter a single word, I realized that this had been the greatest, the most painful experience of my whole life, and that I shall carry it with me untarnished to my last day.'[7] He did, and he manifested it time and again.

16. GUSTAV MAHLER

During this period from 1879 to 1897, the period of a moon-node, he had been striving constantly to make the opera house a true institution of art. When his activities in Hamburg came to an end, he was appointed general director of the Imperial Opera House in Vienna at the age of 37. There he remained almost for a decade, and no one who was privileged to share in his most wonderful time, can ever forget the experience. Everything in Mahler had become a challenge. He created a completely new style of both performance and production by unifying music, scenery and acting. Together with Alfred Roller, who designed the scenery, he created opera presentations of unprecedented power. The greatest among these were *Don Juan, Fidelio,* and *Tristan and Isolde.* To quote Paul Stefan again:

> The aim of Mahler and Roller was to completely renew the very foundation of the repertoire. The last German operas were born out of the spirit of a mature art, and their significance for all future times appeared in the fact that in their new beauty was now revealed a new style.

And Mahler's widow, Alma Maria, confirmed this: 'The opera performances were festivals. Mahler knew no limits. Absolutely nowhere! "I only like people, who exaggerate, not those, who understate," he said. Roller was present in our house constantly, for lunch, for dinner. And there was never any other topic than the new scenery for this or that opera.'[8] However this time too came to an end. In 1907, when the opposition against him had become too strong, he offered his resignation which was accepted.

Many factors had contributed to this decision: the death of his dearly loved daughter at the age of five; he himself had become the victim of a severe heart ailment and other clouds began to gather on the sky of his destiny. When he told Bruno Walter of his resignation, he said: 'During these ten years I have completed my circle.' Thus one of the most glorious epochs in theatre history had ended.

From then on Mahler's farewell song began. The New York Metropolitan Opera offered him an excellent contract as guest conductor. He accepted it, greatly appreciating the way he was honoured and helped. Whatever he requested — and it was by no means little — was granted. He came to New York in the winter of 1908–9, returning again the next year and once more in 1910–11 but then he fell ill. The sickness virtually defeated him. He returned to Europe in February 1911; from Paris he went to Vienna, where he died, less than 51 years old, on May 18.

The flame of his musical summons was extinguished, having burst forth again in a last brilliance just a few months earlier. This was in Munich, where he conducted the performance of his Eighth, the *Symphony of the Thousand*. The exaltation and devotion shown him by thousands was the heartfelt reward for the sacrifice of his life, which the people understood and accepted, though only half consciously. It was a 'hosanna,' followed by a 'Crucify him!' Bruno Walter, his faithful friend, recalls:

> What a moment, when greeted by thousands in the gigantic exhibition hall, and he stepped upon the podium, before the thousand singers and musicians, at the zenith of his life, yet already marked by destiny's imminent recalling, when his work called upon the *Creator Spiritus* in whose fire it had originated, when a thousand lips formed the summons of his life's yearning — *Accende lumen sensibus, infunde amorem cordibus!* After the last sound of the symphony faded away and the rapturous roar of applause reached him, he ascended the steps of the platform to the children's choir who were shouting with joy, and he shook hands with every single one of them, walking all the way along their ranks.
>
> It was the children from whom he was taking leave, because he loved their innocence and their devotion, just as he himself had been filled with love and devotion.[9]

This was the very same evening, September 12, 1910, on

16. GUSTAV MAHLER

which Rudolf Steiner gave the last lecture in his cycle on the Gospel of St Matthew. There he said,

> And human nature has proved capable of receiving the Son of God. This Son of the living God promised to remain united with the Earth's spiritual existence until the Earth achieves its goal — when all human beings will be filled with the substance and being of Christ, to the degree that they accept his presence within them ... We must experience this idea in all humility ... and when we do, our feeble strength will inevitably increase and lead us ever upward toward our divine goal.[10]

This was the nature of Gustav Mahler's striving. In imitation of the Christ, he was walking toward his divine goal. His work was a challenge to mankind so that the earth's mission might be fulfilled.

Mahler's work as the conscience of his time

Mahler was born into a middle-class Jewish family in Kalischt in Bohemia (now Kalište), the second child among twelve, and Iglau (Jihlava) was the place where he spent his childhood.[11] The impression of the far-stretching Bohemian-Moravian plains strongly influenced his childhood: the broad and fertile fields of grain, the hills so characteristic of that region, here and there dark forests, brooks and rivers. The land had been permeated by the warm faith of the Bohemian-Moravian Brethren, who had lived and worked there for centuries. 'Ever and again one is captured by the spell of this scenery and is filled with the feeling of the deep Sabbath stillness of the spirit, so that it is hard to believe, that there can be another part of the world which can help so greatly those souls longing for ethical rebirth.'[12] This world was the womb out of which Mahler's music grew. Of this landscape Rainer Maria Rilke, the poet said:

> Much am I moved
> With Bohemian's song,
> Softly it slips to the heart
> Weighs it so deeply down.
>
> Much though hast
> Journeyed far over lands
> Yet over years does it still
> Come to your mind.

Again and again in his music Mahler recalls the melodies of his Bohemian homeland. In his compositions can be heard the sounds of the musicians who played their violins, their double-basses and their trumpets every Sunday in the taverns for young people's dances; in them echo also the bugle calls of the old Austrian army, for Iglau, like so many small towns in those times was a garrison.

When Mahler was 15 he entered the Academy of Music in Vienna, and from then on he was bound by the all-pervading spell of this city of music and by its surroundings, the famous enchanting Viennese Woods. He was a frequent visitor at the home of Anton Bruckner, joined the Wagner Association and became a friend of Hugo Wolf. There with all his heart he plunged into the sea of music which had been formed during the last century. What better place could one have chosen for composing and for completing what a Mozart and a Haydn had started?

Mahler began his creative activity with the song, taking it with him through his own musical development, and returning to it again at the end of his life and work. Whatever he created was a song at the same time, or was a metamorphosis of the human singing voice. Always in a new form, the human voice breaks forth from the sea of sounds, is heard high above it, and leads to ever loftier heights, fulfilling in its sound what the music had promised earlier. This close interweaving of the human voice with the powerful sounds of the instruments is one of the most important features of Mahler's music.

His first composition, which he still recalled in later years, was a kind of oratorio for which he had written the words himself. He called it: *Das klagende Lied* (The Song of Lament); he took the words from an old fairy tale (The Little Singing Bone) and wrote it around 1879. The title itself points to the deepest origin of Mahler's work: the song. This first composition was followed by the *Lieder eines fahrenden Gesellen* (Songs of a Wayfarer) to which he also wrote the lyrics, which sound as if they could have originated in a collection of old folk songs. However, Mahler came to know these only much later. He was so deeply immersed in the atmosphere of folk songs that he imitated them, without even knowing them! And when he had become familiar with them, he used a whole series of them for new compositions.

The First Symphony is a musical paraphrase and an elaboration of the *Lieder eines fahrenden Gesellen.* In the Second, Third and Fourth Symphonies, the voices of the soloists as well as the chorus resound at the decisive places; they summon the listener to the higher life. How is it possible to discuss these works without going into details about every single movement? How can their spell, their power of expression, their greatness of their annunciation, be dealt with adequately in only a few lines?

If in Brahms the earth itself resounds, if in Bruckner the angelic hierarchies begin to sing, in Mahler it is always the human being who is the centre of the composer's revelation: man's quest for death and resurrection (in the Second Symphony), his relationship to all being of nature, to forest and flowers, animals and children (Third), man's delight and joy in a life of faith (Fourth). In the next three monumental works, the Fifth, Sixth and Seventh, however, man suffering, shaken by his own innermost being, stands silent in the sea of thundering music around him. The Fifth leads him into the deepest depth of space; the Sixth, the tragic one in the very foundation of his heart; and the Seventh is a call into the far future. But from neither side is man approached by grace and salvation. He errs and searches and doubts, and his life is a constant question about the meaning of his existence. And then the overwhelming power of the Eighth! It consists of only two movements, but again it is filled with the human voice. Choirs resound, from a thousand lips flows the *Veni Creator Spiritus*. Not often has the invocation of the Holy Spirit been heard with such a tremendous power.

His widow, Alma Maria, recalled,

> he first wrote down the whole chorus from memory, with the words half forgotten; however, words and music refused to harmonize, the music had become broader than the words. In frantic excitement he wired to Vienna, requesting the complete Latin text by return telegram. Now the complete text harmonized exactly with the music. Intuitively he had composed music for the complete stanzas without even having seen them.

Pursuing this tempest of his creative activity, he took the whole last scene of Goethe's *Faust,* basing the second movement of his Eighth upon it. Here the choruses, the soloists' voices and the orchestra unite in such a perfect beauty and in such power, that it is as if man and the whole cosmos become one again. In this Symphony mankind is elevated to the Tenth Hierarchy. It recognizes itself as the creature becoming a creator.

At the same time that Mahler was at work on his Eighth Symphony in August 1906, Rudolf Steiner gave one of his great fundamental lecture cycles. What in Mahler streamed out as musical creation, was offered to mankind in sublime clarity, by the spiritual researcher. The spirit of mankind began to find itself.

Mahler was now 46 years old. In retrospect, his widow related, 'this was the last peaceful summer. Then followed years of horror and of the destruction of everything we had built up.'

From then on everything became a farewell. Again the old song resounded. Now it was called *Das Lied von der Erde* (The

Song of the Earth). This work combined six songs, assembled to form a whole; songs which tell of the splendour and suffering, of the fullness and loneliness of man on the dear earth; deeply stirring sounds, a farewell of one who is leaving for good. The *Lied von der Erde* is followed by the Ninth Symphony which becomes an epilogue. Mahler then tried to force destiny again and began the Tenth, but there he sang: *Ach, ach, ach! Leb wohl, Mein Saitenspiel!* (Alas, Alas, Farewell my Harp!). His work had ended.

Wherever it resounds, it awakens the listeners' hearts. It is as if concealed bells call, appealing to the conscience of the listener, 'O man know yourself!' And again, Mahler's music carries the message which he once formulated in a letter to his wife: 'Now perhaps you will feel — or even know — what I think of human works. They are in truth transient and mortal; however, what man makes of himself, out of is own forces, what he becomes as a result of his indefatigable striving and living — this is what remains.'

It is true that there is music more sacred, more beautiful, more powerful than that of Mahler; there are better modulations of the themes, mightier fugues, more ingenious orchestrations; but there is no music which reaches the moral forces resounding through Mahler's works like the voices of archangels on Judgment Day. Here mankind itself hears the words of its conscience. They sound forth, they interpret, they demand, and it is only the deaf in spirit who would not be deeply touched and stirred by them. A voice in the wilderness had appeared, admonishing his fellow human beings: 'Repent, for the Kingdom of Heaven is at hand!'

Before the storms of the twentieth century began their destruction, before the beginning of the First World War which led to all subsequent catastrophes, Gustav Mahler returned to the realm for which he had been yearning all his life.

Epilogue

The powerful stream of German music originated in the sources of Bach: in Mahler, it returns into the ocean of eternity. It flowed for two centuries: from the birth of Haydn to the death of Mahler. There are no followers; his disciples are simply tributaries on the delta of this river, as it were. Only in a completely new source, be it in the near or the far future, at some place not yet known to us, will the new stream of music spring up. Until then, there will be many musicians and they will make music; however, they are unlikely to be touched by the true musical inspiration. They will be either followers or forerunners.

The stream, which was completed in Mahler, carried with it the sounding waters of life in the form of sonatas and symphonies. The unity of the fugue gave birth to the twofold thematics in which resounded the evolution of the world and of mankind. In Haydn and Mozart the stream was still flowing in eternal youth; in Beethoven and Schubert it had grown to the strength of the youth and of a mature man. It lost some of its power in Schumann; it was dreaming in Mendelssohn, suffering in Brahms and fulfilled itself in Bruckner. In Mahler, it returned to the ocean of the spirit, from which Bach once had drawn the inspiration for his works. These nine names symbolize, as it were, the nine symphonies which feed this stream with its water. Each of those nine tried to complete himself in this ninefoldness: Haydn and Mozart overflowed with youthful forces, others contributed only four or five symphonies, but Bruckner and Mahler fully reached their goal, as did the greatest among them, Beethoven.

This stream had been flowing during the two centuries of separation from the Spirit: the epoch of rationalism, of agnosticism and of materialism. It kept human hearts alive, not allowing them to die spiritually. It was music alone which gave man a last presentiment of a heavenly existence and of a divine omnipotence. But then the turning point of 1879, 1899 and 1909 had taken place.

When in 1879 the Archangel Michael again started to guide human destiny, when in 1899 the Dark Age of the Kali Yuga came to an end after five thousand years, when in 1909 the Christ appeared again in the realm of earth, then the stream of music returned into the cosmic sea of the Spirit. This return is closely connected with Mahler's destiny. He once said: *My life is nothing but a yearning nostalgia.* It was in the year 1879 that he started his activities. His task was to challenge mankind and again and again to remind it of its true goal. As a conductor he was a fighter for Michael. His music is the ever-renewed attempt to comprehend, to interpret and to represent the voices which still resound from the ending Kali Yuga. He tried to burst open the gates of the Light Age by the power of his compositions. His Eighth Symphony welcomed the new era in which man will be able to see the Resurrected Christ in the circumference of the earth. Then once again he embraced and used all musical means of expression in the *Lied von der Erde* (Song of the earth). With him the stream of music takes its leave before it disappears. In Mahler it has fulfilled itself; it vanishes with him. Like the sun, the knowledge of the Spirit arises, bathing his disappearance in a golden light.

The stream of music has reached its end; the brightness of the new revelation of the Spirit ascends. A living witness of this appeared in Bruno Walter, when he said of Rudolf Steiner's science of the spirit, 'Here is living and active the salvation which Hölderlin, the great poet, had in mind: I too have been blessed by it.'[13]

Alma Mahler-Werfel with a picture of Gustav Mahler

17

Alma Mahler-Werfel and Lou Andreas-Salomé

Alma Mahler-Werfel (1879–1964), née Schindler, was a Viennese socialite who married Gustav Mahler. After his death she married Walter Gropius, the architect, and following a divorce, married the writer Franz Werfel. She had a number of affairs with other well-known artists including Oskar Kokoschka. Karl König knew Alma Mahler well in Vienna and kept in touch with her in later years. Lou Andreas-Salomé (1861–1937), a Russian-German writer and psychoanalyst, was born in St Petersburg and travelled widely.

At the beginning of December 1964, Alma Maria Mahler-Werfel died in New York at a ripe old age. She was 85 years old and had experienced and suffered more than most of her contemporaries. At roughly the same time there appeared a biography of Lou Andreas-Salomé, another, older contemporary who, however, had a similar destiny.[1] The births of the two women were separated by eighteen and a half years, the period of a moon-node. Lou Salomé was born on February 12, 1861 — two weeks before Rudolf Steiner — in St Petersburg. She was the daughter of a high-ranking Russian general. Alma Mahler came into the world on August 31, 1879 in Vienna. At this same time Rudolf Steiner entered the Technical College in this city as a young student.

Both women not only avidly and inwardly participated in the cultural life of their time but were wholly integrated within it, because they were very closely connected with artists and thinkers. The great signs of a spiritual renewal which was pervading all the arts and philosophy of that time were experienced by these women as though in their own bodies and souls. Their roles can only be compared with those played a hundred years before by certain wives of the Romantics, such as Caroline Schlegel-Schelling and Dorothea Schlegel, the daughter of the philosopher Moses Mendelssohn. Here too a significant women's destiny was an intimate part of the work and the burdens, the call and the renewal of a whole, albeit brief period.

Of the two, Lou Salomé was the stricter, more serious and also harder working personality. For years she was only interested in the intellectual activities of the people she met. She went through these experiences as though untouched by them. Berlin, Paris, Zurich and later also Vienna were her stopping-places. She got to know the most significant people everywhere. In Berlin she associated with the circles of the brothers Heinrich and Julius Hart. She knew Gerhart Hauptmann and took an active part in the founding of the *Freie Volksbühne* (People's Theatre). She wrote articles and reviews for the *Freie Bühne,* the *Neue Deutsche Rundschau,* the *Magazin für Literatur* and many other leading journals of that time. In Vienna she knew Arthur Schnitzler, Peter Altenberg and Hugo von Hofmannsthal and was later a pupil of Sigmund Freud and collaborated with him.

However, her first significant encounters were her brief, but intense friendship with Friedrich Nietzsche and her longer-lasting connection with his pupil, Paul Rée. This was at the beginning of the 1880s. Some time later she married — without their being a real relationship but under a strange compulsion — the Professor of Persian Languages and Dialects, Friedrich Carl Andreas. He was a curious person, who combined Dutch,

17. ALMA MAHLER-WERFEL & LOU ANDREAS-SALOMÉ

Lou Andreas-Salomé

Malayan, Persian and German blood. She yielded to his magical influence and bore his name.

A few years later — shortly before the end of the century — came the encounter in Munich with Rainer Maria Rilke, who was 14 years younger than herself. He was at the time 21 years old, whereas she had reached the middle of her life. She became a friend, mother, lover and teacher to the shy young man. Through being with her his dreams were clarified and acquired definite substance. René (as he was named) became Rainer. For many years he continued to have an inner loyalty, reverence and devotion for her. 'Without the influence of this extraordinary woman my whole development would not have been able to take the paths which have led to so much.'[2]

Several years after this she came to know the Swedish psychologist and psychiatrist Poul Bjerre in the house of Ellen Key. They developed a fascination for one another and shared their life's destinies over a short period of time. Bjerre was not exactly a pupil of Freud, but he admired the great pioneer of depth psychology. Through him she came to Freud and in 1911 became his pupil. This friendly connection lasted unsullied until Salomé's death. Freud had great respect for the gifted and often brilliant way in which she described and interpreted his work in writing. He, who bestowed praise only rarely, gave it to her in abundance.

This is a brief sketch of the life of this remarkable personality. She died surrounded by just two of the friends she met towards the end of her life, alone and forsaken amidst a Germany being overwhelmed by darkness, in 1937. Her last words strike a note of hopelessness: 'When I allow my thoughts to roam, I see no people ... Death is therefore the best thing.'[3]

Alma's life was totally different, and yet similar. She grew up in Vienna. Her father was a well-known and popular painter and through him she grew up from childhood in a society of artists and musicians. As a girl she loved the painter Gustav Klimt, and she would have married him if her mother had not intervened.

So she was kept for the great love and the deepest sorrow of her life: her brief marital union with Gustav Mahler. She met him at the house of the famous anatomist Zuckerkandl when he was already a well-known conductor and musician. Mahler, who was nearly twenty years older, fell in love with the charming young girl — she was 22 at the time — and they married very shortly afterwards. In her book about Gustav Mahler this awakening of their mutual affections is enchantingly described.[4]

This marriage lasted for ten years; it was an arduous task for the young woman to be at the side of the great, self-willed and jealous artist. Two children were born, one of whom died young. Alma Mahler accompanied her husband on most of his concert tours. In 1911 she returned to Europe from America with her mortally ill husband. He died at a relatively young age after a short illness.

Shortly afterwards she became acquainted with the much younger painter Oskar Kokoschka. A painful love affair developed in a turbulent way, and the two of them lived together amidst ever new torments which they inflicted on each other. The older woman became the mother as well as the lover of the young artist who was constantly growing through her and through her presence.

Then the well-known architect Walter Gropius entered Alma Mahler's life. In autumn 1915 they married; Alma remained in Vienna while her husband did his military service as an officer on the German front. The first child of this marriage — the daughter Manon — came into the world in November 1916.

One year later — through the publisher Jacob Hegner and the author Franz Blei — she got to know Franz Werfel, a young 27-year-old writer. On January 5, she wrote in her diary: 'This profound musical bond and inner closeness with Franz Werfel is almost lethal. It must be that I love him, and the music is protecting us. The last days with their rich fullness through Gustav Mahler's music and Mengelberg sang of love … love.'[5] After Gropius had released his wife, she married Werfel.

This marriage was a lasting and self-generating source of happiness in being together. Alma was intimately involved with her husband's literary work. She went with him into exile by way of France and Spain to America with those forced to leave Central Europe. Werfel then died in California — when not much older than Gustav Mahler — on a Sunday afternoon in 1945.

Alma was now 66 years old; and from then on she remained a widow and looked back at the diversity of her lives with Mahler, Kokoschka, Gropius and Werfel. A great musician, a painter of genius, a leading architect and a famous writer had been her husbands, sons and masters.

Some disparaging remarks have been made about her, and her autobiography has been condemned. However, when she wrote it she was over seventy years old, and the way that it was extracted from her would be a story in itself. She was different from the picture that this autobiography conveys of her.

Their characters

What was seeking to find expression in the lives of these two women? Is it not extraordinary that each of them encouraged, inspired, filled with enthusiasm and stood by the side of so many remarkable men?

One of them went from Nietzsche to Rée and from there to Rilke and on to Bjerre and Freud. The first two were thinkers, the last two psychotherapists, and the one who stood between them was one of the great poets of his time. How deeply have three of them — Nietzsche, Rilke and Freud — influenced their epoch! Each one of them brought about a restructuring of outmoded concepts and ideas in their respective fields of philosophy, poetry and psychology. Lou Salomé acted as a godmother for these endeavours. Through meeting with her, Nietzsche was inspired to write *Thus Spoke Zarathustra*, a book that was born of despair and torment; and it was when she was with him that the idea of 'eternal recurrence' came to him. Rilke's poetry acquired a completely new diction once he had come to maturity and manhood through this intriguing woman. He found himself and his own style. *The Book of Hours,* which pioneered a new century of poetry, arose in connection with their visit together to Russia and echoed what they had experienced there. What Lou signified for Freud cannot be stated with any degree of clarity, but he felt invigorated in her midst and accepted her as a pupil. She remained his faithful admirer until her death.

The second of these two women went from Mahler through Kokoschka and Gropius to Werfel. Each of them was convinced that she was his muse and enabled him to create. Mahler's symphonies — from the first to the tenth — were composed during his time with Alma. Likewise Kokoschka — in this respect like Rilke — came to himself and to his distinctive style through this woman. The birth of the Weimar Bauhaus under Gropius's leadership came about during his relationship with Alma. Similarly, Werfel wrote novels and plays at her side, with her help and through her devotion.

Such women's destinies are barely conceivable. They break through the surface of history only at particular times of human evolution in order to help to bring about what the forces that fashion history are seeking to achieve. Two women appear who have, in a womanly way, entered fully into the cultural life of their time. They deny their own talent in order to make themselves available to help those who are greater than they.

One of these women, Lou, was the more tragic because, for all her devotion, she was unable to sacrifice herself. She appeared in her own dazzling light which exhausted and confused the others around her. She remained youthful right into old age. But her girlishness was a cold light and an icy flame which caused many to perish. Bjerre gave his verdict about Lou in a distinctive way when he was an old man:

She was an unusual person — this was immediately apparent. She had the gift of putting herself directly into another person's world of thoughts, especially when she loved him ... In my long life I have never met anyone else who understood me so quickly, so well and so completely as Lou. And then there was an astonishing openness about her observations. She spoke with the greatest equanimity about the most delicate and personal things ... I also remember being horrified when she told me of Rée's suicide.

"But have you really no pangs of conscience?" I asked her.

She laughed and said that pangs of conscience are a sign of weakness. This may have been bravado, and yet Lou seemed totally unconcerned about the consequences of her actions. *In this respect she was more a force of nature than a human being* ... True, she could flare up, but only for moments and with a strange, cold passion. Nietzsche was absolutely right when he said that Lou was an 'evil person.' But evil in Goethe's sense: 'A part of that power that is constantly doing good ...'

She activated my thoughts like a catalyser. Yes, she destroyed marriages and human lives, but in the cultural domain her proximity had a fructifying and creative influence ... People grew when they were near her.[6] [Emphasis added.]

This enables one to understand Lou existence. She must have had something about her that justified the destiny of her bearing the name 'Salome,' the name of Herodias's daughter who so enchanted Herod Antipas that he wanted to give her half his kingdom. But she demanded the head of John the Baptist. Good and evil lived in such close proximity in Lou that she could bring about each through the other. True passion never glowed within her; it merely flickered and died. She derived satisfaction through intellectual insight into spiritual relationships. She was good at analysing the soul; but she was indifferent to actual person.

Every year she returned like a wounded animal to her home in Göttingen after her extensive travelling; but as soon as spring knocked at the door she had to be off again. To Vienna, Paris, Munich ... for new adventures and encounters.

At the end of his observations Bjerre says, 'She told me she had been pregnant once but neither could nor wanted to be a mother. Perhaps there were deeper reasons why motherhood was denied to her ... A woman who becomes a mother sacrifices herself in a certain sense for her child. But this was just what Lou was unable to do. She could not make a sacrifice.'

She was someone who took, took where she thought she could connect herself more intensely with life; but people who as individuals in their own right went through all the joys and sorrows of earthly life were barely accessible to her. Human existence was, rather, an interesting experience which could be stowed away as in a botanist's vasculum so as to be arranged in this woman's catalogue of memories according to the principles of a psychologically –based philosophy.

Nevertheless — and perhaps precisely because of this — she went about amongst her contemporaries as someone who was both strange and delightful. She passed through her circles and groups, associations and social organizations as though there were no connections of either destiny or conscience in all that was being experienced in them. She was an emissary from another world and conducted herself in accordance with her extra-territorial relationship to the earth.

Alma Mahler exemplified the opposite pole. She was the epitome of devotion; she became a mother four times and lived and suffered with and for her children. The earth was by no means alien to her; on the contrary, she loved it — and Mahler's *Lied von der Erde* is a vibrant expression of Alma's soul and her essential orientation. She was a portion of Demeter and Erda, and she poured out this mother-earthly power of abundance and her bestowing nature over the men who were devoted to her and often completely captivated by her.

Lothar Schreyer has described her as she appeared in later years to those who knew her. When he met her at the beginning of the 1920s, at the time of the Weimar Bauhaus, as the wife of Gropius and as Werfel's lover, he was captivated by the greatness of this woman. He relates:

> I have already met many unusual women. Each of these great personalities, most notably the mistress and fellow member of the *Sturm,* Nell Walden, lived in a closed soul-world. *This singular woman ... was open to all manner of different worlds. It seemed as though all streams of life, angelic, demonic and all imaginable kinds of human ones, radiated through her* and she wove a symphony out of all these forces, surprising even herself ... I knew how Kokoschka had painted her. But I could not recognize this picture in her when she sat opposite us beside the burning candle, whose light played over her face.[7] [Emphasis added.]

This description gives a first picture of Alma's appearance. A few days later Schreyer met her in a larger group of people and continues his description as follows:

> When Gropius spoke about the slander [against the Bauhaus], Alma Gropius's expression became belligerent, Amazon-like. Her eyes flamed in confidence of victory amidst a slightly reddening countenance. The fighter with virginal power soon became a vengeful goddess, blazing with a cruel smile. Then a smug woman sat there, who was enjoying her triumph to the full, and finally she became the charming hostess of a superior party game, whose words and looks ensnared us all in the net. We were all captivated by her being ... *A gentle, sensuous beauty pervaded us which was wholly impersonal.* It seemed to me

that I had been enabled to behold *das Weib an sich* [essential womanhood], and this image changed from the virginal to the maternal and back to the virginal, while in between there shimmered the image of the wife. But this was not the wife of Walter Gropius but a life's companion in her essential nature, the female leader of a secret society of men and women ... I finally believed that I knew Alma Mahler–Gropius to be the image of Natura, who ceaselessly bestows and transforms herself in her sanctity. [Emphasis added.]

It now becomes all the more clear what Schreyer and many others also experienced in Alma Mahler: that as yet natural power which surrounded her in its fullness as *natura naturans*. She, too, was not wholly herself, no more than was Lou Salomé. For 'all streams of life, angels, demonic and all imaginable kinds of human ones,' seemed to stream through her. But what in Lou appeared as an 'I' that was entangled in itself and was deaf and blind to other people was, in Alma, bestowing power and streaming devotion. In her a fullness of soul expended itself that had not wholly achieved human and personal fulfilment. In Lou, on the other hand, the intellectually stimulating brilliance of her own intelligence, which was, however, lacking in heart-forces, suffocated the truly human aspect of her nature. What was the destiny of these two women?

Their times

The further we are from the turn of the century, the more clearly does the spirit and the form of that period come to expression. What was still a richness that was too close to observe a few decades ago has now begun to acquire contours and bear headings which make it possible for one to have some initial understanding of this time. What was taking place in Europe and America, and indeed in the most civilized countries of the world, when the nineteenth century ended and the twentieth century began? What were people trying to discover in order to present an answer to the barely conscious stirrings and awakening impulses living in the inner depths of their existence? An old world had come to an end; this had happened completely and absolutely. The outworn forms had to be broken up in order that something new could take their place.

Lyell, Darwin, Haeckel, the materialists Büchner and Moleschott together with many others had brought about this process of reducing everything to ruins. Nietzsche shattered the values of the past and caused what remained to fall to pieces. The new and the old vied with one another for supremacy. The 'new' tried to find modern forms. The initial attempts towards finding forms for creative energy began in the art nouveau movement in architecture, crafts, poetry and literature. But the waves of the old always burst through; mysticism, romanticism, veneration of heroes, religious Baroque and medieval Gothic: they all appeared in a new guise. Poetic, artistic and musical mannequins passed us by like a fashion show of past cultural history and presented themselves in their glittering robes: Maeterlinck and Klimt, Klinger and Ernst Hardt and hundreds more. Many true artists and poets also fell victim to this deception.

For those who were truly searching, however, those who placed themselves at the service of the Time Spirit, there was — although they were barely conscious of it — something more to life than fame, recognition and getting noticed. They tried to give answers to the inner questions that were constantly living within them. One of these questions is clearly formulated in the subtitle of Lothar Schreyer's book, *What is the Image of Man?*

'Who am I?' This is what people began to ask themselves after the foundations of their belief and trust in the existence of their world had been taken away from them, a process which began from the sixteenth century onwards and gradually became ever stronger. What technology constantly set forth before them embodied only the outward manifestation of the soul's inner world, so that the ancient words, 'Know yourself!' could be heard as though in the thunder and lightning of this storm of the new century's beginning.

The mighty sequence of the public lectures which Rudolf Steiner gave during the first two decades of this century in Berlin — often on a weekly basis — were a constant attempt to furnish souls with ever new and ever more powerful answers to these questions; for to receive such answers was the principal demand of that time.

The question itself, however, had two aspects. One had to do with gaining a new understanding of the nature of the individual human being. What is to become of him who, after all, stands at the pinnacle of natural development? Where does his path lead, now that he appears to himself as naked and bare, as a highly developed animal and nothing more? What is this individual and his property? Rudolf Steiner worked intensively with this question before the turn of the century. His encounters with the philosophy of Nietzsche and Stirner and the endeavours of John Henry Mackay, together with his own book *The Philosophy of Freedom,* offered a way forward. In an article that he wrote in 1899 entitled 'Idols and Confessions, he refers briefly to a sentence which is of particular relevance to us here:

> Lou Andreas-Salomé, in her novel *Im Kampf um Gott* (In the Battle for God) which touches upon the deepest tasks of the culture of our time, has expressed this thought: 'The highest achievement of human creativity is that, by gazing upwards, it is able to create in a manner which transcends itself.' The education of the past few centuries has been energetically working on not allowing anyone to think that the world of the ideal is a creation of man ... This has now changed. Reality has proved to be victorious in our consciousness. We shall gain an

understanding of the ideal only insofar as we are able to find its roots in the natural world itself ... Truth is more important to us today than anything else. We shall reveal it completely if we find the capacity to destroy things of value which have for centuries been regarded as holy.[8]

Nietzsche's idea of the 'superman' arose from these endeavours. He is 'the sovereign individual who knows that he can only live out of his own nature, and who sees his personal goal in a way of life that corresponds to his essential being.'[9] From this also arose Stirner's individual anarchism, which was reformulated at the turn of the century by J.H. Mackay. This has to do with understanding the self-conscious I and the creative faculties of man which develop from it.

Lou Andreas-Salomé tried to bring an image of this striving to realization. She wanted to make manifest what this aspect of the quest for a new image of man represented. As a Russian, Lou had the quality of an individual anarchist whose life revolved around herself.

But then there was also a further aspect of great significance which began to burn in human hearts. It could in essential terms be called 'the social question,' which had never before presented itself so acutely and directly to human beings in the whole development of history. It could also be defined as the question of 'the individual and community.' Individual people were longing for a new brotherhood and sisterhood; they founded associations and societies. The *Wandervogel* movement came into being; artists got together; work colonies formed in Worpswede and Hellerau. The Blaue Reiter in Munich, the Secession and the *Hagenbund* in Vienna, the *Sturm* in Berlin and the Bauhaus in Weimar — just to name a few — sought to bring these fraternal connections and community impulses into being. Schreyer describes the intentions that Gropius had very clearly when he says:

Gropius's impulse was not only to do with building a factory but with establishing a home for human beings in the true sense. He knew that the task of an architect and master builder is to create the housing that is appropriate for any particular new community of a modern age. The easily misunderstandable and greatly misunderstood designations 'cathedral of socialism' and 'machine for living' were intended to mean both the community and its home. Gropius hoped to be able to develop a home for human beings of our time out of his community of trainees, initially for it and around it. It was clear to him that for the completion of this building he first needed the new human community.[10]

Schreyer additionally speaks of Max Berg, the architect of the Centennial Hall in Breslau (Wroclaw), and says of him that he sensed 'that the new human community for which he longed would only come if human individuals found their inner image of man and a new community were formed out of the togetherness of such people.'

This was the other problem of the age. Rudolf Steiner worked, wove and was actively creative also here. The First Goetheanum could be called the 'true Bauhaus' of our time, because those people who had struggled to find their 'inner image of man' were to gather together there in community.

But it was not only Gropius who concerned himself with this struggle; Mahler, Kokoschka, Werfel and many others shared a similar endeavour. Social problems were a matter of the greatest urgency for them, and Alma, as *natura naturans,* the image of a woman who, as a mother, was forming a community and engendering togetherness, became their star. Something was being lived out in her that was reminiscent of the age-old matriarchy, when the woman was still a priestess and an emissary of the gods.

Why did they all — those around Lou Salomé who wished for the renewing of the human individual, and those around

Alma Mahler who aspired towards the revivifying of human communities — fail in their objectives? Because none of them found the path to a Christianity of our time, to the new revelation of Christ. They all remained 'pagans.' They sought religion; they also longed for the spirit. But the will to change was not sufficiently strong and unremitting. Thus all of them — after their powerful beginnings and initial impulses — lost their way. Nietzsche became insane, Rée committed suicide; Rilke's inspiration faded and his last words spoke of hell. Freud became a cynic and a slanderer of everything to do wit the spirit. Only Lou survived, hardened, care-worn and completely isolated.

Mahler was consumed with his longing for the earth; Werfel wore himself out with compassion and sentimentality, Gropius built veritable 'machines for living' and Kokoschka struggled continually with the picture of the Christian city and Christian people.

What descended upon them and succeeded them was a political, social and scientific anti-Christianity. The first battle for the spirit, for brotherhood and for the image of man had been lost for them. Lou and Alma were like the standards of this battle, leading the way forward; but the monogram of the Christ impulse did not appear on their flag. Just as Lou became hardened, so Alma became witty and scintillating and then faded away. Both became the servants of powers that must be regarded as anti-Christian. In Lou the warmth of heart that could have transmuted the I striving to individualize itself into a serving vessel did not develop. Alma did not attain that strength of heart forces out of which the moderating element of an essential clarity of insight can arise. Thus both lacked that human middle realm which would have been so necessary for a truly responsible human existence at that time.

18

Robert Owen

Robert Owen (1771–1858) was a Welsh social reformer, best known for his model manufacturing community at New Lanark in Scotland.

Owen's biographers

Around the end of 1905 and the beginning of 1906 Rudolf Steiner published a series of three articles under the title 'Theosophy and the Social Question, in the journal *Luzifer-Gnosis* which he edited.[1] Here he tried to give the first basic indications of what theosophy as represented by him had to say regarding the social problems which were then current.

In the second article he begins with a consideration of the views of Robert Owen, whom he calls 'one of the noblest of social reformers.' The third article, however, which also contains a description and formulation of the Fundamental Social Law, features a full discussion of this remarkable personality. The first sentence read as follows:

> Robert Owen may in a sense be regarded as a genius of practical social activity. He possessed two qualities which may well justify this designation: a circumspect eye for socially useful organizations and a noble love for mankind. One has only to consider what he has

Robert Owen

accomplished by means of these two faculties in order to appreciate their full significance.

After these introductory sentences Rudolf Steiner subjects the life's work of this friend of humanity to a detailed study and, on the strength of Owen's ideas and enterprises, develops that Fundamental Social Law of social life, of which he says that it 'holds good for all social life with the same absoluteness and necessity as any law of nature within a particular field of natural phenomena.'

At the same time as these articles appeared, the hitherto two most detailed and important books on Robert Owen's life and work were published, one in England and one in Germany.[2] Frank Podmore, the author of the English biography makes the following remarks in his foreword:

> Robert Owen died in 1858. Up to January 1905, four biographies of him, and four only, had appeared, all in English — the last having been written more than twenty years ago. When, in 1901, I formed the intention of adding another to the list, I was moved less by a sense of the inadequacy of the work of my predecessors, than by my own desire to treat of so congenial a theme. In a word, I made up my mind, as I supposed, to write because I wanted to write. But a subsequent series of coincidences has led me to question whether in following my own pleasures I was not the unconscious instrument of larger forces.

Podmore then describes how in 1902 and 1903 he met several people (in England, France and Germany) who similarly felt inspired by the idea of writing a biography of Robert Owen. Out of all these initiatives these two biographies duly appeared. Almost simultaneously, however, in 1902 the first full account of the great community experiments that Owen carried out in America appeared, and in addition, a long sequence of hitherto missing letters of this social reformer were found in a wooden box, thus supplying important insights into his thoughts.

Rudolf Steiner's three articles should be viewed as a culmination of all these undertakings. They crown these attempts at that time to bring Owen's work to people's attention. It can hardly be doubted that behind all these wishes and aspirations there was a spiritual intention which was taken up by Rudolf Steiner and gave him a solid basis for formulating and presenting his social ideas.

The times of Owen

Robert Owen was born on May 14, 1771. The date of his birth determined a significant part of his earthly destiny, for he entered into an epoch which was at once an end and also a new beginning. Many historical streams meet one another at this time. On the one hand there was the wave of the Enlightenment led by the French rationalists and the English philosophers, and on the other, a stream of religious expectations pervaded human hearts.

The intentions of Voltaire and Montesquieu found their fulfilment in this historical moment; for in 1772 the French Encyclopaedia, which had been initiated twenty years before, was completed. The knowledge of the time was thereby put firmly in its coffin. At the same time a start was made with publishing the Encyclopaedia Britannica. This was one aspect of the world-outlook of that time.

However, a large part of European humanity was imbued with an altogether different mood. The movements for a deepening of inner religious life brought together under the name of Pietism, which went back to the beginning of the eighteenth century, had most probably run their course. The Wesley brothers, the founders of Methodism, were now old. The noblest representative of German Pietism, Gerhard Tersteegen, had died on April 3, 1769, and Count von Zinzendorf, the founder of the

18. ROBERT OWEN

Bohemian Brethren, had departed from earthly life in 1760. But new elements were beginning to take up these aspirations to counteract rationalism in a different form.

At the time of Owen's birth Oberlin had made a beginning with his peace project in Steintal near Strasbourg. Pestalozzi was struggling with his task as an 'educator of the people' and had started his work in Neuhof. Matthias Claudius had taken on the editorship of the *Wandsbeck Bote,* and at the same time Goethe was in Strasbourg, where he met Herder. The North American states had made their Declaration of Independence and were battling with England for their freedom. The Count of St Germain was appearing at the courts of Europe and trying to ward off the disaster of the impending French Revolution whose nature he could discern. Emanuel Swedenborg died at this same time, leaving behind a legacy which became a very considerable influence on his contemporaries and successors.

During the same historical phase the Industrial Revolution took its first mighty steps in England, and this giant's progress was beginning to cause the whole world to shake. In 1769 James Watt patented his improved steam engine, which would from then on totally transform economic life in all manner of directions.

Thus an extraordinary variety of forces and aspirations were working together: political, economic, religious and intellectual impulses were meeting and beginning a task which would be of decisive significance for mankind's immediate future. Around the end of the eighteenth century and the beginning of the nineteenth century, some fundamental decisions were to be made in Europe, and the immediate preparations for these had begun. Robert Owen was born into the midst of these events.

A whole series of personalities whose destinies would have a determining influence on the coming events came to the earth at the same time as he did. Napoleon and Alexander von Humboldt were born in 1769. They were followed in 1770 by Friedrich Hegel, Hölderlin and Beethoven. In the same year as Owen

Friedrich Creuzer saw the light of day; and shortly afterwards, in 1772, Friedrich Schlegel and Novalis arrived on earth. The French Utopian and forerunner of socialism, Charles Fourier, was also born then. This is a true gathering of spirits as the turn of the century was approaching. Each of them was a discoverer, who would open up new realms of earthly and spiritual existence. Each followed his own life's path, and yet a similar destiny can be sensed in all of them as a common prevailing mood.

Early years

Owen's place of birth was Newtown in Montgomeryshire, Wales. As a Welshman he had a strong measure of the Celtic nature; his father was a master saddler and his mother was descended from a family of Welsh farmers. He was the sixth of seven children. In his autobiography, which he wrote at the age of eighty-five and which appeared in 1857, he describes his childhood in detail. He must have been unusually precocious. He went to school at the age of five and by the time he was seven had learnt everything that the teacher in Newtown was able to impart to him. He mastered reading, writing and arithmetic so well that he was at this age made the teacher's class-assistant and thus became an educator while still a child.

At this time he began reading a quantity of books and specifically struggled through a number of religious texts. This occurred under the influence of three young women who wanted to convert the child to Methodism. He himself wrote regarding these studies:

> I read and studied the books they gave me with great attention; but as I read religious works of all parties, I became surprised, first at the opposition between the different sects of Christians; afterwards at the deadly hatred between the Jews, Christians, Mahommedans,

> Hindoos, Chinese, etc. etc., and between these and what they called Pagans and Infidels. The study of these contending faiths, and their deadly hatred to each other, began to create doubts in my mind respecting the truth of any one of these divisions.[3]

Owen was at the time no more than nine years old and one may well ask where he derived the maturity for such judgments and doubts while he was still a child. Perhaps this had to do with experiences which Owen himself describes in considerable detail. While he was still very young he was on three occasions in immediate danger of death. On each occasion he lost consciousness for a short while but was saved by some miracle. This threefold loss of consciousness brought about by illness and accidents might have been responsible for the extraordinary acceleration of his intellectual development.

When he was ten years old he left his parental home and went to see his older brother in London, and after a short stay there moved to Stamford in Lincolnshire, where he started an apprenticeship at a drapers shop. He did well there. His masters, Mr and Mrs McGuffog, received him into their own family. The working hours were very long, but in the early morning he had time to pursue his private studies. 'I was all this time endeavouring to find out *the true religion* and was greatly puzzled for some time by finding all of every sect of which I read ... claim for themselves to be in possession of *the true religion*.'

These questions and searchings continued to occupy him for several years until, in his fourteenth year, he came to certain definite conclusions, which came to be of seminal significance for the whole of his later life. He writes about this as follows:

> It was with the greatest reluctance, and after long contests in my mind, that I was compelled to abandon my first and deep-rooted impressions in favour of Christianity. But being obliged to give up my faith in this sect, I was

at the same time compelled to reject all others, for I had discovered that all had been based on the same absurd imagination, 'that each one formed his own qualities — determined his own thoughts, will, and action — and was responsible for them to God and to his fellow-men.' My own reflections compelled me to come to very different conclusions. My reason taught me that I could not have made one of my own qualities — that they were forced upon me by Nature; that my language, religion, and habits were forced upon me by Society; and that I was entirely the child of Nature and Society; that Nature gave the qualities, and Society directed them. Thus was I forced, through seeing the error of their foundation, to abandon all belief in any religion which had been taught to men. But my religious feelings were immediately replaced by the spirit of universal charity — not for a sect or a party, or for a country or a colour, but for the human race, and with a real and ardent desire to do them good.

Owen's life-principles are summed up in these few sentences. He never changed them, but continued to represent and defend them in many thousands of lectures and addresses and battled for them in innumerable newspaper articles and pamphlets. That he had already arrived at these convictions at the age of fourteen, and thereafter only added some variations while not changing the main theme, is a sign of his early maturity, but also of his intellectual entrenchment.

For Owen, man is the product of the world that surrounds him. Nature provides him with his own basic qualities, which are almost the same for everyone. Hence the environment must be arranged in such a way that right results grow out of these qualities. At the same time every religious belief must be eradicated; but — and this is what was so extraordinary about the beliefs of this young man — the way to achieve this is to replace it with 'the spirit of universal charity.'

At the time when Owen was pondering these very primitive notions, Goethe was writing 'Die Geheimnisse' (The Mysteries). It was in the spring of 1785, and in both contexts — albeit in totally different forms — the same aspiration can be discerned: the overcoming of individual religions through a renewed conception of man. The churches and sects which the young Owen encountered cast a veil for him over true Christianity, with the result that he was no longer able to distinguish the outer garment from the actual reality. But in his innermost heart he was striving for a higher Christianity, a Christian religion that is rooted in the will and in deeds and seeks to do what is good. Robert Owen did not succeed in raising this impulse to the sphere of knowledge.

New Lanark

After a few years' apprenticeship Owen left Stamford and went for a while to London. From there he came to Manchester, where he soon established his own little workshop manufacturing components for the newly invented mechanical looms. Shortly afterwards he was in charge of a large mechanical spinning mill and had 500 workers under him. He now encountered the dreadful working conditions of that time: working hours of 14 to 15 hours every day in small, antiquated, airless rooms; the workers' total dependency on the whims of the overseers; alcoholism, dirt and undernourishment were common features. The greatest evil was child labour. Parents sent their children to the spinning mills from the age of five. They were allotted a working day of 12 to 13 hours with an hour's break for lunch, during which they had to clean the spinning machines. The food was brought into the machine-halls for the children. In the evening between seven and nine o'clock they could, as a generous mark of favour, participate in school lessons if they were still able to do so.

The details of this cruelty and his efforts over many decades to combat it cannot be described here. Owen remained a champion for improving work conditions and abolishing child labour.

He soon reached a leading position in his profession and, as an inspector of a number of factories, visited Scotland. There he met his future wife, whose father, David Dale, owned several cotton mills in and around Glasgow, including New Lanark. With the help of several sponsors Owen became a partner and was installed as its manager. He married on September 30, 1799 and on January 1, 1800 he started his new task. On this same day Schiller wrote his remarkable verses 'The Commencement of the New Century' where he asks:

> Where will a place of refuge, noble friend,
> For peace and freedom ever open lie!
> The century in tempests had its end,
> The new one now begins with murder's cry.

And then comes the cry:

> Although thine eye may every map explore,
> Vainly thou'lt seek to find that blissful place,
> Where freedom's garden smiles for evermore,
> And where in youth still blooms the human race.[4]

Through Owen's activities in New Lanark this 'blissful place' which Schiller longed for was created for a brief span of time. By constantly overcoming obstacles which his sponsors and managers presented him with he succeeded in creating a model community of human beings in this little manufacturing town.

Owen's first aim was to shorten the working hours. Then he saw to it that the places where the workers lived became clean and hygienic. He established a co-operative association, where for little money better groceries, clothes and household goods could be bought. After some initial mistrust had been overcome, his unremitting and untiring example had a rousing effect. He managed almost entirely to do away with the consumption of alcohol, and finally he arrived at the point of fulfilling his highest aim: he built a school-house and made it possible for all children up to the age of 12 to receive regular tuition and, as they grew older, to work in the factories only for short hours.

For Owen the school was the place where a person's character was formed most decisively. The workers' children were able to attend school from their second year, and so Owen became the first in Europe — alongside Pastor Oberlin and Pestalozzi — to set up kindergartens. The greatest emphasis was placed on small children playing rather than learning. All who visited the school reported of the cheerfulness and the happy mood that reigned in the classrooms. 'They appeared perfectly happy, and as we entered the little creatures ran in groups to seize their benefactor by the hand, or to pull him by the coat, with the most artless simplicity.'

The older children learned through visual instruction. Large slates on which a number of plants, animals and rocks were portrayed hung in the classrooms. Giant geographical maps were put up on the walls in the halls, and it was said that the children learned their lessons in a playful fashion. They were urged to test and consult one another, and everything proceeded without punishments or teasing. None of the teachers were allowed to raise even a hand against a child or even admonish it with a loud word.

All children had to appear at school in white clothes, which were made available by the factory. In the morning lessons there was a focus on rhythmical exercises, dancing and singing.

No textbooks were used. The children learnt through visual practice and mutual help. In the school's heyday, between 1810 and 1820, there were regularly between 500 and 600 pupils attending lessons.

Thus it is understandable that visitors came to New Lanark from throughout the world. That 'place of refuge' that Schiller and many others were dreaming of at that time seemed to be taking shape there. Helene Simon rightly said:

> For twenty years New Lanark delighted many thousands if its visitors. Among them were kings and their ambassadors, high spiritual dignitaries, deputations from cities, parliamentarians and scholars ... The order, cleanliness and charm of this community, the moral quality and harmonious creativity, cheerfulness and self-confident politeness of its people were the result of Owen's efforts ... In the course of a few years he had nurtured a spirit of solidarity of interests, which made the New Lanark workers to a certain degree a self-governing community.[5]

Owen's persistent will to awaken the good in every single person, his dogged enthusiasm, his social skill and above all the lasting example that he himself gave through the impeccable way that he led his own life made the miracle of New Lanark possible. It was the only time that Owen was able to carry through a community-building project successfully over a number of years. He was now convinced of the truth of his ideas and demands and expected that the whole world would imitate his experiment in New Lanark.

The community experiment in America

After the end of the Napoleonic Wars the countries of Europe again began to take over their share in supplying overseas markets; and as a result there was a significant shrinking of British exports, and production — especially in spinning and weaving — was cut back. A wave of unemployment engulfed the industrial areas of the Midlands and Scotland. There were no trade unions, no unemployment benefit, and the poverty and hardship of the workers grew to an immeasurable degree.

Owen, who through his success in New Lanark had become one of the most respected and well-known industrialists and benefactors of his country, considered that his moment had come and developed a very detailed plan eliminating unemployment. He conceived the idea of community settlements of 1500 to 2000 people who would develop self-sustaining enterprises. None of the members would receive any direct payment for their work; instead, everything would flow to the community, which in its turn would cater for all needs, including the education of children, so that a care-free life would be made possible for all.

This plan was worked out in great detail and conveyed to the highest places in government and Christian churches. *The Times* devoted a remarkably long sequence of approving articles to these ideas, and parliamentary presentations and long debates were held regarding the possibilities of such communal experiments. Owen was untiring in drawing up petitions; he visited offices and ministries, dined with influential people and was a welcomed and honoured guest wherever he went. But again and again he forfeited the extraordinary opportunities that were open to him by proclaiming his strict atheism and by his fixed refusal to collaborate with the religious element in the settlements that he planned.

There are a whole number of drawings and sketches for the layout of such community buildings. The idea was to have a massive square of houses. Three sides of this complex would contain dwellings for married and unmarried members. The fourth block was to be used for store-rooms, workshops and so forth. The square enclosed by the living accommodation was conceived as the place for the community buildings: schools, library, dance-halls, function rooms and huge dining-rooms. For all meals, all entertainments and all studies were envisaged as being inclusive of the whole colony.

Despite all his efforts, Owen did not succeed in raising sufficient state or private money to be able to begin with building and running a settlement of this kind.

In 1824 the opportunity suddenly arose of buying a whole village settlement in America, in Indiana. This community-based entity had been founded ten years previously by a religious sect of Württemberg peasants, the Rappists, and developed into a model economy. Some mills, smaller factories and dwellings for nearly ten thousand people were available, together with a large amount of farmland and woods. The autocratic leader of the sect, Georg Rapp, had decided to destroy the well-being of his Brothers and get them to begin again elsewhere.

Owen heard of this resolve and seized the opportunity to realize his ideas in New Harmony. With his own money he acquired the whole settlement and the 20,000 acres of land that belonged to it, for which he paid $150,000 (then £30,000). In January 1825 he came to America and began to give a great number of lectures and addresses about his plans. On February 25 and March 7 he spoke in the House of Representatives in Washington and always demanded that people come to New Harmony in order to begin with the establishing of the first real and true human community based on equality and brotherliness.

Nearly a thousand people took up his call. In April most of the houses were occupied. None of those who arrived were subjected to even the merest test as to their suitability for the settlement. Each one was accepted and greeted without selection. On April 25 Owen gave his first address, explaining that New Harmony was a kind of stopping-place which should embody the transition from the old to the new social order; for there would still be inequalities in living situations, in the work to be carried out and also in the remuneration. There was, nevertheless, the absolute expectation that over the course of the coming years the whole life of the colony would have developed to the point of acquiring a communistic social order.

In the first year everything went so well that Owen, on returning from a trip to Europe, immediately set about giving a final form to this community. The articles of union included, under the general title 'The New Harmony Community of Equality,' the following stipulations: 'All the members of the Community shall be considered as one family, and no one shall be held in higher or lower estimation on account of occupation. There shall be similar food, clothing and education ... and, as soon as practicable, all shall live in similar houses, and in all respects be accommodated alike. Every member shall render his or her best service for the good of the whole.'

A year after this declaration the whole enterprise was in a state of collapse. Certain groups, guided by national or ideological principles, had broken away and formed independent splinter colonies. The necessary tasks were no longer being carried out, and Owen saw himself forced to dispose of larger and smaller parts of the whole property with considerable financial losses.

His enthusiasm, nonetheless, did not wane. He even proclaimed that out of the one colony many others had been formed, which would gradually bring the essential core of truth to maturity.

His mind conceived of still greater undertakings. In Mexico an enormous piece of land was offered to him by the government in order that he might establish a huge colony there. He accepted, went to Mexico as well, but everything ran into the sand. The realm of peace that he planned for this place was never even inaugurated.

Owen had gone through great trials. On returning to England, he began to pursue his aims with an even more intensified power.

The last years

Owen's further life and work appears astonishing and to a certain extent incomprehensible, but also admirable. He went through a string of new disappointments, which were caused by the constantly repeated failure of his initiatives, through the collapse of the associations and co-operatives that he had established. But every failure only spurred him on with renewed encouragement. He tried to summon members of the working class throughout the country to the cause of a future social order. He saw himself as their educator, as their inspirer, as their father. His impulses were persistent, but his ideas and suggestions were unpredictable. He gradually changed from a reformer into a utopian.

His preaching became ever larger in scale, more all-embracing and more illusory. His will was not merely unbroken but became ever more powerful. He brought about the first co-operative societies, the first workers' insurance schemes and the trade union movement. Hundreds of thousands regarded him as their saviour and then turned away from him.

Around 1835, first in a journal and then also in a work in three volumes, he began to proclaim 'The New Moral World':

> The Rubicon between the Old Immoral and the New Moral World is finally passed; and Truth, Knowledge, Union, Industry and Moral Good now take the field, and openly advance against the united powers of Falsehood, Ignorance, Dis-Union and Moral Evil. The sword of Truth and Moral Good is now unsheathed, and will not be returned to its scabbard until Falsehood and Moral Evil shall be driven from the abodes of men ... The First Coming of Christ was a partial development of Truth to the few, conveyed, of necessity, in dark sayings, parables and mysteries. The Second Coming of Christ will make Truth known to the many, and enable all to enjoy the endless benefits in practice, which it will assure to mankind. The time is therefore arrived when the foretold Millennium is about to commence, when the slave and the prisoner, the bondsman and the bondswoman, the child and the servant, shall be set free for ever, and oppression of body and mind shall be known no more.

One of his friends, Francis Place, wrote in a letter dated January 7, 1836: "Mr Owen has this day assured me, in the presence of more than thirty other persons, that within six months the whole state and condition of Society in Great Britain will be changed and all his views will be carried fully into effect.'

In all this there is an inextricable tangle of rationalism, utopianism, materialism, religious sensibility, primitive views about man's being and an excessive fondness of the truth of his own convictions. Everything is, however, regardless of its truth or falsehood, imbued with an utterly purposeful will that pursues one aim alone: the good.

Owen never called for a class struggle; although he characterized the social classes with precision, he wanted freedom to reign amongst human beings. He entrusted the responsibility for proclaiming the 'New Moral World' to an 'Assembly of all Classes and all Nations.'

In the last years of his life he converted to spiritualism and took up this cause with the same enthusiasm as all his previous battles. The spiritual world was for him only a 'refined material' world where the departed live. He was present at many seances and was totally convinced that there is a life after death.

He spent his last months in the town of his childhood. He felt drawn back to the place where he had been born. There he died, in the early morning of November 17, at the age of 87. His last words were: 'Relief has come.' This can be interpreted in various ways. It could signify relief in the sense of making things easier, alleviation from pain; but for a dying man it probably meant 'liberation, redemption has come.'

Review

Robert Owen's life was remarkably rich and many-sided. Trying to interpret it would be an impossible exercise. It was a life that was thoroughly will-oriented and, hence, was seminal in its nature. One can have the impression that everything that Owen thought had little relevance for the future. This is probably why he was so precocious and completed his studies and reflections when he was still only young. Thereafter he became a 'genius of practical social activity,' as Rudolf Steiner describes him.

In this respect — as a master of deeds and activity — he had a lot of resemblance to two of his immediate contemporaries, Napoleon and Beethoven. The former was carried to fame in battle and eventual downfall on the waves of the French Revolution. The latter was lifted up on the wings of German music and rose — towering above all others — to the highest achievements. Both died in the 1820s — Napoleon in 1821, in the solitude of imprisonment, and Beethoven in 1827, in the separate world in which his deafness had placed him.

Owen was gripped and carried away by the storms of social upheaval. Like Napoleon he made conquests, and he created social works of art of the greatest significance. At the time when the other two masters of the will had resigned themselves to leaving the earth, Owen went to America to try out his experiment of New Harmony. After this a new phase began, which was probably a continuation, but at the same time a new beginning. For he now entered into the shadow-zone of those towering clouds which, with the year 1841, spread over the whole earth. Rudolf Steiner often spoke of

> how the middle of the nineteenth century, especially the 1840s, represented a significant turning point in the spiritual development of European and American humanity ... how this time was in a certain sense the culmination of the development of materialistic thinking on the earth, the climax of the development of what one might call an intellectual understanding of external, dead facts which does not want to grapple with what is living.

In the background of these developments there was a spiritual battle which lasted for decades and ended in 1879.

> This battle came to an end through certain spiritual beings who had acted as rebels in the spiritual world during these decades being first overcome and then cast down into the sphere of human evolution as spirits of darkness in the autumn of 1879.[6]

18. ROBERT OWEN

The last third of Robert Owen's life fell under the shadow of this battle; it was the time when he was subject to utopian, prophetic and spiritualistic blindness. But his heart continued to be an organ of devotion that sought to sacrifice itself for the whole of humanity. Even though in the *Communist Manifesto* Marx and Engels called the dreams of the first socialists a 'minor version of the New Jerusalem' and, hence, looked down with scorn on Fourier, Saint-Simon and Owen, it would not be untrue to detect a chiliastic note in these movements. They all had a premonition of, and were aspiring towards, the culmination of the millennium, and Owen, too, was in his innermost soul a chiliast. Were not Napoleon and Beethoven as well? The imminent spiritual battle, that 'war in heaven,' kindled the darkness of the Napoleonic War, but also the light of the Ninth Symphony. But Owen, without being able to express it properly, was filled with that Fundamental Social Law which Rudolf Steiner formulated:

> The well-being of a community of human beings working together becomes greater the less the individual claims the fruits of his work for himself, that is, the more of these fruits he passes on to his fellow workers and the more his own needs are satisfied not out of his own work but out of what has been done by others.[7]

This was what Owen aspired to achieve. It lived in his visions of the future and impelled him to ever renewed attempts to bring it about. But only spiritual science, which rose like a great light in the aftermath of that battle in the spirit-world which was fought out in the middle of the nineteenth century, could make this idea a reality. Henceforth there also exists the demand 'to create institutions of such a kind that no one can ever claim the fruits of his own labour for himself but that they all, as far as possible without exception, go to the benefit of the community.'

Harry, Graf Kessler

19

Harry, Graf Kessler

Harry Clément Ulrich Kessler (1868–1937) was an Anglo-German count, diplomat, writer and patron of modern art.

In autumn 1961 the diaries that Count Harry Kessler had kept between 1918 and 1937 were published by Insel Verlag. Although only a selection of the whole was published, it was still a substantial volume of over 750 pages. The publisher must have reckoned with very low sales, for the purchase price was remarkably high. However, the book became a bestseller, and several editions were printed in a few months.

Suddenly, apparently without any reason, Count Kessler became a famous author 24 years after his death. He died in total solitude on December 4, 1937 in Lyon. He had been born in Paris in 1868, so that he came to this earth in France and also departed from it there. But the question remains: who was this man who, quite unexpectedly and in a way that no one could have foreseen, emerged from his oblivion and held up the story of his life before the eyes of many thousands of people like a mirror? If it had not been a mirror, his numerous readers would not have seized hold of his books with such a degree of intensity. Is it possible to make sense of what they actually found by reading the books? Did they find themselves? Or was it something similar to *À la recherche du temps perdu?*

In the 1920s Kessler was called 'the red Count,' because he

cared about the lot of the workers. He had also developed some new ideas for establishing a League of Nations, which was to be composed not of state representatives but of supranational organizations such as trade unions, churches, scientific and artistic associations. For some years he was also the president of a league for peace and dabbled in politics; but he met with little success there.

He was a fringe figure in world history who had Weimar as his base but lived in Berlin and was at home in Paris, London, Vienna and Rome. He knew most of the leading politicians between 1920 and 1930. He was also on friendly terms with many artists and frequented the circles of the important figures of his time. Walter Rathenau and Albert Einstein, Hugo von Hofmannsthal and Aristide Maillol, Bruno Cassirer and Auguste Rodin belonged to these circles. He knew them all and moved between them as one who moderated between them and was affiliated to them.

His roots reached far back into the culture and social fabric of the nineteenth century. His father, who was ennobled in Paris as a banker, came from Switzerland and grew up in Hamburg. His mother, the child of a noble family, came from Ireland. Thus the various colours of the European spectrum met in this child and were interwoven into a manifold tapestry as regards gifts and predispositions.

His mother, Alice, had a particularly strong influence on the growing child. She was enchantingly beautiful, to the extent that the visitors to the spa in Bad Ems climbed onto chairs and tables in order to see her when she went by, and she was revered and given preferential treatment by Wilhelm I on account of her charm; and so she was her son's image of the ideal. 'In this many-coloured and flowing fairy-tale world [in which the child lived] was my mother. She continued to be the firm measure and focus of everything well beyond the time of fairy tales until I was twelve or thirteen. She seemed to me to be a synthesis of all perfections that I saw in other women.'[1]

19. HARRY, GRAF KESSLER

The first part of the memoirs simply has to do with this mother. The whole magical world of the last decades of the nineteenth century is evoked here. Wealth and property, journeys and balls, concerts and celebrations, parties on a grand scale with princes and kings, inventors and musicians flowed by. A fairy-tale world of good fortune surrounded this woman, who was later stricken with illness, paralysis and blindness and pined away in a lonely castle in Brittany.

His mother gave him a further special gift from her Irish heritage: premonition through second sight. An old legend was linked with her ancestors which the son relates, adding: '[These ghost stories] awoke within me a feeling for the unfathomable mystery that is present everywhere behind the world, endows it with its worth, and at the same time takes it away, making it in the same moment meaningful and meaningless, powerful and powerless. This sense of the relative impotence of the real world with respect to a ghostly, but stronger other reality hovering behind it was my Celtic heritage.' This is an important insight into the underlying theme of this life.

His father was Swiss; the family came from St Gallen. He found an Irish wife. Did he reach back through her to where his ancestors had come from? To St Gallus and St Columbanus?

Harry attended three schools in succession. He was initially a pupil at a private school in Paris, of which he had only the worst memories. This school put him off France and the world of the French for many years. His parents then took him to a particularly exclusive preparatory school, St George's School in Ascot, England, which was at the time led by the well-known English headmaster, Rev Herbert Sneyd-Kynnersley. Only the sons of the privileged nobility of England were admitted to it. Approximately forty boys between eight and fourteen were together there. Winston Churchill was one of his fellow pupils. There he was educated in such a way that he acquired the foundations of what he and his companions were later to be: the prototype of the English 'gentleman.' Sport and games, fairness and fearlessness, clarity of thought, and complete power one's own feelings were practised and drilled there.

The young Kessler very soon perceived the two-track nature of this method and noticed that there was a huge disparity between what was professed and what was done, between teaching and practice. So he was pleased when after two years he arrived at the Johanneum in Hamburg. There he encountered, not exactly under ideal conditions, the Germany of that time. But little by little the true Germany began to reveal itself to him.

> By degrees something of the free, great humanity of Goethe and the German Romantics began to penetrate the bourgeois and pastoral fog. Even in this state of imperfection it gripped and intoxicated me. I owe it to these qualities that in the difficult struggle that now flared up between my English character and my German blood, the German element won. Every German word became sacred to me in its beauty and intimacy, its sound and fragrance. In this secret domain, my relationship to the German language acquired the profundity of a deeply moving amorous adventure ... I recited to myself the songs of the angels that stole away Faust's immortal soul and certain poems by Goethe and Hölderlin again and again, tasting them with my lips and hearing them with my ears, overwhelmed by their colour and music.

This testimony proclaims Kessler's reception into the spiritual domain of Germany. His intimate relationship to the German language which now opened up in his soul like a blossom connected him directly with the being of the German folk spirit. For language is the garment which is woven by the folk spirit.

He then also found friends and friendships among his fellow pupils of a kind that were uniquely possible among young Germans at that time. An enchanting feeling for the world and for life in general opened up in the growing boy. He swam and

19. HARRY, GRAF KESSLER

walked, wrote poems and had night-long discussions; he was imbued with the happiness of maturing and developing.

After finishing at school he went to university — first to Bonn and later to Leipzig, in order to study psychology and ethnology with Wilhelm Wundt. It was the end of the 1880s, and his encounter with Nietzsche's works now became the decisive experience in this young man's development. This time of the end of the century, when a soul and spiritual awakening began to take place everywhere, became also for Kessler the decisive phase of his maturation. It was the time when Ibsen and Zola were starting to be active; naturalism in literature began to be a prominent force; and a new wind was starting to blow in the sphere of culture. Dostoyevsky's influence had become discernible, and the young generation — insofar as they had an openness to the present and were endowed with sufficient time — came under these influences. Kessler reports:

> The way that Nietzsche influenced us, or, to be more precise, took possession of us, could not be compared with any other contemporary thinker. He did not merely address one's reason and imagination. His influence was more extensive than this, deeper and more mysterious. His ever more strongly reverberating echo signified the advent of a mystic into the age of rationalism and mechanization. We were as though enchanted and transported away by him from this ice-bound phase of history.

And then — with the help of a quotation from Nietzsche's fragment *The Will to Power* — Kessler finds very striking words to describe the feelings that were living in the hearts of his generation. These are words that magnificently describe this very special state of being:

> We were surrounded by a new landscape. Together with him [Nietzsche] we had entered a new world where we felt equally at home, because some of the greatest

Germans — Beethoven, Goethe, Fichte, Hölderlin — came towards us beneath these foreign stars, in this new light, as if it were their true home ... We were only beginning to get a feeling for it [this new world], but almost without our having taken note of where we were its sons were around us; not merely our great forebears but those newly born from it and looking towards the future, those bearing the first buds which in the 1890s gave the weary autumn of the old world the radiance of an early spring; at the time they were all still solitary, isolated individuals but who resembled one another as brothers, without their being able to say which were the traits that betrayed their family likeness ... Companions, ready to stand up for each other even before they knew one another properly.

But who were these 'knights in the spirit' who are spoken of here? Had Kessler found them and taken the new step which he intuited and yearned for? He indicates that he still wants to speak of 'those who have influenced Germany's evolution more deeply than the official schools of thought promoted from above.' This intention of his was unfortunately not carried through. One can only presume that some of those in his immediate and further vicinity were listening. He indicated as much in a caustic remark in his diary after a discussion that he had in his home in Weimar on February 21, 1919 with Nadolny, who would later be the German ambassador in Moscow:

> I have the impression that the National Assembly is likely to be something in between a beer garden and a conclave; that is, high politics in the style of a beer garden, and its lesser negotiations conducted in the higher and more refined atmosphere of a college of cardinals. This strikes a strange note in my house, which was hitherto full of memories of van de Velde, Hofmannsthal, Edward

Gordon Craig, Maillol, Rodin, Bodenhausen, Ludwig von Hofmann and Nietzsche; like a factory chimney in a country landscape.²

These were some of those he had in mind and then found: the painter von Hofmann, the stage designer Craig (son of the great English actress Ellen Terry), the poet Hofmannsthal, the architect van der Velde, the sculptors Maillol and Rodin, and Eberhard von Bodenhausen, the art historian. They were all devoted to, and entrapped by, art nouveau, and if one were to trace their roots further back one would arrive at Hans von Marées, John Ruskin and William Morris.

There were, however, also other circles which scarcely had any connections with this particular one but nonetheless belonged to it, thus for example the group of the Munich *Kosmiker,* the Cosmic Circle, with Alfred Schuler, Ludwig Klages and Karl Wolfskehl, among whom also Stefan George and the solitary Ludwig Derleth should be counted. Then there were the circles around Gerhart Hauptmann and the Hart brothers, the Worpsweder Group and isolated individuals like Rilke and Mombert. Many of these should be mentioned, for they all stood expectantly at the threshold of the century, and few of them managed the breakthrough to a great, all-encompassing activity.

Kessler, too, remained — necessarily — a fringe figure. Art nouveau, with all its social ideals, ceased to make fine gestures. Some pictures, furniture, pottery, valuable books — this was all that survived. This experiment came to nothing because the social conditions which might have welcomed it did not exist. This noble cultural stream did not find the foundations for its growth.

What had happened? Why did Kessler and those who were with him and around him remain so lacking in influence? Why did world history pass them by? I venture an answer: because they were meant for something other than what they found. It is also true that Kessler was one of those many people who were destined to be the bearers and leaders of a German

Central Europe, whose development and rightful unfolding were prevented by destructive and retarding influences in the course of the nineteenth century.

These misdeeds began already in 1812, when the new-born heir to the house of Baden 'died,' and as Kaspar Hauser was tormented, denied recognition and later murdered. When he died on November 17, 1833 in Ansbach as a result of his severe injuries, a part of history in process of becoming was put out of joint and shattered.

Thirty years later, in August 1864, Ferdinand Lassalle was shot by the frivolous bullet of his opponent in a duel. This, too, was a form of murder.

Because these two great men sacrificed their lives far too early, a substantial part of the 'unwritten' history of Central Europe could not become a reality. Bismarck, who had been chosen to establish a kind of 'social kingdom' in Germany together with these two was alone left behind. Thus he had to connect himself with Prince Wilhelm, the future King of Prussia and German Kaiser, and inject 'blood and iron' into the politics of Central Europe.

On several occasions Rudolf Steiner referred to this historical opportunity which did not come to fulfilment, and Karl Heyer has endeavoured to bring together the historical documents. In his book about Kaspar Hauser this is demonstrated with absolute clarity. There is no need to enter into the details here; they can be read in Heyer's book. But it becomes apparent from the available evidence that this triumvirate of European destiny: the heir to the house of Baden, the North German *Junker* and the Silesian Jew, were destined to create those social conditions whereby the seeds of the new spiritual stream would have fallen on fertile soil at the end of the century.

If this had happened, Nietzsche's struggle would have been elevated and redeemed in Rudolf Steiner's philosophy of freedom; the phantasmagoria of the Munich *Kosmiker* would have found some proper foundations instead of leading to National

19. HARRY, GRAF KESSLER

Socialism; and art nouveau would, in addition, have been spiritually pervaded by Goetheanism and made more strongly effective as a movement.

A truly social, non-Marxist Central Europe would have been able to be receptive to the utopian dreams of a William Morris and put them into effect. But the First World War came about instead, and the lights went out over Europe and have not been rekindled even today.

In the course of his childhood and youth Kessler gained access through his mother whom he revered above all else to those personalities who, under different circumstances, might have had a determining influence on his destiny. Because the old Kaiser Wilhelm I had succumbed to the charms of his mother, regular meetings took place between the Kaiser and the Kesslers, and young Harry was often part of these. But the old Prince Bismarck also heard about the enchanting young countess, and so he likewise entered the circle of the child's life.

However, at a later point, when Kessler was a student in Leipzig, there was a further decisive meeting with Bismarck. A year after the chancellor's dismissal, the German student body addressed some words of gratitude and loyalty to Bismarck, and the young Kessler — at the head of a student delegation — had the task of paying the former chancellor this tribute. This took place in Kissingen in August 1891. The day after the official ceremony, the old prince invited a small group of students — including Kessler — to see him in private. What then occurred was a conversation about the future of Germany, which left Kessler with a sense of depression. Although the prince's magical powers of rhetoric were displayed to the young listeners ('one could easily find oneself setting his tempestuous performance to music,' Kessler writes in his memoirs), the content was thoroughly unsatisfying.

'You see, the longer one listened, one was forced to acknowledge that what he said applied to a generation that belongs to the past ... everything was backwards-looking ... He clearly had nothing to say to us youngsters.' Then he goes on to report at greater length what Bismarck had spoken about; and indeed, everything was oriented towards the past, just memories and illusions.

Kessler concludes his book by saying that he picked up the reverberations of this encounter when looking at Erfurt Cathedral, and asks himself:

> What did Bismarck give his all-powerful state by way of spiritual impulse — ideas, ideals and dreams? One thing was definitely apparent, and there was something great about it — the maintaining of German unity ... One only had to open one's eyes in order to see that the fire [of the spirit] was no longer sufficient to complete the casting, that is, to weld the power of the German spirit and that of the Prussian state into a whole. Did the project fail, as happened under the Hohenstaufens?

And he ends with this sentence: 'The mighty phenomenon [Bismarck] which was still so illumined by lightning flashes stood well behind on the path that we youngsters followed into the future with some trepidation but ready for battle.'

Yes, there was a real group of them gathered there and ready to fight. But the one who should have become their model and ought to have been a bearer of the German Folk Spirit had lost his way. This empire that he had founded was a pipe-dream, because he lacked the inner strength. This was replaced by outward power and rattling of sabres. But those who bore the mantle of the state were those whom no one would ever have asked to do so, such as Bülow and Holstein, Bethmann and Wilhelm II.

So it happened that the swan knights, who were ready to fashion the inner empire, to address social problems in a spiritual context and to reach out into the wider world, did not get a chance. Their destiny gripped hold of a gaping void, and so they began to lose themselves, to squander and dissipate their lives. A *l'art pour l'art* came about, pursued in small circles; and, in forgetfulness of their true task, they became involved purely with themselves.

Other forces surged threateningly forth and destroyed what still remained by way of beauty and truth. Kessler himself did not give up; he tried — until 1933 — to intervene and assist wherever he could still hope for understanding. But it was too late. The counter-picture of the new Germany emerged, made use of the distorted image of Bismarck as a lever to gain power and founded that 'millennium' which tore Europe to shreds.

Kessler died alone in exile. At his last Christmas festival in 1936, he invited the village children and their teachers to his home and gave them all presents.

On the last day of this year he made the following entry in his diary: 'In the evening listened with Wilma [his sister] to the New Year's Eve celebrations from Berlin. Around midnight, Berlin time, the Berlin church bells pealed movingly in a foreign land. Around midnight, French time, the Paris bells answered them. At the same moment Biederle [his dog], who had been asleep in front of the fire, climbed onto my lap as if to bring me his good wishes for the new year.'

So began the last year of his life. In this foreign country a faithful dog was the only one who still congratulated his master. The tragedy of the swan knights was great and mighty in its implications. They were there, but their home had been seized by enemies and robbers, and they no longer had a place on the earth.

Is it our conscience which begins to call out when we hear Kessler's destiny speak from his books? Does it prick us because we hear there the voice of a lost Germany? Does the folk spirit speak from them out of his exile and sense of betrayal, trying to gather together the hearts of his individual members? However it may be, this man was a true German, because he had Europe and the whole wide world as his home but bore the true Germany in his soul.

Helen Keller

20

Helen Keller

Helen Adams Keller (1880–1968) was an American author, political activist and lecturer. She was born deaf and blind, but learned to communicate through the work of her teacher, Anne Sullivan.

Helen Keller's spirituality

In her book *My Religion,* Helen Keller presents herself as a follower of Emanuel Swedenborg, the great Swedish seer, and of his teachings. She writes in a very appealing way about this man, who became the herald of new worlds, and he, the robust advocate of earthly human rights, acknowledges her belief in supersensible beings and worlds. Indeed, for her the kingdoms of which Swedenborg reported so fully were a reality which she had always dimly sensed and known.

Helen Keller became acquainted with Swedenborg's writings while she was still young. It was one of her many friends and helpers who first referred her to Swedenborg; since this time she based her picture of the world on Swedenborg's perceptions and derived lasting instruction and uplift from them. At the end of the book, which is devoted wholly to Swedenborg, she writes:

> I cannot understand the poor faith that fears to look into the eyes of death. Faith that is vulnerable in the presence

of death is a frail reed to lean upon. With steadfast thought I follow sight beyond all seeing, until my soul stands up in spiritual light and cries, 'Life and death are one.'

And then she adds some words which sound like a confession and should be read and assimilated by those who are still able to see and hear. The blind and deaf Helen Keller says:

> I cannot imagine myself without religion. I could as easily fancy a living body without a heart. To one who is deaf and blind, the spiritual world offers no difficulty. Nearly everything in the natural world is as vague, as remote from my senses as spiritual things seem to the minds of most people.

In these words something of Helen Keller's true being manifests itself; for she shows herself to be a human spirit to whom the earthly world is almost as far away as the kingdoms of the spirit are to us. She is blind and deaf to her physical surroundings and yet she stands upright in a space that opens out as a twilight world between the physical and spiritual domains. Despite being attached to the world of appearances, which she is unable fully to experience, she inclines to a spiritual world in which she trusts but which is nevertheless denied to her as is the world of light and sound.

Thus she stands like a lighthouse in that twilight realm where the earth meets the sea of the spirit. The breakers of the spirit crash against the coast of the earthly world. Helen Keller can experience this intuitively, and the light that she radiates is fed by the oil of Swedenborg's perceptions.

It is a strange and remarkable destiny which is thus revealed, and perhaps in what follows a certain insight can be given into the inner halls of this existence.

20. HELEN KELLER

Childhood

Helen Keller was born on June 27, 1880 in the little town of Tuscumbia in the North American state of Alabama. Her earthly life began in this land well-endowed with fertility and growth-forces, on the bank of the mighty Tennessee River to the west of the Allegheny Mountains. It was a subtropical landscape that surrounded the child, who, like John the Baptist, was born at midsummer.

She describes her earliest environment — her parental home, the garden, flowers and clouds — with much love. She must have been a very precocious and self-willed child, for she could speak some words as early as six months. In February 1882, when she was 19 months old, she fell ill.

> The doctor thought I could not live. Early one morning, however, the fever left me as suddenly and mysteriously as it had come ... I fancy I still have confused recollections of this illness. I especially remember the tenderness with which my mother tried to soothe me in my waking hours of fret and pain, and the agony and bewilderment with which I awoke after a tossing half sleep, and turned my eyes, so dry and hot, to the wall, away from the once-loved light, which came to me dim and yet more dim each day ... Gradually I got used to the silence and darkness that surrounded me and forgot that it had ever been different.[1]

In spite of this loss, which banished this child into outward darkness and silence, she remained inwardly connected to the world. She must have gone through a very rapid process of adaptation, for Helen was soon able to make herself understood to a certain extent and to express her wishes and aspirations through a few gestures. It is also apparent from her writings that the richness of the surrounding world became a strong experience for her and that she could not only perceive but also distinguish flowers and animals, people and material objects.

Moreover, she developed a highly refined sensitivity to the vibrations of the noises that surrounded her. Thus she writes: 'One day some gentlemen called on my mother, and I felt the shutting of the front door and other sounds that indicated their arrival.' When she had deliberately locked her mother into the pantry and the poor woman had to knock for hours until she was heard by the maid and was released from her dungeon, she records this incident as follows: 'She kept pounding on the door, while I sat outside on the porch steps and laughed with glee as I felt the jar of the pounding.'

She also had playmates with whom she could engage — an older girl and a dog, who were her constant companions. Thus the world was dark and dumb, but this child's nature was so wakeful and lively that she constantly sought experiences that she could access from the senses that still remained to her.

It is very probable that the illness that led to her loss of sight and hearing was meningoencephalitis, an inflammation of the brain and its membranous coverings. The central parts of the brain remained healthy, and so the character, spontaneity and enthusiastic love of knowledge of this child were maintained.

One thing was lacking, however: the capacity to be able to communicate to others in such a way that mutual communication could be possible. 'The few signs I used became less and less adequate, and my failures to make myself understood were invariably followed by outbreaks of passion ... After a while the need of some means of communication became so urgent that these outbursts occurred daily, sometimes hourly.'

When this condition became more and serious, Helen's mother remembered having once read the story of Laura Bridgman in Charles Dickens's *American Sketches;* she had been taught by her teacher Dr Howe in such a way that she managed to gain proper contact with the world around her despite being blind and deaf. Her parents then took Helen to an eye specialist in Baltimore who referred her on to Dr Alexander Graham Bell in Washington, and through this remarkable personality the doors opened which became for Helen the gateway to the world. Al this happened around her sixth year and came to a culmination on March 3, 1887, when her teacher Anne Mansfield Sullivan arrived in Tuscumbia to take on Helen Keller's education and training.

A completely new destiny-circle opened up to the child in her meetings with all these people; and this must now be characterized.

Perkins Institution for the Blind

Graham Bell recommended to Helen's father that he apply to the Perkins Institution for the Blind in Boston. Mr Keller wrote to the Director of this institution, Michael Anagnos, who promised to send a teacher with the appropriate training to educate little Helen to Tuscumbia.

The Perkins Institution was world-famous at that time, for it was here that its founder had instructed the deaf-mute and blind Laura Bridgman. This Dr Samuel Gridley Howe was an unusual personality. He was born in Boston in 1801, studied medicine and went immediately after finishing his studies to Greece to take part in the struggle for freedom against the Turks. He spent six years there and then retuned in order to collect some funds in his native land for the impoverished Greeks. With the capital that he had put together he went back and founded reception camps and colonies for Greek paupers at Aegina and on the Gulf of Corinth. In 1831 he returned to Boston and began to take an interest in educating the blind. After another shorter journey to Europe he took on some blind children in need of education, and out of this the Perkins Institution arose.

Laura Bridgman was entrusted to him for instruction by her parents in 1837. She was eight years old at the time, and Dr Howe began to give her access to the world of words by placing the names of things on objects in raised lettering; by doing this he wanted the name and the object in question to be simultaneously discernible by the sense of touch. To begin with he used the whole word, and only when Laura began to understand after some time did he separate the words into the individual letters, thus developing an awareness of the alphabet. Laura gradually learnt to write and read raised lettering, and this great success became a world sensation.

Dr Howe was gradually able to expand his institute and to do a great deal of good. He also began to take a significant part in educating children with developmental disablities, and in this respect had a connection with the great pioneer of Swiss curative education, Johann Jakob Guggenbühl. Through Dr Howe's energy the first educational establishments for children with developmental disablities in America were established.

According to the descriptions of his contemporaries he must have been a fascinating, radiant and exceptionally kind individual. He died on January 9, 1876.

His successor as Director of the Perkins Institution was Michael Anagnos, a Greek, and a friend and pupil of Dr Howe since the time of his Greek adventures.

When the letter from Helen Keller's father arrived, a young, half-blind girl who had over a period been trained as a teacher for the blind was at the Perkins Institution. She was the child of Irish immigrants, and her father was an alcoholic. The girl and her brother came to the poorhouse and were kept there under very difficult circumstances; brother and sister lived together with old and unkempt outcasts.

At the age of fourteen the girl then came to the Perkins Institution in Boston through the help of a physician. Her condition improved with instruction and medical care, and Mr Anagnos, who respected her, decided that she should undertake the education of little Helen. This was a decision of destiny, for this young woman was Anne Mansfield Sullivan. She had entered the Perkins Institution at the age of fourteen in Helen's year of birth. Seven years later, as a twenty-one-year-old, she became the seven-year-old Helen's companion. As preparation for her new task she studied the drawings that Dr Howe had done over the years of his treatment of Laura Bridgman. For six years Anne and Laura had lived together in the same cottage at the institute.

It was in this way that Anne Sullivan became the bearer of that spiritual tradition which had become established at the Perkins Institution. Through Dr Howe this institute also became a kind of focus for American cultural life at that time. Poets and philanthropists, preachers and thinkers were drawn by the mystery of blind people and especially by the destiny of Laura Bridgman. That a person, without being able to hear or see, could become able to comprehend language and come in contact with the surrounding world represented a huge step forward in understanding for that time, for the currently dominant philosophical conceptions based on John Locke, David Hume and Immanuel Kant, according to which the experience of the senses had become the foundation for everything that could be grasped conceptually, was reduced *ad absurdum*.

One cannot but view these events taking place in Boston as a significant preparation for the renewal of the cultural life of mankind. At this time a deed was quietly unfolding which would be of fundamental significance for a very large number of people.

Awakening to words

Helen Keller's writings, above all the letters of Anne Sullivan to her friend which have been preserved, enable one to have an overview of the first steps in educational development that were taken then. The child and her teacher soon became an inseparable unity, and out of this destiny-laden relationship there arose the miracle that was accomplished in the space of a few months. For it was the first months that were of such decisive significance for Helen Keller's spiritual development.

This little girl had nothing in her that suggested a blind child. 'There's nothing pale or delicate about Helen. She is large, strong and ruddy, and as unrestrained in her movements as a young colt.'[2] In the first days after her arrival the young teacher did not have an easy time of it. The child was completely unbridled, and the parents — because of a mixture of compassion and pride — were wholly incapable of exerting even the slightest measure of authority over Helen. Screaming, kicking, hitting and throwing herself on the floor were examples of her constant attempts to enforce her own will, and when the teacher applied strictness and force she came up against the opposition of the parents.

But her perseverance overcame all resistance, for she knew 'that the education of this child will be the distinguishing event of my life, if I have the brains and the perseverance to accomplish it.' But there was still quite some way to go. 'She has tyrannized over everybody, her mother, her father, the servants, the little darkies who play with her.' And Miss Sullivan wrote as follows about Helen's behaviour and appearance: 'I have seen her smile only once or twice since I came. She is unresponsive and even impatient of caresses from anyone except her mother. She is very quick-tempered and wilful ... One thing that impresses everybody is Helen's tireless activity. She is never still a moment.'

Immediately after arrival the teacher began to instruct the child by trying to teach her the names of things by forming the letters with her fingers. She used every opportunity to awaken in Helen the sense of a word's meaning through the sensation of touch. With her astonishingly quick powers of comprehension Helen soon managed to unite words together with their objects. But this was a kind of mechanical memory-feat. She now knew that many things have a sign, but the significance of the names, the meaning of the word, was as yet incomprehensible to her.

At any rate, the teacher's determined consistency had lessened Helen's unbridledness:

> The wild little creature of two weeks ago has been transformed into a gentle child. She is sitting by me as I write, her face serene and happy, crocheting a long red chain of Scotch wool ... She lets me kiss her now, and when she is in a particularly gentle mood, she will sit on my lap for a minute or two; but she does not return my caresses.

On April 5, 1887, there took place that event which has since then become so famous, and which for the child signified the awakening to a new life. On this day Helen understood through a direct intuition that every object and being in the world also has a name and that it is the name that designates and defines everything. On the morning of this day the teacher had tried to explain to the child the difference between milk and water and spelt the word 'w-a-t-e-r' in her hand. After breakfast

> we went out to the pump-house, and I made Helen hold her mug under the spout while I pumped. As the cold water gushed forth, filling the mug, I spelled 'w-a-t-e-r' in Helen's free hand. The word coming so close upon the sensation of cold water rushing over her hand seemed to startle her. She dropped the mug and stood as one transfixed. A new light came into her face.

Helen Keller herself wrote of this moment:

> Suddenly I felt a misty consciousness, as of something forgotten — a thrill of returning thought; and somehow the mystery of language was revealed to me. I knew then that 'w-a-t-e-r' meant the wonderful cool something that was flowing over my hand. That living word awakened my soul, gave it light, hope, joy, set it free!

The sound 'water' had a special significance in Helen's life, for she writes at the beginning of her autobiography: 'Even after my illness I remembered one of the words I had learned in these early months. It was the word "water," and I continued to make some sound for that word after all other speech was lost.'

It was probably not without significance that it was the word 'water' which awakened Helen's spirit and kindled in her the sense of thought; for it was about water that Christ spoke to the Samaritan woman: 'Whoever drinks of the water that I shall give him shall never thirst' (John 4:14). These words were spoken at a well, and it was also a well where Helen Keller's awakening took place. The day was April 5, which according to esoteric traditions was the date of the first Easter Sunday.

Such considerations are an important part of doing justice to the event that had taken place there; for something happened in Helen Keller at that time which will be of star-like significance for generations of people.

Experience of the world

However, on the same day something else happened which was of great importance for Helen Keller's life. She describes it as follows:

> As we returned to the house every object which I touched seemed to quiver with life. That was because I saw everything with the strange, new sight that had come

to me. On entering the door I remembered the doll I had broken. I felt my way to the hearth and picked up the pieces. I tried vainly to put them together. Then my eyes filled with tears; for I realized what I had done, and for the first time I felt repentance and sorrow.

Thus on the day when the world of names opened up for this child, her heart became receptive to moral values. The meaning of beings and objects unfolded simultaneously with their worth in the context of world events.

Henceforth everything in existence had its place and its order. Everything beyond this depended on hard work, on the power of endurance and the loyalty that needed to be developed. For the ground had now to be prepared! Helen Keller recognized herself as a being who could call all other beings with their names. The Holy Spirit had touched her and enabled her to stand erect as a human being. Neither eyes nor ears, nor any other of the senses, are necessary to bring about what took place then. It was a step from creature to creator that was being taken here. The soul had become conscious of the spirit.

Helen's progress from now on was breath-taking. Her vocabulary increased every day; her thirst for knowledge was almost unquenchable, and through the medium of language she won for herself a mental picture of the world. Already in June she began out of herself to write letters that were still very clumsy and were composed of one- or two-word sentences. Flowers and animals, people and events became for her questions about whys and wherefores.

In the August of that year she learnt the basic facts of the birth and death of the beings of nature and experienced chicks hatching from the egg and the miracle of new-born puppies. Miss Sullivan was now convinced of her mission:

> Something within me tells me that I shall succeed beyond my dreams. Were it not for some

> circumstances that make such an idea highly improbable, even absurd, I should think Helen's education would surpass in interest and wonder Dr Howe's achievement. I know that she has remarkable powers, and I believe that I shall be able to develop and mould them. I cannot tell how I know these things. I had no idea a short time ago how to go to work; I was feeling about in the dark; but somehow I know now, and I know that I know. I cannot explain it; but when difficulties arise, I am not perplexed or doubtful. I know how to meet them; I seem to divine Helen's peculiar needs. It is wonderful.

Such words give one a sense of the mood that pervaded the collaboration between pupil and teacher at that time. It was as if a spirit-wind was blowing around them both, giving the child wings of understanding and experience and the teacher sure guidance.

Helen's powers of imaginative perception were beginning to unfold. When she was told that her little sister's eyes were blue, she asked: 'Are they like wee skies?'

Thus she was finding her place in the world of language, in the world of abstract concepts and the world of imagination. Her progress was maintained, and a year after her meeting with Anne Sullivan she made her first journey to the Perkins Institution in Boston. This is how she writes about it:

> We had scarcely arrived at the Perkins Institution for the Blind when I began to make friends with the little blind children. It delighted me inexpressibly to find that they know the manual alphabet. What joy to talk with other children in my own language! Until then I had been like a foreigner speaking through an interpreter. In the school where Laura Bridgman was taught I was in my own country.

From then on she was to have her 'own country' as a place to stay for many years. She visited the school there with her teacher's help, became a companion to the other children and had the experience of being accepted as part of a community.

This summer also brought her for the first time an experience of the ocean, as she spent her holidays at Cape Cod. This first great and consciously experienced journey was of far-reaching significance for Helen:

> As I recall that visit north I am filled with wonder at the richness and variety of the experiences that cluster about it. It seems to have been the beginning of everything. The treasures of a new, beautiful world were laid at my feet, and I took in pleasure and information at every turn. I lived myself into all things. I was never still a moment; my life was as full of motion as those little insects that crowd a whole existence into one brief day.

The child now experienced that she could immerse herself with her soul into all objects and beings and learn about them with at least the same intensity as people who could see and hear. Without being able to see, she felt the way that the things around her appeared spatially; and without her being able to hear, the inner substances of beings quivered in her soul. For she had learnt through 'understanding' not to keep her soul imprisoned in the house of her body but to communicate with the surrounding world. What is otherwise wholly brought about through the gates of the senses occurred in the case of this child out of an eagerness for knowledge and a true mania for getting to know things. She longed with every fibre of her being to learn about the world in all its richness. This enabled her to overcome the barriers set by her blindness and deafness and made it possible for her in a very direct way to make the world of experience her own.

This happened pre-eminently when she was with other people. She had a direct access to what anyone around her was feeling. Thus, to give one of many possible examples, Miss Sullivan described the following event in a report about the year 1888:

> On one occasion, while walking on the common with her, I saw a police officer taking a man to the station house. The agitation which I felt evidently produced a perceptible physical change, for Helen asked, excitedly, 'What do you see?'

At this time it was also established that direct contact with other people by, for example, holding someone else's hand made it easier for her to understand what was going on around her.

The liveliness of her experiences of nature is apparent from the description that she gives of her first experience of winter:

> I recall my surprise on discovering that a mysterious hand had stripped the trees and bushes, leaving only here and there a wrinkled leaf. The birds had flown, and their empty nests in the bare trees were filled with snow. Winter was on hill and field. The earth seemed benumbed by his icy touch, and the very spirits of the trees had withdrawn to their roots, and there, curled up in the dark, lay fast asleep.

When one day she was walking through a snowy forest, she experienced the radiant light of winter: 'The trees stood motionless and white like figures in a marble frieze. There was no odour of pine-needles. The rays of the sun fell upon the trees, so that the twigs sparkled like diamonds and dropped in showers when we touched them. So dazzling was the light, it penetrated the darkness that veils my eyes.'

This is not the description of a 'blind' person but of someone whose power of vision — even without the use of her eyes — has penetrated into her field of perception. This is what was remarkable about Helen Keller's life, that she was able to achieve a union with the world that lies beyond eye and ear.

People around Helen Keller

In the meantime, however, people's attention had been drawn to this child prodigy. American reporters tried to set everything in motion which could make this sensation even more sensational. What was taking place in silent seclusion was dragged brutally into the limelight. Michael Anagnos did all he could to distort to the point of incredibility what was in any event the immense progress made by the boarder at his institute. From this time onwards Helen Keller was a 'public event.' Again and again she was questioned, examined and observed. What helped to shield her from arrogance and delusions of grandeur was solely her uninhibited openness which she had for all people.

Through her popularity, however, she also had the possibility of meeting many important people. One of the most crucial events for her was her connection with Bishop Phillips Brooks. He was at the time a preacher at the Trinity Church in Boston and one of the greatest preachers of his day. He gave the famous funeral oration for President Lincoln. This man introduced Helen to the world of religious thought. She later said of him:

> Only those who knew Bishop Brooks can appreciate the joy his friendship was to those who possessed it. As a child I loved to sit on his knee and clasp his great hand with one of mine, while Miss Sullivan spelled into the other his beautiful words about God and the spiritual world ... Once, when I was puzzled to know why there were so many religions, he said: 'There is one universal religion, Helen — the religion of love.'

She also met the famous Scottish preacher Henry Drummond, the author of two significant anti-Darwinistic works. One of them, *Natural Law in the Spiritual World,* tried to present a unified picture of the world that embraced both nature and the spirit-world. In 1893 he gave the Lowell Lectures in Boston, out of which he subsequently wrote his book, *The Ascent of Man.* It was at this time that Helen Keller met him. 'I knew Mr Henry Drummond, and the memory of his strong, warm hand-clasp is like a benediction.'

Another friendship of long duration connected her with Dr Edward Everett Hale. He was a preacher, author, youth-leader, philanthropist and journalist, all in one; a strong and warm personality who through his direct and simple religiosity became the helper of thousands of young and old people. He died in 1909 aged 85 and was to the end Helen's protector and friend.

Alexander Graham Bell was one of the first of those who gave spiritual and physical help to Helen Keller. He was a Scot, from a family that had traditionally been involved with language and speaking. His grandfather was a famous speech therapist, and his father Melville Bell was the inventor of 'visible speech,' a new method of educating deaf mutes, which was particularly successful at that time. In 1870 father and son came to Boston and established there a private educational establishment for deaf mutes. Out of his work with the problems of educating deaf and dumb people Graham Bell constructed the first telephone device in 1875. (He knew nothing of the previous attempts at constructing such a device by the German, Johann Philipp Reis, fourteen years earlier.) From these beginnings there evolved the technical application of the modern telephone. The Bell Telephone Company was founded, and by 1881 none of the larger states in America was without a telephone network.

When Graham Bell saw little Helen for the first time in 1886, he was not only a famous, but also a very rich, man. However, he gave a large part of his means for the help and support of education for the deaf and dumb. When he was awarded the Alessandro Volta Prize by the French Government for his inventions (its value was 50,000 francs), he added a further 100,000 dollars to this and the Volta Bureau was founded as a result. It was a foundation 'for promoting and spreading knowledge about deafness.' From this foundation there later arose many different subsidiary organizations in America for caring for and educating the deaf and dumb.

Helen Keller said of him: 'His dominating passion is his love for children. He is never quite so happy as when he has a little deaf child in his arms. His labours in [sic] behalf of the deaf will live on and bless generations of children yet to come; and we love him alike for what he himself has achieved and for what he has evoked from others.'

The first director of the Volta Bureau was John Hitz, to whom Helen Keller owed her acquaintance with Swedenborg's teachings. He was 'one of the friends I loved most.' She goes on to write about him:

> I met Mr Hitz first in 1893, when I was about thirteen years old, and that was the beginning of an affectionate and beautiful friendship which I cherish among the dearest memories of my life. He was always deeply interested in all I did — my studies, my girlish joys and dreams, my struggle through college and my work for the blind. He was one of the few who fully appreciated my teacher and the peculiar significance of her work not only to me, but to all the world. His letters bore testimony to his affection for her and his understanding of what she was to me — a light in all dark places.[3]

A lasting friendship developed between the old Swedenborgian and the young girl. Summer after summer John Hitz visited the little country estate of Wrentham, where Helen Keller was living with Miss Sullivan, and in the course of their long walks introduced the deaf and blind girl to the spirit's kingdoms of light, as Swedenborg was enabled to behold them. He translated many of Swedenborg's works into Braille in order that Helen could read them.

'Many friends have done wonderful things for me,' writes Helen Keller, 'but nothing like Mr Hitz's untiring effort to share with me the inner sunshine which filled his silent years. Each year I was drawn closer to him, and he wrote to me more constantly as the days passed.'

Then this friend died suddenly at her side, after he had come to fetch her from the station in Washington, where she had come to visit him. 'He was full of joy as he embraced me, saying how impatiently he had awaited my coming. Then, as he was leading me from the train, he had a sudden attack of heart trouble, and passed away. Just before the end he took my hand, and I still feel his pressure when I think of that dark time.'

All these men surrounded Helen Keller's path of life. They guided this girl like spiritual godparents on her gradual journey into the world of the knowledge and experiences which opened up to her in so powerful a way. They were men in whom the power of tradition had been linked with the radiance of a new epoch. They still bore within themselves the heritage of the nineteenth century, but on their brows there shone the spirit-sun of a future revelation. Helen Keller, the child of the world, stood in their midst.

Helen Keller's spirit

After her schooling at the Perkins Institution was over, Helen entered a grammar school for girls. At this time she was 16 years old and had prepared herself to master the entire curriculum of her age. She read Greek and Latin classics in the original, was able to understand German and French literary works and was completely at home in mathematics and scientific subjects.

At the beginning of the new century she began her university studies at Redcliffe College; against the advice of the professional body she succeeded in gaining admission to this college which at this time had particularly high standards. She studied modern languages, political economy, the history of philosophy and much else besides. However, her carefree and open nature did not blend well with the life and teaching of universities as they were then, and she found harsh words to express the disappointment that the 'fossilization of study' caused her.

Nevertheless she graduated like any other student. While she was still a student, she started working on her book, *The Story of My Life,* which appeared soon after it was finished and made a considerable impression. Over the years it has been translated into almost fifty languages and, hence, made its way to the hearts of nearly all people on earth who wanted to hear its message. Fifty languages! This means that it took all continents by storm. But this was always one of the great aims that lived within Helen Keller as a lofty ideal: to be able to serve and help all people throughout the world without distinction. The ideal of all mankind as a great brotherhood was to her a holy image towards which she aspired.

Immediately after completing her university studies Helen and Miss Sullivan settled down in the little country house in Wrentham near Boston. A room had been set aside where Helen could study:

> A bas-relief of Homer hung on the wall, so that she could feel the features of the great blind poet, the bitter traces of a mind acquainted with sorrow; and she imagined him chanting his lines of life, love and war as he groped his way from camp to camp. She felt that Greek was the loveliest language that she knew anything about — the violin, as she called it, of human thought; and she read it until the tips of her fingers bled. She arranged her braille library in the study, with Plato and Aeschylus also in Greek and with Tacitus, Catullus, Plautus and Horace in Latin.[4]

This intimate connection with Greece and its essential nature was something that she retained. She also reports of an important experience in this regard:

> I had been sitting quietly in the library for half an hour. I turned to my teacher and said, 'Such a strange thing has happened! I have been far away all this time, and I haven't left the room.'
> 'What do you mean, Helen?' she asked, surprised.
> 'Why,' I cried, 'I have been in Athens.'
> Scarcely were the words out of my mouth when a bright, amazing realization seemed to catch my mind and set it ablaze. I perceived the realness of my soul and its sheer independence of all conditions of place and body. It was clear to me that it was because I was a spirit that I had so vividly 'seen' and felt a place thousands of miles away. Space was nothing to spirit! In that new consciousness shone the presence of God, Himself a Spirit everywhere at once, the Creator dwelling in all the universe simultaneously. The fact that my little soul could reach out over continents and seas to Greece, despite a blind, deaf and stumbling body, sent another exulting emotion rushing over me.[5]

When in 1946 she travelled through Greece in order to visit the war-disabled blind soldiers, she stood on the Acropolis; and one of her biographers describes this moment: 'She felt the serene atmosphere in which Pallas Athene moved and men had received visits from the gods, and she realized once more how far these Greek associations had gone to form her own mind and her own spirit.'[6] And she studied Plato with such intensity that he had an almost similar influence on her as Swedenborg.

Thus Dr Howe had probably had some kind of a premonition when he had gone to Greece and had worked there, and had returned to Boston filled with this same spirit in order to lay the foundations for what was to come so richly to fulfilment in Helen Keller.

In Wrentham she also increasingly concerned herself with modern socialism. She studied the books of Marx, Kropotkin,

Engels and others at some length. But hers was not a political socialism but an impulse towards help, unification and brotherhood that embraced all human beings. Her heart belonged to the outcast and the downtrodden, the oppressed and the subjugated. She stood up quite openly for the equality of races. Wherever one was stronger, she took the side of the weaker.

Above all, however, she was filled with a breadth of vision that few people at that time had in so great a measure. In this respect she was inspired by the same impulse that also lived within her great fellow-countryman, Walt Whitman.

> O take my hand Walt Whitman!
> Such gliding wonders! Such sights and sounds!
> Such join'd unended links, each hook'd to the next,
> Each answering all, each sharing the earth with all.

These famous introductory words to Whitman's hymn *Salut au monde* could also be by Helen Keller.

This great hymn, where the poet takes the whole world — the seen, experienced, heard and suffered world, with all its people and their destinies — into his heart, this world-encompassing poem in which a new dawn shines forth, is the expression of Helen Keller's innermost will. Her later life sought to bring about what is expressed in the concluding verses of this hymn:

> What cities the light or warmth penetrates I penetrate those cities myself,
> All islands to which birds wing their way I wing my way myself.

> Toward you all, in America's name,
> I raise high the perpendicular hand, I make the signal,
> To remain after me in sight forever,
> For all the haunts and homes of men.[7]

Helen Keller's life was latterly a constant service to the blind people in the world. She spoke at hundreds of congresses and in thousands of meetings. She answered tens of thousands of letters and collected hundreds of thousands of pounds, dollars, yen and francs through her voice wrenched from the prison of her body and used them for building schools, institutes and workshops in service of the blind.

Above all, however, she spoke with innumerable people — with the blind and the deaf, the disabled and the burdened, the humiliated and the insulted. She always remembered their lucid appeals, their faith, their humour and their confidence. For her, 'tolerance is the greatest spiritual gift.'

Emissary of the spirit

Rudolf Steiner spoke several times about Swedenborg and explained from many different points of view what kind of clairvoyant insight had been granted to this great spirit. In a lecture of May 8, 1917 he describes him in the following way:

> Swedenborg points out ... that it is evident to the spiritually enlightened that the soul by virtue of its inner forces is related to a spiritual sun in the same way as the body is related to the physical sun, but that everything of a physical nature is dependent upon the soul and spirit. Thus he explains in, I would say, a new way what we have referred — when speaking of the mysteries — to as the sun mystery, that mystery of which Julian the Apostate had a dim recollection when he spoke of the sun as a spiritual being ... To the extent that this was possible, Swedenborg restored the sun mystery for his time through his imaginative faculty of knowledge.[8]

And in another lecture he describes Swedenborg's gift of seership in these words:

20. HELEN KELLER

> On looking deeply into Swedenborg's personality, we find that ... in his forties [when his clairvoyant gift suddenly appeared] he developed an overwhelming love for all he had learnt up to that time. There can hardly be anyone in the world who came to love knowledge for its own sake as much as Swedenborg did. It was this love for knowledge as such that enabled him at a certain point in his life to gain insight in his own way into the spiritual world.[9]

Two aspects of Swedenborg's underlying intentions are touched upon here which are also of significance for understanding Helen Keller's cast of mind. For there can be no doubt that, in her, love of knowledge — true *philo-sophia* — had, as in Swedenborg's case, developed to a remarkable degree. But she did not arrive through this at an imaginative understanding of the spiritual world. In her, love of knowledge was transformed into an intuitive activity in the service of other people.

However, Helen Keller also aspired towards the sun mystery which Swedenborg tried to reveal for his time. Little by little she struggled for a new understanding of the Bible, and only with Swedenborg's help did she begin to enter into that hidden and yet clearly evident sun-land, in which understanding and vision merge into one. But what made her into this relentless pursuer of knowledge?

Helen Keller was born on June 27, 1880, at a time of the yearly cycle which John the Baptist had also chosen for his birth. It followed from this that her soul began its journey into incarnation at Michaelmas 1879. This was the time when an event of the greatest importance took place in the world of spirit. At this moment the archangel known by the name of Michael took on the leadership of mankind in order to guide its destiny and history through the coming four hundred years.

In every Michael epoch, however, this Sun Spirit inspires human beings in such a way that they have the aspiration to experience the whole world as a unity, that they endeavour to overcome the forces of inheritance and nationalism and try to experience brotherliness out of a striving towards freedom:

> All people will be brothers
> Where thy gentle wings abide.[10]

One of the roots of Helen Keller's spiritual existence is to be found here. The sun power of Michael that unites all beings was active within her, and from it she received the potential that she had for helpful deeds.

When she became ill at the age of nineteen months she overcame her hereditary forces in this illness. But she paid for this victory with the loss of her sight and hearing. Expressed in pictorial terms, her sensory head was demanded as a sacrifice. But she uplifted her supersensible head and thereby became the standard-bearer of a new epoch for humanity; in her own way and together with many she inaugurated the Michael age. She is a modern Baptist figure, who embodied the dawn of a new epoch not through the word but through inner and outer deeds.

Shortly after her sixteenth birthday, on July 8, 1896, she gave a first address at the meeting of the American Association to Promote the Teaching of Speech to the Deaf. Through what she said she made it apparent how infinitely difficult it became for her to acquire even the first rudiments of speech. And then she said:

> I can remember the time before I learned to speak, and how I used to struggle to express my thoughts by means of the manual alphabet –how my thoughts used to beat against my finger tips like little birds striving to gain their freedom, until one day Miss Fuller [her speech teacher] opened wide the prison-door and let them escape. I wonder if she remembers how eagerly and gladly they spread their wings and flew away. Of course, it was not

easy at first to fly. The speech-wings were weak and broken, and had lost all the grace and beauty that had once been theirs.'[11]

In this spirit-imbued picture the girl Helen Keller depicts a person who can speak as a being from whose confined space the birds of thoughts soar up on the wings of speech and fly to other people — a truly Johannine imagination.

At the end of her address she calls out to her mute sisters and brothers: 'Sometime, somewhere, somehow we shall find that which we seek. We shall speak, yes, and sing too, as God intended we should speak and sing.'

Only an emissary of the spirit who has something essential to say to her fellow human beings can speak in such a way.

'O Life, Life, Wondrous Time ...'

Afterword by Alfons Limbrunner

Karl König was inwardly and outwardly devoted to man. His mission, if so grand a word may be allowed here, was 'the child in need of special care,' the person with special needs. Born in Vienna in 1902, he studied medicine, and found his way to Rudolf Steiner's anthroposophy quite early in life through Goethe's scientific writings. When still only 19 years old he made the following note in his diary: 'The world-spirit is to be found within the human spirit.'[1] He received his first impressions of the developing field of curative education through meeting the Dutch physician Ita Wegman in Arlesheim, Switzerland. Along with other pioneers of curative education, he started working at Pilgramshain in Silesia, an estate that was run on biodynamic agricultural principles; but he then returned to Vienna where, through his medical practice, he formed a group of young people — mostly of Jewish origin — to study spiritual science. When Hitler invaded Vienna and Austria, he emigrated with some of them to England by a circuitous route. From there, the 'Candle on the Hill' lit in Camphill, Scotland in 1940 became the symbol of a movement which now comprises nearly a hundred centres worldwide. Until his death in Überlingen, Germany in 1966, he was one of the most tireless advocates of people with special needs. He also gained recognition and respect within scientific circles by giving talks and through his various publications.

König's interest in man was broad and diverse. As a well-educated person of his time he was also interested in history, and even more so in people who 'had made history.' He endeavoured 'to discover the intentions of the people concerned, to grasp their their significance for the present and to encompass their possible metamorphoses for the future with his own intentions.'[2] His specific concern was to engage with the century at whose threshold — at the dawn of a new age — he himself had been born.

Through König's essays we can get a sense of this world of yesterday, as well as the transformation of the world. The paintings by Adolph von Menzel further depict this mood reflected by the middle and upper middle classes, but also by the position of the working class as a new social norm. In the essay 'A Study of the Year 1861,' which forms part of the introduction to this book, and explores the year Rudolf Steiner was born, it is made clear that König considered this year to be an important nodal point in the history of Europe and the wider world in the nineteenth century: 'One can find almost the entire history of the second half of the nineteenth century concentrated as though in a concave mirror in this year 1861, and from there one can follow the threads that link past and future events with one another' (p. 13).

König maintained that 'the history of the nineteenth century is still to be prperly written,' and he compared this era to the legendary myth of the Trojan War (p. 321). The old had to be destroyed in order for the new to emerge. Whether this epic has been written, now that more than half a century has elapsed since König's own research, is not yet clear. However, there is extensive literature and historical research that goes far beyond the information available to König at the time.[3]

It has become common to talk about 'the long nineteenth century' within Germany and Europe spanning the time from the decisive outbreak of the French Revolution to the catastrophe of First World War. It was a century of industrialisation, imperialism, accelerated growth of world populations and mass migrations across the whole of Europe. All this was accompanied by extraordinary technical inventions and discoveries: railways, motor cars, steam ships, photography, cinema, electric light, X-Rays, the telegraph and telephone, and much more. It was also the century during which nations were shaped, a new middle class became established, along with its culture and conflicts; and essentially, it was the century that saw the beginnings of democracy, linked with the introduction of structures for a socially ordered state. It was indeed a time when some highly gifted scientists and artists were living: 'A Milky Way of geniuses, who, even as very young people, accomplished the most astounding feats. Europe was young and vibrant during this epoch, and alive with a drive for action.'[4]

The triumph of the exact sciences, and materialistic thinking based on the natural sciences, had begun. It was the dawning of a world without mysteries. Rudolf Steiner and Karl König frequently pointed out that this led to elements of one-sidedness, the consequences of which have become markedly obvious in today's world. These developments also prevented initiatives by other thinkers, who had played an important role within Goethe's intellectual circle. There were medical practitioners, historians and philosophers, for example Carl Gustav Carus, Joseph Ennemoser, Lorenz Oken und Ignaz Troxler, whose names are almost forgotten today. They all considered the world, the earth and human beings to be part of one inclusive organism. 'It was their endeavour to arrive at an intuitive knowledge of the world, to focus their attention not on details but instead direct it towards the whole, to discover the macrocosm within the microcosm, and to unify the polarities of existence through synthesis in a higher third element.'[5] These people — the representatives of the Goethean world view, of that forgotten, German cultural stream — considered it important to raise questions that are regarded as increasingly relevant again by people today.

It is said that König had the ability to notice connections between people and times that had not previously been discovered. Hans Müller-Wiedemann, his biographer suggests, that his motivation to write the various 'life portraits' was further linked to personal experiences:

> It was as though they emerged — imperceptibly at first — out of his own biography and connected him with his subject. In this endeavour König searched in particular for the central theme of a biography, that which points towards the esoteric, inner stream of history — viewed as a web of karmic relationships between people — for which the outer events of a human life are symptoms. An experience of this kind would not let him go until he had so illuminated the destiny of the life concerned that it became transparent in the stream of history and the karma of mankind.[6]

Taking a brief look at the portraits of Adalbert Stifter, Gustav Mahler and Sigmund Freud may further exemplify this. The portrait of this extraordinary composer was written in 1960, the year of Mahler's centenary. König had listened to Mahler's Second Symphony already as a young man in Vienna and in his diary described it as an almost 'ecstatic experience.'[7] König felt deeply connected with Gustav Mahler's destiny and music. Throughout his life, during good times and bad, this music accompanied him on a deep level. How else would he have come to write the sentence that concludes the essay on the great composer: 'The powerful stream of German music originated in the sources of Bach: in Mahler, it returns into the ocean of eternity. It flowed for two centuries: from the birth of Haydn to the death of Mahler. There are no followers; his disciples are simply tributaries on the delta of this river, as it were.' (p. 382).

Of all the essays included in the present volume, the one on Freud and his psychoanalytical theory is König's most comprehensive study of a particular individual. He shows himself to be an opponent of Freud's, not least also because of his own studies towards a more imaginative and spiritual approach to psychology, which were published in his book, *The Human Soul*. There can be no doubt that König owes some important insights to this fellow Austrian, who, like himself, emigrated to England. One can get the sense that the way he describes Freud's 'search for truth' at the end of his essay is disproportionate — that 'his path to the Mothers was deceptive and actually led him to Satanic illusions.' In the words Mephistopheles says to Faust 'into an untrodden domain which none can enter, a path into what has not been asked for, and which none would request.' Freud's psychoanalysis has greatly changed and enriched the world, and therefore also the way we feel and think about ourselves to this day. One does not need to be a follower of his teachings, but none of the modern psychoanalytical approaches — not even the ones considered 'anthroposophical,' 'transpersonal,' or 'spiritual' — can disregard some of Freud's specific insights. However, they can of course be developed much further, based on a wider understanding.

Adalbert Stifter was a central element in König's life, as he seemed to feel a close affinity with him.[8] König felt connected to Bohemia and to the inner picture of a spiritual East. In 1937 he went on a journey to Stifter's home country, and described the Bohemian landscape to be of 'quiet, but resigned beauty.' He visited Oberplan, Stifter's birthplace, and devotedly re-read his stories and novels. 'This gave new strength to an impulse which played a significant part in the founding and development of Camphill. Reverence for mankind, for the laws working in nature, and devotion to small things: these became the basic rules of existence.'[9] Karl König pointed out that there was a recurring theme in Stifter's stories, expressed symbolically by snow, the colour red, and roses. In this essay, he further quoted Rudolf Steiner's meditative verse about the 'blossoming roses of the soul, whose red shines into the heaviness of earth,' the words with which Müller-Wiedemann concluded his biography on Karl König.

In 1955, König published a further essay on 'Adalbert Stifter and Curative Education,' where he even declared him as be a brother and fellow traveller to us modern human beings. In König's view the deeper teachings of the poet, as they were described in *Bunte Steine* (Coloured Stones) — the stories 'Granite,' 'Limestone,' 'Tourmaline,' 'Rock Crystal,' and 'Muscovite,' including the introduction on the 'law of gentleness' — constituted the guiding principles, or 'the true morality of curative pedagogy.' He suggested that the stories expressed the core value of curative education: that any human being, in spite of their specific characteristics, should be treasured, so as to uphold their eternal human spirit, no matter how strange their actions and behaviour may be. König interpreted the deeper meaning to be discovered in the stones' names as follows: 'How else would one define the kind of law and order achieved through spiritual striving, if not by the names of stones? If moderation and good habits have been established through inner practice, they will remain in the depths of the soul as precious crystals and orderly form.'[10]

König's biographical studies can, on the one hand, be understood and read in terms of filling the abstractions of historical writing with the vitality of actual lives, but also as a way of developing and sharing a true social understanding of man. Rudolf Steiner referred to this necessary 'social understanding of man' in his lecture on: 'How can the soul-needs of the present be met?'[11] Steiner suggested that what was needed were many positive images on how people actually developed, a kind of 'natural history of individual human development.' It would furthermore be important to take a loving interest in that life story, to actually tell it and share it.

Life stories and biographies are always 'interpreted' history. Within the collection of essays in this publication, one can see that König managed to formulate some truly original, but also bold, interpretations that have remained controversial, both in the past and at the present time, and some details of which may be in need of correction. His understanding of and way of working with his subject-matter led him always to establish contemporary connections as well as those of content between specific events and people, which is something the reader cannot always comprehend. For König, there is no such thing as coincidence, everything has significance; things correspond from far back in the past and far ahead into the future. Objective information is interwoven with the images that have been stirred and awakened within the writer. König's work is generally full of empathy and warmth, and goes far beyond the psychological interpretations and the non-committal curiosity so common in certain biographical images of our time. They respect the greatness and uphold the dignity of the people portrayed; people, who together with countless others, transformed this period of world history.

It is said that König took a deep interest in Rainer Maria Rilke's work, and would occasionally give small volumes of poetry as a gift to close colleagues. Rilke, who in this publication of essays is only briefly mentioned within the portrayal of Lou Andreas-Salomé, published a marvellously timeless poem in 1913/14. In its incomparably poetical way, it reflects what runs like a 'dramatic red thread' through König's life. It is the substance that life, that destiny is made of:

> O life, life, wondrous time
> Extending from one contradiction to another
> Treading tediously on its way
> Until suddenly, with wings outstretched
> Indescribably far, like an angel
> Life is there in its inexplicable majesty.
>
> Of all existences that can be ventured
> Is there one more glowing and more bold?
> We stand our ground and push against our boundaries
> And thereby wrench in the unknown.

Notes

Original publication dates

The chapters were originally written in German as individual essays. The list below shows the original German name and place and date of first publication.

1. A Study of the Year 1861: *Vor hundert Jahren. Zur Phänomenologie des Jahres 1861,* in *Die Drei,* 1961, Vol. 31, No. 6.
2. Samuel Hahnemann: *Samuel Hahnemann und seine Zeit,* in *Beiträge zur Erweiterung der Heilkunst,* 1955, Vol. 8, No. 1 & 2, and in *Die Drei,* 1955, Vol. 25, No. 2
3. Ernst Baron von Feuchtersleben: *Der Goetheanist Ernst Freiherr von Feuchtersleben,* in *Beiträge zur Erweiterung der Heilkunst,* 1956, Vol. 9, No. 3 & 4.
4. Charles Darwin: *Charles Darwin und das Schicksal des Darwinismus,* in *Die Drei,* 1959, Vol. 29, No. 1.
5. Rudolf Wagner: *Rudolph Wagner und der Materialismusstreit in Göttingen,* in *Die Drei,* 1964, Vol. 34, No. 3.
6. Rudolf Virchow: *Rudolf Virchow. Zu seinem 60. Todestag,* in *Die Drei,* 1962, Vol. 32, No. 6.
7. Carl Ludwig Schleich: *Besonnte Vergangenheit. Zum 100. Geburtstag von Carl Ludwig Schleich,* in *Beiträge zur Erweiterung der Heilkunst,* 1959, Vol. 12, No. 6.
8. Justinus Kerner: *Aus Justinus Kerners Gedichten und Gedanken. Zu seinem 100. Todestag,* in *Die Drei,* 1962, Vol. 32, No. 2.
9. Josef Breuer: *Dr Joseph Breuer 1842–1925,* in *Beiträge zur Erweiterung der Heilkunst,* 1957, Vol. 10, No. 5 & 6, and in *Wiener Klinischen Wochenschrift* at the same time.
10. Sigmund Freud: *Sigmund Freud zu seinem 100. Geburtstag,* in *Die Drei,* 1956, Vol. 26, No. 4 & 5.
11. Adalbert Stifter: *Adalbert Stifter zu seinem 150. Geburtstag,* in *Die Drei,* 1955, Vol. 25, No. 5.

12. Wilhelm Dilthey: *Wilhelm Dilthey, zu seinem 50. Todestag,* in *Blätter für Anthroposophie,* 1961, Vol. 13, No. 10.
13. Karl Eugen Neumann: *Auf den Spuren Karl Eugen Neumanns. Zum 100. Geburtstag des Übersetzers buddhistischer Texte,* in *Die Drei,* 1965, Vol. 35, No. 5.
14. Marie Eugenie Delle Grazie: *Die Dichterin Marie Eugenie Delle Grazie,* in *Die Drei,* 1964, Vol. 34, No. 5.
15. Grant, Hildebrand, Dohrn, Marées: *Charles Grant, Adolf Hildebrand, Anton Dohrn, Hans von Marées. Schicksale im Schatten des Darwinismus,* in *Die Drei,* 1963, Vol. 33, No. 2, 3 & 4.
16. Gustav Mahler: *Gustav Mahler. Ein Wort zu seinem 100. Geburtstag,* in *Die Drei,* 1960, Vol. 30, No. 3. Published in English in *Free Deeds,* Vol. II, No. 5.
17. Alma Mahler-Werfel and Lou Andreas-Salomé: *Das Ringen um den Menschen zur Jahrhundertwende. Alma Mahler-Werfel, Lou Andreas-Salomé,* in *Die Drei,* 1965, Vol. 35, No. 2.
18. Robert Owen: *Robert Owens Persönlichkeit. Zu seinem 100. Todestag,* in *Die Drei,* 1958, Vol. 28, No. 6.
19. Count Harry Kessler: *Harry Graf Kessler, ein Deutscher, der seine Heimat suchte,* in *Die Kommenden,* 1962, Vol. 16, No. 17.
20. Helen Keller: *Die Geistgestalt Helen Kellers,* in *Das Seelenpflege-bedürftige Kind,* 1956, Vol. 3, No. 1.

Individual Spirit and Spirit of the Age

1 König, *My Task,* p. 41.
2 See Steel, 'Motives for the Social Impulses in Karl König's Life,' in König, *Becoming Human.*
3 König, *My Task,* p. 28.

1. A Study of the Year 1861

1 Schneider, 'Das Schicksal Friedrich Wilhelms IV' in *Macht und Gnade.*
2 Münch, *Böhmische Tragödie.*
3 Palacký, *Österreichs Staatsidee* (quoted in Münch, *Böhmische Tragödie.*)
4 Quoted from Tschuppik, *Franz Joseph I.*
5 Croce, *Geschichte Europas im 19. Jahrhundert.*
6 Morazé, *Das Gesicht des 19. Jahrhunderts.*
7 Bachofen, *Das Mutterrecht,* Vol. 1.
8 Whitehead, the chapter entitled 'God,' *Science and the Modern World.*
9 Whitehead, *Adventures of Ideas,* chapter entitled 'Philosophic Method.'
10 This and the following quotations relating to Tagore come from Chakravarty, *A Tagore Reader.*
11 Steiner, *Autobiography,* pp. 61ff.

NOTES

12 Steiner, *The Riddles of Philosophy*, p. 451.
13 Steiner, *The Philosophy of Spiritual Activity*, 'The Consequences of Monism.'
14 Steiner, *Geschichtliche Symptomatologie*.
15 Steiner, *Geistige und soziale Wandlungen*, lecture of Feb 6, 1920.

2. Samuel Hahnemann

1 English translation in Hahnemann, *Lesser Writings*.
2 English translation in Hahnemann, *Lesser Writings*.

3. Ernst Baron von Feuchtersleben

1 Friedell, *Kulturgeschichte der Neuzeit*.
2 Hadow, *Oxford History of Music*, 1904, Vol. 5, 'The Viennese Period.'
3 This and the following quoted from Neuberger, *Der Arzt Ernst Freiherr von Feuchtersleben*.
4 Quoted from Guttman, *Feuchterslebens ausgewählte Werke*.
5 Quoted from Guttman, *Feuchterslebens ausgewählte Werke*.
6 Quoted from Neuberger, *Der Arzt Ernst Freiherr von Feuchtersleben*.
7 Schönbauer, *Das Medizinische Wien*.
8 Schönbauer, *Das Medizinische Wien*.
9 Steiner, *Geisteswissenschaft und Medizin*, lecture of March 21, 1920.
10 Neuberger, *Der Arzt Ernst Freiherr von Feuchtersleben*.
11 Steiner, *The Karma of Materialism*, lecture of Sep 25, 1917.
12 Steiner, *Goethe's Secret Revelation*, lecture of Oct 24, 1908.
13 This and the following quotation from Steiner, *Goethe's Secret Revelation*, lecture of Oct 24, 1908.
14 Steiner, *Die Kunst der Rezitation und Deklamation*.
15 Steiner, *From Symptom to Reality*, lecture of October 25, 1918.
16 Steiner, *Physiologisch-Therapeutisches*, lecture of April 7, 1920.

4. Charles Darwin

1 Translation by Cecil Harwood.
2 Steiner, *The Fall of the Spirits of Darkness*, lecture of Oct 14, 1917.
3 Quoted from Barlow, *The Autobiography of Charles Darwin*, p. 122.
4 Barlow, *The Autobiography of Charles Darwin*, pp. 119f.
5 Haeckel, *Die Naturanschauung von Darwin, Goethe und Lamarck*.
6 Soret, *Zehn Jahre bei Goethe*.
7 Oken, *Lehrbuch der Naturphilosophie*.
8 Steiner, *Geistige und soziale Wandlungen in der Menschheitsentwickelung*, lecture of Feb 1, 1920.
9 Quoted from Bölsche, *Ernst Haeckel*.
10 Barlow, *The Autobiography of Charles Darwin*, pp. 130f.
11 *Life and Letters of Charles Darwin*, (edited by his son, Francis Darwin), Vol. 3, p. 133.

12 Barlow, *The Autobiography of Charles Darwin*, pp. 139, 138.
13 Barlow, *The Autobiography of Charles Darwin*, pp. 87, 94f.
14 Steiner, *The Fifth Gospel*, lecture of Oct 1, 1913.
15 Steiner, *Autobiography*, p. 263.

5. Rudolf Wagner

1 Steiner, *The Riddles of Philosophy*.
2 Wagner, *Menschenschöpfung und Seelensubstanz*.
3 In Degen, 'Die Naturforscherversammlung zu Göttingen und der Materialismusstreit' (The Naturalists' Assembly in Göttingen and the Dispute about Materialism), *Naturwissenschaftliche Rundschau*, July, 1954.
4 Wagner, *Menschenschöpfung und Seelensubstanz*.
5 Steiner, *The Riddles of Philosophy*, chapter entitled 'The Struggle over the Spirit.'
6 See the obituary by his son Adolph Wagner, Göttingen 1864.
7 Koller, *Johannes Müller*.
8 Wagner, *Über Wissen und Glauben*.
9 Reprinted in Steiner, *Methodische Grundlagen. der Anthroposophie*.
10 Steiner, *The Riddles of Philosophy*, p. 280.
11 Steiner, *The Fifth Gospel*, pp. 19f.

6. Rudolf Virchow

1 Waldeyer-Hartz, *Lebenserinnerungen*.
2 Quoted from Unger, *Virchow*.
3 Quoted from Unger, *Virchow*.
4 Steiner, *From Symptom to Reality*, lecture of Oct 25, 1918.
5 Schleich, *Those Were Good Days*.
6 Steiner, *Methodische Grundlagen der Anthroposophie*.
7 Steiner, *Gesammelte Aufsätze zur Kultur- und Zeitgeschichte*.
8 Steiner, *From Symptom to Reality*, lecture of Oct 25, 1918.

7. Carl Ludwig Schleich

1 This and the following quotations – unless otherwise indicated – are from Schleich, *Besonnte Vergangenheit*, (An English translation was published as *Those Were Good Days.)*
2 A. Wettley, 'Die wissenschaftliche Odyssee des Chirurgen Carl Ludwig Schleich 1859–1922' (The Scientific Odyssey of the Surgeon Carl Ludwig Schleich), *Med. Klinik* 54, 29/1959.
3 Steiner, *Gegenwärtiges und Vergangenes im Menschengeiste*, lecture of April 13, 1916.
4 Schleich, *Die Wunder der Seele*.
5 Steiner, *Karmic Relationships*, Vol. 4.

8. Justinus Kerner

1. Kerner, T. *Das Kernerhaus und seine Gäste.*
2. Kerner, *Das Bilderbuch aus meiner Knabenzeit.*
3. Kluckhohn, 'Friedrich von Hardenburgs Entwicklung und Dichtung.'
4. Steiner, *Soul Economy and Waldorf Education,* lecture of Jan 1, 1922.
5. Kerner, *Das Bilderbuch aus meiner Knabenzeit.*
6. Steiner, *Biographien und biographische Skizzen.*
7. Quoted from 'Justinus Kerners Leben und Schaffen' in *Justinus Kerners sämtliche poetische Werke,* Vol. 1.
8. Varnhagen, R. *Ein Frauenleben in Briefen,* (likewise the following quotation).
9. Translated by Constance Naden, *The Complete Poetical Works.*
10. Kerner, T. *Justinus Kerners Briefwechsel.*
11. Kerner, *The Seeress of Prevorst,* p. 52f. Subsequent quotes from pp. 53, 57, 73, 74.
12. Kerner, *Die Seherin von Prevorst.*
13. Liebbrand, *Romantische Medizin.*
14. Kerner, *The Seeress of Prevorst,* pp. 52f.
15. Bock, *Boten des Geistes.*
16. Kerner, T. *Justinus Kerners Briefwechsel.*
17. Kerner, T. *Justinus Kerners Briefwechsel.*
18. Steiner, *Biographien und biographische Skizzen.*

9. Josef Breuer

1. Billroth, *Lehren und Lernen der medizinischen Wissenschaften.*
2. Schönbauer, *Das medizinische Wien.*
3. Mach, *Grundlinie der Lehre von den Bewegungsempfindungen.* Breuer, 'Über die Function der Bodengänge des Ohrlabyrinthes,' (The Function of the Semicircular Canals of the Inner Ear), *Medizinische Jahrbücher* 1874, Vol. 1; 'Beiträge zur Lehre vom statischen Sinn,' (Towards Understanding the Sense of Balance), *Medizinische Jahrbücher* 1875, Vol. 1, No. 2. Crum Brown, 'On the Sense of Rotation and the Anatomy and Physiology of the Semicircular Canals of the Internal Ear,' *Journal of Anatomy and Physiology,* Vol. 8, 1874.
4. Goltz, 'Physiologische Bedeutung der Bodengänge des Ohrlabyrinthes,' (The Physiological Significance of the Semicircular Canals of the Inner Ear), *Pflügers Archiv für Physiologie* 3, 1870.
5. Wodak, *Kurze Geschichte der Vestibularisforschung.*
6. Steiner, *Kunst und Kunsterkenntnis,* lecture of Oct 28, 1909. English published as 'The Being of the Arts' *The Golden Blade,* 1979.
7. Freud, *Selbstdarstellung,* (likewise the following quotation).
8. Freud, *Aus den Anfängen der Psychoanalyse,* (also the following quotation).
9. Steiner, *Autobiography,* pp. 131f.

10. Sigmund Freud

1. Freud, *An Autobiographical Study*.
2. Susman, *Gestalten und Kreise*.
3. Reik, *The Inner Experience of a Psychoanalyst*.
4. This information comes from Jones, *Sigmund Freud*, Vol. 1.
5. Freud, *An Autobiographical Study*.
6. See Spehlmann, *Sigmund Freuds neurologische Schriften*.
7. Only a small proportion of the letters to Freud's fiancée have been published in Jones, *Sigmund Freud*.
8. Steiner, *Psychoanalysis and Spiritual Psychology*, lecture of Nov 10, 1917.
9. See *Blätter des jüdischen Frauenbundes für Frauenarbeit und Frauenbewegung*, 7/8, 1936.
10. Steiner, *Psychoanalysis and Spiritual Psychology*, lecture of Nov 10, 1917.
11. Freud, *The Origins of Psychoanalysis*.
12. Sachs, *Freud, Master and Friend*.
13. Binswanger, *Ausgewählte Vorträge und Aufsätze*.
14. Weizsäcker, *Natur und Geist*.
15. Sachs, *Freud, Master and Friend*.
16. Weizsäcker, *Natur und Geist*.
17. Jones, *Sigmund Freud*, Vol. 2.
18. Sachs, *Freud, Master and Friend*.
19. Susman, *Gestalten und Kreise*.
20. See especially Freud, *Beyond the Pleasure Principle*.
21. Friedell, *Kulturgeschichte der Neuzeit*, Vol. 3.
22. Freud, *An Autobiographical Study*.
23. Freud, *Moses and Monotheism*.
24. Rudolf Steiner, *Heilfaktoren für den sozialen Organismus*, lecture of April 3, 1920.
25. Sachs, *Freud, Master and Friend*.
26. Bock, 'Christsein vor dem Zeitgewissen.' In *Die Christengemeinschaft*, 10/1955.

11. Adalbert Stifter

1. All quotations from Stifter are taken from Fürst, *Adalbert Stifters Ausgewählte Werke*, or from Stifter, *Betrachtungen und Bilder*, the letters from Seebass, *Briefe. Privat, Adalbert Stifter,* has also been drawn upon.
2. Rehm, *Nachsommer – Zur Deutung von Stifters Dichtung*.
3. Steiner, *Verses and Meditations*, translated by George and Mary Adams.
4. Steiner, *Das Künstlerische in seiner Weltmission*, lecture of June 8, 1923.
5. Steiner, *From Symptom to Reality in Modern History*.

12. Wilhelm Dilthey

1 This and the following quotations are from Misch, *Der junge Dilthey.*
2 Dilthey, *Gesammelte Schriften,* Vol. 5.
3 Foreword to Misch, *Der junge Dilthey.*
4 From the Georg Misch's introduction to Dilthey, *Gesammelte Schriften,* Vol. 5.
5 Inaugural lecture in Basle, 1876 in Dilthey, *Gesammelte Schriften,* Vol. 5.
6 Address on his seventieth birthday, Dilthey, *Gesammelte Schriften*, Vol. 5.
7 Dilthey, *Gesammelte Schriften*, Vol. 6.
8 Steiner, *A Psychology of Body, Soul and Spirit.*
9 Steiner, *The Riddles of Philosophy,* p. 424. Following quotations from pp. 426, 427, 428f, 445.
10 Steiner, *Mitteleuropa zwischen Ost und West,* lecture of Feb 17, 1918. (English: *The Mission of the Archangel Michael.)*
11 Steiner, *Die spirituellen Hintergründe der äusseren Welt.* lecture of Oct 14, 1917. (English: *The Fall of the Spirits of Darkness.)*
12 Steiner, *The Riddles of Philosophy,* p. 451.
13 In *Esoteric Christianity and the Mission of Christian Rosenkreutz.*

13. Karl Eugen Neumann

1 Jost, *Ludwig Derleth. Gestalt und Leistung,* Stuttgart 1965.
2 This and the following quotations are taken from the third volume of the monumental edition which is now available of Neumann's translations. Neumann, *Übertragungen aus dem Pali-Kanon.*
3 Rudolf Steiner referred on several occasions to the biographical significance of the moon node periods (18 years and 7 months) in a person's life. See the lectures of Nov 4 and 5, 1916 in *The Karma of Vocation.*
4 Neumann, *Der Wahrheitspfad.*
5 Letter of Feb 11, 1902.
6 Steiner, *Biographien und biographische Skizzen.*
7 Wagner, *Gesammelte Schriften,* Vol. 6.
8 Steiner, *The Gospel of St Mark,* lecture of Sep 15, 1912.
9 Steiner, *The Background to the Gospel of St Mark,* lecture of March 13, 1911.
10 Steiner, *The Gospel of St Mark,* lecture of Sep 15, 1912.
11 See Heyer, *Wer ist der deutsche Volksgeist?*
12 Steiner, *The Background to the Gospel of St Mark,* lecture of March 13, 1911.
13 See the three lectures given in May 1912, in Steiner, *The Spiritual Foundation of Morality.*

14. Marie Eugenie Delle Grazie

1 Pinder, *Das Problem der Generationen.*
2 Soergel and Hohoff, *Dichtung und Dichter der Zeit,* Vol. 1.
3 Pinder, *Das Problem der Generationen.*
4 Steiner, *Autobiography,* p. 89.
5 Lemmermeyer, *Erinnerungen.*
6 Steiner, *Autobiography,* p. 85f.
7 Steiner, *Autobiography,* p. 89f.
8 This and the following quotations are from Delle Grazie's autobiographical novel, *Eines Lebens Sterne.*
9 Steiner, *Gesammelte Aufsätze zur Literatur.*
10 Jodl, *Bartholomäus von Carneris Briefwechsel.*
11 Steiner, *Gesammelte Aufsätze zur Literatur.*
12 Steiner, *Die Welt der Sinne und die Welt des Geistes.* (English: *The World of the Senses and the World of the Spirit.*)
13 Steiner, *Methodische Grundlagen der Anthroposophie.*
14 Steiner, *Gesammelte Aufsätze zur Literatur.*

15. Grant, Hildebrand, Dohrn, Marées

1 Quoted from Heuss, *Anton Dohrn.*
2 The letters quoted are from Sattler, *Adolf von Hildebrand und seine Welt.*
3 In Marées, *Die Fresken in Neapel.*
4 Kuttner, *Hans von Marées.*
5 From Goethe's play, *Iphigenie in Tauris,* translated by Anna Swanwick.
6 Sattler, *Adolf von Hildebrand und seine Welt.*
7 Steiner, *Das Innere der Erde,* lecture of April 21, 1906.
8 Goethe, *Reisetagebuch,* entry of Sep 29, 1786.
9 Goethe, *Iphigenie in Tauris,* translated by Anna Swanwick.
10 Sattler, *Adolf Hildebrand und seine Welt.*
11 This and the following quotation are from Heuss, *Anton Dohrn.*
12 Kurz, *Florentinische Erinnerungen.*
13 This and the following quotations are from Sattler, *Adolf von Hildebrand und seine Welt.*
14 Kurz, *Florentinische Erinnerungen.*
15 This and the following two quotations are from Heuss, *Anton Dohrn.*
16 Steiner, *The Riddles of Philosophy,* pp. 329f.
17 Fiedler, *Hans von Marées.*
18 Meier-Graefe, *Hans von Marées.*
19 Fiedler, *Hans von Marées.*
20 Kuttner, *Hans von Marées.*
21 See Steiner, *The Fall of the Spirits of Darkness.*
22 Meier-Graefe, *Hans von Marées.*
23 Fiedler, Hans von Marées.

NOTES

24 Steiner, *Geistige und soziale Wandlungen,* lecture of Feb 6, 1920.
25 Steiner, *Kunst und Kunsterkenntnis,* lecture of Sep 12, 1920.
26 Steiner, *Wonders of the World,* lecture of Aug 18, 1911.

16. Gustav Mahler

1 This chapter was translated by Stephan Michael Engel, and of the Rilke poem by Carlo Pietzner.
2 Specht, *Gustav Mahler.*
3 Walter, *Gustav Mahler.*
4 See Adler, *Gustav Mahler.*
5 Stefan, *Gustav Mahler.*
6 Walter, *Thema und Variationen.*
7 Mahler, A. *Gustav Mahler, Briefe 1879–1911.*
8 Mahler, A. *Gustav Mahler. Erinnerungen und Briefe.*
9 Walter, *Gustav Mahler.*
10 Steiner, *According to Matthew,* lecture of Sep 12, 1910, p. 227.
11 König's mother also came from a Jewish bachground in Iglau. In the year she was born, 1880, Mahler took up his first position as conductor in Bad Hall.
12 Eckstein, *Comenius und die Böhmischen Brüder.*
13 Walter, Bruno, *Von der Musik und vom Musizieren.*

In August 1960 Bruno Walter wrote to Karl König who had sent him a copy of the article on Mahler (the letter is in the Karl König Archive):

Nothing could have given me greater pleasure than your kind letter of July 28, which also included what you called 'a small contribution' towards the centenary of Gustav Mahler. You will understand that I have been following those celebrations in America and Europe with the greatest pleasure; I myself have supported the events in New York and Vienna, and have tried, as far as possible, to stay informed about the way the public received them or commented on them. However, none of the articles I read can compare to the depth of understanding of Mahler's character and work, or the spiritual integrity that is so apparent in the essay you wrote for *Die Drei;* I read it as soon as it was published and took it in with a true sense of joy ...

The impressions engendered by your essay on Mahler leave little room for me to doubt that you have known Mahler personally, or that the most important impressions were gained in Vienna, and that you yourself are indeed from Vienna??? Anyway, the picture that emerges from your essay on Gustav Mahler clearly shows that it can only have come from the Viennese era.

17. Alma Mahler-Werfel and Lou Andreas-Salomé

1 Peters, *My Sister, My Spouse.*
2 In a letter written by Rilke to Maria von Thurn und Taxis.
3 Peters, *My Sister, My Spouse.*
4 Mahler, *Gustav Mahler, Erinnerungen und Briefe.*
5 Mahler-Werfel, *Mein Leben.*
6 Peters, *My Sister, My Spouse.*
7 Schreyer, *Erinnerungen an Sturm und Bauhaus.*
8 Steiner, *Gesammelte Aufsätze zur Literatur.*
9 Steiner, *Friedrich Nietzsche, Fighter for Freedom.*

18. Robert Owen

1 These three articles have been published in English as a single essay entitled *Anthroposophy and the Social Question.*
2 Simon, *Robert Owen. Sein Leben und seine Bedeutung für die Gegenwart.* Podmore, *Robert Owen. A Biography.*
3 This and the following quotations are, where unless otherwise indicated, from Podmore, *Robert Owen.*
4 Schiller, *Poems of the Third Period,* translator unknown.
5 Simon, *Robert Owen.*
6 Steiner, *The Fall of the Spirits of Darkness,* lectures of Oct 14 and 26, 1917.
7 Steiner, *Anthroposophy and the Social Question.*

19. Count Harry Kessler

1 Unless otherwise noted, quotations are from Kessler, *Gesichter und Zeiten.*
2 Kessler, *Tagebücher.*

20. Helen Keller

1 Keller, *The Story of my Life.*
2 This and the following quotations are taken from Anne Mansfield Sullivan's letters reprinted as a supplement to Keller, *The Story of My Life.*
3 Keller, *My Religion.*
4 Van Wyck Brooks, *Helen Keller, Sketch for a Portrait.*
5 Keller, *My Religion.*
6 Van Wyck Brooks, *Helen Keller, Sketch for a Portrait.*
7 Whitman's *Leaves of Grass.*
8 Steiner, *Building Stones for an Understanding,* lecture of May 8, 1917.
9 Steiner, *The Evolution of Consciousness,* lecture of Aug 25, 1923.
10 Schiller, 'Ode to Joy.'

11 From 'A Supplementary Account of Helen Keller's Life and Education', in Keller, *The Story of My Life*.

Afterword: O life, life ...

The afterword as well as the poem by Rilke was translated by Christine Reyneke-Frey

1 Müller-Wiedemann, *Karl König*, p. 42.
2 Richard Steel in König, *Becoming Human*, p. 24.
3 For instance, Riemeck, *Mitteleuropa;* Kocka, Jürgen, 'Das lange 19. Jahrhundert. Arbeit, Nation und bürgerliche Gesellschaft in Vol. 13, Gebhardt, *Handbuch der deutschen Geschichte;* Osterhammel, *Die Verwandlung der Welt*.
4 Seibt, Gustav, 'Generation Bonaparte' In *Süddeutsche Zeitung*, Dec 17, 2010.
5 Riemeck, *Beispiele goetheanistischen Denkens*, p. 6.
6 Müller-Wiedemann, *Karl König*, p. 409f.
7 Müller-Wiedemann, *Karl König*, p. 340.
8 Limbrunner, Alfons, 'Die große, heitere Blumenkette des Schicksals. Karl König und Adalbert Stifter: Versuch einer Zusammenschau' in *Info3*, 9, 2002.
9 Müller-Wiedemann, *Karl König*, p. 114.
10 König, 'Adalbert Stifter und die Heilpädagogik,' in *Das Seelenpflegebedürftige Kind*, 1, 1955.
11 Steiner, *Wie kann die seelische Not der Gegenwart überwunden werden?* lecture of Oct 10, 1916.

Bibliography

Adler, Guido, *Gustav Mahler,* Leipzig and Vienna, 1916.
Bachofen, J.J. *Das Mutterrecht,* Basel 1948.
Barlow, Nora (ed.) *The Autobiography of Charles Darwin,* Collins, London 1958.
Billroth, Theodor, *Lehren und Lernen der medizinischen Wissenschaften an den Universitäten deutscher Nation* (Teaching and Learning Medical Sciences at the Universities of the German Nation), Vienna 1867.
Binswanger, L. *Ausgewählte Vorträge und Aufsätze,* Bern 1955.
Bock, Emil, *Boten des Geistes. Schwäbische Geistesgeschichte und christliche Zukunft,* (Emissaries of the Spirit. Swabian Cultural History and Christian Future), 3rd edition, Stuttgart 1955.
Bölsche, Wilhelm, *Ernst Haeckel,* Berlin (no date).
Chakravarty, Amiya (ed.) *A Tagore Reader,* Macmillan, London 1961.
Croce, Benedetto, *Geschichte Europas im 19. Jahrhundert,* Zurich 1947.
Diepgen, Paul, *Geschichte der Medizin,* Berlin 1955.
Dilthey, W. *Gesammelte Schriften,* Stuttgart 1957.
Eckstein, Friedrich, *Comenius und die Böhmischen Brüder,* Leipzig (no date).
Fiedler, Conrad, *Hans von Marées,* Munich 1953.
Francis Darwin (ed.) *Life and Letters of Charles Darwin,* John Murray, London 1887.
Freud, Sigmund, *Aus den Anfängen der Psychoanalyse,* Imago, London 1950. (English: *The Origins of Psychoanalysis).*
—, *An Autobiographical Study,* Hogarth, London 1935.
—, *Beyond the Pleasure Principle,* London & Vienna 1922.
—, *Jenseits des Lustprinzips,* Vienna 1921. (English: *Beyond the Pleasure Principle.)*
—, *Moses and Monotheism,* 1932 (3rd ed 1951).
—, *The Origins of Psychoanalysis,* London 1954.
—, *Selbstdarstellung,* 1925. (English: *An Autobiographical Study).*
Friedell, E. *Kulturgeschichte der Neuzeit* (A Cultural History of Modern Times), Munich 1931.

Fürst, Rudolf (ed.) *Adalbert Stifters Ausgewählte Werke,* 6 vols. Insel Verlag, Frankfurt 1959-62.
Gaismaier, J. (ed.) *Justinus Kerners sämtliche poetische Werke,* Leipzig (no date).
Gebhardt, *Handbuch der deutschen Geschichte,* Stuttgart 2001.
Goethe, *Iphigenie in Tauris* (translated by Anna Swanwick) Arthur Hindes, New York (no date).
Grazie, Marie Eugenie delle, *Eines Lebens Sterne,* Leipzig 1919.
Guttman, R. *Feuchterslebens ausgewählte Werke* (Feuchtersleben's selected works), Leipzig 1907.
Hadow, William Henry, *Oxford History of Music,* 1904.
Haeckel, Ernst, *Die Naturanschauung von Darwin, Goethe und Lamarck* (The View of Nature common to Darwin, Goethe and Lamarck), 1882.
Hahnemann, Samuel, *Lesser Writings,* Tr. R.E. Dudgeon, B. Jain, New Delhi 2004.
Hecker, Hellmuth, *Karl Eugen Neumann. Erstübersetzer der Reden des Buddha, Anreger zu abendländischer Spiritualität,* Hamburg 1986.
Heuss, Theodor, *Anton Dohrn,* Tübingen 1962.
Heyer, Karl, *Kaspar Hauser und das Schicksal Mitteleuropas im 19. Jahrhundert,* Stuttgart 1964.
—, *Wer ist der deutsche Volksgeist?* Stuttgart 1961.
Jodl, Margarete (ed.) *Bartholomäus von Carneris Briefwechsel mit Ernst Haeckel und Friedrich Jodl,* Leipzig 1922.
Jones, Ernest, *Sigmund Freud, Life and Work,* London 1953.
Jost, Dominic, *Ludwig Derleth. Gestalt und Leistung,* Stuttgart 1965.
Keller, Helen, *My Religion,* Hodder & Stoughton, London 1927
—, *The Story of my Life,* 1903; restored edition supplemented with Anne Sullivan's letters, Modern Library Inc. 2004.
Kerner, Justinus, *Das Bilderbuch aus meiner Knabenzeit,* in J. Gaismaier (ed.), *Justinus Kerners sämtliche poetische Werke,* Vol. 4, Leipzig (no date).
—, *The Seeress of Prevorst,* T. Catherine Crowe, Partride & Brittan, New York 1885.
—, *Die Seherin von Prevorst,* Leipzig (no date). (English: *The Seeress of Prevorst).*
Kerner, Theobald (ed.) *Justinus Kerners Briefwechsel mit seinen Freunden,* Stuttgart 1897.
Kerner, Theobald, *Das Kernerhaus und seine Gäste* (The House of the Kerners and its Guests), Stuttgart 1894.
Kessler, Harry, *Gesichter und Zeiten,* Fischer, Frankfurt 1935 (republished as *Erinnerungen,* 1961).
—, *Tagebücher 1918–1937,* Insel, Frankfurt 1961.
Kluckhohn, Paul, 'Friedrich von Hardenburgs Entwicklung und Dichtung' (Friedrich von Hardenburg's Development and Literary Work). Introduction to *Novalis, Schriften,* Vol. 1, Stuttgart 1960.
Koller, Gottfried, *Johannes Müller,* Stuttgart 1958.

König, Karl, *Becoming Human: A Social Task,* Floris Books 2011.
—, *My Task,* Floris Books 2008.
—, *The Human Soul,* Floris Books 2006.
Kurz, Isolde, *Florentinische Erinnerungen,* Munich 1911.
Kuttner, Erich, *Hans von Marées,* Zurich 1937.
Lemmermeyer, Fritz, *Erinnerungen* (Memories), Stuttgart 1929.
Liebbrand, Werner *Romantische Medizin,* Hamburg 1937.
Mach, Ernst, *Grundlinie der Lehre von den Bewegungsempfindungen* (Outline of the Theory of Sensations of Movement), Leipzig 1875.
Mahler, Alma Maria (ed.) *Gustav Mahler, Briefe 1879–1911,* Berlin & Vienna 1924.
—, *Gustav Mahler. Erinnerungen und Briefe* (Reminiscences and Letters), Amsterdam 1940.
—, *Mein Leben,* Frankfurt am Main 1960.
Mann, Golo, *Deutsche Geschichte des 19. und 20. Jahrhunderts,* Frankfurt 1958.
Marées, Hans von, *Die Fresken in Neapel.*
Meier-Graefe, Julius, *Hans von Marées,* Munich 1912.
Misch, Clara (ed.) *Der junge Dilthey. Ein Lebensbild in Tagebüchern und Briefen,* Stuttgart 1960.
Morazé, Charles, *Das Gesicht des 19. Jahrhunderts,* Düsseldorf 1959.
Müller-Wiedemann, Hans, *Karl König. A Central European Biography,* Camphill Press 1996.
Münch, Hermann, *Böhmische Tragödie,* Brunswick 1949.
Naden, Constance, *The complete Poetical Works,* Bickers & Son, London 1894.
Neuberger, M. *Der Arzt Ernst Freiherr von Feuchtersleben. Gedenkrede gehalten in der Gesellschaft der Ärtze in Wien am 23. 3. 1906* (Doctor Ernst Baron von Feuchtersleben, commemorative address given at the Society of Viennese Physicians on 23 March 1906).
Neumann, K.E. *Übertragungen aus dem Paili-Kanon,* 3 vols., Zurich and Vienna 1957.
—, (tr.) *Der Wahrheitspfad. Ein buddhistisches Denkmal* (The Path of Truth, A Buddhist Memorial), 2nd ed, Munich 1921.
Oken, L. *Lehrbuch der Naturphilosophie* (Manual of a Philosophy of Nature), Jena 1831.
Osterhammel, Jürgen, *Die Verwandlung der Welt. Eine Geschichte des 19. Jahrhunderts,* Munich 2009.
Peters, H.F. *My Sister, My Spouse, a Biography of Lou Andreas-Salomé,* Norton, New York 1962.
Pinder, Wilhelm, *Das Problem der Generation,* 2nd ed, Munich 1961.
Podmore, Frank, *Robert Owen. A Biography,* Hutchinson, London 1906.
Privat, Karl (ed.) *Adalbert Stifter – Selbstzeugnisse, Briefe und Berichte,* Berlin 1946.
Rehm, Walter, *Nachsommer – Zur Deutung von Stifters Dichtung,* Bern 1951.
Reik, Theodor, *The Inner Experience of a Psychoanalyst,* London 1949.

Riemeck, Renate, *Beispiele goetheanistischen Denkens. Der Mensch als geistiges Wesen,* Basle 1974.

—, *Mitteleuropa. Bilanz eines Jahrhunderts,* Frankfurt 1983.

Sachs, Hanns, *Freud, Master and Friend,* Harvard University Press, Cambridge, Mass., 1944

Sattler, Bernhard (ed.) *Adolf von Hildebrand und seine Welt. Briefe und Erinnerungen,* Munich 1962.

Schleich, C.L. *Aus Asklepios Werkstatt,* Stuttgart and Berlin 1916.

—, *Besonnte Vergangenheit,* Berlin 1930 (English: *Those Were Good Days*).

—, *Those Were Good Days,* London and New York 1936.

—, *Die Wunder der Seele,* Berlin 1934.

Schneider, Reinhold, *Macht und Gnade,* Wiesbaden 1954.

Schönbauer, Leopold, *Das medizinische Wien,* Vienna 1947.

Schreyer, Lothar *Erinnerungen an Sturm und Bauhaus,* Munich 1956.

Seebass, Friedrich (ed.) *Adalbert Stifter – Briefe,* Tübingen 1936.

Simon, Helene, *Robert Owen. Sein Leben und seine Bedeutung für die Gegenwart,* Jena 1905.

Soergel, Albert and Curt Hohoff, *Dichtung und Dichter der Zeit,* Düsseldorf 1961.

Soret, Frédéric, *Zehn Jahre bei Goethe,* Leipzig 1929.

Specht, Richard, *Gustav Mahler,* Berlin 1913.

Spehlmann, Rainer, *Sigmund Freuds neurologische Schriften* (Sigmund Freud's Neurological Writings), Berlin 1953.

Stefan, Paul, *Gustav Mahler,* Munich, 1912.

Steiner, Rudolf, Collected Works (CW) / German Gesamtausgabe (GA) volume number.

—, *According to Matthew, The Gospel of Christ's Humanity,* Anthropsophic Press, USA 2003.

—, *Anthroposophie, Psychosophie, Pneumatosophie* (GA 115) (English: *A Psychology of Body, Soul and Spirit*).

—, *Anthroposophy and the Social Question*.

—, *Art in the Light of Mystery Wisdom* (part of CW 271) ??.

—, *The Arts and their Mission* (CW 276) Anthroposophic Press, USA 1986.

—, *Aus der Akasha-Forschung. Das Fünfte Evangelium* (GA 148) (English: *The Fifth Gospel*).

—, *Autobiograhy. Chapters in the Course of my Life 1861–1907.* (CW 148) Anthroposophic Press, USA 1999.

—, *The Background to the Gospel of St Mark* (CW 124) Anthroposophic Press, USA 1985.

—, *Bausteine zu einer Erkenntnis des Mysteriums von Golgotha* (GA 175). (English: *Building Stones for an Understanding of the Mystery of Golgotha*).

—, *Biographien und biographische Skizzen 1894–1905* (GA 33) Dornach 1967.

—, *Building Stones for an Understanding of the Mystery of Golgotha* (CW 175) Rudolf Steiner Press, UK 1972.

—, *The Christ Impulse and the Emergence of Consciousness*, GA 116, Dornach 2006.
—, *Destinies of People and Nations*, GA 157, Dornach 1981.
—, *Esoteric Christianity and the Mission of Christian Rosenkreutz* (CW 130) Rudolf Steiner Press, UK 2005.
—, *Das esoterische Christentum und die geistige Führung der Menschheit* (GA 130) (English: *Esoteric Christianity and the Mission of Christian Rosenkreutz*).
—, *The Evolution of Consciousness* (CW 227) Rudolf Steiner Press, UK 2007.
—, *Exkurse in das Gebiet des Markus-Evangeliums* (GA 124). (English: *The Background to the Gospel of St Mark*).
—, *The Fall of the Spirits of Darkness* (CW 177) Rudolf Steiner Press, UK 2008.
—, *The Festivals and their Meaning*, Rudolf Steiner Press, UK 2002.
—, *The Fifth Gospel* (CW 148) Rudolf Steiner Press, UK 1998.
—, *Friedrich Nietzsche, ein Kämpfer gegen seine Zeit* (GA 5). (English: *Friedrich Nietzsche, Fighter for Freedom*).
—, *Friedrich Nietzsche, Fighter for Freedom* (CW 5) Garber Books, USA 1985.
—, *From Symptom to Reality in Modern History* (CW 185) Rudolf Steiner Press, UK 1976.
—, *Gegenwärtiges und Vergangenes im Menschengeiste* (GA 167) (not translated).
—, *Geisteswissenschaft und Medizin*, GA 312. (English: *Introducing Anthroposophical Medicine*).
—, *Geistige und soziale Wandlungen in der Menschheitsentwickelung* (GA 196) (English: *What is Necessary in These Urgent Times*).
—, *Gesammelte Aufsätze zur Kultur- und Zeitgeschichte 1887–1901* (GA 31) Dornach 1966.
—, *Gesammelte Aufsätze zur Literatur 1884–1902* (GA 32) Dornach 1971.
—, *Geschichtliche Symptomatologie* (GA 185). (English: *From Symptom to Reality in Modern History*).
—, *Die gesunde Entwicklung des Leiblich-Physischen als Grundlage der freien Entfaltung des Seelisch-Geistigen* (GA 303) (English: *Soul Economy*).
—, *Goethe's Secret Revelation*, (CW 57) Rudolf Steiner Publishing, London (no date).
—, *Goethe's Theory of Knowledge. An Outline of the Epistemology of his Worldview* (CW 2) Steinerbooks, USA 2008.
—, *The Gospel of St Mark* (CW 139) Anthroposophic Press, USA 1986.
—, *Heilfaktoren für den sozialen Organismus* (GA 198).
—, *Individuelle Geistwesen und ihr Wirken in der Seele* (GA 178) (English: *Psychoanalysis and Spiritual Psychology*).
—, *Initiations-Erkenntnis* (GA 227). (English: *The Evolution of Consciousness*).
—, *Das Innere der Erde* (GA 97). (English: *The Interior of the Earth*).
—, *The Interior of the Earth* (CW 97) Rudolf Steiner Press, UK 2007.
—, *Introducing Anthroposophical Medicine* (CW 312) Anthroposophic Press, USA 1999.

—, *Das Karma des Berufes des Menschen in Anknüpfung an Goethes Leben* (GA 172) (English: *The Karma of Vocation).*
—, *The Karma of Materialism* (CW 176), Anthroposophic Press, USA 1985.
—, *The Karma of Vocation* (CW 172) Steinerbooks, USA 2009.
—, *Karmic Relationships,* Vol. 4 (CW 238) Rudolf Steiner Press, UK 1997.
—, *Die Kunst der Rezitation und Deklamation* (GA 281) (not translated).
—, *Kunst und Kunsterkenntnis* (GA 271).
—, *Das Künstlerische in seiner Weltmission* (GA 276) (English: *The Arts and their Mission).*
—, *Luzifer-Gnosis. Grundlegende Aufsätze zur Anthroposophie und Berichte aus 'Luzifer' und 'Luzifer-Gnosis' 1903–1908* (GA 34).
—, *Das Markus-Evangelium* (GA 139). (English: *The Gospel of St Mark).*
—, *Mein Lebensgang* (GA 28) (English: *Autobiography).*
—, *Menschliche und menschheitliche Entwicklungwahrheiten. Das Karma des Materialismus* (GA 176). (English: *The Karma of Materialism).*
—, *Methodische Grundlagen der Anthroposophie. Gesammelte Aufsätze zur Philosophie, Naturwissenschaft und Seelenkunde 1884–1901* (GA 30) Dornach 1961.
—, *The Mission of the Archangel Michael* (CW 174a) ??.
—, *Mitteleuropa zwischen Ost und West* (GA 174a) (English: *The Mission of the Archangel Michael).*
—, *Die Philosophie der Freiheit* (GA 4) (English: *The Philosophy of Spiritual Activity).*
—, *The Philosophy of Spiritual Activity* (CW 4), Rudolf Steiner Press, UK 1992.
—, *Physiologisch-Therapeutisches auf Grundlage der Geisteswissenschaft. Zur Therapie und Hygiene* (GA 314) (not translated).
—, *Psychoanalysis and Spiritual Psychology* (CW 178) Steinerbooks, USA 20??.
—, *A Psychology of Body, Soul and Spirit* (CW 115) Anthroposophic Press, USA 1999.
—, *Die Rätsel der Philosophie* (GA 18) (English: *The Riddles of Philosophy).*
—, *Reincarnation and Karma* (part of CW 34) Anthroposophic Press, USA 1992.
—, *The Riddles of Philosophy* (CW 18) Anthroposophic Press, USA 1973.
—, *Soul Economy. Body, Soul and Spirit in Waldorf Education* (CW 303) Steinerbooks, USA 2003.
—, *The Spiritual Foundation of Morality* (CW 155) Anthroposophic Press, USA 1995.
—, *Die spirituellen Hintergründe der äusseren Welt. Der Sturz der Geister der Finsternis* (GA 177) (English: *The Fall of the Spirits of Darkness).*
—, *Theosophische Moral* (GA 155). (English: *The Spiritual Foundation of Morality).*
—, *Truth-Wrought-Words,* (tr. Arvia MacKaye Ege) Anthropsophic Press, USA 1979.

—, *Verses and Meditations*, (tr. George and Mary Adams) Rudolf Steiner Press, UK 1972..

—, *Wahrspruchworte* (GA 40). (Partial English: *Verses and Meditations*, and *Truth-Wrought-Words*).

—, *Die Welt der Sinne und die Welt des Geistes* (GA 134). (English: *The World of the Senses and the World of the Spirit*).

—, *Weltenwunder, Seelenprüfungen und Geistesoffenbarungen* (GA 129). (English: *Wonders of the World*).

—, *What is Necessary in These Urgent Times* (CW 196) Steinerbooks, USA 2010.

—, *Wie kann die seelische Not der Gegenwart überwunden werden?* lecture of Oct 10, 1916.

—, *Wo und wie findet man den Geist?* (GA 57), (English: *Goethe's Secret Revelation*).

—, *Wonders of the World, Ordeals of the Soul and Revelations of the Spirit* (CW 129) Rudolf Steiner Press, UK 1983.

—, *The World of the Senses and the World of the Spirit* (CW 134) ??.

Stifter, Adalbert *Betrachtungen und Bilder*, Vienna 1923.

Susman, Margarete, *Gestalten und Kreise* (Figures and Circles), Zurich 1954.

Tschuppik, Karl, *Franz Joseph I*, Dresden 1929.

Unger, Hellmuth, *Virchow*, Hamburg 1953.

Van Wyck Brooks, *Helen Keller, Sketch for a Portrait*, London 1956.

Varnhagen, Rahel, *Ein Frauenleben in Briefen*, Weimar 1917.

Vierchow, Rudolf, *Cellular Pathology*, Churchill, London 1860.

Wagner, Richard, *Gesammelte Schriften* (Collected Works), Vol. 6, Leipzig (no date).

—, *Menschenschöpfung und Seelensubstanz*, Göttingen 1854.

—, *Über Wissen und Glauben*, Göttingen, 1854.

Waldeyer-Hartz, W. von, *Lebenserinnerungen*, Bonn 1921.

Walter, Bruno, *Gustav Mahler*, Frankfurt 1957.

—, *Gustav Mahler*, Da Capo Press, 1970.

—, *Thema und Variationen*, Stockholm 1947, (English: *Theme and Variations, An Autobiography*).

—, *Theme and Variations, An Autobiography*, London 1947.

—, *Von der Musik und vom Musizieren* (About Music and Music Making), Frankfurt 1957.

Weizsäcker, Victor von, *Natur und Geist*, Göttingen 1955.

Whitehead, A.N. *Adventures of Ideas*, 1933 (2nd ed, 1941).

—, *Science and the Modern World*, Cambridge 1925.

Whitman, Walt, *Leaves of Grass*, 1855.

Wodak, E. *Kurze Geschichte der Vestibularisforschung* (A Short History of the Research on the Vestibule), Stuttgart 1956.

Zotz, Volker, *Auf den glückseligen Inseln. Buddhismus in der deutschen Kultur*, Theseus, Berlin 2000.

Index

Entries in *italics* refer to illustrations.

Abbe, Ernst (1840–1905, German physicist and entrepreneur) 325f
Abraham, Karl (1877–1925, German psychiatrist) 227, 231f
Adalbert of Bavaria, Prince (1828–75) 160, 186
Adam, Adolphe (1803–56, French composer) 36
Aeschylus (c. 525–c. 455 BC, Greek dramatist) 451
Agassiz, Louis (1807–73, Swiss geologist) 101f
Alexander Christian Friedrich (1801–44, Count of Württemberg) 160
Alexander II (1818–81, Russian Czar) 19
Altenberg, Peter (1859–1919, Austrian writer) 386
Anagnos, Michael (1837–1906, Perkins Institution for the Blind) 437f, 447
Andersen, Hans Christian (1805–75, Danish writer) 116, 119
Andreae, Johann Valentin (1586–1654, author of Chymical Wedding) 75
Andreas, Friedrich Carl (1846–1930, Geman Orientalist) 386
Andreas-Salomé, Lou (1861–1937, German Russian–born psychoanalyst and writer) **385–400,** *387*
Annunzio, Gabriele D' *see* D'Annunzio
Arnim, Bettina von (née Brentano) (1785–1859, German writer, sister of Clemems Brentano) 61, 91, 184, 263
Asch, Max (colleague of Carl Ludwig Schleich) 151

Bach, Johann Sebastian (1685–1750, German composer) 380
Bachofen, Johann Jakob (1815–87, Swiss jurist and anthropologist) 21, 34, 284
Baer, Karl Ernst von (1792–1876, Baltic German naturalist) 258, 364
Bahr, Hermann (1863–1934, Austrian writer) 300, 303, 315
Balzac, Honoré de (1799–1850, French novelist) 36
Bamberger, Eugen von (1858–1921, German–Austrian physician) 215
Baranovska, Marie *see* Dohrn, Marie
Bárány, Robert (1876–1936, Austrian neurobiologist) 197
Bauernfeld, Eduard von (1802–90, Austrian dramatist) 60, 63
Bauhaus (German school of art between world wars) 390, 398
Beer-Hofmann, Richard (1866–1945, Austrian witer) 301
Beethoven, Ludwig von (1770–1827, German composer) 60f, 258, 382, 405, 418f, 426
Begas, Reinhold (1831–1911, German sculptor) 156
Bell, Alexander Graham (1847–1922, inventor of telephone, educator of deaf) 437, 448
Bell, Alexander Melville (1819–1905 inventor of Visible Speech, father of Alexander Graham) 448
Berg, Max (1870–1947, German architect) 399

485

Bergmann, Ernst von (1836–1907, Baltic German surgeon) 148
Berlioz, Hector (1803–69, French composer) 22, 36
Bernheim, Hippolyte (1840–1919, Alsatian neurologist) 214, 219
Bierbaum, Otto Julius (1865–1910, German writer) 150, 156, 301
Billroth, Theodor (1829–94, German–Austrian surgeon) 193f, 202, 204
Bindemann, Hermann (friend of Schleich) 156
Binswanger, Ludwig (1881–1966, Swiss psychiatrist) 225
Bismarck, Otto von (1815–98, German statesman) 15, 18, 138–40, 148, 428–30
Bjerre, Poul (1876–1964, Swedish psychiatrist) 388, 390f, 393
Blaue Reiter (group of expressionist artists 1911–14) 322, 396
Blavatsky, Helena Petrovna (1831–91, founder of Theosopy) 258
Blei, Franz (1871–1942, Austrian writer) 389
Blumenbach, Johann Friedrich (1752–1840, German physician) 109, 112
Blumhardt, Johann Christoph (1805–80, Lutheran pastor) 217
Bock, Emil (1895–1959, Christian Community priest) 186, 236
Böckh, August (1785–1867, German philologist) 273
Böcklin, Arnold (1827–1901, Swiss artist) 360
Bodenhausen, Eberhard von (1868–1918, German art historian) 427
Bodenstedt, Friedrich von (1819–92, German writer) 312
Bois-Reymond, Emil du (1818–96, German physician) 110, 116, 193, 210f, 322
Bölsche, Wilhelm (1861–1939, German writer) 233
Bonaparte, Napoleon *see* Napoleon
Bonaparte, Princess Marie (1882–1962, French psychoanalyst) 221
Bonaventura (probably pseudonym of Ernst Klingemann 1777–1831) 175f
Bopp, Franz (1791–1867, German linguist) 273

Brahms, Johannes (1833–97, German composer) 261, 263, 379, 382
Braun, Otto (1897–1918, German writer) 364
Brendel Mendelssohn, Dorothea *see* Schlegel, Dorothea
Brentano, Clemens (1778–1842, German poet) 184, 263, 278
Brentano, Franz (1838–1917, German psychologist) 210
Breuer, Josef (1842–1925, Austrian physician) **189–205**, *191*, 216, 218–21, 223
Bridgman, Laura (1829–89, first American deaf–blind person to gain education) 436–39, 444
Brion, Wilma de (née Kessler) (1877– after 1937, sister of Harry Kessler) 431
Brooks, Phillips (1835–93, American Bishop of Massachusetts) 447
Brown, Alexander Crum (1838–1922, Scottish organic chemist) 195f
Brown, John (1735–88, Scottish physician) 164n
Brücke, Ernst Wilhelm von (1819–92, German physiologist) 110, 116, 192, 195, 198, 202, 210f, 213, 218, 322
Bruckner, Anton (1824–96, Austrian composer) 284, 378f, 382
Brühl, Carl (1820–99, Austrian anatomist) 209
Büchner, Ludwig (1824–99, German physiologist) 116, 121, 124, 396
Bunsen, Robert (1811–99, German chemist) 91, 188

Carneri, Bartholomäus von (1821–1909, Austrian writer) 306, 313
Carus, Carl Gustav (1789–1869, German physiologist) 185, 263, 461
Cassirer, Bruno (1872–1941, Berlin gallery owner) 422
Catullus, Gaius Valerius (*c.* 84–*c.*54 BC, Roman poet) 451
Cavour, Camillo Benso, Count of (1810–61, leading figure in Italian unification) 18
Cezanne, Paul (1839–1906, French painter) 360

INDEX

Charcot, Jean-Martin (1825–93, founder of modern neurology) 213f, 216, 223, 229
Charlemagne (c.742–814, Emperor) 334f
Chopin, Frédéric (1810–49, Polish–French composer 36, 322
Chrobak, Rudolf (1843–1910, Austrian gynecologist) 202
Churchill, Winston (1874–1965, British statesman) 423
Claudius, Matthias (1740–1815, German poet) 184, 405
Cohen, Hermann (1842–1918, German philosopher) 279f
Conradi, Hermann (1862–90, German writer) 300
Conrad-Martius, Hedwig (1888–1966, German mystic) 102
Conz, Philipp (1762–1827, German poet) 169
Corot, Jean-Baptiste Camille (1796–1875, French painter) 355
Cosmic Circle *see* Kosmiker
Craig, Edward Gordon (1872–1966 theatre director and designer) 427
Creuzer, Freidrich (1771–1858, German philologist) 406
Crum Brown, Alexander *see* Brown, Alexander Crum
Cullen, William (1710–90, Scottish physician) 42
Cuvier, Georges (1769–1832, French naturalist) 100, 117, 258, 364

Dahn, Felix (1834–1912, German writer and historian) 157
Dale, David (1739–1806, Scottish mill owner) 410
Danhauser, Josef (1805–45, Austrian painter) 60
D'Annunzio, Gabriele (1863–1938, Italian writer) 300
Dante Alighieri (1265–1321, Italian poet) 353
Darwin, Charles (1809–82, English naturalist) 89, **91–108**, *93,* 123f, 188, 258, 270, 306, 325, 364, 366, 396
Darwin, Erasmus (1731–1802, English physician, grandfather of Charles) 99
Däubler, Theodor (1876–1934, German writer) 283

Debussy, Claude (1862–1918, French composer) 300
Dehmel, Richard (1863–1920, German poet) 148, 150, 156f, 300
Delacroix, Eugène (1798–1863, French artist) 36
Delle Grazie, Marie Eugenie *see* Grazie, M E Delle
Derleth, Ludwig [no von] (1870–1948, German writer) 283, 427
Dickens, Charles (1812–70, English novelist) 436
Dieffenbach, Johann Friedrich (1792–1847, German surgeon) 130
Diepgen, Paul (1878–1966, German medical historian) 21, 136
Dilthey, Karl (1839–1907, German archeologist, brother of Wilhelm) 274
Dilthey, Wilhelm (1833–1911, German philosopher) *262,* **263–81**
Dittus, Gottliebin (possessed girl cured by Blumhardt) 217
Doblhoff, Anton, Baron von (1800–1872, Austrian statesman) 67
Dohrn, Anton (1840–1909, German Darwinist) 104, 324–27, *328,* 329f, 332f, 337, 339, 341, **346–51**, *347,* 366
Dohrn, Carl August (1806–92, German entomologist, father of Anton) 348f
Dohrn, Marie (née Baranovska, wife of Anton) 351
Dostoyevsky, Fyodor (1821–81, Russian writer) 425
Drossbach, Maximilian (1810–84, Dutch philosopher) 124
Drummond, Henry (1851–97, Scottish evangelist) 447f
du Bois-Reymond *see* Bois–Reymond, Emil du

Ehmann, Friederike *see* Kerner, Friederike
Eichendorff, Joseph Freiherr von (1788–1857, German poet) 185
Einstein, Albert (1879–1955, German theoretical physicist) 422
Eitingon, Max (1881–1943, Russian psychoanalyst) 231
Elisabeth of Austria (1837–98, Empress, wife of Franz Joseph I) 18

487

Emerson, Ralph Waldo (1803–82, American writer) 264
Emmerich, Anne Catharine (1774–1824, German mystic visionary) 184
Engels, Friedrich (1820–1895, German social philosopher) 419, 452
Ennemoser, Joseph (1787–1854, German physician and writer) 185, 461
Ernst, Paul (1866–1933, German writer) 301
Eschenmayer, Karl August von (1768–1852, German philosopher & physician) 185
Eucken, Rudolf (1846–1926, German philosopher) 279–81
Exner, Sigmund (1846–1926, Austrian physiologist) 202
Exner, Sigmund (1846–1926, Austrian physiologist) 211

Fairy Tale of the Green Snake and the Beautiful Lily (Goethe's) 79–85
Fechner, Gustav (1801–87, German psychologist) 73
Fercher von Steinwand *see* Steinwand, Fercher von
Ferenczi, Sándor (1873–1933, Hungarian psychoanalyst) 231
Feuchtersleben, Ernst, Baron von (1806–49, Austrian physician) **57–90**, *59*, 117, 119
Feuchtersleben, Helena von (wife of Ernst) 64f, 68
Feuerbach, Anselm (1829–80, German painter) 303, 360
Fichte, Johann Gottlieb (1762–1814, German philosopher) 56, 426
Fidus *see* Höpener, Hugo
Fiedler, Conrad (1841–95, German art historian 327, 333, 345f, 354, 360, 362f, 366
Fiedler, Mary (née Meyer) (1854–1919, wife of Conrad) 366
Flaschlen, Cäsar (1864–1920, German writer) 300
Flaubert, Gustave (1821–80, French writer) 22, 32
Fleischl-Maxow, Ernst von (1846–91, Austrian physiologist) 211

Fliess, Wilhelm (1858–1928, German physician, friend of Freud) 201, 203f, 213, 220, 223f, 229, 233
Fontaine, Pastor (Alsatian visionary) 184
Fourier, Charles (1772–1837, French philosopher) 406, 419
Francis, St (1181–1226) 298
Frank, Johann Peter (1745–1821, German physician) 69
Franz Joseph I (1830–1916, Austrian Emperor) 15, 17f
Frederick the Great (1712–86, King of Prussia) 334–36
Freiligrath Ferdinand (1810–76, German poet) 160
Freitagsgesellschaft (Friday society of learned people started by Goethe) 41
Freud, Sigmund (1856–1939, Austrian founder of psychoanalysis) 89, 192, 198–201, 203f, *206*, **207–37**, 386, 388, 390, 400, 462
Friedell, Egon (1878–1938, Austrian writer) 234
Friedrich III, German Emperor (1831–88, reigned for 99 days) 148
Friedrich Wilhelm IV (1795–1861, King of Prussia from 1840) 14f
Führich, Joseph von (1800–1876, Austrian painter) 60
Fuller, Sarah (1836–1927, American educator) 455

Garibaldi, Giuseppe (1807–82, commander of Italian unification campaign) 18f
Geibel, Emanuel von (1815–84, German poet) 157
George, Stefan (1868–1933, German writer) 283, 322, 427
Gmelin, Eberhard (1751–1809, German mesmerist) 165
Goethe, Johann Wolfgang von (1749–1832) 40f, 44, 47, 58, 77, 86, 101, 124, 144, 167, 169, 183–85, 258, 263, 270f, 294, 307, 335, 405, 409, 426
Goltz, Friedrich (1834–1902, German physiologist) 195f
Graefe, Albrecht von (1828–70, German ophthalmologist) 146

488

INDEX

Grant, Charles (1841–89, Scottish poet and layabout) 324, *328,* 329–31, 333, **337–41,** *338,* 346, 366

Grazie, Marie Eugenie Delle Grazie (1864–1931, Austrian writer) **299–320,** *302*

Greif, Martin (1839–1911, German writer) 312

Greipl, Fanny (Adalbert Stifter's first love) 247f

Grillparzer, Franz (1791–1872, Austrian writer) 60–63

Grimm, Hermann (1828–1901, German art historian) 264, 273

Grimm, Jacob (1785–1863, German philologist, brother of Wilhelm) 60, 184

Grimm, Wilhelm (1796–1859, German author, brother of Jacob) 60, 185

Gropius, Alma *see* Mahler–Werfel, Alma

Gropius, Walter (1883–1969, German architect) 389–91, 394, 398–400

Grote, Ludwig (1893–1974, German art historian) 330

Guggenbühl, Johann Jakob (1816–63, Swiss physician) 438

Hadow, Sir William Henry (1859–1937, English educational reformer & musicologist) 61

Haeckel, Ernst (1834–1919, German naturalist) 94, 102, 106, 114, 116, 121–24, 138–40, 188, 260, 270, 306, 313f, 322, 325, 337f, 349–51, 358, 396

Haen, Anton de (1704–76, Dutch–Austrian physician) 69

Hagenbund (Austrian group of artists formed 1899) 398

Hahnemann, Melanie (née d'Hervilly-Gohier) (1800–1878, French homeopath, second wife of Samuel) 35f, 38f

Hahnemann, Samuel (1755–1843, German physician, founder of homeopathy) **35–56,** *37*

Halbe, Max (1865–1944, German dramatist) 301

Hale, Edward Everett (1822–1909, American Unitarian clergyman) 448

Halévy, Fromental (1799–1883, French composer) 36

Hamerling, Robert (1830–89, Austrian writer) 304, 312

Hammer-Purgstall, Joseph von (1774–1856, Austrian orientalist) 58

Hansen, Carl (1833–97, Danish hypnotist) 214

Hansson, Ola (1860–1925, Swedish–German writer) 150

Hardt, Ernst (1876–1947, German writer) 396

Hardy, Robert Spence (1803–68, author of *Eastern Monachism*) 287

Hart, Heinrich (1855–1906, German literary critic, brother of Julius) 386, 427

Hart, Julius (1859–1930, German poet, brother of Heinrich) 386, 427

Hartleben, Otto Erich (1864–1905, German writer) 150, 156, 300, 315

Hauffe, Friederike *see,* Prevorst, seeress of

Hauptmann, Gerhart (1862–1946, German writer) 283, 291, 300, 301f, 314, 386, 427

Hauser, Kaspar (?1812–1833) 185, 258, 263, 428

Haydn, Joseph (1732–1809, Austrian composer) 60, 382

Hebbel, Friedrich (1813–63, German writer) 65

Heckenast, Gustav (1811–79, Hungarian publisher) 243f

Hegel, Georg Wilhelm Friedrich (1770–1831, German philosopher) 56, 184f, 258, 263, 270–72, 280, 405

Hegner, Jakob (1882–1962, Austrian publisher) 389

Hellingrath, Norbert von (1888–1916, German literary scholar) 364

Helmholtz, Hermann von (1821–94, German physician) 110, 116, 146, 193, 210f, 322

Henckell, Karl (1864–1929, German writer) 300

Herder, Johann Gottfried (1744–1803, German philosopher) 124, 405

Hering, Ewald (1834–1918, German physiologist) 194

Herod Antipas (20 BC – AD 39, son of Herod the Great) 392

Herodias *(c.* 15 BC – AD 39, granddaughter of Herod the Great) 392

489

Hervilly-Gohier, Melanie d' *see* Hahnemann, Melanie

Herwegh, Emma (1817–1904, German revolutionary, wife of Georg) 341

Herwegh, Georg (1817–75, German revolutionary poet) 341

Heuss, Theodor (1884–1963, first president of Federal Republic of Germany, writer) 348f

Heyer, Karl (1888–1964, German anthroposophical hostorian) 428

Heym, Georg (1887–1912, German writer) 301

Hildebrand, Adolf von (1847–1921, German sculptor) 324—27, *328,* 329f, 332f, 227–40, *338,* **341–46,** *342,* 351, 366

Hippocrates of Cos *(c.*460 – *c.*370 BC, ancient Greek physician) 48f, 53f

Hirsch, Ernst *see* Reinhold, Ernst

His, Wilhelm (1831–1904, Swiss anatomist) 274

Hitler, Adolf (1889–1945) 227

Hitz, John (1828–1908, superintendent of Volta Bureau) 449f

Hofmann, Ludwig von (1861–1945, German artist) 427

Hofmannsthal, Hugo von (1874–1929, Austrian writer) 283, 291, 311, 353, 386, 422, 426f

Hölderlin, Friedrich (1770–1843, German poet) 38, 184, 363, 383

Hölderlin, Friedrich (1770–1843, German poet) 172, 263, 277, 304, 405, 426

Hölty, Ludwig (1748–76, German poet) 169

Holz, Arno (1863–1929, German poet and playwright) 300

Homer (around 850 BC, Greek poet) 451

Höpener, Hugo (1868–1948, German artist, known as Fidus) 283

Horace, Quintus (65–8 BC, Roman poet) 451

Howe, Samuel Gridley (1801–76, American physician and educator of the blind) 436–39, 444, 452

Huch, Ricarda (1864–1947, German writer, using pseudonym Richard Hugo) 300, 315

Hufeland, Christoph Wilhelm (1762–1836, German physician) 43, 45–50, 52, 54, 56

Hugo, Richard *see* Huch, Ricarda

Hugo, Victor (1802–85, French writer) 22, 36

Humboldt, Alexander von (1769–1859, German naturalist and explorer) 15, 91, 185, 263, 405

Humboldt, Wilhelm von (1767–1835, German linguist, philosopher and diplomat) 58, 273

Hume, David (1711–76, Scottish philosopher) 439

Huxley, Thomas (1825–95, English biologist) 94, 102, 358

Hyrtl, Josef (1810–94, Austrian anatomist) 192

Ibsen, Henrik (1828–1906, Norwegian playwright) 322, 425

Immermann, Karl Leberecht (1795–1840, German dramatist) 78

Jäger, Georg Friedrich von (1785–1866, German naturalist) 171

Janet, Pierre (1859–1947, French psychologist) 214

Joachim, Joseph (1831–1907, Austrian composer) 264

Jonas, Ludwig (1797–1859, German theologian) 267

Jones, Ernest (1879–1958, British psychoanalyst) 200, 228

Jost, Dominic (1922–94 , Swiss professor of German literature) 282

Julian the Apostate *(c.*331–363, Roman Emperor, philosopher) 454

Jung-Stilling, Johann Heinrich (1740–1817, German writer) 184

Kainz, Josef (1858–1910, Austrian actor) 314

Kandinsky, Wassily (1866–1944, Russian painter) 301

Kant, Immanuel (1724–1804, German philosopher) 100, 120, 137, 439

Kaposi, Moritz (1837–1902, Hungarian physician) 202

Karl August (1757–1828, Grand Duke of Sachsen–Weimar) 43, 47, 307

INDEX

Kaulbach, Wilhelm von (1805–74, German painter of murals) 360
Keller, Gottfried (1819–90, Swiss writer) 147, 322
Keller, Helen (1880–1968, American deaf–blind author and political activist) *432,* **433–57**
Kerner, Friederike 'Rickele' (née Ehmann) (1786–1854, Justinus' wife) 160, 175
Kerner, Justinus (von) (1786–1862, German poet and medical writer) **159–188,** *161,* 217
Kerner, Theobald (son of Justinus) 162, 186
Kessler, Alice (née Blosse-Lynch) (1844–1919, mother of Harry) 422
Kessler, Count Harry (1868–1937, Anglo–German diplomat) *420,* **421–431**
Kessler, Wilma *see* Brion, Wilma de
Key, Ellen (1849–1926, Swedish writer) 388
Khayyam, Omar (1048–1131, Perisan poet & philosopher) 58
Kirchhoff, Gustav (1824–87, German physicist) 91, 188
Klages, Ludwig (1872–1956, German philosopher) 283, 427
Klee, Paul (1879–1940, German painter) 301
Kleinenberg, Nikolaus (1842–97, German zoologist) 325f, *328,* 329–33, 366
Kleist, Heinrich von (1777–1811, German writer) 340
Klemm, Wilhelm (1881–1968, German writer) 301
Klettenberg, Susanne von (1723–74, German religious writer) 167
Klimt, Gustav (1862–1918, Austrian Jugendstil painter) 300, 388, 396
Klinger, Max (1857–1920, German symbolist artist) 396
Klopstock, Friedrich Gottlieb (1724–1803, German poet) 169
Knauer, Vincenz (1828–94, Austrian theologian) 306
Kokoschka, Oskar (1886–1980, Austrian artist) 389–91, 394, 399f

Kosmiker (Cosmic Circle) (early 20C Munich group of writers around Alfred Schuler) 283, 427f
Köstlin, Heinrich (1787–1859, German physician) 171
Kris, Ernst (1900–1957, Austrian–American psychoanalyst) 223
Kropotkin, Peter (1842–1921, Russian anarcho–communist) 452
Krüdener, (Baroness Barbara) Juliane von (1764–1824, Baltic German mystic) 184
Kühn, Sophie von (1782–97, financée of Novalis) 41, 167
Kummer(in), Maria Gottliebin (1756–1828, German visionary) 184
Kürnberger, Ferdinand (1821–1879, Austrian writer) 57
Kurz, Isolde (1853–1944, German writer) 340, 344

Lamarck, Jean-Baptiste (1744–1829, French naturalist) 99, 271
Lang, Melchior (blind healer) 175
Lange, Friedrich Albert (1828–75, German philosopher) 349f
Langenbeck, Bernhard von (1810–87, German surgeon) 148
Langerhans, Robert (1859–1904, German pathologist) 156
Lanner, Joseph (1801–43, Austrian composer) 60
Lassalle, Ferdinand (1825–1864, German socialist) 30
Lazarus, Moritz (1824–1903, German philosopher) 265
Leibbrand, Werner (1896–1974, German psychiatrist & historian) 182
Lemmermeyer, Fritz (1857–1932, Austgrian writer) 304
Lenau, Nikolaus (1802–50, Austrian poet) 60
Lenau, Nikolaus (1802–50, Austrian poet) 160
Lenbach, Franz von (1836–1904, German painter) 354
Lenin, Vladimir (1870–1924, Soviet leader) 227
Lessing, Gotthold Ephraim (1729–81, German philosopher) 86, 124, 270f, 277

491

Lincoln, Abraham (1809–65, US President) 20, 447
Liszt, Franz (1811–86, Hungarian composer) 322
Locke, John (1632–1704, English philosopher) 439
Löns, Hermann (1866–1914, German writer) 301
Lorenzo, Guiseppe de (1871–1957, Italian orientalist) 285f, 289
Louise Philippe I (1773–1850, King of France) 36
Ludwig, Carl (1816–95, German physician) 110, 112, 116, 193, 210f
Ludwig, Otto (1813–65, German dramatist) 124
Luther, Martin (1483–1546, German religious reformer) 265
Lyell, Charles (1797–1875, Scottish geologist) 96f, 100–102, 306, 396

Mach, Ernst (1838–1916, Austrian physicist) 195f
Mackay, John Henry 1864–1933, Scots-born German writer) 397f
Macke, August (1887–1914, German painter) 301, 364
Maeterlinck, Maurice (1862–1949, Belgian writer) 300, 396
Mahler, Gustav (1860–1911, Austrian composer) 368, **369–83,** 389–91, 399f, 462
Mahler-Werfel, Alma Maria (née Schindler) (1879–1964, Viennese socialite, wife of Gustav Mahler, and later of Walter Gropius and Franz Werfel) 375, 380f, *384,* **385–400**
Maier-Graefe, Julius (1867–1935, German art critic) 363
Maillol, Aristide (1861–1944, French Catalan artist) 422, 427
Makart, Hans (1840–84, Austrian painter) 360
Malthus, Rev Thomas Robert (1766–1834, English social researcher) 97
Mann, Golo (1909–94, German writer) 13f
Marc, Franz (1880–1916, German painter) 301, 364
Marées, Hans von (1837–87, German painter) 324, 326f, *328,* 329–33, 337, 339, 341, 344–46, *352,* **353–67,** 427

Marriot, Emil (1855–1938, pseudonym of Emilie Mataja, Austrian writer) 306f
Marwitz, Bernhard von der (1890–1918, German writer) 364
Marx, Karl (1818–83, German sociologist) 89, 92, 261, 419, 452
Mataja, Emilie see Marriot, Emil
Matthison, Friedrich von (1761–1831, German poet) 169
Max(imilian) Joseph (1808–88, Duke in Bavaria) 160
Mayer, Karl (1786–1870, German poet) 160, 171
Mazzini, Giuseppe (1805–72, Italian politiician) 18
Meckel, Johann Friedrich (the Younger) (1781–1833, German anatomist) 271
Mendelssohn, Dorothea see Schlegel, Dorothea
Mendelssohn, Felix (1809–47, German composer) 382
Mendelssohn, Moses (1729–86, German philosopher) 386
Mengelberg, Willem (1871–1951, Dutch conductor and composer) 389
Menzel, Adolph von (1815–1905, German artist) 460
Merezhkovsky, Dmitry (1865–1941, Russian novelist) 301
Mesmer, Franz Anton (1734–1815, German physician, magnetism) 184, 214
Metternich, Prince Klemens von (1773–1859, Austrian politician) 67
Metternich, Princess Pauline von (1835–1921, promoter of Richard Wagner) 22
Meyer, Conrad Ferdinand (1825–98, Swiss writer) 322
Meyer, Mary see Fiedler, Mary
Meyerbeer, Giacomo (1791–1864, German opera composer) 36
Meynert, Thomas (1833–92, German psychiatrist) 212, 215
Michaelis, Caroline see Schlegel, Caroline
Misch, Georg (1878–1965, German philosopher) 269
Mohaupt, Amalie see Stifter, Amalie

INDEX

Moleschott, Jacob (1822–93, Dutch physiologist) 116, 122, 124, 396
Mombert, Alfred (1872–1942, German writer) 283, 427
Mommsen, Theodor (1817–1903, German historian) 273
Montesquieu, Chalres-Louis (1689–1755, French political thinker) 404
Morgenstern, Christian (1871–1914, German poet) 154
Mörike, Eduard (1804–75, German Romantic poet) 117, 119, 263
Morris, William (1834–96, English designer and socialist) 427, 429
Mozart, Wolfgang Amadeus (1756–91, Austrian composer) 60, 382
Mulford, Prentice (1834–91, Californian author) 233
Müller, Johannes Peter (1801–58, German physiologist) 110, 119f, 130f, 146, 210f, 322
Müller-Wiedemann, Hans (1924–97, German physician and Camphill coworker) 462f
Müllner, Laurenz (1848–1911, Austrian philosopher & rector) 304, 306–10, 313f, 316, 318
Munch, Edvard (1863–1944, Norwegian painter) 300
Musset, Alfred de (1810–57, French novelist) 36
Mussolini, Benito (1883–1945, Italian Fascist leader) 227

Nadolny, Rudolf (1873–1953, German diplomat) 426
Napoleon (1769–1821, French general and emperor) 116, 257, 405, 418f
Napoleon III (1808–73, ruler of Second French Empire) 15, 19
Nazarene movement (early 19C group of German romantic painters) 322
Nestroy, Johann (1801–62, Austrian playwright) 60
Neuberger, Max (1868–1955, Austrian medical historian) 66, 73
Neumann, Angelo (1838–1910, Austrian stage director, father of Karl Eugen) 285
Neumann, Karl Eugen (1865–1915, Austrian oriental translator) **282–298**

Neumann, Wilhelm (1837–1919, Austrian theologan) 306
Newman, John Henry (1801–90, English Cardinal) 322
Niebuhr, Barthold Georg (1776–1831, German historian) 273
Nietzsche, Friedrich (1844–1900, German philosopher) 279, 322, 358, 386, 390, 396–98, 425, 427
Nothnagel, Hermann (1841–1905, German physician) 216
Novalis (Georg Friedrich von Hardenberg) (1772–1801, German Romantic writer) 41, 44, 46, 167, 184, 277, 363, 406

Obenauer, Karl Justus (1888–1973, professor of German studies) 167
Oberlin, Jean-Frédéric (1740–1826, Alsatian pastor and philanthropist) 183f, 405, 411
Oken, Lorenz (1779–1851, German naturalist) 100, 461
Oppolzer, Johann von (1808–71, Austrian physician) 193
Owen, Robert (1771–1858, Welsh social reformer) 91, **401–19**, *402*

Palacký, František (1798–1876, Czech historian, politician) 17
Pappenheim, Bertha (1859–1936, Austrian–Jewish feminist, patient of Breuer) 200f, 217f
Paracelsus (1493–1541, Swiss physician) 45f, 49, 54
Pasteur, Louis (1822–95, French microbiologist) 91
Paul, St *(c.* 5–67, Apostle) 235f
Pestalozzi, Johann Heinrich (1746–1827, Swiss educator) 184, 405, 411
Piloty, Ferdinand von (1828–95, German painter) 360
Pinder, Wilhelm (1878–1947, German art historian) 299, 303
Place, Francis (1771–1854, English social reformer) 416
Platen, August von (1796–1835, German dramatist) 58
Plato *(c.*424–*c.*347 BC, Greek philosopher) 451f

493

Plautus, Titus Maccius (c. 254–184 BC, Roman playwright) 451
Podmore, Frank (1856–1910, English author) 403
pre-Raphaelites (mid 19C group of English painters and poets) 322
Preuss, Wilhelm Heinrich (1843–1909, German philosopher) 277
Prevorst, seeress of (Friederike Hauffe, 1801–29) 179–85, 187, 217
Prowe, Carl (friend of Schleich) 156
Przybyszewski, Stanislaw (1968–1927, Polish writer) 150

Rademacher, Johann Gottfried (1772–1850, German physician) 45–50, 52, 54, 56
Raimund, Ferdinand (1790–1836, Austrian dramatist) 58, 60f
Rank, Otto (1884–1939, Austrian psychoanalyst) 231f
Ranke, Leopold von (1795–1886, German historian) 267, 273
Rapp, Georg (1757–1847, Founder of religious sect Harmony Society) 414
Rathenau, Walter (1867–1922, German foreign minister in Weimar Republic) 422
Rauscher, Joseph Othmar von (1797–1875, Cardinal and Archbishop of Vienna) 310
Rée, Paul (1849–1901, German philosopher) 386, 390, 392, 400
Rehm, Walther (1901–63, Professor of German literature) 243
Reik, Theodor (1888–1969, Austrian psychoanalyst) 209
Reimer, Georg Ernst (1804–85, Berlin academic publisher) 130
Reinhold, Ernst (1886–1964, or E.R., pseudonym of Ernst Hirsch, Oriental scholar) 285n
Reis, Johann Philipp (1834–74, German scientist, inventor of telephone) 448
Rembrandt van Rijn (1606–69, Dutch painter) 355
Rilke, Rainer Maria (1875–1926, Austrian poet) 377f, 388, 390f, 400, 427, 465
Ritter, Heinrich (1791–1869, German philosopher) 273

Rodin, Auguste (1840–1917, French sculptor) 422, 427
Rokitansky, Carl (1804–78, Bohemian–Austrian pathologist and philosopher) 69–73, 192
Rolland, Romain (1866–1944, French writer) 301
Roller, Alfred (1864–1935, Austrian stage designer) 375
Roser, Karl von (1787–1861, Wurttemberg statesman) 171
Rückert, Friedrich (1788–1866, German poet) 58, 185
Ruskin, John (1819–1900, English writer and art patron) 427

Sachs, Hanns (1881–1947, Austrian psychoanalyst) 224, 227, 236
Saint-Hilaire, Etienne Geoffrey (1772–1844, French naturalist) 100, 258, 271
Saint-Martin, Louis Claude de (1743–1803, French philosopher) 184
Saint-Simon, Claude Henri, Count of (1760–1825, French socialist) 419
Salome (c. AD 14 – c. 70, daughter of Herodias) 392
Salomé, Lou see Andreas–Salomé, Lou
Sand, George (1804–76, pseudonym of Amantine Dupin) 36
Savigny, Friedrich Carl von (1779–1861, German jurist and historian) 273
Schack, Count Adolf Friedrich von (1815–1894, German poet and art collector) 354
Schelling, Friedrich (1775–1854, German philosopher) 41, 56, 110, 184f, 263, 270f, 280
Scherer, Wilhelm (1841–1886, Austrian professor of German literature) 190, 266
Schickele, René (1883–1940, Alsace German–French writer) 301
Schiller, Friedrich (1759–1805, German writer) 40f, 44, 86, 167, 169, 257, 270f, 410f
Schlaf, Johannes (1862–1941, German writer) 300
Schlegel, August Wilhelm (1767–1845, German writer, older brother of Friedrich) 41

INDEX

Schlegel, Caroline (née Michaelis) (1763–1809, German writer, August Wilhelm's wife) 41, 386
Schlegel, Dorothea (née Brendel Mendelssohn) (1764–1839, German writer, Friedrich's wife) 41, 360, 386
Schlegel, Friedrich (1772–1829, German poet, younger brother of August Wilhelm) 41, 78, 184, 267, 406
Schleich, Carl Ludwig (159–1922, German surgeon and writer) 137, **143–58,** *145*
Schleiermacher, Friedrich (1768–1834, German theologian and philosopher) 265, 267, 270f
Schmerling, Anton von (1805–93, Austrian statesman) 17
Schmidt, Johann Caspar *see* Stirner, Max
Schnitzler, Arthur (1862–1931, Austrian writer) 300, 386
Schönbauer, Leopold (1888–1947, Austrian surgeon) 193
Schönerer, Georg von (1842–1921, Austrian nationalist politician) 18
Schönlein, Johann Lukas (1793–1864, German naturalist and physician) 74
Schönlein, Johann Lukas (1793–1864, German physician) 130
Schopenhauer, Arthur (1788–1860, German philosopher) 15, 58, 287, 292–94, 296
Schreyer, Lothar (1886–1966, German artist, editor of *Der Sturm*) 394–96, 398
Schröer, Karl Julius (1825–1900, Austrian professor of German literature) 64, 260, 264
Schubert, Franz (1797–1828, Austrian composer) 60, 63, 258, 382
Schubert, Gotthilf Heinrich von (1780–1860, German physician and naturalist) 15, 185, 263
Schuler, Alfred (1865–1923, German mystic) 283, 427
Schumann, Clara *see* Wieck–Schumann
Schumann, Robert (1810–56, German composer) 382
Schwab, Gustav (1792–1850, German writer and pastor) 160

Schwind, Moritz von (1804–71, Austrian painter) 60, 63
Secession (Modernist art group late 19C early 20C) 398
Sefan, Paul (1879–1943, Austrian music historian) 373, 375
Seligman, Romeo (1808–92, Austrian medical historian) 64, 68
Semmelweiss, Ignaz Philipp (1818–65, Hungarian pioneer of antiseptics) 21
Sibelius, Jan (1865–1957, Finnish composer) 301
Simon, Helene (1862–1947, German biographer of Owen) 411
Škoda, Josef von (1805–81, Bohemian–Austrian physician) 69f, 73, 192f
Sneyd-Kynnersley, Rev Herbert (1848–96, English headmaster) 423
Soergel, Albert (1880–1958, German historian of literature) 288
Soliman, Angelo (1721–96, Nigerian royal servant in Austria) 63
Spaun, Joseph Baron von (1788–1865, Austrian nobleman) 63
Specht, Pauline (1846–1916, friend of Rudolf Steiner) 202f
Specht, Richard (1870–1930, Austrian writer) 370
Spencer, Herbert (1820–1903, English philosopher) 94
St Germain, Count (?1712–?1784) 49, 405
Stadler, Ernst (1883–1914, Alsace German writer) 301
Stalin, Joseph (1878–1953) 227
Steffeck, Carl (1818–90, German painter) 355
Stehr, Hermann (1864–1940, German writer) 300, 315
Stein, Lorenz von (1815–90, Austrian sociologist) 192
Steiner, Bernhard (1930s German biologist) 102
Steiner, Rudolf (1861–1925) 75, 81, 84, 89, 102f, 106-8, 115, 120–24, 134f, 138f, 141, 155–57, 168, 171, 180, 187f, 197, 202, 216, 220, 235, 255, 259, 261, 277–81, 292–97, 305, 307, 314, 316f, 318, 320, 334, 337, 350, 365, 367, 377, 380, 383, 386, 397, 399, 401, 403f, 417–19, 428, 454

495

Steinwand, Johann Fercher von (1828–1902, Austrian writer) 284
Stendahl, Marie-Henri (1783–1842, French writer) 36
Stifter, Adalbert (1805–68, Austrian writer) 22, 32, 60, 116, 119, *238,* **239–261,** 303, 462f
Stifter, Amalie (née Mohaupt) (1811–83, wife of Adalbert) 248
Stirner, Max (1806–56, German philosopher, pseudonym for Johann Caspar Schmidt) 397f
Stöhr, Adolph (1855–1921, Austrian psychologist) 306
Stoll, Maximilian (1742–87, German–Austrian physician) 69
Stramm, August (1874–1915, German writer) 364
Strauss I, Johann (1804–49, Austrian composer, father of Johann II, Josef and Eduard) 60
Strauss, David Friedrich (1808–74, German theologian) 160
Strauss, Richard (1864–1949, German composer) 300, 303
Strindberg, August (1849–1912, Swedish writer) 151f, 156f
Stross, Alfred (1860–88, Austrian composer) 306
Sturm, Der (Expressionist journal, gallery and art school, 1910–31) 394, 398
Sullivan, Anne Mansfield (1866–1936, American teacher of Helen Keller) 437, 439–446, 449
Sun Yat-sen (1866–1925, Chinese revolutionary) 301
Susman, Margarete (1872–1966 German writer) 209, 232f
Swedenborg, Emanuel (1688–1772, Swedish philosopher) 181, 184, 405, 433, 452, 454f
Swieten, Gerard van (1700–1772, Dutch physician) 69
Swoboda, Hermann (1973–1963, Austrian psychologist) 222f

Tacitus, Publius Cornelius (AD 56–117, Roman historian) 451
Tagore, Rabindranath (1861–1941, Bengali polymath) 23–28

Tauber, Melanie (Viennese girl courted by Marée) 362
Terry, Ellen (1847–1928, English actress, mother of Gordon Craig) 427
Tersteegen, Gerhard (1697–1769, German religious reformer) 404
Theoderic the Great (454–526, king of Ostrogoths) 19
Thylmann, Karl (1888–1916, German artist and poet) 364
Tieck, Ludwig (1773–1853, German writer) 41
Toulouse-Lautrec, Henri de (1864–1901, French painter) 300
Trakl, Georg (1887–1914, Austrian writer) 364
Trendelenburg, Friedrich Adolf (1802–72, German philosopher) 273
Troxler, Ignaz (1780–1866, Swiss physician and philosopher) 461

Uhland, Ludwig (1787–1862, German poet and historian) 160, 171, 185, 187
Usener, Hermann (1834–1905, German philologist) 265

Varnhage von Ense, Karl August (1785–1858, German biographer) 160, 171–73
Varnhage von Ense, Rahel (wife of Karl August) 173
Varnhagen, Rahel (1771–1833, German–Jewish writer) 78, 360
Velde, Henry van de (1863–1957, Belgian architect and designer) 300, 426f
Victor Emmanuel (1820–78, Italian king) 19
Vierordt, Karl von (1818–84, Geman physiologist) 116
Virchow, Rudolf (1821–1902, German physician, politician) 72, 91, 115f, *126,* **127–42,** 146, 148
Virgil (70–19 BC, Roman poet) 353
Vischer, Friedrich Theodor (1807–87, German writer) 160
Vogt, Carl (1817–95, German scientist) 110, 113–16, 118, 122, 124
Volta, Alessandro (1745–1827, Italian physicist) 448

INDEX

Voltaire, François-Marie Arouet (1694–1778, French Enlightenment philosopher) 404

Wagner, Richard (1813–83, German composer) 22, 38f, 285, 292f, 295f, 322, 374,
Wagner, Rudolf (1805–64, German physiologist) **109–25,** *111*
Walden, Nell (née Rosmund) (1885–1975, editor of *Der Sturm*) 394
Waldeyer-Hartz, Heinrich Wilhelm von (1836–1921, German anatomist) 127f, 150, 211
Waldmüller, Ferdinand Georg (1793–1865, Austrian painter) 60
Wallace, Alfred Russel (1823–1913, British naturalist) 98, 101f
Walter, Bruno (1876–1962, Austrian conductor) 370, 374–76, 383, 475n
Wandervogel (German youth movement from 1896 onward) 284, 398
Watt, James (1736–1819, Scottish inventor) 405
Weber, Carl Maria von (1786–1826, German composer) 185
Wedekind, Frank (1864–1918, German writer) 300, 315
Weikard, Melchior Adam (1742–1803, German physician) 164
Weininger, Otto (1880–1903, Austrian philosopher) 222f
Weizsäcker, Viktor von (1886–1957, German founder of psychosomatic medicine) 226–28
Werfel, Alma *see* Mahler–Werfel, Alma
Werfel, Franz (1890–1945, Austro-American writer) 389–91, 399f
Werner, Karl (1821–88, Austrian theologian) 306
Wesley, Charles (1707–88, leader of Methodist movement, brother of John) 404

Wesley, John (1703–91, founder of Methodist movement, brother of Charles) 404
Whitehead, Alfred North (1861–1947, English mathermatician) 23–25, 27f
Whitman, Walt (1818–92, American writer) 452
Widenmann, Gustav (1812–76, German physician and writer) 124
Wieck-Schumann, Clara (1819–96, German musician & composer) 38, 322
Wilhelm I (1797–1888, German Emperor, reigned from 1861) 15, 18, 422, 428f
Wilms, Max (1867–1918, German pathologist and surgeon) 146
Wolf, Hugo (1860–1903, Austrian composer) 378
Wölfflin, Heinrich (1864–1945, Swiss art historian) 300
Wolfskehl, Karl (1869–1948, German writer) 283, 427
Worpsweder Group (late 19C, early 20C artistic community) 398, 427
Wundt, Wilhelm (1832–1920. German physician and psychologist) 425

Yat-sen, Sun *see* Sun Yat-sen
Yeats, William Butler (1865–1939, Irish poet) 301

Zinzendorf, Count Nikolaus Ludwig von (1700–1760, German founder of Bohemian Brotherhood) 404
Zola, Emile (1840–1902, French writer) 32, 425
Zuckerkandl, Emil (1849–1910, Austrian anatomist) 389
Zweig, Stefan (1881–1942, Austrian writer) 291

Karl König's collected works are being published in English by Floris Books, Edinburgh and in German by Verlag Freies Geistesleben, Stuttgart. They are issued by the Karl König Archive, Aberdeen in co-operation with the Ita Wegman Institute for Basic Research into Anthroposophy, Arlesheim. They seek to encompass the entire, wide-ranging literary estate of Karl König, including his books, essays, manuscripts, lectures, diaries, notebooks, his extensive correspondence and his artistic works. The publications will fall into twelve subjects.

The aim is to open up König's work in a systematic way and make it accessible. This work is supported by many people in different countries.

Overview of Karl König Archive subjects

Medicine and study of the human being
Curative education and social therapy
Psychology and education
Agriculture and science
Social questions
The Camphill movement
Christianity and the festivals
Anthroposophy
Spiritual development
History and biographies
Artistic and literary works
Karl König's biography

Karl König Archive
Camphill House
Milltimber
Aberdeen AB13 0AN
United Kingdom
www.karl-koenig-archive.net
aberdeen@karl-koenig-archive.net

Ita Wegman Institute for Basic
Research into Anthroposophy
Pfeffingerweg 1a
4144 Arlesheim
Switzerland
www.wegmaninstitut.ch
koenigarchiv@wegmaninstitut.ch